The Ranger Companies Of Bandera County

> When the Indians made a raid into this section
> the minutemen and citizens would take the trail.
>
> Amasa Clark
1825-1927

Earl S. Hardin, Jr

The Ranger Companies Of Bandera County

Earl S. Hardin, Jr

Published by

Positive Imaging, LLC
bill@positive-imaging.com
http://positive-imaging.com

On the cover: The tracking guide points the way, artwork by **Dusan Arsenic**

All Rights Reserved

No part of this book may be reproduced, transmitted or downloaded in any form or by any means, electronic or mechanical, including copying, photocopying, recording or by any information storage and retrieval system without written permission from the author, except for the inclusion of brief quotations in a review.

ISBN: 9781944071899

Copyright   2019   Earl S. Hardin, Jr.

To Mr. Graves who told his class they would write a county history and we did.

Contents

Introduction and Texas Ranger Synopsis ... ix

Maps

Bandera County 1850s & 60s ... xiii

The Upper Nueces River 1870 ... xv

The West Texas Frontier Mid 1870s ... xvii

Chapters

1. The West Texas Frontier ... 1
2. Bandera City and The Frontier ... 21
3. Bandera County and The Frontier ... 51
4. The First Ballantyne's Rangers and Tumlinson's Company ... 65
5. Bandera County In The Year of Secession ... 77
6. The Frontier Regiment: Montel's Company ... 111
7. The Mounted Regiment: Lawhon's Company ... 141
8. The Bandera Home Guardes (Mitchell's Company) ... 167
9. The Reconstruction Years ... 191
10. State Police and Reserve Militia ... 205
11. The Frontier Force: Sansom, Kelso, and Richarz ... 215
12. The Second Ballantyne's Rangers and Phillip's Company ... 269
13. The Frontier Battalion and The Special Force ... 287
14. The Last Minutemen ... 311

Appendix ... 323

Sources ... 351

Introduction

This is a military history of the settlement of Bandera County. As a cross-section history of the Texas Rangers from the mid-1850s to the early 1880s, the story is mostly of rangers and Indians, but also of soldiers, settlers, lawmen, and outlaws. In the time and region covered, rangers were sometimes called upon to deal with outlaws, but they were generally meant to counter Indian raids. There is some overview history of the settlement of the West Texas Frontier and, perhaps, some genealogical information for area residents.

The first chapter presents historical orientation of the region beginning briefly with the Spanish era and surveying relative events up to the founding of Bandera City. The succeeding chapters outline the full-time and minuteman companies of rangers that operated in and around Bandera County, an area and time first described in vivid, but sometimes inaccurate, details by A.J. Sowell, a Texas Ranger who became a writer. He interviewed surviving pioneers and, in 1900, published <u>Early Settlers and Indian Fighters of Southwest Texas</u> (known in short as <u>Texas Indian Fighters)</u>. Another journalist-historian, J. Marvin Hunter, published <u>The Pioneer History of Bandera County</u> in 1922.

Elsewhere the story of these rangers is scattered among autobiographies, oral histories, newspaper articles, and archival documents. In order to transcribe documents as closely as possible, original spellings, in most instances, have been left intact, including "fs" for today's "ss". Editorial comments or corrections are enclosed in brackets. Ellipses to indicate material omitted from quotations are enclosed in brackets. Quotations from Levi Lamoni and Sophia Wight are mostly as edited by Davis Bitton. Muster rolls are transcribed as completely as possible, but some muster roll transcriptions are composites of more than one roll and some are merely summarized. First and middle names, where they have been known, have been added to the list of names for the first Ballantyne's Rangers and for Mitchell's Company.

Texas Ranger Synopsis

At times on the Texas frontier there were only minuteman or militia companies and at other times there were only full-time ranger companies. Sometimes a thin screen of full-time companies would be backed up by minuteman companies. Usually any companies were enrolled for a specified time, "unless sooner discharged." Frequently they served only one or two months before disbanding; some remained in service a year or more, but none were ever permanently standing companies until 1874.

Frontier Texans generally preferred a regiment or battalion of full-time ranger companies along the line of settlement. During the early days of the Republic, separate full-time companies ranged across the frontier at various times. Later a ranger battalion of full-time "spy companies" under Major Jack Hays was backed up by minuteman ranger companies. When Texas became a state of the Union, ranger companies were sometimes called into service by the U.S. Army. Though raised by the state, they were under U.S.Army direction. Later companies were under state control. Minuteman companies were common across the Texas frontier in the mid1850s and in 1860. As the Civil War broke out the state's full-time Mounted Rifleman companies protected the Texas frontier until they were turned over to the Confederacy at the end of 1861. Another full-time ranger organization, the Frontier Regiment, served during 1862 and reorganized as the Mounted Regiment in 1863 before being turned over to the Confederacy. The Frontier Organization of minuteman rangers provided frontier defense for the remainder of the war (1864-65). The turmoil of the post-Civil War years emphasized the need in Texas for law enforcement officers whose jurisdiction extended beyond county lines. When Military Reconstruction ended, Governor Davis set up the organizations that foreshadowed the role of rangers as law enforcement officers: The State Police 1870-72 and the Frontier Force 1870-71. Many frontier counties raised minuteman ranger companies 1872-82. The "Redemption" government of 1874 disbanded Governor Davis' organizations, but found the need to adopt similar measures by organizing the Special Force of State Troops and the Frontier Battalion.

Much Texas Ranger history is outside the realm of this study including all ranger history after 1882 by which time the organization was primarily concerned with law enforcement. The Frontier Battalion disbanded in 1901. Ranger companies continued to be raised by the state, but some were marred by corruption and political intrigue. A reformation occurred in 1935 when the Texas Rangers and the Highway Department were placed under the Department of Public Safety.

Maps

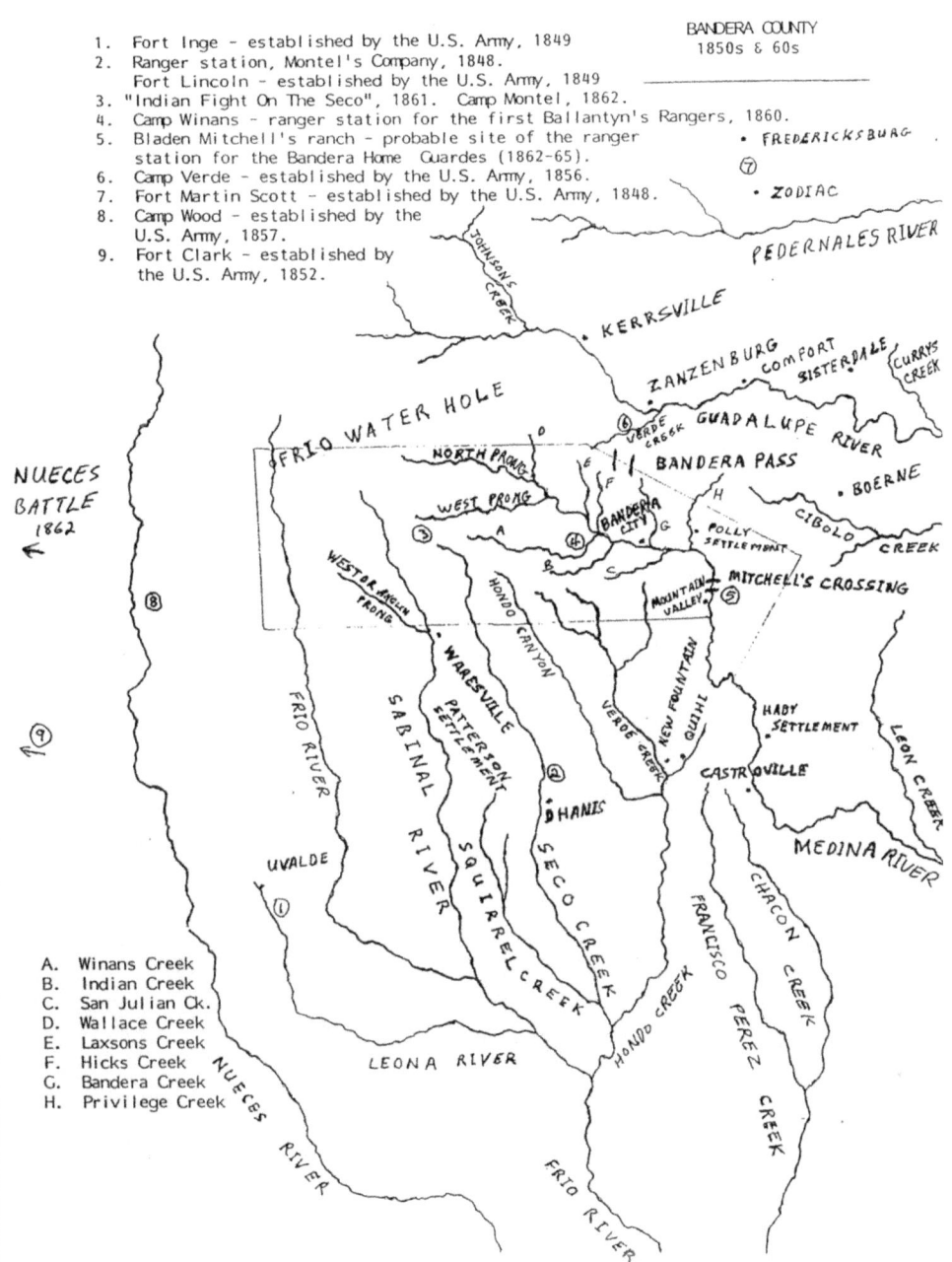

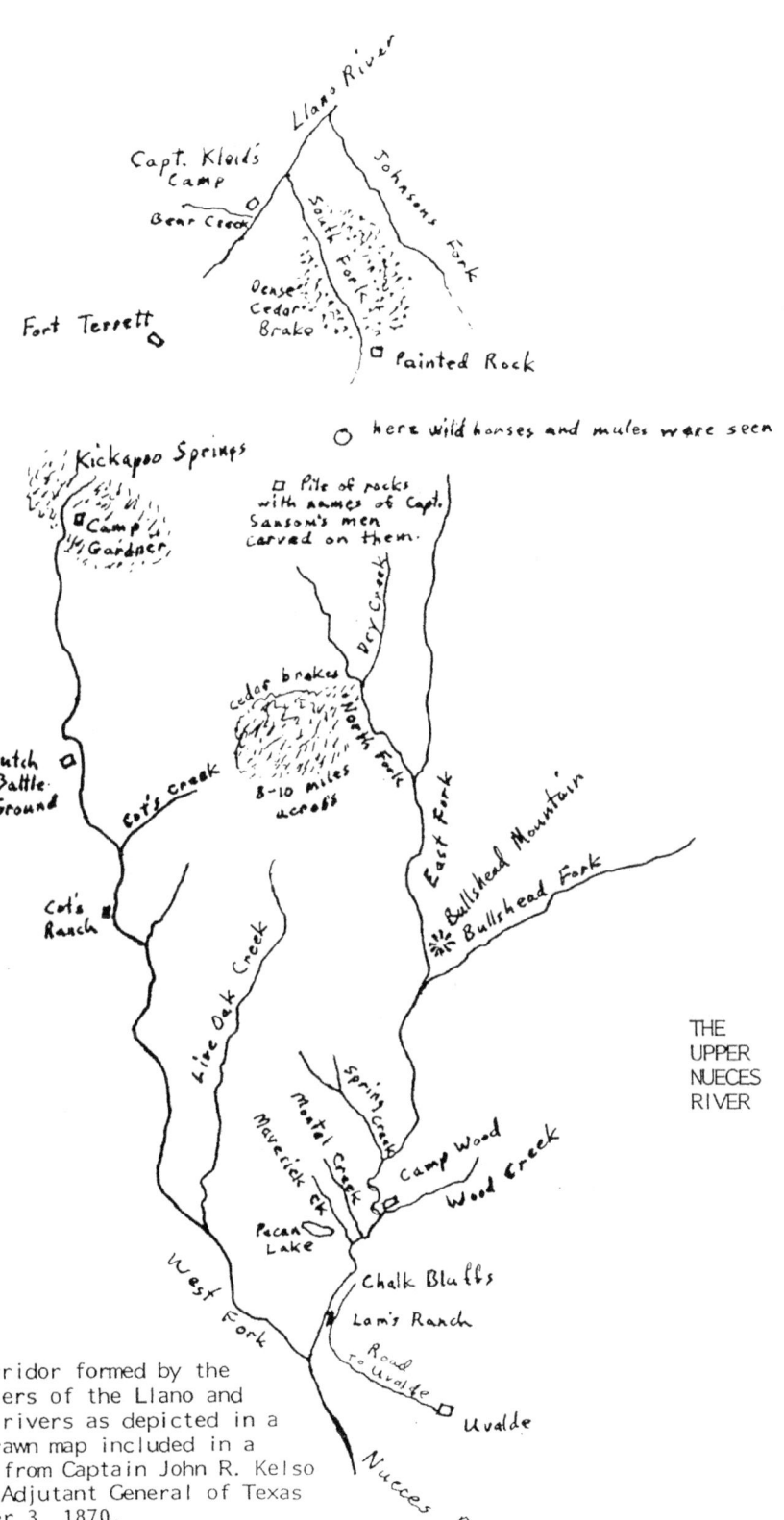

THE UPPER NUECES RIVER

The corridor formed by the headwaters of the Llano and Nueces rivers as depicted in a hand-drawn map included in a report from Captain John R. Kelso to the Adjutant General of Texas December 3, 1870.

THE RIO GRANDE AT EAGLE PASS
MID 1870s

1

The West Texas Frontier

The settlement history of Bandera County begins in the tumultuous era that was termed "Manifest Destiny" in 1845 as the great western migration began. Emigrants from the United States set out for Texas or the Oregon Territory. While land in the United States was $1.25 an acre, land in Texas could be had for 5-10 cents an acre. Most of the Mormons in Illinois were moving to Utah, although a small contingent under Lyman Wight had set out for Texas. The annexation of the Republic of Texas in 1845 and the end of the U.S.-Mexican War in 1848 quickened the pace of the westward movement. The émigrés from the United States were driven by nationalism, the economic cycles, and by individual circumstances. Conditions in Europe insured more immigration.

The middle or western frontier of Texas began to expand during this time. Henri Castro's Colony, the German Adelsverein project, and Elder Lyman Wight's Mormon Colony spearheaded the westward movement in Texas. Father Leopold Moczygemba's Panna Maria settlement brought Polish immigrants. Many other settlers came as families or individuals from Kentucky, Tennessee, and many of the southern United States. Some war veterans and others from the northern United States settled in Texas. They came to a land already rich in history.

The first European to see some of the region that became Bandera County may have been Alvar Nunez Cabeza de Vaca, shipwrecked on the Texas coast in 1528. On his long overland quest to reach Spanish settlements, according to some of the speculative versions of his route, he once camped in or near the Sabinal Canyon.

Luis de Carvajal led an expedition that unsuccessfully searched and dug for silver in the Hondo Canyon around present-day Tarpley. He or other Spaniards may have been responsible for the enigmatic carving of the date 1577 in a cave in that area.

La Salle's French settlement attempt prompted Spanish attention to Texas. The navigational book written by Spanish scholar Pedro Medina in 1545 aided Alonso de Leon as he led his expedition across a wide and unknown land. In 1690 de Leon crossed and named the Medina River.

Long before the Spanish came, Tonkawa Indians were living across Central Texas. They were well-located in a "land of good water" on the trade route between North and South America. Their four-foot bows were highly prized trade items with the Indians living to the south. The Tonkawas declined in numbers as European diseases were transmitted from the south and east. Wars with new Indian neighbors further decimated the Tonkawas.

A series of migrations by different peoples plunged the region into nearly constant turmoil for over 200 years. Spanish settlers, missionaries, and soldiers moved up from the south. The 1680 Pueblo Revolt against Spanish rule in New Mexico speeded the transmission of horses to the various Native American people who became known as the Plains Indians. Apaches, among the first Indians to become a mounted people, moved into the Southwest from the eastern Rocky Mountains. Shortly after that some Shoshone (or Snake) people, also originating in the Rocky Mountains and greatly adapted to horseback warfare, came down to the southern plains where they became known as Comanche. Later small groups of Kickapoos and Delawares came as refugees from their homelands in the northeastern United States to near the end of their 200-year-long migrations.

It is only a slight exaggeration to say that whenever the Spanish were raided by unknown Indians, they asked their Indian friends who that was and their friends would answer in their own language, "the enemy." From the Spanish pronunciation of these words are derived the names Apache and Comanche. Like most Indian groups, they each simply called themselves "The People." First the Apaches and then the Comanches became a barrier to the northern expansion of New Spain.

An Apache-Comanche war erupted for control of the southern buffalo range. The Eastern Apache bands, including the Lipans or Lipaños, bore the brunt of the fighting and suffered heavy losses as the Comanches raided their summer farming settlements. The Spanish settlements and missions unwillingly provided horses for both the Apache and the Comanche war efforts.

Spanish missions and a presidio were established along the San Antonio River where Coahuiltican Indians lived. Later 15 families and four bachelors from Spain's Canary Islands arrived at the port of Veracruz, Mexico, and traveled overland to the future city of San Antonio. Near the end of their journey, while they camped near the Medina River, Lipan Apaches stole much of their livestock. The

Canary Islanders reached the Presidio San Antonio de Bexar March 9, 1731. Nearby they founded the Villa de San Fernando, but the 55 *Isleños* eventually mingled with the few hundred *Bexareños* already living in and around the presidio and missions to meld into San Antonio de Bexar.

To the north and northwest of San Antonio is an elevated land from which flows many rivers, each separated by a rough divide of steeply ridged hills. The Hill Country of Texas was mostly grass lands when the Europeans arrived. Live Oaks could be found scattered about, singly or in mottes. Huge cypress trees lined most rivers and creeks. Cedar (*Ashe juniper*) survived the frequent grass fires of late summer by clustering in "brakes" at the headwaters of some of the rivers and among rough terrain. The Lost Maples nestled near the headwaters of the Sabinal and Medina rivers.

Among the animals found in the Hill Country were panthers, bears, and wolves. An occasional jaguar prowled the cedar brakes. Feral cattle, descendants of a Spanish breed and usually described as "mostly black or brown", were numerous. These wary animals only went to water at night. When threatened, the bulls would form a circle around the cows and calves. They were hunted for sport as big game and rangers on scout sometimes shot them for food.

The geography of the upper Medina River valley determined that the area would never be on a main thoroughfare of civilization, but always an area of strategic military importance as long as there were Indian raids on the West Texas Frontier. In horseback times the practical traveler, whether Native American or European, followed the trails over the passes through the divides. Peggy Tobin described *La Puerta de la Bandera* in the Fall 1992 issue of the <u>Bandera County Historian</u>:

> Bandera Pass, the V-shaped natural passage through the long ridges separating the Guadalupe and Medina River valleys in the hill country of Texas, has given its name to the county wherein it lies, to the nearby county seat, and to two creeks in the county. While many legends abound, all having to do with battles carried on by warring Indian tribes, fighting each other or the Spaniards of San Antonio de Bexar, no documented origin of the name has been found nor a date for its discovery by expeditions from Bexar or the Rio Grande.

One of the legends concerning the origin of the name of the pass illustrates the Spanish meaning: Banners were said to have been placed there to mark a treaty boundary between the Spanish and Apaches. Another legend has a General Bandera defeating the

Apaches in a battle at the pass. One candidate for European discoverer of Bandera Pass is Captain Jose Urrutia whose troop of Spanish soldiers scouted the region for Lipan Apaches in 1739.

The pass is 50-75 feet lower than the surrounding hills and is about 100 yards wide and 500 yards long. Only a few other routes provide north-south access between the valleys of the Guadalupe and Medina rivers. In the settlement era these routes were little more than horse trails over the rough hills. One of these trails, north of Wallace Creek in northern Bandera County is traversed today by State Highway 16 and must be driven at speeds of 5-10 MPH in an automobile. From the area of the headwaters of the Medina and Sabinal rivers, trails over or around the hilly Frio/Sabinal divide gave access to the valley of the Frio River at a place known as the Frio Water Hole. The rivers and creeks drain southeasterly from the area of Bandera County forming canyons through the hills. The canyons open onto rolling prairie from which Indian raiders could spread through the settlements.

In the Eighteenth Century, the Apaches were losing their war against the Comanches. The Lipan Apaches were separated from other Apache bands who were pushed westward from the southern plains. The Lipans in Texas had only their former enemy, the numerically diminished Tonkawas, as a fierce, but inconsequential ally. In 1757 the Lipan Apaches made a bid to ally themselves with the Spanish against the Comanches. A mission and presidio were built on the San Saba River. An army of Comanches wiped out the mission. The presidio was abandoned. Spanish retaliatory efforts against the Comanches failed. Although another Spanish mission was established for the Lipans in 1762 near present day Camp Wood, the Lipan-Spanish alliance did not last much longer. In spite of Spanish and Apache efforts, Comanche control extended from present-day Kansas in the north and through the Texas Plains to the Hill Country in the south where the southernmost band became known as the Penatekas, the Honey-eaters, because of the many wild bee hives that could be found in the region.

The Comanches, as most Native American people at that time, associated other people with their geographic location rather than their flag of allegiance. Among circumstances that determined a different Comanche approach to New Mexico than to Mexico and Texas included a series of Spanish-New Mexican military victories against the Comanches between 1716 and 1779. Followed up by skillful diplomacy, the eventual result was the establishment of peaceful trade between Comanches and the New Mexico settlements, the

Comanchero trade. The Comanches continued to raid into Texas and deep into Mexico.

In later years bands of Indians displaced from the eastern United States, Delawares and Kickapoos, sometimes appeared in the Medina River Valley. The Delaware Indians were living along a river in the present states of Delaware and New Jersey when Jamestown was founded. The English named the river and bay after Sir Thomas West, the third Lord de la Warr, governor of the Virginia Colony in 1610. The inhabitants of the Delaware River Basin called themselves *Lenni Lenape*, the common people. Over the next couple of hundred years they migrated across the country, settling successively in the areas of Pennsylvania, Ohio, Indiana, Missouri, Kansas, and finally Oklahoma, while a few groups pushed on into Texas.

Delaware encampments were variously reported to be on the Pedernales, Guadalupe, and Medina rivers during the early 1850s. These friendly, but wary, people were an important element of the frontier Indian trade at that time. Jim Shaw, whose Delaware name meant Bear Head, often was interpreter for the Texas Indian Agent, Major Robert S. Neighbors. Most of the Texas Delawares moved to the Brazos Reservation in 1854. In 1859 they were moved to the Indian Territory.

The name of the Kickapoo Indians evolved from the sound of the word *Kiwigapawa*, meaning "he moves about". Around 1600, when first noticed by Europeans, they were living between Lake Michigan and Lake Erie where they had been pushed from the east by the Iroquois Confederacy. The Iroquois were attempting to maintain a monopoly on the fur trade. Like the Delawares, the Kickapoo fought on various sides in the fur trade wars and the colonial and frontier wars of the French, English, and Indians, including the French and Indian War, Pontiac's War, Tecumseh's War, and the War of 1812.

The Kickapoo followed a similar historical migration to that of the Delawares, but came to use their knowledge of European economics, warfare, and international intrigue more aggressively. Originally a farming and hunting people, the Kickapoo settled in East Texas with the Caddo and Cherokee farming communities, shortly before Stephen Austin's colonizing project began. Spanish administrators welcomed the Kickapoo as additional troops against marauding Indians and European competitors. Admiring the Spanish military traditions, the Kickapoo began addressing their chiefs as *capitan*.

In the late 1830s the Indians in East Texas were driven from their lands and the Kickapoo began living a more nomadic life, ranging from the southern Indian Territory to Mexico just below the Rio Grande. They were welcomed in Mexico as a buffer to the raids of the Lipan and Mescalero Apaches, Comanches, and other Plains Indians. They became extensively involved in the frontier Indian trade and developed a near monopoly on trade with the Comanches. Weapons, tobacco, cloth, and other items were furnished to the Comanches in exchange for the only payment the Kickapoo would accept: horses and mules. Many Comanche raids on the Texan and Mexican frontiers were motivated by the need for more horses and mules to meet the high prices of the Kickapoo traders.

Beginning in the early 1820s the Spanish and then the Mexican government promoted impresario settlement projects as a way of populating the eastern portion of the state of Cohuila and Tejas. The Austin Colony, situated below the Comanche plains mostly between the Brazos and Colorado rivers, had difficulties with the Karankawa Indians of the Texas coastal regions. In 1822 the Mexican governor ordered the settlers to form two militia districts, each with a civilian *alcalde*. The following year Stephen F. Austin raised a mounted ranging company. In a land remote from any effective military or political force, European militia traditions, filtered through time and the United States and Mexico, found a natural place to evolve into a tradition known as Texas Rangers.

The ranger concept may have originated in the Scottish borderlands, but as it developed in Texas much was adapted from the Mexican and Indian cultures of the open prairies. Ranger companies during the Texas Revolution were mostly deployed as scouts or to aid the refugees of the Runaway Scrape. Texians who had grown up in the forested United States learned hard military lessons from the Mexican light cavalry on the Texas prairie. The Anglo-celtic rangers and cattlemen in the Republic of Texas adopted Hispanic riding style and perspective.

Some men who became well-known in the Bandera region participated in the Texas Revolution or were drawn to Texas by the adventure and opportunity of a new land. Ben Highsmith, who left the Alamo as a courier, and William Ware, a captain in Sam Houston's army, fought in the San Jacinto Battle. William Ware founded Waresville in 1852 and Ben Highsmith settled in Bandera County in the 1880s. Hendrick Arnold, a free black frontiersman, served with his father-in-law, Erastus (Deef) Smith, as a scout for the Texian Army at the Battle of Bexar 1835 and at the Battle of San Jacinto 1836. Texian soldiers were paid with land and the Hendrick Arnold Survey covered part of the area that became Bandera City in 1853.

He died in the 1849 cholera epidemic and is buried south of San Antonio along the Medina River.

Three men whose enterprise eventually founded the town of Bandera City also arrived in Texas during this time. Charles de Montel, a German (originally Scheidemontel) who came to Texas by way of Pennsylvania, arrived and enlisted, according to some accounts, in time to serve as one of the men to guard General Santa Anna. John James from Nova Scotia, delayed by an illness, arrived too late for the war. Both men became surveyors of the Bexar Territories.

After graduating from Transylvania College in Kentucky, John Hunter Herndon set out for Texas, arriving in Houston in 1838. He became a lawyer and married Brazoria County heiress, Barbara Calvit. He was among the movers and shakers of Antebellum Texas economics and politics and by 1860 had become the wealthiest man in the state.

From 1835, the Lipan Apaches were divided in their search for allies against the Comanches as some took opposite sides with Mexico or Texas during or after the Texas Revolution. Many bands changed sides frequently over the years, but the stalwart chiefs Flacco and Castro were each given the rank of colonel in the Texian Army. Castro and 15 of his men became an official Texas Ranger company for a few months in 1839. During the late 1830s the Lipan Apaches in Texas found many occasions to test their new allies against the Comanches. Noah Smithwick was living near Bastrop:

> In the winter of 1839 a party of Lipan Indians out on a hunt discovered an encampment of Comanches up on the San Gabriel, about fifty miles from the city of Austin. The Comanches and Lipans were inveterate enemies, so the Lipans, too weak to attack the camp alone, hastened into the settlements and gave the alarm, offering to assist in dislodging the Comanches. There were no troops in the vicinity, and knowing that if the Comanches were allowed to remain they would soon be making predatory incursions into the settlements, we at once decided to make up a party to go against them. Colonel John H. Moore being the leading spirit in the plan, was given command. Captain Eastland raised a company of thirty men at LaGrange. Bastrop raised a company of about the same number, electing me its captain. To this number was added the full fighting force of the Lipans, under command of Chief Castro, assisted by his son, Juan Castro, young Flacco and Juan Seis.

The Republic of Texas could not long afford a standing army

and raised ranger companies during intervals of heavy Indian raids and for other contingencies. Erastus (Deef) Smith, Houston's chief of scouts during the Revolution, was captain of one of the ranger companies operating around San Antonio in the early days of the Republic. Henry Karnes was another. His company had a fight with Comanches on Seco Creek in 1838. Both men were instrumental in developing the ranger tactics for single-shot firearms that produced an effective Indian fighting force for Texas. John Coffee (Jack) Hays, a ranger who served in each of these companies, later developed aggressive tactics for use of the Colt revolver. He was 19 and an experienced surveyor when he joined Smith's company.

Fierce fighting between Texians and Comanches between 1836 and 1840 left both sides badly mauled. March 19, 1840 a meeting between Penateka Comanche leaders and Texas military officials in San Antonio might have led to better relations between these peoples. Instead both sides arrived with rigid expectations and the result was increased animosity. The interpreter at the meeting was not the best and a disagreement arose over the number of captives the Comanches where supposed to return to the settlements. Troops were called in to arrest the chiefs. The ensuing Council House Fight left 35 Indians dead, including 12 Penateka leaders. The Comanche women and children not killed in the melee were jailed pending further negotiations. Seven San Antonians were killed and 10 or more wounded. John James was in the Council House and narrowly escaped death or injury when an Indian lunged at him with a knife. A man named Jim Dunn pulled him back and shot the Indian through the head.

In an August 1840 raid encouraged by agents from Mexico, Chief Buffalo Hump led 400-1,000 Comanche and Kiowa to the Texas Hill Country to begin a campaign through the heart of the Texas settlements. Skirting San Antonio and coming into the settlements near Gonzales, they sacked Victoria, and raided all the way to Linnville on the Texas coast, the Linnville Raid. On their return to the north, the Indian raiders were defeated by Texas militia at Plum Creek. The ranger skills that would become legendary were well-developed by this time. After this defeat the Penateka Comanche mostly made camp north of the Red River and their raiders into Texas came in smaller groups, usually no more than 50 individuals to a group, often breaking into smaller groups or reforming into larger groups as conditions necessitated.

In most Indian cultures, any warrior who could find followers could organize and lead a raid. After drawing Texian blood and/or capturing sufficient numbers of horses, they would ride hard for 24-

48 hours to put distance between themselves and the settlements, then continue at a more leisurely pace through wilderness sanctuary. Riding a succession of horses gave them an advantage over pursuing rangers or soldiers who usually had no extra horses to fall back on when their mounts tired. Raiders sometimes set grass fires to cover their trails. The many roaming buffalo herds could further obscure a trail.

At close range the Indian's bow and arrows were often more than a match for the ranger's muzzle-loading, single-shot, ball-and-cap, black-powder rifle. An Indian could send many arrows flying while a ranger poured a measure of powder down the barrel of the rifle, wrapped a lead ball with a patch of greased cloth and rammed it down the barrel hard against the powder and then had to cock the hammer and place a small, easily dropped, copper percussion cap onto a small metal tube protruding where the hammer strikes. Then he could take aim. Some rangers and settlers preferred the more versatile double-barreled, muzzle-loading shotgun. Although loaded by a similar ritual and shorter in range, it did provide two shots. A ranger or militia company engaging Indians had to take care not to fire all its rifles at once. Captain Karnes made sure no more than a third of his men fired at the same time.

Samuel Colt patented his revolver pistol design in 1836. He opened a factory in Patterson, New Jersey. Colt pistols and carbines were purchased for the Texas Navy in 1839. Texas Rangers got most of their Patterson Colt five-shooting pistols in 1844 from the disbanded Texas Navy. Jack Hays and his rangers made effective use of the first revolver, but they needed a sturdier, larger caliber weapon. Around 1846 Samuel Walker, a former ranger and then a U.S. Army officer went to Washington to complete negotiations with Samuel Colt for a six-shooting pistol that became known as the Walker Colt.

The six-shooting pistol often gave the settler a defensive edge and, in the hands of rangers like Jack Hays, became an effective offensive horseback weapon. The Colt pistols of that time were the ball-and-cap type, meaning that each chamber of the cylinder had to be loaded by the same procedures as for the barrel of a muzzle-loading rifle. A lever below the barrel of the pistol facilitated the ramming of the ball into each chamber. Percussion caps were placed on metal nipples at the rear of each chamber.

Although some of the five-shooting Patterson Colt rifles found their way to Texas, repeating rifles, particularly the cartridge-firing type, were not widely available in the region until after the Civil

War. Smith and Wesson had developed metal-cased cartridges for pistols in the late 1850s, but these were not widely available in Texas until the early 1870s.

Jack Hays was 23 when he became a ranger captain. He raised a succession of companies during the 1840s, often with some of the same men and some of them later became ranger captains. Captain Hays and company camped on Leon Creek west of San Antonio in the spring and summer of 1841. They had many engagements with Comanches in and around the valley of the upper Medina River. Captain Hays and a detachment of his company united with Captain Flores and his rangers to fight 10 Comanches just south of present-day Utopia. Another fight took place at the head of the Sabinal River.

An ambush in June 1841 (dates vary from 1841-44) that might be an apocryphal tale, became known as the Battle of Bandera Pass. Captain Hays was leading 40 rangers through the pass to scout the Guadalupe valley when around 100 Comanches sprang their ambush. The rangers fought the Indians to a draw and both sides withdrew to bury their dead. Five rangers are said to be buried on the south side of the pass. The chief and perhaps other Comanches are said to be buried on the north side. Among the survivors in this story, William A.A. (Big Foot) Wallace settled on Chacon Creek in the area that became Medina County and owned land along Wallace Creek in the area that became Bandera County. Ben Highsmith settled in Bandera County in the 1880s. Both men are known to have served in some of the various companies that Jack Hays raised.

During 1841 a Texian army, including John H. Herndon as major of a brigade, was sent to the Rio Grande in response to the most recent threat from Mexico. Flacco the Younger and another Lipan Apache accompanied the Somerville Expedition. Some of the men, including Big Foot Wallace, were not satisfied with merely showing the flag along the border and went on to Meir and the drawing of the beans. As the main portion of the army, with Major Herndon, returned to San Antonio, two men from Somerville's army killed Flacco and his companion for their horses. Noah Smithwick was sent to tell Flacco the Elder (or Flacco Colonel) that his son was killed by Mexicans. Chief Flacco who had been a faithful ally of Captain Hays, learned of the cover-up attempt by the Texas government and moved his band into Mexico.

In 1844 Henri Castro brought European settlers, largely Alsatians, to populate a land grant west of San Antonio. Captain Hay's ranger company was stationed in San Antonio and often provided protection as the new town of Castroville went up along the Medina

River. In the tradition of Stephen Austin's and other impresarios' land settlement projects, the Castro Colony and the German Adelsverein project (which founded New Braunfels and Fredericksburg) were models for future settlement in the West Texas area. Various individuals founded many of the Hill Country towns with smaller-scaled projects.

John James and Charles de Montel, as surveyors for Bexar County, were involved in Henri Castro's project. Charles de Montel met his future wife, Justine Pingenot, among the Castro colonists. They married November 11, 1845. He established a ranch north of Castroville and engaged in the Indian trade around the new town. The Bexar County surveyors were paid with land in those days and both men had accumulated large holdings. John James had already established a successful land business in San Antonio. He married Emaline Polley in 1847. After she died of cholera in 1848, he married Annie Milby of Brazoria County in 1851.

These two and other assistant Bexar County Surveyors went into the extensive Bexar Territories in surveying parties indistinguishable from ranger scouts: Both went well-armed, only their purpose and the surveying equipment differed. Robert Hays was the Bexar County Surveyor. His brother, Jack Hays, worked as a surveyor when not in the ranger service and had been Bexar County Surveyor himself. John James was the next Bexar County Surveyor and held other county offices at various times.

Nicholas Haby spent most of 1845 in Castroville in an A.J. Sowell account that recalls that some of the Indians were friendly at that time. Much of the Indian trade was in turkeys and deer hams. Indian and settler alike enjoyed the horse races and the young braves "performing some brilliant but daring and dangerous feats of horsemanship. These were mostly Lipans, but sometimes the Comanches and Kickapoos would come in, especially when a new treaty was to be made with them." A.J. Sowell's account of Jacob Haby describes friendly Lipan and Delaware Indians living along the Medina River in the mid1840s. The account of the Huffman family relates their necessity of trading with Indians for meat and that 500 lived along the Medina River near Castroville.

In the last years of the Republic of Texas, full-time ranger or "spy" companies served as scouts to notify minuteman companies when Indian raiders were seen approaching the settlements. Buck Barry described this use of coordinated ranger companies:

> When I returned to the falls of the Brazos, I joined the little army of the Republic of Texas, numbering two hundred and

fifty men, commanded by Major Jack Hays. I was placed in Captain Thomas J. Smith's company that was assigned to the protection of that portion of the frontier between the Brazos and the Trinity Rivers, a day's ride above the settlements.

The "spy companies" each had 30 men divided into three squads. Each squad patrolled a section of the frontier line each day in an effort to detect Indian raiders. "In case we discovered Indians or their trail going toward the settlements," Barry recalled," it was our business to beat them there and notify the minutemen of their coming." The frontier counties at this time were organized into minuteman ranger companies that were prepared to respond to the reports of the full-time spy companies.

When the Republic of Texas became the State of Texas in 1845, frontier defense became a Federal responsibility. The U.S. Army began building forts to protect mail routes and the line of frontier settlements, but there were never enough soldiers provided for all the army's tasks. The treaty ending the U.S.-Mexican War (1848) stipulated that the United States would stop the Plains Indians from raiding into Mexico. The U.S. Army's dragoons or "mounted rifles" were not sufficient in numbers nor were they sufficiently skilled in light cavalry tactics to deter many Indian raids. However, raids upon Texas settlements by Comanches and other Plains Indians increased as raids into Mexico became more difficult.

In 1846 the first treaty between the United States and Texas Indians defined official relations for the next few years. Lipan chiefs Costelito (Costilietos?) and Soli refused to sign the treaty and moved their bands to Mexico. Buck Barry was still in the ranger service during the transition to statehood and was present for the treaty negotiations:

> The tribe of Lipans who had befriended Texas in all her struggles was there. This tribe had no sins to atone for when Texas was annexed, for the Lipans were annexed, also. But there were two Lipans, young warriors, who had come across two Germans on the head of the Medina, getting timber. As they could not talk English, Spanish, or the Indian Language, they took them to be intruders on Texas soil and killed them, which act they did not deny. So General Butler told the Lipan chief to bring these two young warriors up to be tried for the murder and that he would hold him responsible for the act if he failed to bring up the culprits. The chief told the agent, Butler, that these Germans were not good Texans, as they could not talk like Texans, their clothing was not like that of the Texans, and

they wore wooden shoes. That night the whole tribe ran away and went to Mexico. There were but five of us Rangers and we made no attempt to follow them.

Lipan Apaches in Mexico made raids along the Texas frontier. Kickapoo and Comanche raiders made sure the Lipan Apaches in Texas were implicated, too. In August 1847, somewhere beyond the headwaters of the Guadalupe River Comanche Chief Can-See-Nothing led his raiders and stolen horses through a Lipan Apache camp. The Comanche leader could clearly see what the result would be. Rangers under Lieutenant H.M.C. Brown followed the trail and attacked the Apache camp killing thirty Lipans and taking two hundred horses. The Lipan survivors withdrew to the Pecos River from which Chief Chiquito and his remaining warriors staged a retaliatory raid into DeWitt County. Major Robert Neighbors, the Indian Agent, managed to re-establish peaceful relations with Chiquito which lasted tenuously up to 1854.

Around 1846 some of Jack Hays' former rangers settled at San Marcos, a site the Spanish had attempted to settle several times, but had mostly abandoned due to its proximity to the Comanche Barrier. The town became the county seat of Hays County in 1848. In 1847 John D. Pitts, a former adjutant general of Texas, established a settlement southwest of San Marcos. Many of the people he brought there were from Georgia. Other people came into the area, settling all along a four-mile stretch of the Old San Antonio Road from Purgatory Creek to York Creek. The settlement became known as String Town. Many of the String Town people were waiting for the frontier forts to be completed before moving out onto the frontier. Henry Stevens, born in Tennessee, recalled hunting trips with another Tennessean about 1849:

> On reaching San Marcos I rented a piece of land and began to make preparations to make a crop. I soon got acquainted with a man by the name of Pat Saner, who was a jolly, good hearted fellow, and a great hand to hunt. There were a great many wild cattle in the cedar brakes on the head of a little but very dangerous stream called Purgatory, which flows into the San Marcos River. Deer and turkey were very plentiful then. This man Saner, his brother Tom and myself hunted a great deal the year I was there.

During 1847 Henri Castro founded the last town of his colony and named it D'Hanis after a French businessman who had invested in the project. A group of German idealists formed a commune along

Sister Creek, a tributary of the Guadalupe River. The commune was unsuccessful, but the members remained as the settlement of Sisterdale. At the same time most of the group of Lipan Apaches led by Chiquito and Chipote were on the Pecos River while a smaller group stayed near Fredericksburg. Juan Castro's band of Lipans were on Francisco Perez Creek in Medina County in A.J. Sowell's account of Christian Batot and early Castroville, "The Delaware and Lipan Indians also came and traded with them until the latter became hostile. The Delawares lived over in the Guadalupe valley, near where Comfort is now, but there were no settlers there then."

Except for a few tragic incidents, the Castro Colonists generally got along well with their Indian neighbors, but soon settlers from East Texas and other parts of the United States also began to move into the region. By 1848 the border Indians (Tonkawas, Lipan Apaches, Delawares, and sometimes Kickapoos) were finding it increasingly difficult to live near the expanding Texas frontier. The plight of Juan Castro's Lipans and the European settlers is described in A.J. Sowell's Life of Bigfoot Wallace:

> Although the Indians who lived on the Francisco had been friendly, the time came when they had trouble with the white settlers who had commenced to settle west of the Medina and which ended in an open rupture. A fight or two took place and the Lipans moved into the mountain country towards the Northwest and made many raids on the whites. In one of these raids they got a mule and horse of Bigfoot Wallace, besides many horses and mules belonging to other settlers. This was in 1848. [...] When the Lipans arrived at their camp which was at what is now called "Frio Water Hole" on the divide at the head draws of the river, "Chepeta," the chief's daughter, recognized the horse and mule of Wallace and was greatly agitated, and warned her people to look out, that Bigfoot would be after them sure.

A year later Big Foot Wallace and Ed Westfall led a militia group of Medina County men against the Lipan Apaches in a desperate fight that ended in defeat for Juan Castro's band.

As Comanche raids also began to increase during this time, Charles de Montel captained a ranger company stationed on Seco Creek one mile from D'Hanis. The following year Fort Lincoln (1849-51) was established by the U.S. Army in place of the ranger station. Richard Irving Dodge was a young second lieutenant when he was stationed at the "little two-company frontier post, exposed to the wiles and machinations of the most cunning, the most mischievously artful, of all the United States Indians, the Comanches." Patrols from Fort Lincoln often ranged far to the north of the post as Lieutenant Dodge remembered:

> I was returning with my command from a long scout; our route led through the Guadalupe mountains, by the Bandera Pass. These mountains were at that time infested by hostile Indians, who secure in their fastnesses, watched the plains below, pouncing upon settlements or unwary travelers and hurrying with their plunder through the Bandera Pass to their secure retreats.

Lieutenant Dodge felt that the pass was "at that time the most dangerous locality in Texas." He described being separated from the patrol he was leading and then pursued by Indians north of the Guadalupe River. He had a good head start:

> The mule responded nobly, and, as if comprehending the necessity for extra effort, fairly flew over the ground for the next five or six miles. The Guadalupe was crossed, then the Verde, and yet no sign or sound of pursuit.
> The race so far had been on a broad Indian trail, through woods and thickets, but from the timbered fringe along the Verde to the summit of the Pass, was a three-mile slope of bare prairie. Until I could get through the Pass I was obliged to keep the trail, the mountains being elsewhere almost impassable; but once through it I was safe, for then, leaving the trail, and plunging into ravines and thickets of the Medina river, I could elude pursuit until night should give me the opportunity to reach my post. When about half way over this bare ground, to my inexpressible delight, I ran into the trail of my command, but had hardly time to congratulate myself when several Indians emerged in full pursuit, from the thickets of the Verde.

The Indians turned back upon reaching the tracks of the other soldiers. Lieutenant Dodge crossed over Bandera Pass and lived to become a colonel and to publish his memoirs in 1883.

In 1850 Seminole and Negro-Seminole Indians left the Creek Reservation in Indian Territory, passing through Texas on their way to Mexico. Under chiefs Wild Cat and John Horse they established a military colony at El Nacimiento on lands granted by the Mexican government in exchange for defense of the Northern Mexican Frontier against filibusters and marauding Indians.

The various Lipan bands were still looking for reliable allies against the Comanches. Lieutenant Dodge told of a band of Lipans on the Pedernales River that became hostile and moved to Mexico. The varying numbers of Lipans signing the 1850 and '51 treaties may reflect the waivering allegiances as some bands moved between the frontiers of Mexico and West Texas. Document 98, Volume 3, <u>Texas Indian Papers</u> lists the Lipan Chiefs who signed the 1850 treaty: Chi-ci-to, Chi-po-ti, Ye-keh-tas-na, Keh-rauch. The Lipans signing the 1851 treaty (Document 103): Chicito (little Captain), Coyote (Wolf), Quaco, Chapote, Manuel, Colonel Lamos, Captain John Castro, Captain John Flaco, Manuel Hernandes. By the end of 1854 Lipans would sign no more treaties with the U.S.

Along the West Texas Frontier Indian agent Robert Neighbors strived to maintain peace with the border Indians, but grievances accumulated on both sides. Most of his time was taken up dealing with Comanches. Kickapoos further complicated the situation as they tried, against treaty stipulations, to maintain trade relationships with the Comanches. From 1850 to 1852 John H. Rollins, a Whig Party appointee, was Supervising Indian Agent for Texas as relations with the border Indians deteriorated. In contrast to Major Neighbors' practice of going out to meet the Indians in their home grounds, Agent Rollins required the Indian leaders to come to him. A letter from Rollins to General G.M. Brooke September 25, 1850, illustrates the agent's heavy-handed approach to dealing with Indians. [Document 94, Volume 3, <u>Texas Indian Papers</u>:]

> This party is under the control of the Civil Chief Che-ke-to and the war chief Cha-po-ta, both old men of much influence and strongly attached to the whites. The larger portion of the Lipan are encamped on the Pecos where they made corn this year and the accounts as to these are not very full or satisfactory. They are under the control of some sub-chief and are reported entirely friendly, but Cha-po-ta acknowledged that he had not seen any of them for three months and he could not, of course, know much of their present pursuits or feelings. I directed Cha-po-ta to bring his party back to Llano and to notify the other band that if they intended to be friendly they must <u>all</u> be upon that river by the 15th of November. He said he would inform them at once but he could not say positively that they would come, <u>he thought</u> they would. [...] I informed the Kickapoo that they must leave the country in two months as they were intruders. I informed the Lipan that such of them as did not come to the Llano would be treated as Comanche in the event of a War.

Rollins was replaced in January 1852 with another Whig appointee, Major George Thomas Howard. Meanwhile Major Neighbors had been elected to the Texas legislature and served on the committee for Indian affairs. Howard, with a reputation as an old Indian fighter, had been a supporter of Mirabeau B. Lamar's politics during the Republic, while Neighbors had favored Sam Houston's Indian policies. Neighbors was re-appointed Supervising Indian Agent by the Democrats in 1853. Howard stayed on as a disgruntled subagent.

In the wake of the U.S.-Mexican War, a U.S. Boundary Commission was sent to map out the new southern boundary of the United States. The descriptions given by members of the Boundary Commission suggest Agent Rollins was misinformed about the roles of the two Lipan chiefs. On October 24, 1850, the U.S. Boundary Commissioner, John Russell Bartlett, was nine days west of Fredericksburg when he met Chipote, the civil chief, and Chiquito, the war chief:

> This chief [Chipote] was about sixty years of age, rather corpulent, owing to the life of ease which he gave us to understand he had been leading, and was mounted on a mule so disproportionately small, as to present a most ludicrous appearance. He had a pleasant, benevolent countenance, and bore so striking a resemblance to the portraits of General Cass, that every one noticed it. He was well dressed in a suit of deerskin, with his bow and arrows slung across his back: these were enclosed in a beautiful case made of the skin of the American leopard, and he wore a pouch of the same material by his side.
> In mien and conduct the old chief was extremely dignified and self-possessed, although his Indian gravity was not proof against the jovial conduct and expressions of our little company, all of whom took an interest in this first specimen of the wild denizens of the prairie that we had met with.

His only description of Chiquito was that he was "about the age of Chipota, and similarly dressed." John Cremony, the U.S. Boundary Commission's interpreter, described Chiquito in more detail:

> About two hours after camping, we were joined by four more Lipans, the leader being named Chiquito, a Spanish term, signifying "the little one." He was tall, thin, sinewy, and had the appearance of having been possessed of more than ordinary powers of endurance. The likeness of this chief to General [Andrew?] Jackson was quite as remarkable and striking as

that of Chipota to General [Lewis] Cass, and was a general subject of remark.

The Boundary Commission party continued westward, crossing the Comanche War Trail near Comanche Springs. Major Robert H. Emory, in charge of the military escort, reported a distant view of an estimated four hundred warriors returning from their raids into Mexico with a herd of 1,000 horses. Later the Boundary Commission, which had taken the new "northern" route from Fredericksburg to Franklin (El Paso), met the freighters of Coons' Train, which had taken the more established "southern" route from San Antonio on their way to supply the U.S. Army posts around Franklin. The freighters were stranded at the last water hole along the route that had water that year and were waiting for barrels of water for the men and livestock to be set up along the rest of the route. Amasa Clark was among the freighters and the event was described in his reminiscences as well as in the Boundary Commissioner's account.

New York-born Amasa Clark was never a ranger, but his reminiscences illuminate life on the West Texas Frontier. He had been discharged from the U.S. Army shortly after the end of the U.S.-Mexican War. He stayed around San Antonio for a while with some other discharged veterans and became acquainted with Orlando B. Miles and his wife, Diane. O.B. Miles had served in the same regiment as Amasa Clark during the war, but in a different company. He had been an attendant in the army hospital in San Antonio before his discharge. Amasa Clark made several freighting trips and, with O.B. Miles, later tried peddling wares between San Antonio and Victoria. Around 1851, while Miles found work freighting shingles out of the Guadalupe River Valley, Amasa Clark set up a whiskey store in a little settlement on the Guadalupe River north of San Antonio along the road to Fredericksburg. This may have been Joshua Brown's settlement on Curry's Creek. It consisted of a few individuals and the Miles and Brown families as Amasa Clark remembered:

> A party of Tonkaway Indians came in and stopped there, and Willy, the German, sold them some whiskey. The Indians said they were hungry and wanted us to give them beef. They said if we did not give them beef they would kill a cow anyhow. It was a cold rainy day and they went into Brown's house and stayed there. They begged for coffee, but Mrs. Brown told them she did not have any coffee. Night came on and three or four of the Indians stayed in Brown's house, laying around on the dirt floor. Mrs. Brown was afraid to stay there that night, so she

and Mr. Brown with their three children went out to a postoak thicket and spent the night, and I stayed with the Indians. In two or three days Major Nabors, the Indian agent, came and paid for the cattle the Indians had killed for beef, and Major Nabors talked pretty rough to Mr. Willy for selling whiskey to the Indians. The Indians finally left and went over on the Medina River. They camped on Indian Creek in Bandera County, and that is how Indian Creek got its name. Here the Indians had a big camp.

The shortage of cavalry in the U.S. Army was made apparent in the U.S.-Mexican War. While most of the Texas Ranger companies raised for the war were disbanded at its end, a few remained operational in Texas for a time. The commander of the U.S. troops in Texas, General George M. Brooke, called on Governor George T. Wood for three ranger companies beginning in 1849 and continued the practice with Governor Peter H. Bell as he discussed the positioning of ranger companies in a letter written from San Antonio March 6, 1850. [Document 65, Volume 5, Texas Indian Papers:]

> This new company will be ordered here to receive its supplies, and will then be stationed on both sides of the Medina, operating between that river and Fort Lincoln on one side, and on the other, from the Medina towards the Guadalupe, and in the Bandera pass.

The new company was needed due to the transfer of J.B. McGowan's company to another region west of Fort Inge, but detailed information on this era of ranger history is rare. By the end of 1850 General Brooke had asked Governor Bell for six ranger companies. The captains were John S. (Rip) Ford, John Grumbles, J.B. McGowan, Henry McCulloch, R.E. Sutton, and William (Big Foot) Wallace. These ranger companies served as light cavalry for the army.

Captain Wallace's company served out of Fort Inge. The 1850 U.S. Census listed 88 men in his "Texas Ranging Company." His lieutenants were Peter R. Bradey, William H. Powell, and Absolam K. Vansickle. A.J. Sowell recounted that Edward Westfall later served as a lieutenant in Wallace's 76-man company. Much of Wallace's ranging activity was along the Nueces River.

In 1852 the U.S. Army established Fort Clark at Las Moras Springs near present day Bracketville. The springs had been an important stop along the southern branch of the Comanche War Trail. The same year Fort Territt became operational between the headwaters of the Nueces and the Llano rivers. Camp Gardner at Kickapoo Springs (headwaters, West Fork of the Nueces River) may have been a satellite post. The fort was closed in 1853 and the troops moved to Fort McKavett on the San Saba River. This consolidation seemed practical at the time when Comanches were the main threat, but that was before all the Lipan Apaches moved into Mexico and began raiding the West Texas Frontier through the gap between Fort Clark and Fort McKavett. During the 1870s, persons of suspicious character sometimes occupied the Fort Territt grounds.

Indian raids slackened for a while around San Antonio due to the expanding line of U.S. Army forts, increased ranger protection, the 1849 Cholera Epidemic (the Comanches had learned to stay away from sick white men), and other factors. More settlers felt secure enough to move into the areas west and north of San Antonio. The Patterson and Ware Settlements were founded along the Sabinal River in 1852. George Patterson and his extended clan settled about six miles above the present town of Sabinal. About ten miles farther north, William Ware established the site for Waresville. Although he died the following year, his son, Richard Ware, and others settled the area on the Sabinal River that in 1856 was part of Bandera County for about a week before Uvalde County was organized. (Maps erroneously showed Bandera County with a stubby southwestern panhandle for years to come.)

Between 1852 and early 1854 Indians seemed to be a reduced menace along the Texas frontier. Comanches remained a constant threat, but the presence of the army with its Texas Ranger auxiliaries, boosted settler confidence. Furthermore, a project to move all Texas Indians to reservations was supposed to make friendly Indians distinct from hostile Indians.

2

Bandera City and The Frontier: 1853-55

Cypress trees grow wide and tall along the Hill Country rivers and creeks. As the settlement of the West Texas frontier began, cypress shingles and lumber were in great demand. The mostly grass thatched roofs of San Antonio and Castroville changed to mostly roofs of cypress shingles. Hill Country shingles were supplied to many frontier army forts and eventually were shipped as far north as Dallas.

As early as 1846 Joshua Brown and a few other shingle-makers from around Gonzales were exploring the upper reaches of the Guadalupe River for suitable shingle camp sites. They did not stay as permanent settlers at that time, but ten years later Joshua Brown laid out the town site of Kerrsville. The namesake was James Kerr who had been a respected colonial and revolutionary leader in the Gonzales area.

John Hoffman and others from Castroville wrote to Governor P.H. Bell, January 2, 1850. A week before, several people had been killed by Comanches seven miles upstream from their town. [Document 47, Volume 5, Texas Indian Papers:]

> Your Excellency has probably heard of the report, which, a couple of months ago was made to the General at the Headquarters of a party of men, having been chased off, by a body of Indians, from a place at the Medina about 20 miles above this town. Upon which report the General immediately ordered Captain McCowens Company of mounted Rangers out to the Medina.--Capt. McCowen had his camp only about 1/2 miles below, where the above named persons were killed.--At that time, the citizens of Castroville very politely rendered, with a few lines, their thanks to the General for his prompt and kind protection, and at the same time entreated him to continue it; but he did take no notice of our humble prayer and ordered the company away.

(The men mentioned as having been chased out of the Medina River Valley in late 1849 may have been a shingle crew. The letter was signed by John Hoffman, Louis Rath, Charles de Montel, John Lamar, G.L. Haass, C. Monroe, and A. Zimmermann.)

During 1852 O.B. Miles was in charge of a shingle crew for a San Antonio company, Gillis & Wilkins (or Williams). Amasa Clark and other army veterans were among the crew that camped along the Guadalupe River between the present towns of Center Point and Comfort, about ten miles from a Delaware camp. He remembered it this way:

> The Delaware Indians often went over on the Medina River to hunt game. They often told me what a fine hunting region it was over on the Medina River and invited me to accompany them on their hunting trips. Some of our boys, Rufus Brown, McLennon, and others made a trip over here [in 1853] and found three families camped on the Medina, about where the town of Bandera is now located. The families were Milstead, Odem, and Pat Saner. Later the Reece [Rees] family came in.

Eighteen fifty-two was a busy year for John James of San Antonio. With Gustav Theisen he laid out the townsite of Boerne which they named after German political writer Ludwig Boerne. That same year James entered a partnership with Charles de Montel of Castroville, and John H. Herndon of Brazoria County. They formed James, Montel & Company to develop a town to be called Bandera City. The following year the townsite was laid out in a bend of the Medina River south of Bandera Pass. Surveyors, lumbermen, and their families were its first inhabitants. Among the first three families to camp there, the Saners were the only one to stay after the Indian raids of 1854-55.

Amasa Clark, O.B. Miles, and others with the shingle crew on the Guadalupe River came to settle and work in the new town. Charles de Montel's horse-powered circular saw provided jobs for many of the men. A few others worked shingles as their own business. Shingle camps ranged up and down the Medina and Guadalupe rivers and their tributaries for many years. Shingle-making remained at least a seasonal occupation for many people in the region into the 1880s.

James, Montel, & Company seemed off to a good start. John James opened San Antonio's first lumber yard on Commerce Street. Some contracts were made to furnish lumber and shingles for forts being built for the U.S. Army. Freighting the finished products to Castroville, San Antonio, or other destinations took many days wheeling along in ox-drawn freight wagons making 15 miles a day in good weather.

The Texas droughts of the 1850s encouraged farmers and livestock raisers to move into the Hill Country region with its plentiful rivers, creeks, and springs. As Bandera City was being laid out, a widow, Henrietta Rees, and her three nearly-grown sons and one daughter, homesteaded on Bandera Creek about 2 1/2 miles north of the lumber camp. The Ballentynes and others in the Morman Colony that arrived in 1854 were cattle ranchers. After 1857 other ranchers moved into the area including Dr. Edwin Downs, Charles Jack, and Polly Rodriguez. Bladen Mitchell established a horse ranch on the east side of the Medina River at Ten-mile Crossing. By account he had lost around 400 head to Indian raids by 1869 when he switched to cattle. John James' 3500 acre ranch on the north side of the river and east of Bandera City, spread towards Privilege Creek.

Settlers began moving into the southwestern portion of the area that became Bandera County. Aaron Anglin and Gideon Thompson were among the first to move their families upstream from Waresville to live along the West or Anglin Prong of the Sabinal River. Most of the Anglin Prong settlers maintained close ties with the lower Sabinal settlements even after the county lines were drawn, as some were relatives by blood or marriage and some continued to hold land in Uvalde County. Aaron Anglin was among the first Uvalde County Commissioners. A.J. Sowell wrote about Gideon Thompson:

> In the same year [1853] Mr. Thompson moved to his place the Tonkaway Indians came and camped at the mouth of the canyon, under the bluffs at the Blue waterhole. They were a friendly tribe, and assured the whites, when Mr. Thompson and others went to interview them, that they were only there for the purpose of hunting bear. They had also camped before this below the mountains on the river. Here they had planted corn and watermelons.

> About the same time the Lipan Indians camped and pitched their tepees on the Frio River, near the "shut-in".

Also in 1853 Reading W. Black founded Encina at the head of the Leona River. The town was known as Uvalde after 1856. J.D.B. Stillman, a naturalist who wrote for an Eastern magazine, passed through in 1855:

Mr. Black has built a substantial stone building at the head of the river, and has laid out a town, which he calls Encina. A forest of small elms (*Ulmus alata*) and live oaks throws a shadow over the site of the town, grateful in a country where, except on the rivers, one will hardly find trees with foliage heavy enough to afford a shade. Situated as it is on the great thoroughfare to Mexico, and the last suitable situation on good water, it will become an important place.

In late February 1854 Lyman Wight's "Mormon Colony" of Latter Day Saints, variously 150-250 men, women, and children, was meandering southwest from Burnet County. They were the millers, craftsmen, farmers, and stockmen, and their families who had left Illinois in 1845 expecting to be the vanguard of the great Mormon migration.

Elder Wight was known among Mormons as the Wild Ram of the Mountains. As one of the twelve Apostles of the Mormon Church and a colonel of Mormon militia, he led his faithful followers into Texas as he believed the recently assassinated Mormon leader, Joseph Smith, had intended. Brigham Young's vision of Utah as the new Mormon home prevailed and Wight's Colony attracted only a few more Mormons and converts. Along their many travels on the Texas Frontier, the members of the colony had a hand in the building of the new capital city of Austin, sold their mill to Noah Smithwick to establish a short-lived town called Zodiac south of Fredericksburg, then moved to the area of Burnet County, spreading water mill technology through a region where previously most corn had been hand-ground.

After a flood wiped out their Burnet County mill, the Colony set out for another uncertain destination. They were camped just north of Bandera Pass one night when Comanches took a large portion of their horses. The next morning some of the men went after the Comanche raiders and retrieved their horses after a two-day chase. In the meantime, the main party pushed on to the south with their herd of 100-200 head of cattle. The Mormon wagons, pulled by oxen, reached Bandera City March 1, 1854. The Scottish families of Hay, Ballantyne, and Chipman were among them. Others were originally from England, Ireland, or the northeastern United States.

Genealogical studies of the Mormon Colony have shown that Lymon Wight had three current wives, a fourth having died some time before the arrival at Bandera City. He was one of six men in the group to have pleural wives. Except for Orange Wight who was divorced by each of his three wives, succeeding generations of this group of Mormons did not continue the practice.

Lyman Wight's four sons participated in much of Bandera County's early history. Orange Wight was an early advocate among the colony for settling permanently in the Bandera region. Loammi Lemhi Wight served in many of the ranger companies that were raised in Bandera County. Levi Lamoni Wight wrote his reminiscences and left a batch of Civil War letters. Lyman Lehi Wight and his family remained in Bandera City until after the Civil War.

The first Indian raid on the Bandera settlement was made by Lipan Apaches and took place a few weeks after the Mormons arrived. Charles de Montel's 8-10 mill horses were discovered to be missing that morning. The Mormons, camped two miles downstream from Bandera City, found many of their horses were gone, too. A trail was found going up the river and a group of men from both camps organized to go after the raiders. Among the group, Amasa Clark recalled, was Gideon Carter, Irvin Carter, O.B. Miles, Dan Turner, and "several others." Eighteen-year-old Levi Lamoni Wight was one of the several others:

> We was soon on their trail and fowllowed them untill night fall and we could not follow in the dark with any certinty so we held to wait for day light. We had not more than got settled down for the [night] when it commenced raining and rained very hard [with] no let up till morning light apeared.
>
> We resumed our chase, pushing with all the speed that our horses was able to stand, over mountains, through gulches, roiks, and brush. Late in the after noon, we sudenly met 6 of our horses that the Indians had captured making their way back. We rounded them up and took them along with us.

In Amasa Clark's version, Dan Turner was left to cope with the six horses, perhaps following along at a slower pace. Farther along, the men saw two Indians about 200 yards ahead, obviously trailing the lost horses. The Indians saw their pursuers at the same moment and wheeled about. They were chased about one and a half miles before they abandoned their horses and escaped into thick brush. Lamoni Wight recalled, "In this chase I [was] so close to one of the Indians that as soon as he abandoned his horse I was in his saddle. As son as I got time to look at the horse I discovered that I was on my own horse."

The Bandera men continued on the trail for about eight more miles before coming in sight of wigwams about half a mile ahead. As the men charged down a long slope, Lamoni Wight remembered, "The Indians moved slowly about, evedently geting ready for battle. One Indan in the time put saddle on horse and got on him." (According to Amasa Clark, it was a "beautiful white horse.") After a charge of about 100 yards, the men were abruptly halted by a deep ravine and had to go up the hollow to find a suitable crossing. Lamoni Wight continued:

> When we rose the bank, the Indians were in full retreat. [They] went in to a brushey hollow and as we were in possion of every thing, camp, equipeg and all, we did not care to follow. They gave us a few shots however and the Indan that had put the saddle on [his] horse rode him up the side of the mountain a little way, killed his horse, and threw the saddle in to the brush. This might have ben the thought with them, that when we dismounted [to cross the deep ravine] that he was to stampeed all the horses, our sadd[l]e horse and all, while those in camp was to engage us and make their escape in this brushey hollow spoken of. But whatever their plan of battle was, we got every thing they had except their saddles, and went home, leaving the Indians to plan for another campain, which they no doubt completed before the next morning.

Except for some camps near the Frio or Nueces rivers up to the early 1870s, these were among the last wigwams ever built by Indians in the Bandera region. Amasa Clark said that the camp was at a site known as White Bluff on the Medina River upstream from Bandera City. He could not have known it at the time, but this was among the first of many Lipan raids in the region and they would not be the last for a long time to come.

During 1853-54 all Texas Indians were compelled to move to the Clear Fork Reservation on the Brazos River or be considered hostile. Fort Inge and Fort Clark were gathering points for the Lipan Apaches and Tonkawas. Chiquito and Juan Castro were the main chiefs of the only two Lipan Apache bands remaining in Texas on friendly terms. The Tonkawa bands had coalesced under the leadership of Placido. He managed to keep most of his men from warring with anyone but Comanches and Comanche allies.

Unclear events of March and April 1854 launched the two remaining bands of non-hostile Lipan Apaches into a long-term guerrilla war with the West Texas frontier settlers. Major Neighbors blamed agent George T. Howard for the Lipan Apache and Tonkawa fiasco and U.S. Army policies for the continuing Comanche raids.

Although George Howard seems to have mismanaged his responsibilities as an Indian agent, he may have had good intentions in promoting a separate reservation for the Lipans and Tonkawas near Fort Clark or Fort Inge. Good intentions aside, he may have planned to profit from government contracts to supply the reservation. The San Antonio merchant, former Bexar County Sheriff, and sometime ranger, did well enough without them as one of the wealthiest men in Texas by 1860.

Frederick L. Olmstead and his brother were making their journey through Texas in 1854. In March they made an excursion into Mexico. Along the way they hoped to meet Chiquito and Juan Castro at Fort Inge. The brothers were disappointed, but on their return trip to San Antonio, met Juan Castro on the open prairie near Castroville:

> Castro was dressed in a buckskin shirt, decorated profusely with bead-work. Upon his bare head was a wreath of fresh oak leaves. Hanging from the ears were heavy brass rings, and across his face blazed a vermilion streak, including the edge of the eyelids, whose motion had a horrid effect. The eyelashes and eyebrows had, as usual, been pulled. His face was not without some natural dignity and force, but the predominant expression was wily and brutal.

George Howard was supposed to provide escorts for the Indians in his charge and failed to do so. Apparently, some of the Lipan bands were attacked while moving to the forts, although General Smith of the U.S. Army stated his belief that the Indians were induced by Mexican agents to settle in Mexico. Frank Buckelew related this account that might have some bearing on some of the events during the gathering of the Lipans and Tonkawas:

> I later learned from a friend, Mr. Chas de Montel, (the man who colonized the Polish people at Bandera), who was on friendly terms with the Lipan Indians, and well versed in their history, that at this time they were greatly incensed at the "Dutch," a name improperly applied to the German people, on account of the conduct of a party of Germans from Stringtown. These people had been, time and again, robbed of horses and other property, and in some cases the owners were murdered by thieving bands of Indians. Enraged at this insolent conduct on the part of the savages, a number of these German people banded together for the purpose of overtaking one of these bands and punishing them for their thieving and murdering.

In their pursuit of the guilty parties, the whites came upon a camp of Lipan Indians on the Medina River, and believing they had overtaken their enemies, opened fire on them, killing several of their number at the first fire. Owing to the superior forces of the Lipans, the whites fell back, and never renewed the charge.

The Lipans had a "peace treaty" with the whites and were on friendly terms with them. Being innocent of this crime and abiding by the treaty of friendship, they were enraged at the conduct of the whites. They now considered this treaty made void by the hostile action of these German people, and flung aside their treaty obligations and vowed vengeance on the "Dutchman."

More certain events began when 12 Tonkawas raided the Indians already living on the Brazos Reservation and attempted to steal horses. This was about the time the Bandera settlement was raided while some Lipan Apaches raided through the Gallagher Ranch on San Geronimo Creek and along Helotes Creek west of San Antonio. Chief Juan Castro was in San Antonio at the time trying to negotiate an alternate plan to reservation-life. His proposal as he had explained to Frederick Olmstead, was to allow his men to make horse-stealing raids into Mexico and share the profits with the U.S. Government. The Lipan Apaches were not eager to move to any reservation, particularly one so close to Comanche and other Lipan enemies. The reasoning seems justified as Placido was later killed on the reservation by enemies of the Tonkawas and Lipan Apaches. Frederick Olmstead heard the news of the Lipan raids shortly after arriving back at San Antonio:

> The following morning came news that the [Gallagher] ranch had been visited during the night by Indians, who had killed a Mexican shepherd, carried off a second boy, and shot at the third, who brought the news. Later in the day, an express arrived from a settlement [along Helotes Creek] ten miles nearer San Antonio, with intelligence of a similar outrage. The savages had appeared at the house of a settler named Forrester, demanding something to eat. As the poor fellow was entering the cabin to comply, he was shot from behind, and fell dead on the threshold. His wife sprang out at the other door, and, looking back, saw two of her children struck down by hatchets, and a third running to the bushes, the Indians in full

pursuit. She escaped unobserved to the nearest settlement. This occurrence took place within sixteen miles of the town.

Juan Castro and his companions in San Antonio volunteered or were forced to track the raiders. The Lipans' escape route went past the Rees homestead on Bandera Creek a few miles upstream from Bandera City. The family was unaware that hostile Indians had passed so closely until the U.S. Army detachment followed the Indians' trail past the cabin. Meanwhile the tracking continued over Bandera Pass, then west along the Guadalupe River. Beyond the headwaters, the trackers crossed paths with Gideon Thompson and some of the Sabinal men. They were ranging in A.J. Sowell's account, but the Indian agent may have been George Howard rather than the ubiquitous Robert Neighbors:

> The hostile trail led to the head of the Guadalupe River, and when it was taken up was followed rapidly by the trailers. After several day's hard ride over a rough country, the command stopped at the head springs of the Guadalupe to rest their horses a short time, and while so doing the Lipans went a short distance from camp to take observations, and were charged and run back by a squad of white men from Sabinal Canyon. Among these men was Mr. Thompson. They were out on a scout and looking at the country. As soon as matters were explained to them by Major Neighbors, they left and went back towards home and the soldiers continued the pursuit. The trail led around the head of the Nueces River. They next made a dry camp, but had water enough next morning to make coffee, and while it was being boiled the agent sent the Lipan chiefs and two soldiers to make note of the general course of the trail, who were soon to return and report. The two soldiers shortly came back and reported that the chiefs had suddenly left them and galloped away rapidly towards the Palo Pinto. The troops followed on, but when the reserve was reached the Lipans, having been warned of the approach of the soldiers by the chiefs, had hastily gathered up their belongings and decamped into Mexico. One of the chiefs carried off a horse belonging to Major Neighbors, and wanted to take the horses and tent of Linsell [Christopher Lunztel, an agent and interpreter], but were prevented by the Tonkaways, who were always friends of the white man. Strange to say, the old Lipan chief sent the horse of Maj. Neighbors back, but the tribe always remained hostile to the whites and made many raids from Mexico into Texas.

Major Neighbors arrived at Fort Inge April 7, 1854, and tried to sort things out. He found that Agent Howard had imprisoned Chiquito and some of his men in the guard house. The chief supposed to have sent back the horse may have been Juan Castro. His family was also being held at Fort Inge pending his explanation of why the Lipans had left the Indian agent's tracking party. Most of the other Lipans were gathering in San Fernando, Mexico, "in a threatening manner," as Major Neighbors reported to Governor Pease. The Tonkawa warriors who had raided the Brazos reservation were identified, but Governor Pease declined to try them. It was enough that most of the Tonkawas still agreed to go to the reservation. Chiquito and his men were released since none of his band had been involved in the San Geronimo/Helotes Creek raids. On May 3, 1854, Robert Neighbors preferred charges against George Howard for dereliction of duty. The charges were dropped as Agent Howard resigned in 1855.

Most of the Tonkawas and Delawares eventually moved to the Clear Fork Reservation. Chief Buffalo Hump and his hard-pressed Penatekas were the only Comanches to accept the Texas reservation. Comanche raids into Texas increased about this time as even the northern Comanche bands were feeling pressured from all sides. All the Lipan Apache bands were now hostile to the United States and camped in Mexico or along the Pecos River. The Kickapoo bands were divided between Mexico and Indian Territory, and some raided the Texas frontier. Mescalero Apaches and various Plains Indians were scattered in the fray.

J.B. Wernette's statement in an A.J. Sowell account, referring to the 1848-49 Apache and Comanche raids, applies equally to the Lipan Apache raids that began in 1854: "Every light moon now the Indians would come, and when horses were brought to the settlement the Indians would get them." The Rees family on Bandera Creek realized the danger in their proximity to Bandera Pass and, with a few other Bandera settlers, relocated along the Guadalupe River. Some Bandera settlers left the frontier at this time, at least temporarily. The Odems, Milsteads, and others moved closer to San Antonio.

Widow Rees had brought her family from Tennessee to Devine County, Texas, before moving to their homestead on Bandera Creek. The older brothers, Sidney Benner and Daniel Adolphus, had built the cabin, moved their mother, sister, and younger brother to the homestead, and had gone back for the family's cattle in Devine County. When they returned to the cabin, they found a note pinned to the door. The rest of the family had loaded up the ox wagon and moved to the small settlement forming at R.E. Brown's ranch on the Guadalupe River (present-day Center Point). The two older brothers held some of the first county offices when Kerr County was organized a few years later. Alonzo Rees, the younger brother, was active as a ranger for many years. The daughter, Martha, married Kerr County rancher Jonathan Scott.

John F.C. Vles, a New Orleans cotton buyer, owned a large tract of land around Cherry Creek, a tributary of the Guadalupe River. In September 1854 his agent, Ernest Hermann Altgelt, an immigrant from Dusseldorf, Germany, surveyed the townsite of Comfort. The town was soon populated with freedom-minded Germans. The name signified their feelings of political satisfaction with their new country.

Also around 1854 John D. Pitts and James Hughes Callahan formed the Pittsburgh Land Company to develop a town on the Blanco River. Called Pittsburg, the town became Blanco City in 1858 when the Blanco County seat was established across the river.

The Indian raids influenced the formation of many Hill Country towns as people gathered for common safety. Many of the early settlements on the West Texas frontier were more or less planned communities where people could buy a town lot and some acreage in the surrounding countryside. Amasa Clark explained:

> At that remote period there was much vacant land open to homestead by anybody who wanted to take it up. But Indians were numerous and often made raids on unprotected settlers, making it dangerous for those who lived apart from the settlement, and consequently very few people had a desire to take the risk.

While John James was driving a herd of cattle to California in 1855, James, Montel & Company's Bandera City project got some much-needed promotional support from the <u>San Antonio Herald</u>:

> Bandera Valley and City
>
> You ask my opinion of this country. I have seen [much?] of the early settlement of the justly [touted?] Bandera City and Valley. For desirable privileges for stock raising and general farming purposes, probably no section of country can exceed this. The City was founded under the direct patronage of our esteemed (though now absent) fellow citizen John James, and advocated and advanced by Charles de Montel, Esq. This desirable place of residence and adjacent valuable Country, must attract the attention of those wishing to purchase land for per-

manent residence in Texas; adapted as it is not only to the culture of grain, but more particularly to raising of sheep, hogs, and stock generally. Occasionally depredations occur from Indians, but settlers can come with safety and purchase and occupy this delightful country.

As Charles de Montel's horse-powered circular saw continued in operation through 1854, Mormon workers under direction of miller David Monroe built a water-powered grist and saw mill for James, Montel & Company. It was the following year before a mill-race was dug. Eighteen-year-old George Hay was among the Mormons and remembered the times:

> This was a beautiful country then, a wilderness it is true, but inviting and offering our people wonderful possibilities. Charles de Montel had a horse-power saw mill with a circular saw, and the men of the community were nearly all employed in getting out cypress timber and working at the mill. August Pingenot supplied the camp, for Bandera was but a camp then, with game. Here I met Amasa Clark, who was in the employ of Milstead. This was in 1854 [...] Here I also met DeWitt Burney, an uncle to our present district judge [1922]. August Klappenbach kept the commissary for Mr. Montel. Klappenbach afterwards [1855] built the first house in Bandera where he kept a store and postoffice.

The Mormons camped for several months downstream from Bandera City. They were primarily looking for work at this time, finding it in the mill project. Lyman Wight's dream of bringing all the Mormons to settle the Texas frontier was long dead. Excommunicated from the Mormon body in Utah, he kept an eye on the liberal revolution against President Santa Anna in Mexico. He had hopes of entering Mexico to convert the people he believed to be the Lost Tribes of Israel. Near the end of May 1854, a school house was built in the new town and it looked like the Mormons might stay. One of them, Spencer Smith, made these notations in his diary:

> 26th, Monday, we have concluded to move across the river to take village lots in a new place called Bandera City. We have chosen our lots and commenced a school house today.
> 30th.--Tuesday, we are at work at the school house today.
> 31st.--Wednesday, we finished the school house today.
> June 1st.--Thursday, we are moving over, fixing our tents, etc.
> 5th.--Monday, I commenced teaching school. My scholars are boys over 8 years old.

July 1st.--I have been teaching school since the last date.

In the fall of 1854 the Mormon Colony moved from Bandera City to found Wight's Settlement or Mountain Valley about 12-15 miles downstream on the Medina River. Lyman Wight's reasons for moving were probably myriad, but a greater distance from Bandera Pass might have been one of them. Levi Lamoni Wight later recalled:

> We went down the Medina about 15 miles below Bandera and put in a farm, leasing the land. The Indans continued to torment us untill they at last left us with out a horse or mule, haveing succeded in robing us abcetully of 50 head in all [and] killing a great many oxen and cows.

In 1855 most of the U.S. Army's mounted rifleman companies in Texas were called away to Kansas where the national conflict was foreshadowed. Jayhawkers fought Bushwackers. The expansion of United States territory as a result of the U.S.-Mexican War brought the debate about the expansion of slavery in the country to a head. It was widely assumed that Texas would be the next "Bleeding Kansas". One of the purposes of Frederick Olmstead's Journey Through Texas was to attract free-soil settlers to Texas. Southern organizations countered abolitionist positions and lobbied for expansion of slavery. The Knights of the Golden Circle formed throughout the South in 1860 and provided the Confederacy with the nucleus of an army the following year.

Meanwhile on the West Texas frontier, the Indian raiders came in generally small groups to streak down the rivers and creeks into the settlements, collecting as many horses as they could and lancing or shooting arrows into as many cattle as they could along the way. When the opportunity presented, they captured children to replenish their dwindling numbers or to sell for ransom in Mexico. Any outnumbered settlers unlucky enough to encounter one of these bands were likely to be attacked. Any warrior who could raise a following could lead a raid and motivation was culturally and circumstantially provided.

Timing their Hill Country arrival to coincide with the nights of the light (full) moon, the Lipan raiders set out from Mexico or the Pecos or Devil's rivers often on foot across a harsh, dry land and many of them preferred the lighter weapons of bows and arrows to the heavier firearms. A leather quiver could hold an unstrung bow, 50-60 arrows, and fire-making equipment. Other Lipans carried anything from an old flintlock rifle to a six-shooter. Their use of firearms was limited by availability of powder, shot, percussion caps, and repair facilities.

The Lipan Apache arrows at this time were mostly tipped with metal arrowheads procured from blacksmiths in Mexico. Lipans sometimes fashioned their own from scrap metal from wagon wheels or other discarded metal. Herman Lehman, a captive of the Mescalero Apaches, described their use of flint arrowheads in the 1870s.

The Lipan quiver often carried a broom-handled size piece of sotol for making fire. A stick of dogwood or wild china would be placed into a small hole in the sotol. A rapid back and forth spinning of the stick produced glowing dust. The sotol was discarded when all the space for holes was used up. Frank Buckelew was a young captive of the Lipans when he saw them use this method in 1866, "I had seen these pieces of sotol before, as early settlers had found them quite often. The general belief was that they were the Indian's method of moulding bullets, and we called them Indian bullet moulds. Now I learned they were his means of making fire." He said some used flint and steel, but most Lipans he observed used the sotol method.

Frank remembered 10-12 foot lances among the Lipan armaments and observed other accouterments of a Lipan raider, "The 'Indian water bag' was made from a portion of the stomach of a beef. This was closed at the top by means of a draw-string of buckskin and was usually fastened to the belt, so as to hang on the left hip. The water oozing from this sack, kept this hip always wet."

The Lipans did not ordinarily ride bareback, but made saddles of wood and covered them with blankets. Their saddles were roughly fashioned after the Spanish style.

He described average Lipan male attire as a breechcloth with leggings and moccasins. In cold weather a buckskin shirt and a heavy wool blanket were added. Even in warm weather, a blanket might be carried on a raid for bedding. There was a particular way of wearing the blanket as Frank recalled, "It was folded in the middle the length way and thrown over the shoulder and around the neck, allowing one end to hang down my back."

On the left side of his head a Lipan man's hair was cropped short just above his ear, while on the right side his hair grew long, nearly to the ground when loose, but was ordinarily brought up in a loop and tied off with red string. His hair would usually be adorned with a few feathers and perhaps trinkets of various sorts. The bare left ear sported six to eight holes, which were filled with rings on ceremonial occasions. Ordinarily a Lipan man wore only a pair of earrings. Paint was frequently applied to the face and body.

Lipan women also wore earrings, usually a pair made of copper wire and beads. They wore a top made from a whole doe skin with a hole for their head to go through and the tail left on and hanging down the back. A knee-length deer skin skirt, leggings, and high-top moccasins completed their usual attire. Frank remembered the younger women dressed somewhat differently:

> The young squaws were more careful about their dress, and beaded them elaborately. The bottom of their skirt was fringed with beads and on the bottom of this fringe were little tin jingles. On dress occasions they wore a piece of deer skin draped from the waist and reaching to the ankle. This was beaded and had fringe with the little jingles on it, and when they walked there was quite a tinkling noise. Their hair was worn in one long plait that hung down the back, but on dress occasions it was worn loose.

The land around the Panna Maria settlement southeast of San Antonio proved too little for the many Polish immigrants who settled all along the way from Galveston and Indianola to San Antonio. February 3, 1855, 16 families from the Silesian region of Polish Prussia arrived in Bandera City. Among them were Adamietz, Anderwald, Dlugosz, Haiduk, Jureszki, Oborski, and others. They had been recruited by Charles de Montel in San Antonio with the cooperation of Father Moczygymba. More families from Silesia, including some who had previously settled in Panna Maria, came to Bandera City later in the year. They were mostly farmers and craftsmen. Polish midwives, such as Mrs. Samuel Adamietz, were an instant asset to the frontier community. Many of these men and women found their first work in their new country in the construction of the mill race for the water-powered mill which had lain idle since its completion. They were not generally poor people, but it often took all they had to book passage to Texas and then to buy land in the new country. Many bought land on the installment plan from James, Montel & Company. Constantina (Pyka) Adamietz, a young girl at the time, later recalled that winter:

> Then, as now, this was a beautiful country, but it was a wilderness. Game was plentiful and we did not lack for meat. Indians were also numerous, and often we heard of the raids they made in other parts of the country, killing people and stealing horses, and they soon began coming into our settlement.

Indeed, Indians were raiding quite a few Texas settlements. The Clear Fork Reservations were not the simple solution many Texans had imagined. Lyman Wight appealed from "Medina River Camp" to Indian Agent Robert Neighbors March 18, 1855:

> I take it upon me to record to you another, yea, two more Indian depridations of the most savage character on the 16th inst. they took the opportunity while we were at dinner and drove off 16 horses all we had but one and that was gone from home. this prevented our following them as they had got an hour or more the start and our nearest neighbors 11 miles off and no way of sending an express as most of us was down with sickness. the 17th we spend in hunting our cattle and got them into a yard late in the evening. this morning the 18th we found 2 of them cut to pieces in a savage manner and 25 oxen drove off. we thought last fall when we gave you such a list of Indian depridations that we were perfectly broken up as that was our feeling then. it will be useless to describe them at this time. It seems very curious to us that troops are raised and sent five or six hundred miles from where an Indian ever roamed and leave our frontiers without protection. at Fredericksburg, Guadaloupe, and all along the Medina is one continued scene of depridations.

Major Neighbors replied to Lyman Wight, March 26, 1855, "I shall pass through your settlement in a few days with the Tonkaway Indians on their way to the Indian reservation and will try and see you. Your petition in regard to losses of property shall be submitted to the Indian Bureau at Washington." The enormity and difficulty of Major Neighbors' task is illustrated by an article in the San Antonio Herald April 26, 1855:

Indians Stampeded

> The Agents had collected the Tonkawa Indians in the vicinity of Fort Inge for the purpose of transporting them across the country. But on arriving there with the teams for that purpose, it was found that the Indians had all been stampeded, by a party of citizens who went to their camp for the purpose of attacking them. Such things are to be regretted as they lead the Indians to suspect the integrity of the Agents, in promising them peaceful homes. The Indians have since been found and collected within thirty miles of Fort Clark, whence they will be conveyed to the reserve, where there are already collected between eight hundred and a thousand. In fact, within thirty days from the time Maj. Neighbors reached Fort Belknap for that purpose, eight hundred Indians were collected on the reserved lands in

the vicinity of that post. The Major is confident that before September, he will have all the Texas Indians located, and that no more depredations will be committed unless it is done by outsiders. Some few of the Comanches stampeded last winter, have come in.

Seminole, Kickapoo, and some Lipan Apache bands accepted military colonies in northern Mexico where they provided something like ranger service against Comanche raids and also stimulated the local economies of sparsely settled regions. The Seminoles under Wild Cat inflicted severe casualties on the Lipan Apaches who raided in Mexico between 1850 and 1861. The Seminoles made one known raid into Texas in 1851 in response to an incursion by Texas slave hunters. The military colonies gave the appearance of government sanction for raids into Texas. Although there are documented instances of Mexican agents attempting to influence Indians to make raids into Texas, most of the Indian raids from Mexico were made by Lipan Apache, Mescalero Apache, and Kickapoo Indians unassociated with the colonies. The Northern Mexican Frontier was just as harassed by Indian raids as the West Texas Frontier and mostly by the same Indians: Lipan and Mescalero Apache, Comanche, Kiowa, and Kickapoo. The governments on both sides of the Rio Grande were obligated by the Treaty of Guadalupe Hidalgo to stop Indians from raiding across their borders. The truth was that neither government had the ability to do that for many years to come, although the U.S. Army had significantly reduced the Comanche raids into Mexico by 1857.

In the meantime, raiders found ready markets for Texas horses in Mexico, often around Santa Rosa. Sometimes they ransomed or sold human captives there and elsewhere along the border. When the Kickapoos organized the raiding after the Civil War both cattle and horses were sold or traded there. The perception from Texas was expressed in a letter General Persifer Smith wrote to the military commander of Coahuila in December 1855:

> More than a year since a tribe of Lipans which had formerly been under the care of an Indian Agent of the United States in Texas were persuaded by some of the authorities of Coahuila to move to that State and when Major Neighbors the Indian Agent endeavored to visit them and persuade them to return he was not permitted by those authorities to communicate with them. These Indians were put under the protection of the civil and military authorities then in power in Coahuila and they

commenced at once a series of murders and robberies on this side of the river which has continued up to this time.

Bexar County citizens petitioned Governor E.M. Pease July 12th, 1855. [Document 137, Volume 3, Texas Indian Papers:]

After the murder of the Forester family [on Helotes Creek] and the Sheperds at the rancho of Mr Gallagher (within three hours ride of the above named city) [along San Geronimo Creek] the Indians for a few months abstained from making further incursions upon our immediate portion of the frontier, but about the last of October 1854 they killed Mr Williams, on the Medina, and committed the most fearful atrocities upon his family—

[The petition describes numerous raids all around San Antonio in which lives and livestock were taken, including "almost all the horses on the upper Medina."]

These are but a few of the depredations which have been committed immediately around us, within the last year--and we have not thought it necessary to mention many others in the vicinity of Fredericksburg, the upper Guadalupe and the more advanced portions of the frontier, because, we suppose that you may be informed of them from other sources, and because it would fill many papers to give even a passing mention of them all--

From time to time small expeditions, composed of private citizens, (who have been obliged to leave their fields untilled and their homes unprotected,) have been started in pursuit of the authors of these depredations, but they have been with a very few exceptions compelled to return without success--yet in every instance in which they have been pursued, they have proved to be Indians, and not white men or Mexicans as asserted by those whose duty it is to know better--

(Among the 122 signatures are Thos L. Odom and A.G. Milsted, as well as Wm.A.A. Wallace, H. Castro, Peter Gallagher, John N. Seguin, C. Hummel, and S.A. Maverick.)

Constantina Adamietz commented on early days in Bandera City:

I can recall many tragedies of those times, for the Indians made frequent raids into this settlement and stole horses. One night they stole some horses from Herman Thallman's stable that was located near where the Davenport store now [1922] stands.

They got the horses by removing several logs from the stable. One night Gideon Carter, a Mormon, was carrying a little child in his arms and, with his sister, was going to visit a neighbor. An Indian concealed behind a tree or in a fence corner shot Mr. Carter through the body with an arrow. He ran to the home of O.B. Miles where the arrow was pulled out. Carter recovered and afterward went to Utah. Albert Haiduk also had a narrow escape from death. One night he thought he heard some cattle breaking into his corn field, and when he went to investigate he found it was Indians. He ran back to the house, but was wounded with an arrow before he could get inside. The Indians got all of his horses.

During the reduction of U.S. troops in Texas, Indian raids increased steadily along the Texas frontier. July 25, 1855, Governor Pease sent a letter to the "Citizens of Bexar County," passing along General Smith's explanation of why the army could do no more. [Document 138, Volume 3, <u>Texas Indian Papers</u>:]

> I have rec'd a letter from Genl Smith dated the 15th inst. in which he says he will send a party of Mounted Riflemen to the neighborhood where the recent depredations were committed as soon as the Command of Major Simenson returns from the duty he is now engaged in--In mean time I will direct Capt. Callahan to station a part of his company, as soon as it is raised, at such point as will enable them to give protection to the settlements of Bexar and Medina counties, should these not prove sufficient to give security to the settlers, I shall not hesitate to call out other volunteers.

Governor Pease called out at least six full-time ranger companies and many minute-man ranger companies during his two terms. These companies served anywhere from two to six months and at different times. They were under the governor's control rather than the military's. The first full-time company was Callahan's Mounted Volunteers in 1855.

James Callahan, an early settler of Gonzales and Seguin, was 40 years old and an experienced ranger. He had just moved his family to Pittsburg (Blanco). On July 20, 1855, he was commissioned to raise a ranger company for a three-month duration. The 88 men of the company were mostly gathered from Seguin, San Marcos, and Austin. Ages of the men ranged from 16 to 44. Twenty-one-year-old John William Sansom was among the privates. Born in Alabama and raised in Washington County, Texas, he was an early settler of the Currys Creek area. A future Bandera County sheriff, twenty one-year-old Valerius P. Sanders, enrolled from Cibolo. Yet another future Bandera County sheriff, twenty-seven-year-old Fabian Lucius Hicks, just arrived in Texas from North Carolina, joined the expedition to Mexico.

Captain Callahan set up his base camp in Bandera City, renting two buildings, one for supplies and the other for use as a hospital. He paid John Ridley $26.25 for seven weeks rent. Ridley also supplied the company with corn.

That Callahan perceived Commanche raiders as the main threat is shown by his deployment of two detachments to northern Gillespie County. A third detachment made a token patrol through Medina County where citizens had long complained of Indian raids. Meanwhile he made plans to take the company into Mexico for an undisclosed purpose. He kept Lieutenant Edward Burleson Jr in his confidence writing to him on August 31 that they must keep the matter as secret as possible and "have the provisions here as soon as possible for we cannot go until we get them for I want to be off by the 10 certain."

The idea of a raid into Mexico to attack the Lipan Apaches might have found wide support along the Texas frontier. Attacking guerrilla fighters in their home base was already a proven and effective ranger tactic against Comanches, but it was not a good time for the settlers to be left without a force of rangers on the home front as illustrated by this excerpt from the September 8, 1855 <u>San Antonio Ledger</u>:

> August 29, F.W. Petmesky, while in search of oxen, near Bandera Pass, discovered two Indians, and immediately went to the house of Mr. Miller, to give the alarm; from thence to the house of Mr. F.C. Jones. Passing Allison's, warning was given. They soon saw fourteen or fifteen Indians on horseback. Petmesky and Jones, with Mrs. Miller and Mrs. Jones, and children fled to the house and secured the doors. The Indians assailed it with arrows, but without success; continuing their attack one hour. The mothers amused themselves by moulding bullets. Five or six Indians were taken off, supposed to be mortally wounded. The savages stole fourteen horses. No one in the house was injured.
> [...]
>
> September 5, at the farm-house of Mr. Caruthers, on the Medina, a man was killed by aboriginal tourists.

Juan Rodriguez, and party, on the Rio Frio, lately attacked a party of Lipans, and killed two. The Lipans were fifteen in number. Mr. Rodriguez is an old citizen, and knew the party to be Lipans.

In the following article Mr. Lakey was John L. Leakey who was among the early Patterson and Waresville settlers. Mr. Hodges was John S. Hodges, a miller and early settler in the Currys Creek area that became Blanco County and later Kendall County. Luntzell was Christopher Luntzel, an Indian agent, interpreter, and a signer of the 1855 petition to form Bandera County. Hass was probably the Castro colonist, G.L. Haass, who signed an 1850 Medina County petition to Governor Bell. Among other newsmakers in the <u>San Antonio Herald</u> September 11, 1855 were Callahan's rangers and Charles de Montel:

Bandera City--More Indian Depredations

The Indians again paid this place a visit on the 3d inst., stealing three horses. Mr. C. de Montell, with two or three others, followed their trail three days, but did not succeed in overtaking them. On their return, were about thirty miles from home, they struck a fresh trail going west, which they took and were nearly up [with the] party when they met a small body of Rangers, who had met the Indians and killed one, (a Lipan,) and captured two horses and two mules branded with the Government Brand. The party saw three or four fresh trails going up the country, all with numbers of animals. The Indian killed was known to be a Lipan by Messrs. Montell, Luntzell and Hass. One year ago, at Bandera City, there was a school with forty children, a thriving village, and situated as it is in a most healthy part of the country, bid fair to be a prosperous town. To Indian depredations alone is its decline owing. This, and other contiguous settlements, will have to be abandoned, unless some protection is afforded to the Settlers. A company at the head of the Hondo would protect all the lower settlements, as in almost every case the Indians come in by the head of the Hondo or Medina. We have no doubt as soon as practicable, Gen. Smith will give the matter his attention, and would recommend the settlers not to abandon their homes for a time at least. On the 30th ultimo, the Indians came to Mr. Hodges place on Currey's Creek in daylight, and drove off about twenty head of horses. Mr. Hodges and his negro followed them, and as they crossed the Guadalupe, the negro shot one of them. Supposing themselves pursued, the Indians fled leaving nine head of horses.

About the same time we learn that a party of Callaghan's command of volunteers, had a brush with the Indians, higher up on the Guadalupe. They struck a trail and followed it for some distance, but finding no fresh signs, they returned. When near the Guadalupe, on their return to camp small parties went out in search of game. Two killed a bear, and went to camp for help to bring it in. When they returned the bear was gone. Seeing a fresh Indian trail, they followed it three miles and came up with a party of five Indians on whom they charged bringing down one and severly wounding another, judging from the amount of blood. The Rangers followed the Indians a short distance, but it being nearly night they gave up the chase. Returning to where the first Indian fell, they found him gone. They tracked him a short distance by the blood, which satisfied them he was mortally wounded. They took from the Indians four horses and one mule, and also the bear, saving their supper.

The Indians visited Mr. Lakey's, on the Savinal, on last Saturday morning, before daylight, and stole a mule and brood mare.

William E. Jones was a Federal Judge who frequently provided Governor E.M. Pease with the perspective of the frontier from his ranch near Hodges Mill (Currys Creek). His letter to Governor Pease September 22, 1855, informs about ranger activities and the frontier situation in general. [Document 148, Volume 3, Texas Indian Papers:]

On the 30 August a party of Indians were trailed by a party of Capt. Callahan's Company up the Guadalupe River and overtaken about thirty miles above the San Antonio and Fredericksburg Road--Two Indians were wounded and all their horses Six in number taken--Among other articles taken from this party was a shirt, apparently suited to a boy 12 or 14 years of age, with holes through as if made by a lance, or arrow.--
On 7th Septr another party of Callahan's Company following a trail between the Guadalupe and Medina overtook a party of Indians--One was killed on the spot--one severely wounded and four horses taken--Both of the above statements were received from persons present and acting in each affair. I think that perhaps both have already been noticed in the newspapers. [...]

I regret to add that on that part of the frontier in which I reside, a great deal of uneasiness is manifested by the people-- property is not considered safe & there is danger that persons in passing about will be attacked by small bands of Indians-- and when they can no longer find horses to steal they may & probably will attack families whose situations are isolated & where there is a probability of getting plunder--Some families have already broken up & left the frontier--
[...]

It is reasonable to expect that the Indians will again return the latter part of this month or during the next.
[...]

It is believed that they are Lipan & Comanche & possibly some of Wild Cats Seminole are engaged in the business with them—
[...]

The Indians generally come in on foot & their presence is not known until they have perpetrated their outrages and are on the retreat--In this way they have penetrated in some places forty miles within the settlements, Stolen horses & made their escape.

A few settlers made trips into Mexico in unsuccessful attempts to buy their horses back. Slaveholders, whose peculiar property rights were protected by the U.S. Constitution at that time, were experiencing similar difficulties trying to retrieve escaped slaves. Slaveholders in Texas commonly believed some 3,000 former slaves lived along the Northern Mexican Frontier. Slave hunters, including Big Foot Wallace at one time, congregated along the Texas border and made raids into Mexico for the usual $50 bounty, which slaveholders paid for the return of an escaped slave. The U.S. government made attempts at extradition treaties and made formal complaints about the Indian raids, but it seemed that nothing could be done for either situation. The frontier settlers were frustrated by the performance of the U.S. Army horse soldiers of the time who were called dragoons or mounted riflemen. Often these troops were mounted on mules rather than horses. September 8, 1855, General P.F. Smith wrote from San Antonio to Colonel S. Cooper, the U.S. Adjutant General:

> The Lipan Indians who are located in Mexico near our border and protected by authorities there, cross constantly in small parties and steal horses and mules. The country being flooded

by late rains, it is almost impossible to trail them, and the Mounted Riflemen who have attempted it have not been successful for that reason.

No funds were immediately available for Callahan's rangers and they had to hope for legislative action at a later date. Other ways to finance the company may have surfaced. A vague set of propositions floating around Texas at the time, to which Captain Callahan seemed not averse if the occasion arose, included striking Indian camps in Mexico or, perhaps, as W.R. Henry advocated, joining Mexican revolutionaries to take control of Northern Mexico or the whole country. F.L. Olmstead spent some time around San Antonio and came away with this opinion:

> Isolated foraying invasions along the border, with vague intentions in this interest, have been frequent. In 1855 a more deliberate plot was laid, and had any respectable support, within Mexican boundaries, been found, the project might have disclosed itself by a decisive trial. The company of rangers under Callahan, which invaded Mexico at Eagle Pass, ostensibly for the chastisement of Indians, was, in fact, upon a revolutionary reconnaissance. The reception it met gave a quick quietus to the scheme.

It was in San Antonio that Captain Callahan met with slaveholders from various parts of the state. Captain Callahan may have heard another way to finance the company. Historian Ron Tyler suggests that by August 1855 a plan had been developed to take the company into Mexico in an attempt to capture escaped slaves or Negro-Seminoles living near or among the Seminole and Negro-Seminole Indians around San Fernando or El Nacimiento. While it is certain that Callahan intended to strike at the Lipan Apache camps, whatever the whole plan might have been, it was kept from the rest of the rangers, with only First Lieutenant Edward Burleson Jr. in the loop. Captain Callahan always maintained that they were trailing Lipan Apaches into Mexico, however unlikely that was on the main San Antonio-Eagle Pass road.

Captain Callahan had an implied authority from Governor Pease to pursue Indian raiders into Mexico. The counties of Bexar and Medina where assigned as Callahan's patrol area, "unless it may become necessary to pursue any marauding parties of Indians that may be found in the neighborhood, in which case you are authorized to follow them up and chastise them wherever they may be found."

The following order from Captain Callahan is in the Adjutant General Records in the State Archives:

                  In camp near Bandera

Sept 12th 55

Special Orders No 2

Lt Ed Burleson

Sir you will proceed to Sanantonio imediately and make any arrangements you can in order to get me as many as fifteen hundred and sixty Rations each of Flower and Bacon

                                      Respectfuly yours
                                        J.H.Callahan
                                  Capt Comd Co T Md vol

To Ed Burleson
Adjt. & Qmaster

Captain Callahan and his Texas Mounted Volunteers left Bandera Pass September 18, 1855, "in pursuit of Lipan Apaches." Their destination could have been the Seminole military colony beyond San Fernando (Zaragosa), Mexico, or more likely, the Lipan Apache camps in the region. As they left Bandera County, the rangers were conveniently met and reinforced by groups of men including some filibusters and slave hunters. Around 130 men were organized into three companies at Encina.

James Callahan captained about 60 men and commanded the battalion. William R. Henry was elected captain of a company of about the same number, but some of the men objected to Captain Henry's filibustering reputation. The result was William Henry as captain of about 35 men and Nat Benton elected captain of another company of about the same number. They reached the Rio Grande September 29 expecting no opposition from Mexican authorities in disarray from the recent revolt against President Santa Anna. Some of the men remained in Eagle Pass, while 111-115 crossed into Mexico.

On October Third near Arroyo Escondido, the rangers clashed with a Mexican military force which had been alerted to the incursion. The heroic action of F.L. Hicks to save a fallen comrade is told in the A.J. Sowell accounts. After an indecisive battle both sides withdrew, the Mexicans toward San Fernando with four dead and three wounded, the Texans to Piedras Negras with four dead and seven wounded. Higher casualty figures can be found in some accounts, but the Texas casualties are confirmed in their muster rolls.

The rangers took over the town of Piedras Negras and evacuated their wounded to Eagle Pass and Fort Duncan. Captain Callahan sent urgent messages to Fort Duncan and San Antonio requesting support and reinforcements. The U.S. Army would only provide cover for a return river crossing and the many volunteers who began pouring into San Antonio, almost on cue, could not arrive in time. On October 5, confronted with the approach of Colonel Manuel Menchaca and 600-800 Mexican troops including a Seminole detachment, Captain Callahan, with about 90 men remaining, may have set fire to the outer houses of Piedras Negras to form a barrier that postponed the confrontation. Another view, according to Seminole tradition, is that warriors shot flaming arrows onto the rooftops to drive the rangers from the town. There were skirmishes on the outskirts. The following evening Captain Callahan realized his hopeless situation and, with the smoldering houses of the town as a smoke screen, withdrew from Mexico.

The Mexican government viewed Callahan's raid in the light of recent negotiations with agents of Texas slaveholders and as a result of the past summer's failed, but widely advertised, filibustering plan of William R. Henry. The diplomatic repercussions of the raid went on for years, but, at that time in Texas, Callahan's statement that he was justly trailing Indian raiders was widely defended by General Smith, Governor Pease, and Texas newspapers, and approved by much of the frontier populace.

Nevertheless, settlers in the Bandera region were adversely affected by the removal of ranger protection. Amasa Clark recalled walking beside his freight wagon the day after the rangers left for Mexico. He was going towards the shingle camps west of town when he met R.N. Davis carrying his daughter's body. (In later times Clark and others somehow remembered her name as Amanda.) The following petition is transcribed from the original in the state archives and can also be found as Document 147, Volume 3, <u>Texas Indian Papers</u>:

Bandarah Bexar Co. Sept. 21, '55

To E M Pease. Gov. Sir.

We the citizens of Bandarah would most respectfully call your attention to our exposed and dangerous condition.

On Wednesday the 19, Ins't a party of thirteen Indians--armed with guns pistols bows & arrows attacked the family of Mr. R.N.

Davis; and shot an arrow through the heart of his daughter Mary-- (aged about 13 years): after having run about too yards she fell dead. His whole family would have been murdered had it not have been for the accidental coming up of a Mr. Stanford and Davidson. Mr Davis' daughter was brought down to this place yesterday evening & buried about 3 Oclock P.M.--There is a trail in different parts of this valley, which must have been made by some thirty Indians. We have ceased our work and are preparing to defend our lives and property in case we are attacked--which we have every reason to believe will be before this petition shall reach you--: but having no horses (having been robbed of every animal) we can not follow them or in any way avenge our wrongs. We are in a manner at their mercy--and if such mercy as the blood of Miss Mary Davis testifies to: Sir, there is too much of the blood of our citizens and of their children spilt in Bexar County by these merciless demons--to longer hesitate between peace and war. If we the citizens of the frontier have any right of protection from our Country, whether federal or State, in the name of God let us have it before it is forever too late.

Your fellow Citizen,

J.P. Daniel
R.H. Davis
L W Thomson
Chr. Luntzel
Charles Montel and Co.
W Ballantyne
M. Gillis
O B Miles
A.W. Stilwel
John Mier
A. Smith
F W Davidson
C.C. Stanford
T.E. Oborske
Amasa Clark

George Montague
B F Bird
Lyman Wight*
Aaron Hurley
James Ballantyne
G M Bird
[continued from left column:]
Samuel Calvert
Andrew Hoffman
T.F. Carter
Lyman Wight*
Meacham Curtis
Levi L. Wight
John L Gressmen
Spencer Smith

T. Kindla
G Carter
George Hay
Joseph Curtis
Richard Bird

Asher Grefsmen
Jeremiah Curtis
Frances Johnson

[* One of these is Elder Lyman Wight while the other would be his son, Lyman Lehi Wight.]

Many of Callahan's men lost horses and equipment during the raid. Among the requests for reimbursement in the Adjutant General Records is this one:

The State of Texas}   Before me the Undersigned
County of Hays}   Authority, personaly appeared

Captain Wm R. Henry to me known who being by me duly sworn upon Oath says that Fabian L. Hicks, late a Private in his Company, lost his Horse during the Engagement with the Enemy at Piedras Negras, Mexico on the 7th October A.D. 1855 Also one SixShooting Pistol lost in the Battle of Escondido on the 3rd day of October A.D. 1855--

Sworn to & subscribed
before me this the 9th—   WRHenry
day of January 1856—   Comdg Comp
  C. Erhard
  Clk. C.C. Hays Co

The men of Callahan's rangers had provided valuable service to the frontier settlements until the last month of their enlistment. As the 1855 Indian raids continued, Medina and Bexar counties raised several full-time companies of rangers without waiting for official support as Governor Pease reported to the legislature January 3, 1856:

I transmit herewith the muster rolls of three small Companies of Mounted Volunteers, one Commanded by William Tom, which was in service on the frontier from the 18th of October to the 16th of November 1855. Another Commanded by W.G. Tobin, which served on the frontier from the 12th of October to the 15th of November

1855. the other Commanded by Levi English, whose precise term of service is not known to me.

These Companies were Voluntarily Organized and supported by the Citizens of the frontier, for their defence, during the past Fall, while they were suffering from the Constant attacks of hostile Indians, there being no mounted Troops of the United States near enough to afford any protection.

Small parties of the last named Company had several encounters with and killed many of the Lipan Indians, and all of the Companies were in active service at a time when the frontier settlements were nearly broken up by the incursions of the Indians, and contributed greatly to restore peace and confidence to those settlements,

I think it but an act of justice that they should receive from the State, a reasonable compensation for their services and expenses, and therefore submit the matter to your consideration with the hope that you will make suitable provisions for their payment.

The circumstances under which these Companies were organized and the service they renderd are well known to Messrs Maverick and McCullough of the Senate [and] the Bexar delegation in the House of Representatives to whom reference is made for information on these points.

E.M. Pease

Captain English's Mounted Volunteers served from August 6 to November 13, 1855. According to historian D.E. Kilgore, "On one scout, the volunteers encountered ten Lipans on the headwaters of the Medina River, killed at least five of them, and recovered the horses the Indians had stolen." Peter Tumlinson was in this company as a sergeant or lieutenant. He was a ranger captain in later years.

A.J. Sowell, a ranger-turned-journalist who interviewed Medina, Bandera, and Kerr county pioneers in 1897 and '98, and August Santleben, an early Castroville settler who wrote an autobiography, may have been remembering Callahan's Rangers or the Bexar County minuteman companies when they suggest a minuteman company was raised in Bandera in 1855. However, Governor Pease did authorize minuteman companies for the frontier counties at that time. There are several muster rolls surviving for 1854, '55, and '56 Bexar County minuteman companies, but none for the region that became Bandera County. A.J. Sowell's statement can be found on page 639 of <u>Texas Indian Fighters</u>. August Santleben remembered it this way:

> The Indians were very bad and made raids on the unprotected settlements about Bandera at regular intervals until 1855, when Governor Pease made an effort to check them by authorizing the citizens on the frontier to organize themselves into minute companies under a provision which stipulated they should receive pay only for actual services performed.

In spite of the setbacks caused by the Indian raids, Bandera City during 1855 began transforming from a shingle camp of tents into a town with a few cabins and houses going up. Economic activity expanded as Klappenbach's store began to provide supplies for the region. Soon Oborkse's store was providing competition. With the completion of the mill race, the water mill of James, Montel and Company began cranking out lumber and flour. Some small-scale ranching and farming operations began.

Bandera militia 1854-56 seems generally to have formed spontaneously and without state support in response to specific raids, except perhaps in 1855 when there could have been a state-supported minuteman company. The Bexar County minuteman companies of 1855 served from one to three months.

Among the earliest known formally organized companies in the area that became Bandera County, the Sabinal Settlements raised a minuteman company in 1856 and Bandera County organized a company in 1860.

3

Bandera County and The Frontier: 1856-59

Comal County had organized in 1846 with New Braunfels as its county seat. Medina County with Castroville as its county seat organized in 1848. That same year Gillespie County, where Lyman Wight served part of a term as chief justice, formed around the county seat of Fredericksburg. All other land west of San Antonio to the Rio Grande comprised the Bexar Territories. As Bexar County Tax Assessor-collector, Big Foot Wallace made many trips through Precinct Number 18, which comprised much of the region that became Bandera County.

When the county organized in 1856, the area around Bandera City comprised Precinct One of the new county. The sparsely populated Anglin Prong of the Sabinal River was Precinct Two. The Bandera County election return March 10, 1856, is post scripted, "No election was held in Precinct No. 2, on account of Indian depredations."

While Bandera Pass had been on a traditional Comanche raiding route, U.S. Army activity north of the pass may have shifted the raids more to the west and east. A.J. Sowell wrote a long account of Gideon Thompson and the Anglin Prong settlers:

> In 1856 the Indians made their first raid into Sabinal Canyon. They came in from the south, and entered the valley from the lower side. They first came upon the ranch of John Fenley, where W.B. Wright now lives [1897], and stole two head of stock horses, one mare belonging to the old man, or Uncle Johnnie as he was called, and one belonging to his son Demp. Early that morning Mr. Thompson discovered there was something wrong with his cattle by their actions, and on investigating found a trail of Indians not far from his house. This was the same band that raided Mr. Fenley nine miles below. Mr. Aaron Anglin lived about 400 yards up the creek from Mr. Thompson's, and he was at once notified of the presence of the Indians. John Brown, of Tennessee, an old-time friend, with his family, was living with Mr. Anglin. They had

just come to the country a short time before. These three at once set out in pursuit of the Indians, who had crossed the west prong of the Sabinal 250 yards below Mr. Thompson's house and kept around the foot of a mountain northeast of his place until they struck a spur of the mountain which extended west towards the river.

The raiders got away after a long chase. A few days after the first Bandera County elections, men from the Anglin Settlement, Waresville, and the Patterson Settlement (Sabinal) met at the confluence of Rancheros Creek and the Sabinal River where 38 men formed a minuteman ranger company.

Muster Roll of Captain John M. Davenports Company of Mounted Volunteers Minute Men for the protection of the Sabinal Settlements and this section of the frontier. Organized the 13th day March A.D. 1856

John M. Davenport	Captain
Joseph G. Brown	1st Lieut
R.C. Miller	1st Sergeant
Joseph Townsend	Sergeant

Privates [33]

J. B. Davenport	Silas Webster*
N.M.C. Patterson	John Leaky
J.C. Patterson	Philip Garsee
Wm. A. Brown	Louis Lee
W.H. Pullman	Gideon Thompson*
G.W. Patterson	H.M. Robinson*
Geo. Patterson	J.H. Richardson*
John Bowles	J.F. Robinson*
J.B. Bowles	J.C. Ware
A.B. Dillard	Rofs Kennedy
Greenville Bowles	John Kennedy
D.C. Bowles	J.S. Baremore*
John Davenport	Ambrose Crane
J.M. McCormick	Robert Kincheloe

W.B. Bowles
John M. Finlay
Joel C. Finlay

Jasper Kincheloe
Emory Gibbons

[* possible Bandera County residents (Anglin Prong settlers). James Booker Davenport, first sheriff of Uvalde County, had established a ranch in Bandera County along the Sabinal River at least by 1866, but perhaps was a Waresville resident at this time.

In a note separate from the muster roll, a 34th private, Edward Kennedy, is stated by Captain Davenport to be "entitled to the Same pay as the other privates of my Company of Ninty days and Should have been returned on this Muster Roole for that time of Service."]

General Remarks

1st

On the 20th day of March 1856, a party of Indians supposed to be Comanches, came into the lower Sabinal Settlements and stole 7 head of horses and mules. I took the trail with my men which was followed up to the head waters of the New Esses, then Crossing, we proceeded to the south prong of the Llano, and on arriving there late in the afternoon, discovered the Indians encamped Barbacuing a horse. We charged the Camp, but being on an elevated position and the Indians in a low ravine, discovered our movements and made their escape through a mountain pass, being then dark, and in the morning no trail was visable.

Scout 2nd

On the night of the 16th day of may, a party of Comanchy Indians 8 in number Came into Old Fort Lincoln [residence of H.J. Richarz] and stole 8 head of horses. We took their trail next morning and followed them to the head waters of the Medina river, but owing to a heavy rain, we lossed the trail and could not proceed any further.

Scout 3rd

On the night of the 7th June 1856, there was a party of Indians supposed to be 25 in number Came into the upper Sabinal Settlements, known as the Canion valley. five of them entering the yard of Mr Aron Anglon and killed two dogs. being fired on by John Leaky a private of my Company, who was stopping for the night in Mr. Anglons house and from his exertions the Indians left the yard. I sent five men next morning to hunt for their trail while I was collecting the balance of the men, about three miles south west from Anglons house. the above mentioned five men Came on the Indians in Camp on the Frio Mountain, this being the place where Mr. Leaky and Baremore received their wounds. On the morning of the 9th I took the trail with Twenty of my men and followed it for Eight days, and finally Came up with them in Camp on the Leona river about 30 miles from Fort Inge (south). We Charged the Camp and killed 7 of them which lay on the ground and wounded several others. we also captured 4 head of horses, three shields, 6 quivers with Bows and arrows, 2 Rifle guns and one Government Revolver. We made various others scouts too numerous to report, but all of which Came off with sucess.

I Remain, Sir,
Your obt. Servant

John M. Davenporte
Capt M M Volunteeres

I do hereby Certify on honor that the above Muster Roll is a true and Correct account of the Mounted Volunteer Minute Company that I Commanded in 1856 and 1857 and that the names of Each Officer and Private are accurate and just, and also the remarks set opposite to Each man's name are Correct

Sabinal June 22nd 1858.—John M Davenporte
Capt M. M. Volt. Compy

[The roll was stamped with the seal of Bexar County September 11, 1858, by the Bexar County Clerk, James Smith(?), in his office in San Antonio.]

The story of the "scout 3rd" can also be found in A.J. Sowell accounts and other sources. June 7, 1856, John and Nancy Leakey were staying with Mrs. Anglin while her husband was away on business. The ranger company is not mentioned in the A.J. Sowell account of the Indian raid in Sabinal Canyon:

> Mr. Leakey notified the nearest settlers of the raid, and five men soon collected at Mr. Anglin's house to go in pursuit of them. They were, besides Leakey, Gideon Thompson, Henry Robinson, Silas Webster, and Sebe Barrymore. They decided to follow the Indians on foot, as the mountains were steep and rough for horses. The Indians were supposed to be some distance away by this time and the pursuit would last several

days, but in the end they hoped to come upon them unawares in camp and get the best of them. Mrs. Anglin filled a pillowslip full of provisions, and Mr. Leakey fastened it across his shoulders back of the neck.

The five rangers were ambushed near the top of the divide. Private Leakey covered their retreat with his six-shooter and they were lucky to get back down with only two wounded. The side notations on the muster roll state, "June 8th 1856 [John Leakey was] severly wounded in an Indian fight on the Frio Mountains, receiving six arrow wounds, losing his Rifle valued at $25" and J.S. Baremore was, "severly wounded by a Rifle shot in an Indian fight." According to Myrtle Murray's account of John Leakey:

> After arriving at the Anglin ranch again, Dud Richardson was sent to the Patterson settlement for re-enforcements. An expedition was organized and went in pursuit of the Indians. They were finally overtaken and massacred on the Leona River. Mr. Leakey was taken home to a grateful family. It took about six weeks for him to recover from the wounds received during this battle.

In the A.J. Sowell accounts, John Leakey had borrowed the rifle he lost. He did not know how to operate its double trigger and could not fire it when the Indians attacked. He threw it down and began firing his pistol. After he fell back with the other rangers, an Indian used the rifle to wound J.S. Baremore. Some dismantled metal parts of this rifle were found attached to a shield when Captain Davenport and the other rangers caught up with the raiders. Other parts were found and the rifle was re-assembled at Charles Hummell's gun shop in San Antonio.

John M. Davenport commanded the Mounted Volunteers Minute Men March 13, 1856 to June 1, 1857. Journalist-historian Florence Fenley wrote about him:

> A lover and breeder of fine horses, it was a stroke of fate that decided him to ride a mule that day to a ranch below Sabinal to trade the mule for oxen. On his way back he was overtaken and surrounded by Indians after he was within two miles of his home. He fought like a demon, even firing his gun at them after he fell from his mule, but the savages were on him, scalping him before he died [1859?]. Red hair was a prize they never overlooked.

The Sabinal Settlements were not the only area that found a need for minuteman rangers during March 1856: The people throughout the whole region from the Leona River to the Blanco River were writing to the governor "complaining of their exposed situation and asking protection against the Indians." In his message to the state legislature August 4, 1856, Governor Pease wrote:

> I replied to these communications that no means had be[e]n placed at my disposal for the protection of the frontier, and advised them to organize a Company of Minute Men for their own protection, and that I would urge the Legislature to compensate them for their services and expenses.

The Currys Creek area raised a company of rangers who elected John W. Sansom captain. They were in service from March to about August 1856. Reading W. Black was elected captain of a company of Uvalde County men around the same time. Speaking of these and Captain Davenport's company, Governor Pease told the legislature, "I am well satisfied that these Companies were actually necessary to keep the frontier settlements from breaking up, and they have done good service in their protection."

The 2nd U.S. Cavalry deployed across the Texas frontier in the summer of 1856. Commanded by Colonel Albert Sidney Johnston, the six companies were trained in light cavalry tactics. On July 12, 1856, Captain Albert G. Bracket with Company I established Camp Sabinal on the west bank of the Sabinal River, one mile west of the Patterson Settlement. The post remained active until November 1856.

The citizens around Bandera City probably expected not to need rangers that year. Lieutenant John H. Edson and a company of Mounted Rifles set up Camp Davant at Bandera Pass as a temporary post while Company D, 2nd U.S. Cavalry, commanded by Captain Innis N. Palmer, established Camp Verde (July 8, 1856), north of Bandera Pass on Verde Creek, seven miles from where the stream flows into the Guadalupe River. This cavalry post was also the first and easternmost base of the U.S. government's camel experiment. August Santleben remembered the founding of Camp Verde:

> That year [1855] a company of infantry was stationed by the Federal Government on Verde Creek, but the absurdity of foot soldiers undertaking to cope with the wild nomads of the plains soon became apparent, and they were relieved the following year by a company of dragoons under the command of Captain

Palmer, who erected the necessary buildings and Camp Verde became a permanent station.

The Indians were not deterred by the preparations to resist them, but continued their murderous and thieving raids as before, until the more timid settlers abandoned the frontier through fear of death and the terror of captivity.

San Antonio was the military headquarters for a wide region. The James house on Commerce Street became the center of a social circle that included Captain Robert E. Lee, other officers of the 2nd Cavalry, and Polly Rodriguez.

Jose Policarpo Rodriguez, born in San Fernando, Mexico, grew up around San Antonio where his father had a ranch. By 1847 at the age of 16 he was making a living as a game hunter rather than at the gunsmith trade his father had in mind for him. He made some trips into the Bexar Territories with surveying parties and by 1849 was serving the U.S. Army as mule-handler and tracker in the Whiting Expedition which surveyed a route from Fredericksburg to Franklin. Around 1850 he was with the U.S. Army in Franklin when he met Amasa Clark who had just arrived with Coons' Train. By the time he married Nicolasa Arocha in San Antonio in 1852, he had found the steady job he needed to support a family as a tracker and scout. In 1856 he was on assignment at an army camp on the San Antonio River. The Conquista Crossing, about fifty miles southeast of San Antonio, was an important crossing for Indian raiders. The frontiersman came down with a fever which turned out to be a stroke of luck for the untested troops at Camp Verde. As he recalled, "I contracted chills at Conquista Crossing, and was ordered to go to Camp Verde with Captain Palmore, of the Second Cavalry."

A U.S. soldier, Edward Merritt Ross, returned to New York after the U.S.-Mexican War and married Katherine Delaney. They came to Texas where Mr. Ross taught school in San Antonio and Castroville. He reinlisted in the U.S. Army and served at Camp Verde. After his enlistment was over he established a sheep and cattle ranch on land south of Bandera City. He served a term as chief justice of Bandera County and was a private in the Bandera Home Guards during the Civil War.

Another U.S.-Mexican War veteran, Fred Metzger, had gone to California in the Gold Rush and later traveled to the West Indies. With his friend, John Ecker, he came back to reenlist in the U.S. Army. They served in Company D, part of which was sent to Fort Mason and the other part to Camp Verde. A.J. Sowell's account of Fred Metzger and the 2nd U.S. Cavalry at Camp Verde:

Soon after arriving at their Camp Verde quarters a runner came and informed them that the Indians were in the country, and thirty men were at once sent out under the command of Lieutenant Van Camp, with Polly Rodrigues as quide and trailer. The Indian raid was in the Medina valley, fifteen miles south of the post, and when the troops arrived on the scene a band of settlers led by F.L. Hicks was already on the trail and had fought the Indians at the head of the Medina and defeated them, Mr. Hicks killing the chief in the skirmish. Rodrigues found the body of this chief and scalped him and took his head-dress, and afterwards let the scalp hang attached to his bridle. The soldiers followed on after the Indians three days, but could not overtake them. This was in 1857.

[A.J. Sowell's account of F.L. Hicks gives more details:]

On one occasion Mr. Hicks and a number of others pursued a band of Indians to the head of the Medina river and came so close upon them, the trail being very fresh, Mr. Hicks proposed a halt while he reconnoitered. Going down into the bed of a creek where there was some water, the Indian sign was so fresh that he knew they must be in the immediate vicinity. They had watered their horses there and the water was still muddy; in fact it seemed that they had run away from the water as if they had detected the presence of the white men. Mr. Hicks turned back, as the Indian trail had left the creek and went among the rocks where he could not see it. After getting nearly back to where the Indians had watered their horses he discovered an Indian sitting on his horse on a bluff not more than thirty yards away, looking and listening. Hicks took a quick but steady aim at his side and fired. At the crack of the rifle the Indian uttered a loud squall and went tearing down into a ravine on his horse, and Mr. Hicks could hear him making a noise down there like a buzzard or something of that sort, as you might say, a squawking noise. Hicks quickly reloaded his gun and went back to where he left his horse and the other men. They now went to look for the wounded Indian and the others, but nothing could be seen of them. Blood was found on the trail where the Indian ran his horse after Hicks shot him. But down in the ravine he got with his companions and they carried him away, the trail continuing towards the divide in a very rough country. Mr. Hicks wanted to follow, but the other men refused to go, saying the Indians knew of their presence and would be certain to ambush them somewhere. One of the men in this party had been shot by an Indian with an arrow only a short time before, right in the town of Bandera, just after dark one night. On the way back they met a squad of soldiers from Camp Verde on the trail of the Indians. They went on and found the Indian dead on the trail after they passed the place where he was shot by Hicks.

Polly Rodriguez established a ranch along Privilege Creek east of Bandera City in 1857. With Nicolasa, he moved there from Camp Verde in 1859. He invested in real estate and, as people began to come in, the settlement became known as Polly. Blas Ruiz, Antonio Garcia, Roberto Trevino, and their families were among the first settlers there. The Rodriguez two-story stone house served as a fort in times of Indian raids.

Polly Rodriguez remained on-call for the U.S. Army until the Civil War broke out. He sometimes tracked for minuteman companies including John Sansom's. He gave this account of the culmination of another Indian chase with the 2nd Cavalry in 1857:

> I fired at one, and he left a bloody trail. I was sorry afterwards that I shot him. It was not necessary, as they were already all running. We got the things they left in their camp; but their horses were farther on in a thicket, and, as it was now nearly dark, we feared some one of us would get shot if we went into the thicket after the horses. We returned to our own horses, and next morning came again; but the Indians had also been back and carried off the dead Indian, and also got away with their horses. I told the sergeant that it would be useless to follow them, as they would scatter and we should be able to do nothing. I had scalped the dead Indian before we left him the evening before, because a lady at Camp Verde said to me as I was leaving: "Polly, bring me a scalp."
> I took it to her, but she would not have it. She said in a very frightened voice: "I don't want it. I didn't think you would kill an Indian." I had brought also a beautiful shield and a quiver full of arrows. The quiver was made of panther skin, with the animal's tail hanging from the lower end. The arrows and bow were beautifully carved and painted. I gave them to one of the officers who begged them of me.

The 2nd Cavalry provided an improvement over previous Army protection, but was spread too thinly across the frontier. In 1857 half the 2nd Cavalry left Texas with Colonel Albert S. Johnston to stabilize a situation in Utah. Governor Pease again authorized minuteman companies. In the Hill Country some efforts were made to raise regional ranger companies to supplement army protection, but financial and other problems often got in the way as in this excerpt from a letter from William E. Jones (Blanco County) May 12, 1857, to Lieutenant Governor H.R. Runnels. [Document 146, Volume 5, Texas Indian Papers:]

> A company is now enlisting under the lead of Mr. John S. Hodges, of exclusively young men, principally from the counties of Comal, Blanco, Kerr, & Bandera, and will be ready for reception into Service at any designated day. Most of these men have long resided on the frontier--and have already seen service as rangers & are therefore qualified for immediate active & efficient service from the first day they take the field.

There seems to be no record of this company actually "taking the field", but it could have materialized as a minuteman company or one of Governor Pease's full-time companies. There were also private ranging companies, the last one was raised in Kerr County in 1859.

Although permanent settlement along the West Texas Frontier remained tenuous, ranger companies and the 2nd U.S. Cavalry provided some security and enough confidence along the frontier for further settlement and development around the larger communities. According to the WPA survey of county archives:

> In 1858, the town of Bandera boasted more than 50 families, the best water mill in West Texas and "a superior and commodious hotel," and gave promise of becoming "a place of considerable resort for pleasure seekers and invalids in the summer months." On the public square, building stone was quarried; a good grade of lime brought 60 cents a barrel. Otto Brinkman founded a cabinet and lumber business that was to endure more than half a century. The first Polish church, a building 20 by 30 feet, was erected in this year. Since no priest could be had, the Polish colonists gathered regularly for prayer and congregational singing. Later, a priest from Panna Maria, Karnes County, came to the parish once or twice a month.

While the Lincoln-Douglas debates made news in the northeastern United States, many people were probably having fears, dreams, and premonitions of a coming conflict between the North and South. Among those with premonitions was Elder Lyman Wight whose dreams were enhanced by opium. In 1858 he decided to abandon Mountain Valley and lead his people back to the north. The colony broke up after Lyman Wight's sudden death two days into the journey. Many of the Mormon families returned to Bandera County, but Mountain Valley was not reestablished. The town and Mitchell's Crossing are now under Medina Lake. The Galveston News obituary said Lyman Wight was "the first to settle in five new counties."

On June 19, 1859, Major Samuel Peter Heintzelman, his wife and two children in the wagons, arrived at Camp Verde to take command of the post. He found some of the buildings in poor shape. He set about making improvements while a Sibley tent served as the adjutant's office. In the ensuing months he inspected several sites on both sides of Bandera Pass for a new cavalry camp, eventually settling on Turtle Creek about four miles north of Camp Verde. Camp Ives was established October 2, 1859, with Lieutenant Wesley Owens in command of Company I, 2nd Cavalry. Major Heintzelman's headquarters remained at Camp Verde along with Company A (infantry) and the camels.

In this excerpt from Document 266, Volume 5, Texas Indian Papers, William Jones wrote to (former) Governor Pease telling of 14 Indians raiding through Kerr, Bandera, and Uvalde counties beginning August 18, 1859:

> On the morning of the 19th they turned their course back toward the [Guadalupe] river & down it and killed some horses & rode over all the mountain Points which overlook the farms in the vicinity of the German settlement of Comfort & passing near that place crossed the river & camped that night-- here they killed two horses & captured two belonging to Mr. Cocke-- Next morning they were discovered by Mr. Cocke's sons & believing themselves pursued they left & were seen next morning about day light at the ford of the Medina at Bandera-- after passing that place they killed another horse & still further west they killed a young man named Bushnal or Bushna. He was shot with seven arrows in the breast and scalped down to the eyes.--

Jonathan Scott, Chief Justice of Kerr County at the time, lost some horses in this raid. He gathered some men and got Polly Rodriguez to go along as tracker. The Indians scattered near Uvalde and the trail was given up. The Indians regrouped for one more raid in Uvalde County before leaving the area with Uvalde County men in pursuit. Justice Scott related the incident to Judge Jones while both where in San Antonio.

James B. Cloud, a 32-year-old farmer from Tennessee, was Camp Verde's other guide, but often had more to do with managing camel expeditions than with tracking Indians. The 1859 raids were frequent and Major Heintzelman noted August 23, "The Indians some think & others the runaway negroes & Mexicans have been killing & stealing animals the last few days. Cloud who has charge of our Camels is out with a party of citizens."

The major, ever the professional soldier, expressed little regard for rangers and militia. August 25 he wrote, "Some Indians rode through the streets of Bandera the other night. There is a party in pursuit but in such a manner that there is no prospect of their over taking them." There is mention of P.D. Saner in A.J. Sowell's account of Joseph Ney, Seco Smith, and other Medina County settlers on the trail of Indian raiders in 1859:

> The trail led in a northwest direction to a point on the head waters and mountain creeks of the Medina and Guadalupe rivers. Here the trail suddenly turned towards the southeast, going in the direction of the little frontier town of Bandera, situated on the Medina River. These experienced frontiersmen from D'Hanis soon perceived, from the signs and general direction traveled, that the horses were now in the hands of white men, who were evidently making for Bandera. This surmise was correct, for when Ney and his party arrived at Bandera they found all of the horses in possession of a scout who had just arrived in town a little ahead of them. Captain Saner and other citizens of the town and vicinity had struck a trail of Indians who had been raiding in their settlement, but abandoned it and were returning home when they struck this band of Indians who had raided D'Hanis, and gave them battle. The Indians failed to make much of a fight, and soon abandoned the horses and fled into a cedar brake. While considerable shooting was indulged in by Captain Saner and his men, it was not known if an Indian was killed or wounded, on account of the thick brush and rocks where the skirmish took place. The horses were all collected and driven to Bandera. This fight took place at the point where Ney's men noticed the acute turn the trail assumed, and at once surmised that here the Indians had met with white men and been defeated and the horses recaptured. Captain Saner said his men were tired, thirsty, and hungry when they met the Indians, and after routing them and rounding up the horses, not only those which were taken from Medina County, but as many more which had been stolen elsewhere, came at once back home.

Polly Rodriguez had been absent from Camp Verde for much of 1859 while he got himself established on his Priviledge Creek ranch in Bandera County. When he returned to the post on a more full time basis, he was the "new guide" to Major Heintzelman in his journal entry for November 1:

> Polly our new guide came & reported three Indians stole his horse 14 miles from here. I sent 15 men with him in pursuit. He thinks he can overtake them & that there is a large camp on the headwaters of the Concho.

Major Heintzelman noted November 10, "The Indians are becoming very bold." On November 13 the major had been out to Doctor Charles Ganahl's ranch to investigate a report of an Indian raid when he got the news of the Cortina Raids:

> On our way back we came by Camp Ives & saw Lt. Mower. On our way home an express met me with orders to go to Brownsville. That Cortinas was near there with from 600 to 1500 men. I have about 9 companies, Cav. Art. & Infy. to rendezvous at old Fort Merrill. This company (A) goes also. We expect to leave this evening. I take with me Lt. Thomas & Hd. Qrs.

4

The First Ballantyne's Rangers And Tumlinson's Company

Among interesting events in Bandera County in 1860, Robert Ballantyne married Marinda Minear January 2. John James, a strong advocate of sheep raising and breeding, put 500 Merino sheep on his ranch. John H. Herndon, a Brazoria County planter, lawyer, and entrepreneur, financed the construction of a two-story stone building on Bandera City's Main Street (11th Street today). It was, perhaps, one of the last projects of James, Montel & Company. In March Ballantyne's Rangers formed as events left the frontier sparsely defended by regular forces.

While Texas Rangers and U.S. Cavalry had aggressively defended the Texas frontier during the late 1850s, the 2nd Cavalry's stay in Texas was always tenuous. About half the regiment was temporarily in Utah in 1857 and the whole regiment was almost withdrawn from Texas in 1858. Although remaining in the state until the Civil War, the regiment often had other commitments than frontier defense. The Reservation War in 1859 was one far-away event that affected the distribution of army resources. While northern Comanche bands intensified their raids into Texas, some of the 2nd U.S. Cavalry were diverted to the Brazos Reservations due to civil unrest in that area. John R. Baylor, a former agent on the reservation who had previously defended the reservation Indians, became a vocal advocate of their removal from Texas. Although Texas Ranger Rip Ford investigated and found no basis for claims that the reservation Indians were raiding along the frontier, the two Indian reservations on the Brazos River were closed and all residents were forced to move to Indian Territory. Major Neighbors safely led the reservation Indians to the Indian territory. He was killed by assailants when he returned to Fort Belknap. Buck Barry, a Bosque County rancher, wrote about the Reservation War in his autobiography (pages 106-118) concluding, "The Indians had been moved across Red River into the Territory, but their invasions increased in frequency and they were even more troublesome."

The Nueces Strip between the lower Nueces River and the Rio Grande had been an area of contention since the Texas Revolution.

As the Reservation War was winding down, Colonel Robert E. Lee, Major Heintzelman, and some of the 2nd Cavalry (including Camp Verde's company) were along the Rio Grande fighting the Cortina War (1859-60). Texas Ranger units were also entangled in the border fracas. Among them was "Captain Peter Tumlinson's Company of Mounted Volunteers for suppression of the Cortina disturbances on the Rio Grande frontier" which served from November 12, 1859 to February 10, 1860.

During this time the West Texas frontier was left largely unprotected by regular forces. Governor Houston, who had been elected on a platform of frontier defense, responded to the situation by authorizing county ranger companies.

O.B. Miles had been elected chief justice in Bandera County's first election and was ending his second term in 1860. This administrative official, like the modern-day county judge, presided over the county commissioners court, the administrative body of the county. In the frontier counties of the 1850s and 60s, the chief justice was often the enrolling officer for the local minuteman-ranger company. (The county sheriff was usually responsible for that after the Civil War.)

Muster Roll of the Bandera County Minute Detachment of Texas Rangers, called into the service of the State of Texas by Hon O.B. Miles Chief Justice of Bandera County from the 29th day of March 1860, (date of this Muster) for the term of twelve months unless sooner discharged; And mustered out of the service of said state the 3rd day of July 1860, by said Hon O.B. Miles Chief Justice of Bandera County. by order of [Gen.?] Sam Houston, Governer of the State of Texas.

Name	Rank	Age-When	Where
Robert Ballantyne	Lieut	30 3-29-1860	Bandera City
George Francis Towle	1st Sgt.	24 "	"
August Pingenot	2nd Sgt.	27 "	"
George Hay	1st Corp.	24 "	"
Joseph T. Curtis	2nd Corp.	23 "	"
Richard Bird	Private	18 "	"
Thomas Lark Buckner	"	20 4-19-1860	"
Heber Chipman	"	19 4-23-1860	"

Leonard Estes	Private	30	3-29-1860	Bandera City
Francis Johnson	"	22	"	"
James Thomas McMurray	"	27	"	"
Thomas Lafayette Miller	"	23	"	"
James W. Sier	"	32	"	"
William Charles Wheeler	"	36	"	"
Loami Lemhi Wight	"	20	"	"

Perhaps some unreported personnel changes occurred during the 15-man company's existence. The <u>Pioneer History</u> lists G.W. Lewis instead of Francis Johnson. The U.S. Census taker made a written snapshot of the "Bandera County Rangers" when he came through the region. The lieutenant was out with his maximum authorized force of ten men. Apparently, this information was given to the census taker. The closest he could get to spelling Ballentyne was "Bassandyle." He wrote the lieutenant's age as 34 and country of origin as Scotland. Thomas Buckner, 20, was from Mississippi. Charles Wheeler, 36, New York. Joe Curtis, 23, Missouri. James Sier, 32, Maryland. L.L. White, 21, Missouri. Heber Chipman, 18, Illinois. Frank Johnson, 23, Michigan. Francis Towle, 24, Maryland. L. Estes, 40, Mississippi.

Their ranger station was Camp Winan, presumably along Winan's Creek west of Bandera City. According to Governor Houston's stipulation it would have been "at some central point in the county, and not nearer than five miles of any town."

Each man had a rifle or shot gun, and a pistol, except for James Thomas McMurray who had no pistol at that time. Five state pistols were furnished to the company.

Lieutenant Ballantyne was required to post a $500 bond with the chief justice before receiving state equipment (the five pistols and their accessories). It was not uncommon for ranger commanders to cover company expenses with their own money and hope for reimbursement. An accounting of state records in 1866 (Document 84, Volume 4, <u>Texas Indian Papers</u>) shows the state still owed Robert Ballantyne $97.32 for ranger services.

Ordinarily the state would not make any compensation for use or loss of personal property except for a horse killed by the enemy. Just in case, P.D. Saner and Meachem Curtis were appraisers for the "valuation of horses, horse equipments and arms":

	Valuation in dollars of			
	Horses	Horse-Equipment	Guns	Pistols
Ballantyne	55	17	20	30
Towle	30	25	40	30
Pingenot	50	14	32	30
Hay	60	25	25	27
Curtis	55	15	25	27
Bird	40	15	16	State
Buckner	40	15	26	27
Chipman	40	15	12	27
Estes	50	14	12	30
Johnson	50	15	16	State
McMurry	50	12	43	
Miller	55	20	25	State
Sier	35	15	17	27
Wheeler	80	15	53	State
Wight	40	15	16	State

To The Chief Justices of Texas Counties
Sam Houston, Austin, March 9, 1860

The Chief Justice of each county in danger from the Indians, will organize a Minute detachment in his county, composed of one Lieutenant, two Sergeants, two Corporals, and ten privates, holding an election for the officers, and mustering them into the service of the State. The muster rolls will be filled up in duplicate, and sent forward to the Executive Department.

He will cause the Lieutenant to give bond, with two approved securities, in the sum of 500 dollars, for the safe delivery of the arms which shall come into his hands; he shall also require the Lieutenant to take oath that he will faithfully perform the duties of Quarter master, and account for all supplies which shall come into his hands, either by purchase or otherwise, which, with the bond, shall be filed in the office of the Clerk of the County Court. The Chief Justice will also forward to the Executive a certificate to the effect that the Lieutenant has given bond and made oath as provided.

Upon a detachment of minute men being mustered into service by the Chief Justice of any county in danger, the Lieutenant will receive of the Chief Justice blank provision accounts and monthly returns.

The Lieutenant will act as Quarter-master, and purchase such supplies as are absolutely necessary, and at market prices. He will make out duplicate accounts, and have the Chief Justice to certify on the same that the articles are necessary to sustain the men while on duty, and that the prices are just. This is necessary in order to have ample testimony to support the same when an appropriation is made.

The Lieutenant acting as Quarter-master, will furnish the men with rations, and use strict economy in relation to the supplies.

The Lieutenant will detail two men immediately for arms and ammunition, to Austin, providing them with sacks to carry the same; but he is in no case authorized to employ means of transportation.

The detachments will immediately take the field, and enter upon active scouts, affording protection to the inhabitants of their respective counties. When an Indian trail is found, it must be diligently followed, and if the sign indicates a larger party of Indians than he is able to cope with, he will call, not exceeding ten men to his aid. He will keep a true account of the days of service performed by these men, and on a return from the scout dismiss them. Great care is to be taken that the settlements shall not be left exposed, while on scouts, without due notice to the citizens.

The Lieutenant will maintain discipline among the men. He will establish a camp at some central point in the county, and not nearer than five miles of any town, and will not permit more than two men to be absent at any time except on a scout or detailed duty. His supplies will be kept stored at the county site, in the care of the Chief Justice, and not more than two weeks supply for the men taken to camp at any one time.

Immediately upon taking the field, the Lieutenant will notify the Executive of the same, stating the names of the officers of the detachment, and his post office. He will make monthly returns to the Executive, and in the same will be particularly careful to furnish correct information as to the operations of the detachment.

Horses and other property taken from the Indians are to be returned to their owners without charge. Any member of a detachment charging, or receiving anything in lieu of property so returned, will be dismissed from service without honorable discharge. The Lieutenant will be well satisfied that the person claiming the horses is the real owner; and if not, may require testimony. He will report the disposition made of them in his return.

The Lieutenant will charge upon his first monthly return, to the men receiving the same, the arms delivered; and the same must be accounted for at the close of the service, or they will be deducted from the pay when appropriation is made.

The following General Orders have been issued. Particular attention is called to them. The spirit of them is to be carried out by all rangers in the field.

Sam Houston, Commander-in-Chief.

General Orders to all Texians Commanding in the Military Service Executive Department, Austin, February 18, 1860.

Commanding officers of all Texians in the military service will see that daily patrols pass and repass from post to post when any command is divided into detachments, and stationed at different points along the line of operations. Horses lost, unless in action and killed by the enemy, are not to be paid for, nor will the loss of arms be paid for.

In the police and arrangements of encampments, or stations, the health and comfort of the troops will be secured, if possible. Guards will be regularly detailed and mounted; and besides constant vigilance and care, the moral tone of companies will be a subject particularly confided to the authority of commanding officers.

No horse-racing or gambling is to be permitted or practiced. Nor are any intoxicating spirits or liquors of any kind to be brought within camp or camps, or used; nor will any person, or persons be permitted to bring nearer than five miles any spirits of any kind, or to sell the same to any command or to a member or members composing it.

More than four men will not be permitted to be absent from any command at any one time, "except upon special detailed duty."

Monthly reports and returns of the state and condition of different commands will be made to the Executive Department at this place.

Any member guilty of intoxication or insubordination will be immediately dismissed, without honorable discharge.

These orders are required to be read to all commands upon parade within twenty-four hours after reception.

Sam Houston, Commander-in-Chief of Texas.

Governor Houston had $91,831.57 to spend on frontier defense for 1860-61. He also had legislative approval for an additional line of credit of $200,000. The ranger-militia companies were paid in script against the line of credit. He explained "To the Citizens of the Frontier" March 8, 1860:

> Supplies cannot be purchased and sent forward without money, and hence, the Executive will appropriate the $91,831.57 solely for that purpose. He will keep the troops already mustered in the service as long as the appropriations will justify him in so doing. Should the emergency require their presence longer in the field, he will then muster into service such of them as are willing to rely on the Legislature to pay them. Those who have been mustered into the service will have to take script for their pay, as will also some of those who furnished supplies.

No accounts of the exploits of Robert Ballentyne's first company have turned up, but many of the same men served in Bandera County's Civil War company of rangers (home guards) and are named among the men who responded to post-war Indian raids during the time when militarily organized groups of civilians were not allowed. Sometime during the company's existence J.T. McMurray was wounded by an accidental discharge of a shotgun.

Ballantyne's company was mustered out of service July 3, 1860, subject to recall in time of emergency by the chief justice. From the records of the Adjutant General:

The State of Texas}
County of Bandera }

I OB Miles Chief Juste of Bandera County do Certify that I hav this 3d day of July 1860

Discharged from the Service of the State Lieutenant Robert Ballentyn Company Minute Detachment of Rangers in and for the County of Bandera

Articles turned over was five PitaStals five Scabbard five pair moles [bullet molds] five Scrudrives hevy all the Company property turned over Witnefs my hand and Seal of the County Courte of Bandera County this 3d day of June
AD 1860

OB Miles
Chiefe Justice
B.C.

Although 23 minuteman companies were officially operating in the frontier counties in 1860, other companies raised were unable to meet Governor Houston's standards and among his correspondence are many letters to individuals explaining why this or that company could not be recognized for state support.

Newman M.C. Patterson attempted to raise a minuteman company composed of men from the Sabinal Settlements. He was an early settler in Medina and Uvalde counties and in the western, Frio River portion of Bandera County that became part of Edwards County in 1883 and became Real County in 1913. He promoted several irrigation-settlement projects including, in 1868, the founding of The Ditch, a farming community centered around an irrigation canal connected to the Frio River. The town was later known as Rio Frio. Letter from N.M.C. Patterson to Governor Houston:

Uvalde—January 26th, 1860

Governor Sam Houston

Sir
    after my Respects I take the liberty of addrefsing you with Regard to the Company that has Organized and have Elected me to the Captaincy of the same, sir I am aware that the company has not the number Required by the act pafsed by our Legislature for the protection of our Frontier tho it can be filled in two days notice as the Citizens of Medina, Uvalde, Bandarah and adjoining Counties are vary desirous of you authorising a Company to be Raised in this section, from the fact that they have suffered vary much by the depredations of the Indians within the last three or four years and not only that, but they think that they have more experiance and understand the mode of Indian fighting better than those who live back in the older settled Counties, and sir there is Two other things that I would suggest to your Honor, and the first is that owing to the long and protracted drougths in this country it is intirely uncertain with Regard to farming conciquently it leaves a number of young men without Regular imployment, and the second is a company being permited to be Raised here would have a tendency to satisfy the german portion of our population of the mistake that they have long been laboring under with Regard to their politics, thereby being the means of bringing about a Reconseliation of parties here. Now sir if your Honor should sea proper to Recognise our Company and commission the officers that is now Elected by the Company or if in your Honors wisdom you saw fit to appoint myself or some suitable person

to Raise a Company in this section we would ever feel under obligation to your Honor for the favor.

Your friend and supporter,
N.M.C. Patterson

P.S. Sir if you should sea proper to addrefs me Relative to this matter my place of addrefs is Uvalde, Uvalde County.

N.M.C.P.

Apparently, there was some difficulty in the Sabinal settlements with raising the required number of men for a minuteman company. Peter Tumlinson was commissioned to raise a company of full-time rangers in Atascosa County to protect these West Texas settlements from Indian raids. The 47 men probably included many from Captain Tumlinson's previous company, including his three sons. They served from March 20, 1860 to around the first of June 1860. Captain Tumlinson made this report to the governor:

Sabinal P.O. Uvalde Co. April 2d 1860

To his Excellency Hon. Saml Houston Governor of the State of Texas

Sir

    I have the honor to report to you that I organized a Company of Rangers on the 20th of March agreeable to your Orders in Atascosa County and marched from there on the 28th of March and reached the Sabinal the 12th of April and find the Citizens greatly alarm on account of the late depredations committed by the Indians. I herewith send you certificates of elections of Officers of said Company. I will send you in a few Days a Muster Roll of the Company and a complete report of everything belonging to same.

    I will do everything in my power to protect the Citizens and punish the Indians.

I have the honor to remain your obededient Servant.

Peter Tumlinson

pr B.B. Palmer
acting Secretary to Capt Tumlinson

[In May the Sabinal Canyon settlers petitioned the governor:]

Sabinal Canion Uvalda & Bandara Countys

To your Excelency Sam Houston Govorner of the State of Texas.

 We the under asigned petition your Honour in the most Earnest & Solem Terms to Hear our Request if the Same Be in your power to Keep Capt Peter Tumlinson in His Ranging Service in This Our Frontier Country

 We have Been Very Recently informed That Capt Tumlincon woulde Be discharged in a few Days By Your Order Now in gods name what are we Harrats & plundered people to doo

 Within The Last 12 months Our Sparce populated Country have had So much Stock Stole and destroy that maney good Industrous Citizens have Left Some Riled and We Your Petitioners will unlefs Protected Be forst to Leave and abandon our homes Yes Our Remaining all and What Can or will We do time only must tell if The Ranging protection is taken fom us We must Leave With Them for We have had no peace for a great While untill Capt. Tumlinson Came to Our Relief With His mounted Rangers Which for two month He has had Continually Scouring Our Country - -and We have felt Safe for The first time   Ther has Been Several Indian trails pafs Throug a Rmote potion of our Country But never Ventured in the Settlements Since The Rangers has Been Here

 and from The Continual Scouts Capt. Tumlinson has Kept up We Prefer him to Any Protection That Could Be Sent us We are 40 or more miles from any Sodiers Camp Except Tumlinsons and a little minute Company of no Reliable force & Some of us as much as 55 miles We have a fair prospect for The 1th time in to years for a grain Support and Just Comenced gathering up our Scattered Stock which we dare not doo pryor to Ranging protection   how are We to doo if Left unprotected or What Shal We Say That You may Keep us garded Just as We are

Yours Truly Deu Respect & Haste May 30 AD 1860

W.C. Watson	Laban kelley	[Continued from
L.C. kelley	E.L. kelley	first column:]
James Watson	Jasper Wish	B. Blalock
James obriant	J. kelley	luWis hall
Petr Rheiner	Jackson kelley	Green P. Snow
L.R. Bassham	F.C. hilbern	William Denson
J.C. Ware	D. terney	James Snow
John M. fenley	D.D. Wall	Joseph ursey

J.M. fenley Jun.	Jessy tatum	Levi ursey
B.F. Biggs	G.W. Wall	Soloniel ursey
Henry hutchins	John Ritcherson	
Silas Webster	Dudley Ritcherson	
Gidden thomson		
Aaron Anlin		
Wilson obriant		

Peter Tumlinson was 59 or 60 years old in 1860. Rip Ford said of him, "Captain Tomlinson was a brave old frontiersman, had seen much service and was not much concerned about questions of military import." In 1875 the Texas Legislature authorized reimbursement of $1,445 to Peter Tumlinson for his expenses while commanding his ranger companies on the Rio Grande and on the Sabinal.

Major Heintzelman returned to Camp Verde in May 1860 after service along the Rio Grande. In December 1860, as secession fever rose in the South, he received orders to report to Washington, D.C. In his journal December 19, he noted, "I think that Col. Waite, with the Hd. Qrs. will go to Verde & Capt. King's company. They will be crowded, but it will be pleasant there.

5

Bandera County In The Year of Secession

In 1861 the history of the ranger companies of the Bandera region is entwined in the larger spectacle of the War Between the States. By 1859 the national debate over the abolition or extension of slavery had intensified. Southerners had begun to feel something they called "Northern Tyranny". Although many people living in the frontier counties depended on the U.S. Army for protection, politics could warp their view of the situation. Buck Barry, who owned a few slaves while living in Bosque County where Comanche and other Plains Indians raided frequently, commented on the Republican-controlled Congress:

> They had told our Texas Congressman on the floor of the Representative Hall that they would never vote one dollar for appropriations to move the reservation Indians across Red River or to furnish any more protection to Texas until Texans freed her negroes; that the Indian and the negro were more preferable as citizens than the slaveholder. Such insults made me a secessionist.

The Texas Secession Convention met in Austin on January 28, 1861. Charles de Montel, who owned nine slaves at the time, was the Medina County delegate to the Secession Convention. Edward Merritt Ross, who owned no slaves, represented Bandera County and presented the following credentials to the convention:

State of Texas
County of Bandera

I Edward M Ross, Chief Justice of Bandera County do hereby Certify that at an Election held in Bandera County, on the 8th day of January, 1861, that Edward M Ross, received a majority of all the votes polled, for Delegate to meet in Convention at the City of Austin on the 28th day of January A.D. 1861. I therefore declare the said

Edward M Ross, to be dully Elected Delegate, to represent the County of Bandera in aforesaid Convention.

Given under my hand, and Seal of the County Court of Bandera County this 14th day of January A.D. 1861.
[Seal]

Edward M. Ross
Chief Justice of Bandera Co.

The Convention opened with many speeches and Charles de Montel entered a resolution to limit speaking time. Then the convention divided into committees and got down to business. While Charles de Montel served on the foreign relations committee, Edward Ross served on the steering committee that was "appointed to present business for the consideration of the Convention". The ordinance of secession was adopted and the people of the state had then to vote for or against secession.

As the military situation in Texas became more critical, Colonel Carlos A. Waite was concerned about Camp Verde and the satellite post at Camp Ives on nearby Turtle Creek. These posts had been established as bases of operation against guerrilla fighters and had never been intended as defensive positions. Colonel Waite called in the Camp Ives troops and began building defenses at Camp Verde. He wrote to the Assistant Adjutant General of the Department of Texas in San Antonio January 28, 1861:

> This camp can only be defended, without suffering much loss, by infantry, with long-range muskets or by having artillery. Not having infantry, I respectfully request that one or two pieces of artillery--say 6 pounders, or two mountain howitzers, with a supply of spherical-case shot, canister, and round shot, together with the necessary implements (port-fire, slow-match, etc.)--may be sent here as early as practicable.

General David Twiggs, in command of the Department of Texas, ordered Company A, First Infantry, to Camp Verde February 4, 1861.

As a large portion of the U.S. Army was then in Texas, there was some possibility that the first hostilities of the Civil War could have occurred in Texas. In the uncertainties of the time options being considered by the Federal forces included concentrating troops from Indianola to San Antonio to keep a foothold in Texas.

February 16, 1861, 12 days before the state was to vote on secession, Texan volunteers under Ben McCulloch seized Federal property at San Antonio. General Twiggs, waiting for his home state of Georgia to secede, surrendered the U.S. Department of Texas at San Antonio February 18. Colonel Waite had already been promoted to head of the department, but the orders arrived too late. He rode into San Antonio from Camp Verde on the 18th to find McCulloch's volunteers in control of the town.

As the date for the secession vote approached, a question of some importance along the Texas frontier was, would frontier defense be better under a Federal government or a Confederate government? Many European immigrants who had settled along the Texas frontier remained true to the Union. The statewide vote on February 28, 1861 was 46,129 for secession and 14,697 against. The count was a bit closer in many of the frontier counties:

County	1860 Populations		1861 Secession Vote	
	Free	Slave	For	Against
Bandera	387	12	33	32
Bexar	10,057	1,395	827	709
Blanco*	1,183	98	86	170
Comal	3,837	193	239	86
Gillespie	2,703	33	16	398
Kerr*	585	49	76	57
Medina	1,732	106	140	207
Uvalde	497	27	16	76

* In 1862 Kendall County was organized from parts of Kerr and Blanco counties.

Bandera County, on the western edge of Texas settlement was also about on the western edge of the area of the United States where human bondage was legally practiced. Six men worked as field hands on the 250 cultivated acres on the Charles Jack ranch. The remaining six people were owned in ones or twos and probably worked at household and farm and ranch jobs. A man named Oliver, owned by Charles de Montel, was in charge of the mill horses in Bandera City's early days. Joseph Poor's slaves may have worked as shepherds, perhaps arriving after the 1860 census.

After the vote a few Texans, including John Sansom and Noah Smithwick, offered Governor Houston armed support against secession. There were secret communications between Federal officials and Governor Houston. He resisted secession as long as he could, declined Federal support, and left office peacefully. He informed Colonel Waite:

> I have received intelligence that you have, or will soon receive, orders to concentrate United States troops under your command at Indianola, in this State, to sustain me in the exercise of my official functions. Allow me most respectfully to decline any such assistance of the United States Government, and most earnestly protest against concentration of troops or fortifications in Texas, and request that you remove all such troops out of this State at the earliest day practicable, or at any rate, by all means take no action toward hostile movements till further ordered by the Government at Washington City, or particularly of Texas.
>
> Thine, Sam Houston

Noah Smithwick led a group of Unionists, including five of the Burnet County Mormon families, from Texas to California in a long wagon train pulled by Texas longhorns. About the same time Bethel Coopwood, a lawyer and rancher, led a party of California Secessionists to Texas. According to Chris Emmett in <u>Texas Camel Tales</u>:

> Near the line of Texas and New Mexico this caravan of Texas-bound secessionists espied a cavalcade belonging to the United States War Department. With it fourteen camels were doing service for Uncle Sam. A volley from the Coopwood caravan was sufficient to bring within their control the fourteen camels, and Ben Coopwood diverted his journey into Mexico, taking with him the captured animals, while Bethel went on to San Antonio and reported the capture to the Confederate authorities. He received in return from the Confederacy the authority to retain them as "spoils of war."

The Secession Convention formed a Committee of Public Safety to oversee military operations for the state. In many counties local Committees of Public Safety were also formed. Bandera County seems not to have had a Committee of Public Safety, but among persons of interest on the Medina County Committee of Public Safety were Charles de Montel, James Paul, William A. Burrows, and Gideon Thompson. John Robertson was chairman of the State Committee of Public Safety:

> The committee believe that the people along the whole line of the frontier are true and loyal to the cause of the South, and

look with intense anxiety for the Convention to furnish them with immediate and prompt protection. Encouraged and aided by the enemies of Texas the Indians will, unless timely assistance be furnished, commit the most horrid depredations. With the view of rendering to the frontier this protection, and that it may be accomplished speedily and efficiently, as well also to show the government of the Confederate States, of which we hope soon to become a member, that we are not unmindful of what is due to our people, and as an indication to that government of what is expected for our defense, and particularly to save the lives of our women and children in that region, the committee instruct me to report an ordinance for the raising of volunteer forces, which they hope the Convention will find it expedient to adopt.

Jno. C. Robertson, Chrm'n of the Com. on Public Safety.

Federal troops began converging on San Antonio and then to Indianola for debarkation from the state. The cavalry company at Camp Verde left the post February 21 while the infantry company remained.

The San Antonio commissioners overseeing the transfer of Federal property were Thomas J. Devine, Samuel A. Maverick, and P.N. Luckett:

To Col. C.A. Waite, U.S.A., Comd'g Dep't of Texas

From Office of Commissioners, San Antonio, March 2nd, 1861.

We are credibly informed that after the departure of Capt. Maclin's company from Camp Verde, the soldiers of Company A, 1st Infantry, burned up a chest of saddler's tools belonging to the Federal government, left by Capt. Brackett to be placed in the quartermaster's store. Five days after, on the night of the return of that company to Camp Verde, the men broke into the hospital and after consuming the liquor destroyed all they could not conveniently appropriate to their own use; the night after, they broke into the carpenter's shop and destroyed everything that was not appropriated by them to their own use.

We desire to call your attention to this transaction, as it is not in the spirit or according to the letter of the agreement between Gen. Twiggs and the undersigned. We have to request that this company be removed as soon as possible from Camp Verde. The officers and men of Company A will be held liable for any destruction of property or other outrage which they may fail to prevent or be guilty of.

[From The Journal of the Secession Convention:]

To Hon. Jno. C. Robertson, Chairman of Com. of Safety. Austin, March 6th, 1861. [From Thomas J. Devine "on behalf of the commissioners" sent to San Antonio to negotiate General Twiggs' surrender:]

Having received information on the evening of the 2nd inst. that depredations were being committed on public property at Camp Verde by some of the soldiers of company A, 1st Infantry, U.S.A., a note was immediately forwarded to Col. Waite informing him of the fact and that such depredation was considered a violation of the stipulations entered into between Gen. Twigs and the undersigned and that the officers and men belonging to any company committing any depredations in the future would be held personally liable, and requested Col. Waite to remove the troops from that post without delay. Capt. Frank Hubert's company of Washington county volunteers, numbering twenty-five men under the command of Lieut. Haynes, then in San Antonio, were directed to march next morning at daylight for Camp Verde and there remain for the protection of the public property and buildings until further orders.

[From a report to the Commissioners:]

Hdqtrs, San Antonio, March 2nd, 1861

6. Lieut. Jas. Paul, of Castroville, has orders to repair immediately to Camp Verde with 25 mounted men.

7. Lieut. W. Adams, of Uvalde, has orders to repair immediately to Fort Inge and Camp Wood; 10 mounted men at the former, and 25 mounted men at the latter place, in all 35 men.

[...]

9. Lieut. Benton, Lieut. Paul, and Lieut. Adams furnish their respective detachments with arms and ammunition; also, horses.

Paul's Company formed at Frank's Crossing of Hondo Creek and rode to Castroville. More men, including frontiersman Ed

Westfall, informally joined the company there, increasing its number to 40. R.H. William's account suggests that some temporary sergeants were appointed for the additional numbers. There was a "keen, cold norther blowing" in R.H. Williams' narrative of the capture of Camp Verde (With The Border Ruffians):

> Directly we were mustered, we went into a camp on the Medina River, in an old Mormon settlement, where there were several stone houses and a mill.

That night Captain Paul told the men of their mission to ride at daybreak to take Camp Verde some 40 miles to the north. By sunrise the next morning the company had set out "by bridle-path, along the Medina River, which ran swift and clear between high cedar-clad ridges."

> We were so confident of capturing the position, where we knew there were plenty of stores, that we had traveled with but small provision of rations, carried on pack mules; so that my office of issuer of provender, to 40 hungry men, was not an enviable one for my comrades had but scant food for any officer and none for an orderly sergeant.

> That night we lay in our arms, and those of our enemy were almost in touch. It passed without any attack on either side and at daybreak we fell in and marched to within one mile of the fort. There Paul left the command in charge of the next major sergeant, an old fighting frontiersman [Ed Westfall], whilst he and I rode on to the fort, I bearing a white flag. A sergeant's guard received us and escorted us into the fort, outside which I saw strong picket defenses had been thrown up and I made sure we were in for a fight. Lieutenant Hill, the officer in command, received us very stiffly and said that he meant to hold his post to the last. He had really received orders to retire, as we afterwards learned, but put on a better face to gain better terms.

> Paul assured him that although he might hold out against us for a time, reinforcements were coming and eventually he must surrender; that General Twigg, commanding the district, had already done so at San Antonio, and that therefore fighting would mean only useless loss of life. Our crafty friend was deaf to all reason for a time; but when Paul offered to let all officers and men march out with their horses, arms and personal property, which was what he had been fighting for, Hill at once

agreed and the terms were forthwith settled. Hill was to march out next day and report himself and his command at San Antonio.

So at two o'clock that day [3-7-1861] he marched out and we took possession of the fort, the stores, ammunition, twelve mules, eighty camels and two Egyptian camel drivers, for all of which I had to give a receipt. The camels had been purchased in Egypt by the United States Government for transport across the prairies in the dry season, and answered very well. They were very little trouble as far as the females were concerned, but some of the males were the mischief, especially an old gentleman they christened "The Major". He was evidently possessed by Shaitan and bit and fought like a demon; but we chained him to a strong picket post and peace reigned in the camel corral.

[There are two muster rolls and two pay rolls for Paul's Company in the State Library. The pay rolls are duplicates, but the muster rolls, while sharing the same preamble, each have some different information.]

MUSTER ROLL of 1st Lieut. James Paul's Company of Texas mounted Rangers, mustered into the service of the State, by authority of the Commissioners acting on behalf of the Committee of Public Safety of the State of Texas, at Frank's Crossing of Hondo Creek, Medina County, on the Fourth Day of March, A.D. 1861, and mustered out of service at Camp Verde, Kerr County, Texas, on the 16th Day of May, A.D. 1861.

[The preamble for the pay rolls:]

We the Subscribers hereby acknowledge to have received of C.R. Johns, Comptroller of the State of Texas the sums set opposite our names respetivley, being the full amount of our pay and allowances for the Period stated, having signed Duplicates thereof.

[Information about each man in the company extracted as follows (with biographical information from other sources when available):]

1st Lieutenant

1. James Paul. [Acting under orders received in San Antonio from Colonel Ben McCulloch, he was commissioned February 21, 1861 in

San Antonio for the duration of two months and 17 days. His complexion was dark and he stood five feet ten inches. He was born in England. His occupation was lawyer. He was charged for one pair of shoes, 2 pair socks, two blankets and "rations for myself and for 1 horse only from Mar. 4 to May 16/61." No payments are posted to Lieutenant Paul on the pay rolls.]

Sergeants

2. H.M. Madison. [The First Sergeant was 23 years old. He was enrolled and mustered March 4, 1861 at Frank's Crossing for two months and 14 days. His complexion was light and he stood five feet eight inches. He was born in Tennessee. No occupation is listed. He was charged for one pair shoes and one pair socks. His rate of pay was $20 per month. He was discharged May 16, 1861.]

3. Jas. B. McLamore. [The Second Sergeant was 19 years old. He was enrolled and mustered March 4, 1861 at Frank's Crossing for two months and 14 days. His complexion was light and he stood five feet seven and one half inch. He was born in Mississippi. No occupation is listed. He was charged for one pair shoes and one pair socks. His rate of pay was $17 per month. He was discharged May 16, 1861.]

Corporals

4. Thos. L. Buckner. [The son of Judge E.F. Buckner, the First Corporal was 21 years old. He was enrolled at Bandera and mustered at Frank's Crossing for 2 months and 14 days. His complexion was dark and he stood five feet seven and one half inch. He was born in Mississippi. No occupation is listed. He was charged for one pair shoes. His rate of pay was $13 per month. He was discharged May 16, 1861.]

5. Emanuel Widick. [The Second Corporal was 26 years old. He was enrolled at "Hondo Creek" and mustered at Frank's Crossing for two months and 14 days. His complexion was dark and he stood five feet eleven and three quarters of an inch. He was born in Illinois. His occupation was farmer and stock raiser. He was charged for 1 pair shoes and two pair socks. His rate of pay was $13 per month. He was discharged May 16, 1861.]

Privates

[All were mustered at Frank's Crossing except T.L. Miller and, perhaps, W.C. Wheeler, who are listed as mustered at Camp Verde.

Place of enrollment usually meant place of residence. Their rate of pay was $12 per month. Except for R.H. Williams, they were all discharged May 16, 1861.]

6. Bernard Brooks. [He was one of the original settlers of Quihi; A.J. Sowell spelled the family name "Brucks" in Texas Indian Fighters. He was 25 years old and enrolled at Quihi. His complexion was light and he stood five feet ten inches. He was born in Prussia. His occupation was farmer and stock raiser. No charges were made against his pay.]

7. John Brieten. [He was 17 years old and enrolled at Quihi. His complexion was light and he stood five feet ten inches. He was born in Prussia. His occupation was farmer and stock raiser. No charges were made against his pay.]

8. Wm.A. Burrows. [He was a Medina County resident and served on the Medina County Committee of Public Safety; however, his place of residence on one of the muster rolls for Adams Company later in 1861 was Bandera County. He was 35 years old and enrolled at Frank's Crossing. His complexion was dark and he stood five feet ten inches. He was born in Tennessee. His occupation was farmer and stock raiser. He was charged for one pair cavalry boots and one pair socks.]

9. E.M. Downs. [Edwin M. Downs was a Bandera County medical doctor and rancher. He was 41 years old and enrolled at Bandera. His complexion was light and he stood five feet eight inches. He was born in Vermont. His occupation was physician. He was charged for one pair shoes and one infantry hat.]

10. Henry Gerdes. [He was 19 years old and enrolled at Quihi. His complexion was light and he stood five feet eight inches. He was born in Prussia. His occupation was farmer and stock raiser. He was charged for "1 Harper's Ferry Rifle", one pair shoes and 2 pairs socks.]

11. M.M. Harper. [The Harper Community in Medina County was the remainder of Vandenburg after most of the town moved to found New Fountain. He was 20 years old and enrolled at "Hondo Cr[eek]". His complexion was dark and he stood five feet ten inches. He was born in Alabama. No occupation is listed. He was charged for one Harper's Ferry rifle, one pair shoes, and 2 pairs socks.]

12. R.A. Harper. [He was 21 years old and enrolled at Hondo Creek. His complexion was dark and he stood five feet ten inches. He was

born in Alabama. No occupation is listed. No charges were made against his pay.]

13. A. Lubbecke. [He was 36 years old and enrolled at Vandenburg. His complexion was dark and he stood five feet ten and three quarters of an inch. He was born in Hanover. No occupation is listed. He was charged for one pair shoes and two pairs socks.]

14. R.C. Mott. [He was 21 years old and enrolled at Frank's Crossing. His complexion was light and he stood five feet five inches. He was born in Mississippi. No occupation is listed. He was charged for one pair shoes and one pair socks.]

15. William Mylius. [Although he had signed the 1855 petition to form Bandera County, he was a Medina County resident at this time. He was 30 years old and enrolled at Castroville. His complexion was dark and he stood five feet ten inches. He was born in Saxe Meinenger. His occupation was surveyor. He was charged for one pair shoes and two pairs socks.]

16. C.R. Moore. [He was 20 years old and enrolled at "Guadalupe, Ker. Co." His complexion was light and he stood six feet and one half inch. He was born in Tennessee. His occupation was farmer and stock raiser. He was charged for one pair shoes and one pair "stockings".]

17. August Pingenot. [He was a brother-in-law of Charles de Montel. He alternates with Ferdinand Niggle as number 17 and 18 on the two muster rolls. He was 28 years old and enrolled at Bandera. His complexion was dark and he stood five feet eight inches. He was born in France. His occupation was farmer and stock raiser. He was charged for one pair shoes and one pair socks.]

18. Ferdinand Niggle. [He was 42 years old and enrolled at Castroville. His complexion was light and he stood five feet eight inches. He was born in Switzerland. His occupation was blacksmith and he served as the company's farrier and blacksmith. No charges were made against his pay. He received an additional $29.20 for his extra duties.]

19. C.C. Rine. [He was 21 years old and enrolled at "Hondo". His complexion was dark and he stood five feet nine inches. He was born in Mississippi. No occupation is listed. He was charged for one pair shoes and two pair socks.]

20. V.B. Ridley. [He was 25 years old and enrolled at Frank's Crossing. His complexion was light and he stood five feet eleven inches. He was born in Tennessee. No occupation is listed. He was charged for one pair shoes and one pair pants.]

21. Fockke Saathoff. [He was 21 years old and enrolled at Quihi. His complexion was light and he stood six feet. He was born in Hanover. His occupation was farmer and stock raiser. No charges were made against his pay.]

22. William B. Vanpelt. [He was 25 years old and enrolled at "Hondo". His complexion was light and he stood five feet three inches. He was born in North Carolina. His occupation was farmer and stock raiser. He was charged for one Harper's Ferry rifle.]

23. George B. Vanpelt. [He was 28 years old and enrolled at "Hondo". His complexion was light and he stood five feet two inches. He was born in North Carolina. His occupation was farmer and stock raiser. He was charged for one pair shoes and one pair socks.]

24. Alison Vanpelt. [He was 26 years old and enrolled at "Hondo". His complexion was light and he stood five feet one inch. He was born in North Carolina. His occupation was farmer and stock raiser. He was charged for One Harper's Ferry rifle.]

25. R. Williams. [Listed only as "Williams" on one of the muster rolls, this was Robert H. Williams. He was 27 years old and enrolled at "Medio, Bex. Co." His complexion was dark and he stood five feet eleven inches. He was born in England. His occupation was stock raiser. He was honorably discharged April 20, 1861 and "Was permitted to furnish Substitute, Apr 20, 1861." No charges were made against his pay.]

26. W.C. Wheeler [Listed only as "Wheeler" on one muster roll, William Charles Wheeler, a veteran of Ballantyne's Rangers, may have been one of the men to formally join the company after the capture of Camp Verde. Ditto marks on one muster roll indicate March 4, 1861 as his muster date, but the place is given as Camp Verde. However, his time of service is the same as the rest of the privates who mustered at Frank's Crossing: Two months and 14 days. (R.H. Williams was an exception, being discharged early after serving one month and 17 days.) W.C. Wheeler was 45 years old and enrolled at Bandera. His complexion was not listed, nor was his place of birth. He stood five feet seven and one half inch. His occupation was stock raiser. No charges were made against his pay.]

27. T.L. Miller [Another veteran of Ballantyne's Rangers was recruited as a replacement for R.H. Williams. Thomas L. Miller was not listed on one of the muster rolls. The roll his name appears on has little information filled in. He was 21 years old and enrolled at Bandera. He was mustered at Camp Verde April 20, 1861. He served 27 days.]

[Each of the muster rolls ends with two side by side statements by James Paul:]

> I certify on honor, that the above Muster Roll exhibits the true State of 1st Lieut. James Paul's Company of Texas Mounted Rangers on the 4th Day of March, A.D. 1861; that each man answers to his own proper name in person, and the remarks set opposite the name of each officer and Soldier are accurate and just.

Date, March 4th 1861.

James Paul, Station, 1st Lieut

Comm'dg Comp'y

> I certify on honor, That I have carefully examined the men whose names are borne on this Roll; their horses and equipments, and have accepted them into the Service of the State of Texas, for Temporary Service, from this 4th Day of March, A.D. 1861.

James Paul, Station, 1st Lieut

Mustering Officer

.Date March 4th 1861

[From A.J. Sowell's account of Bernhard Brucks:]

> In 1861 Mr. Brucks joined a company of rangers commanded by Capt. James Paul, and was stationed at Camp Verde. On one scout they got seventy-five head of horses from the Indians which these red thieves had stolen and driven off from the settlers. On another occasion Captain Paul lost his spectacles while on an Indian chase, and when it was over had the whole company looking for the lost glasses. A cedar limb had jerked them off, but a whole company of Texas rangers failed to find them. The famous Indian fighter and slayer of the "Big Foot" Indian, Ed Westfall, was their guide and trailer. Judge Brucks says that Westfall would follow Indians until his horse gave

out, and then would abandon him and continue the pursuit on foot. In one camp they found seventy-five head of horses, but no Indians were around. They were off in the D'Hanis settlement stealing more horses. One shield was hanging on a limb in camp. These Indians were pursued from D'Hanis and the horses recovered which were stolen from that place.

In 1880 Mr. Brucks was appointed county judge of Medina County, and was then regularly elected to that office for fourteen years. He now [1897?] lives at Dunlay, on the Southern Pacific road, and is strong and hearty.

During the days of the Republic of Texas, James T. Paul, by one account, had been an officer in the Texas Navy. He was a lawyer and had served as Henri Castro's private secretary. He had run for District Attorney of the 18th Judicial District in 1856, but lost to G.H. Noonan. He had been a member of Medina County's Knights of the Golden Circle and Commission of Public Safety. After his company disbanded, Lieutenant Paul was promoted to captain and went to Austin, perhaps serving on the Military Board. He died in Castroville in 1897.

The war ended the partnership of James, Montel, and Company. According to Vinton James, his father favored remaining with the Union. If so, this probably put some distance between him and Charles de Montel who favored secession. John Hunter Herndon put much of his fortune into supporting the Confederacy. Many Bandera County residents had mixed reactions to secession, but some had very definite opinions. Polly Rodriguez explained his situation:

> The United States troops left Camp Verde and the State, and we passed under Confederate authority. It was a sad day for me when I had to part from the United States troops. I had been with them for twelve years, and I had seen much hard service with them, and had many good friends among them. Major Wait was in command, and asked me to go away with them, but I could not. It would have been to leave everything behind, and really forsake my family and home.

While most among the Lyman Wight Colony were freesoilers, some who grew to maturity along the Texas Frontier took up the Southern cause. In 1856 Sophia Leyland and Levi Lamoni Wight were the first couple to marry in Bandera County. As a private in Company C, 1st Texas Cavalry, C.S.A., Lamoni Wight passed along a hopeful rumor and expressed a common Southern sentiment in a letter to his wife November 23, 1862:

> England & France [have proposed] tearms of peas betwen the No. & So on wich they have so nigh agred that they [want] a treaty of peas for two months to consult the mater, and I think that the two months will be the win[d]ing up of the mater and then we will be an independent Nation free from Norten Tyrany and I can come home and live in peas and as men pas by me I can look them in the face with a clear concienc and tel my children as they gro up that I have served in a war that has made them free. Let it be sooner or later I shal ever hope for the war to end in this way.

The Polish settlers had been in the country only five years when the war broke out. The Panna Maria Polish are documented as mostly pro-Union, but the sentiments of the Bandera Polish are more obscure. They may have felt some obligation or loyalty to Charles de Montel, a staunch secessionist. Some of the men were drafted and a few may have volunteered. Many served in the county's home guard unit. Constantina Pyka married John Adamietz in 1866 and in 1922 commented on the Civil War years in Bandera County:

> When the Civil War came on we remained aloof from partizanship, but many of our American and German neighbors became involved and some went to war, while others went to Mexico. Men were hung for their sentiments and many disappeared to never be heard of again. These were terrible times.

Amasa Clark married Eliza Jane Wright of Fredericksburg in 1859. He worked at Camp Verde in 1860 and served as a Bandera County constable during most of the war years. (In later times, as a centenarian and veteran of the U.S.-Mexican War, he was a celebrity guest at Fort Sam Houston on ceremonial occasions.) Around 1856, while camping along the road to San Antonio, he had suffered a severe head injury when he and two companions were attacked by robbers. He was still not well enough to serve as a soldier when the war broke out. Nevertheless, he expressed mixed emotions between his loyalty to "the flag that I had followed in Mexico" and "my friends and neighbors [who] were true Southern people, and they believed that they had a right and cause to secede." He said, "As it was I kept my own counsel and did not take sides." He further reminisced about the Civil War years:

There were many dark crimes committed in this fair Southland during those terrible days. Men were hung and their property destroyed just because they dared to stand for the Union; so-called vigilance committees committed many of these crimes under guise of governmental authority, and many innocent men suffered at their hands. Here in Bandera County conditions were not so bad as in some other sections, particularly in Gillespie and Kendall counties.

Charles Montague, educated at the University of Dublin, Ireland, came to South Carolina before moving his family to Bandera County in 1859. He wrote the following letter to William T. Clark, the lieutenant governor who had succeeded Sam Houston:

Bandera County 19th July/61

To His Excellency

Gov. Clark

Austin

I am Sorry to trouble your Hon. about the affairs of our County, but I hope to be excused when I State that the most of our Settlers paid no taxes this year, that a document was handed round to get Signatures for a remodelling of this government, So as to form a Union of the States again, that no officer of the county took the oath of allegience, but the Clerk of the District Court [W.S. Goodwin?], and that a Polander who intertained the Hon Judge Buckner for two nights was cursed next day for intertaing a Secefsionist, and that the judge's buggy wheel was Stolen & his cushin and thrown in the river, that a resolution was pafsed at a meeting of theirs at the mormon field to hang Judge Buckner, Doctor Downs, and myself.

about a fortnight Since, I Sent a man round with a paper for Signatures for the call of a meeting to organize a militia company and take the Oath of aligience of this State and the C.S. There was pretty good attendance, but they posativily refused to take the oath and would not enrol themselves as militia, but formed a home guard, which in case of invasion may prove of a dangerous character.

Will your Hon. give me or any one Else authority to enrol [these?] as a militia company, or give me Such directions as your Hon. may deem advisable under the circumstances.

Your obt. Servant.

>   Chs. Montague
>   Justice of the Peace
>   Bandera County

P.S. Our Souther[n] boys have almost all joined Capt. Adams Company and the Secfsionists are in a minority in the County at this time.

P.S. 2nd. The postmaster in Bandera (a german) has not taken the Oath, and is a great Union man. Hon. Judge Buckner dropt a letter in the office for me and next day I got it, and it was torn open in the Office before I got it. Can this be remedied?

When the county organized in 1856, August Klappenbach, a Bandera merchant, was elected Clerk of the District Court and later held other county offices. About the same time, he married Mina Kuhue of Castroville and formed a partnership with Charles de Montel to run the commissary at Camp Verde. He was appointed by Governor Sam Houston to be the county's first notary public and Bandera's first postmaster.

Sixteen-year-old Charles Montague Jr. left Springhill College, a Jesuit school in Alabama, to enlist in Adams Company. After the war his 10-12 years' service as county clerk left a creditable mark on the history of Bandera County.

In 1857 Doctor Edwin Downs and family established a ranch along East Verde Creek south of Bandera City at Cottonwood Springs. Doctor Downs built a two-story stone house there. It was said that he treated all the patients he could get to. He served in Paul's Company and later was a surgeon in the C.S.A. His son, Edwin L. Downs, served in Adams' Company.

Eliphalet Frazer Buckner, born in Kentucky in 1810, had established a law practice in San Antonio and Castroville in the 1850s. He was elected district judge of the 18th Judicial District in 1856. The district included Bandera, Medina, Atascosa, Uvalde, Kenny, and Maverick counties. In 1860 he bought land and built a house in Bandera County, but left the area in 1862 to move back to Kentucky.

His son, Thomas Lark Buckner, served in Paul's Company, Adams Company, and later went to Austin where by account he was elected lieutenant in a company raised for the C.S.A. He returned to Bandera County after the war and taught school on Bandera Creek.

Judge Buckner's daughter, Betty, can be found in the <u>Journal of the Secession Convention</u> along with several other young Austin ladies presenting a hand-sewn Texas flag to the convention.

While some Bandera County men joined Adams' Company, others, some with Union sympathies, formed the required county militia unit. The election of Bladen Mitchell as captain of the home guards, with his Virginia accent and fervent Southern loyalty, probably deflected suspicions of disloyalty, if ever the question arose.

Adams' Company

Adams' Company served initially at Camp Wood and Fort Inge where they had taken over the Federal properties. After disbanding and reorganizing with new recruits, the company served at Fort Inge, Fort Clark, Fort Lancaster, Fort Stockton, and Fort Davis. William C. Adams and many of his men were from Uvalde County, most others were from Medina and Bandera counties. They formed one of ten companies in a regiment of state troops known as the Second Texas Mounted Rifles. (Another regiment formed for the North Texas Frontier, The First Texas Mounted Rifles.) They were the first in a long pattern of state frontier defense forces that got turned over to the Confederacy.

Garrison of the forts along the mail route and escort of mail between San Antonio and El Paso seems to have been their main assignment. This service necessarily included fighting Indians, but well outside the Bandera region. However, most of the Bandera County men who volunteered for service in the CSA enrolled in Adams Company. The company seems to have had a fight with Mexicans October 15-16, 1861, at Presidio del Norte.

Henry McCulloch became colonel of the regiment when his brother, Ben, opted for other service. Later John S. Ford commanded the regiment, while McCulloch commanded the regiment of Mounted Riflemen on the North Texas Frontier. The state of Texas turned the Texas Mounted Riflemen over to the Confederacy in 1862.

There are five muster rolls extant for Adams' Company. Two are early (March to June 1861) showing William Adams as lieutenant. The later three have Adams as captain. Two of the later rolls, although different musters, are dated June 8, 1861, and the last one is from the C.S.A. enlistment. These rolls are herein numbered I-V. From the first muster roll for Adams Company:

Copy of Col McCulloch's Order

Head Quarters Middle Division
San Antonio Texas

February 21st 1861

Mr. William Adams

    Sir you are hereby authorized to raise thirty five mounted men and Command the Same with the Rank of First Lieutenant   It will be your duty to have your Command Ready to accompany the persons appointed by the Commifsioners to receive the Federal Property at Camp Wood and Fort Inge (your Self and Twenty five men at Camp Wood & one Sergent with nine men at Fort Inge) and Guard the same under his Insctions, making Requisition upon said [receiver?] of the Property for Rations and forage for your Command. You will be notified at what time the R[eceiver?] for your posts will leave for [there?]. You will Report monthly to this office.

                      By order of Col. McCulloch

                              W.T. Michling
                        Capt and ast agt General

    I Certify on Honor that the above is a true copy of an order Received from Col McCulloch on the 27th day of February A.D. 1861.
                                  W.C. Adams
                        First Lieutenant Comdg Co.

Muster Roll of First Lieutenant William C. Adams Company of Mounted Volunteers called into the Service of the State by an Order of Col Ben McCulloch bearing date February the 21st AD 1861. A Copy of Order is herewith Submitted From the 7th day of March AD 1861 for Temporary Service Which Service Ended on the 8th day of June AD 1861.
    [Name and rank from roll I, ages from roll II:]

#	Name	Age	Rank
1.	William C. Adams	37	1st Lt
2.	John M. McCormick	34	1st Sgt
3.	James M. Gordon	34	2nd Sgt
4.	Peter T. Adams	25	Pvt
5.	Martin V. Adams	27	"
6.	James M. Adams	33	"
7.	George Allin	56	"
8.	William J. Adams	27	"

9. Rufus Allen	26	"
10. Elijah A. Bates	48	"
11. James C. Boie	20	"
12. William Bishop	21	"
13. Jonathan W. Cummings	40	"
14. Henry P. Courtny	33	"
15. James C. Dodd	27	"
16. John C. Davis	24	"
17. Daniel Davis	44	"
18. Samuel Evans	20	"
19. C.A. Gillis	23	"
20. Thomas J. Horton	19	"
21. Thomas J. Haynie	19	"
22. Charles Hadley	20	"
23. Jesse J. Lewis	27	"
24. Andrew J. Lewis	26	"
25. William Morriw	28	"
26. Thalis N. McKinney	39	"
27. Thomas J. McKinney	28	"
28. Robert McWood	25	"
29. Daniel L. McGary	28	"
30. James M. Nichols	19	"
31. N.M.C. Patterson	33	"
32. John Reichter	28	"
33. James H. Read	26	"
34. Samuel W. Rowan	35	"
35. John Smith	27	"
36. Benjamin W. Taylor	35	"
37. Jasper Tatrini	18	"
38. Edward D. Westfall	35	"
39. John Weymiller	30	"
40. Mathew D. Wilkins	26	"
41. Ernest Weigle	39	"
42. Philip Waters	26	"

I do hereby certify on Honor that the Muster Roll above hereof is Correct and Just and that the Remarks set oposite each man's name are true and correct--that said company was disbanded on the 8th day of June 1861.

W.C. Adams
First Lieut. Comdg. Co.

[The concluding statement from roll II:]

I certify on honor that I have at Fort Inge, Texas, on this 7th Day of June, A.D. 1861 carefully [?] [?] the names borne on the above Roll caused the stoppages, allowances & remarks to be [?] and properly stated opposite the names of each man, & that I have mustered out of the Service said Company at Fort Inge, Texas on the 7th Day of June A.D. 1861, in order that said Company [?] be mustered into State Service in Col. Fords Regiment by [virtue?] of the ordinance of the Convention of March 18, 1861, Sec. 8, & that said force [became?] [part?] of said Regiment on the 8th Day of June 1861, by being mustered into the Service of the State.

W.C.Adams, 1st Lieut.
Comm/dg Company

[W.C. Adams was mustering officer on the first two muster rolls for Adams Company. The following document is associated with roll III:]

> I certify that I appointed Capt Wm. R. Henry to muster Capt W.C. Adams Co. belonging to the 2" Texas M't'd Rifles previous to the 8" June 1861

Jn. R. Baylor
Lt Col Comd'g 2" Reg M

[Roll III]
MUSTER ROLL of Captain William C. Adams Company, in the 2nd Regiment, of Texas Mounted Volunteers, Comanded by Colonel John S. Ford, called into the service of the State Texas, under the Provisions of Act of The Convention March the 18th 1861, from the 8th day of June 1861, (date of this Muster) for the term of one year unless sooner discharged.

Bandera County In The Year of Secession

Name	Age	Arms	Place of Residence	Rank
1. William C. Adams	37	R & 6S	Uvalde	Capt.
2. John C. Ellis	30	R & 6S	Uvalde Co. Tex	1 Lt
3. Emory Gibbons	28	R & 6S	Uvalde Co. Tex	2 Lt
1. Thomas L. Wilson	34	"has no arms"	San Antonio	**1 Sgt**
2. Thomas H. Haynie	19	"has no arms"	Uvalde, Tex	2 Sgt
3. William A. Burrows	35	"has no arms"	Bandera Tex	3 Sgt
4. George G. Vanpelt	27	R	Medina Co Tex	4 Sgt
1. John C. Davis	24	R	Washington Co	1 Cpl
2. Cleon R. Moore	21	"Pistol"	Kerr Co Tex	2 Cpl
3. Edwin L. Downe	18	"no arms"	Medina Co Tex	3 Cpl
4. John C. Boie	20	"no arms"	Uvalde Co Tex	4 Cpl
5. Leonadas Flemings	18	R	Uvalde Co Tex	1 Bugl
6. Alonzo G. Rufsell	18	"no arms"	Uvalde Co Tex	2 Bugl
1. Benjamin Andrews	36	"no arms"	Bexar Co Tex	Pvt
2. Jacob Andrews	30	6S	Bexar Co Tex	"
3. William Bishop	21	R & 6S	Uvalde Co Tex	"
4. Jacob Beiedieger	26	6S	Medina Co Tex	"
5. Thomas L. Buckner	22	R &6S	Medina Co Tex	"
6. Moses W. Bolt	30	"no arms"	Arkansas	"
7. Henry P Courtney	33	"no arms	Uvalde	"
8. John W. Chitwood	23	"no arms"	Misouri	"
9. James Dawson	24	R & 6S	Uvalde Tex	"
10. Daniel Davis	44	R & 6S	Camp Wood	"
11. Jacob Etter	19	"no arms"	Bexar Co Tex	"
12. Monroe Fleming	35	R & 6S	Uvalde Tex	"
13. James M. Gordon	32	R & 6S	Uvalde Tex	"
14. George T. Haynie	18	"has no arms"	Bandera	"
15. Madison M. Harper	20	R & 6S	Medina Co Tex	"
16. John M. Ingram	36	6S	Gonzales Tex	"
17. Samuel H. Kellog	23	"no arms"	San Antonio Tex	"
18. Andrew J. Lewis	26	R & 6S	Uvalde Tex	"
19. Jefsee J. Lewis	27	R & 6S	Uvalde Tex	"
20. Lewis Lee	39	6S	Uvalde Tex	"

24. Jackson M. Phillips	21	R	Kerr Co	Pvt
25. August Pingenot	29	R & 6S	Bandera Co	"
26. William R. Rufsell	26	R	Uvalde Tex	"
27. James H. Read	26	"no arms"	Uvalde Tex	"
28. John Reichter	28	R	Uvalde Tex	"
29. James W. Sier	33	R & 6S	Bandera	"
30. Emil Schleyer	21	"no arms"	San Antonio	"
31. Gustavus Sauffe	28	"no arms"	Uvalde Tex	"
32. Florintino Soso	33	"no arms"	San Antonio	"
33. William S. Thomas	21	"no arms"	Uvalde	"
34. William B. Vanpelt	25	"no arms"	Medina Co	"
35. David A. Vanpelt	26	R & "pistol"	Medina Co	"
36. John D. Wharton	23	R & "pistol"	Kerr Co Tex	"
37. Earnest Weile	38	R & "pistol"	Medina Tex	"
38. William C. Wheeler	37	R	Bandera	"
39. Mathew D. Wilkins	25	R & 6S	[Penn?]	"
40. Thomas B. Wren	30	"no arms"	San Antonio	"
41. Joseph A. Watton	29	"no arms"	Penn	"
42. William C. Watson	41	6S	Uvalde	"
43. Francis M. Joiner	21	"no arms"	Uvalde Tex	"
44. John Smith	27	"no arms"	Uvalde Tex	"
45. Charles L. Sweitzer	19	"no arms"	Bexar Co Tex	"
21. James B. McLamore	19	R & 6S	Galveston Tex	"
22. Thomas L. Miller	24	"no arms"	Bandera Co	"
23. Charles McWilliams	31	R & 6S	Bandera Co	"

[Roll IV]

MUSTER ROLL of Captain W.C. Adams Company in the Second Regiment, of M R, commanded by Colonel John S. Ford called into the service of the State of Texas under the Ordinances of Convention pafsed March 18 1861, from the Eight day of June 1861, when mustered, to the Twenty fifth day of June 1861, the date of the present Muster. at which time the Company was transferred to Confederate Service.

[differences from previous roll:]

1. John C. Boie is 3rd Corporal and Edwin D. Downs is 4th Corporal. "Downs" is spelled without an "e" on this roll.

2. Leonadas Fleming is the only bugler, Alonzo G. Russell is listed as a private.

3. Private M.V. Andrews, 27, is added to the roll.

4. Private John B. Bowles, 26, is added to the roll.

5. Private Jacob C. Gray, 20, is added to the roll.

6. What appears to be private Charles L. Somtzer or Smitzer, 22, on this roll is Charles L. Sweitzer, 19, on the above roll and Charles L. Sweitzer, 22, on the following roll.

7. Private Earnest Weile above seems to be the same person as Eimitt Weigle on this roll, both 38 (also seen as Ernest Weigle).

8. Private Peter Wallace, 20, is added to the roll.

9. Private Jackson M. Phillips is 23, was 21 on the preceding roll, and 23 on the following roll. His residence is shown as Kerr County. Jack Phillips settled with his family on Winan's Creek in Bandera County during the Civil War. He was a Bandera County Commissioner in 1864 and served in the county's home guard unit. Sometime after the war he served the county as a ranger captain and later as a deputy sheriff. His brother-in-law was Henry Hamilton, the Civil War era Kerr County Sheriff who moved to Bandera County where he was elected sheriff in 1875.]

[Roll V]

MUSTER ROLL of Captain W.C. Adams' Company ("C"), in the Second Regiment, ([blank] brigade), of T.M.R. Volunteers, commanded by Colonel J.S. Ford called into the service of the Confederate States by L.P. Walker, Sect. of War under the Act of Congress, approved February 28th, 1861, from the 31st day of August 1861, when mustered, to the 31st day of October 1861, the date of the present Muster.

Name	Rank	Age	Remarks
Wm. C. Adams	Capt	37	R & 6S
J.C. Ellis	1st Lt	30	R & 6S
Emory Gibbons	2nd Lt	28	R & 6S in arrest

John M. Ingram	2nd Lt	36	6S Elected 2nd
Thos L. Wilson	1st Sgt	34	[blank]
Thos H. Haynie	2nd Sgt	19	on DS at Fort Lancaster, Tex since Aug. 31 61 [fs?] detail.
William A. Burrows	3rd Sgt	35	[detached service - as above
Geo G. Vanpelt	4th Sgt	27	R
John C. Davis	1st Cpl	24	R
Cleon R. Moore	2nd Cpl	21	6S
John C. Boie	3rd Cp;	20	[blank]
John D. Whorton	4th Cpl	23	R & 6S. app/d Corp. July 20 61
Geo P. Haynie	Bugler	18	App/d Bugler Sept. 15 61

Privates

1. Andrews Benjamin	36	[blank]
2. Andrews Jacob	30	6S
3. Adams M.V.	27	Sharp's Rifle, [?] & 6S
4. Allen Rufus	26	R & 6S
5. Bishop Wm	21	R & 6S
6. Beiedeifer Jacob	26	6S
7. Buckner Thos. B.	22	R & 6S on D.S. at Ft Lancaster Tex since August 31 61
8. Bott Moses W.	30	[blank]
9. Courtney H.P.	33	[blank]
10. Chitwood John W.	23	Abst. in conft since July 20 61 at Ft Clark, Tex
11. Downs Edwin L.	18	resgd from Corpl July 19 61 on D.S. at Ft Lancaster Tex since Aug 31 61 [fs.O.?]
12. Dawson James	24	R & 6S
13. Davis Daniel	44	R & 6S
14. Etter Jacob	19	[blank]
15. Elkins John	21	transf from Capt Hammers Co "D" July 1 61 fs. O. [sling?]

16.	Fleming Monroe	35	"gun" & 6S on D.S. at Ft Lancaster, Tex since Aug 31 61 fs.O. Lt Col. Baylor to pay for 1 musketoon
17.	Fleming Leonadia	18	R [on ds to Ft L as above] Reduced to pvt Aug 31 63 from Buglar
18.	Gomas Felician	25	[blank]
19.	Gordon James M.	32	"gun" & 6S
20.	Gray Jacob C.	20	[blank]
21.	Gamer[Garner?] Robt L.	24	musketoon & 6S
22.	Griner Anson J.	18	"gun" & 6S
23.	Harper M.M.	20	R & 6S on D.S. at Ft Lancaster, Tex since Aug 31 61 fs. O.
24.	Holmes Wm	28	sick
25.	Highsaw James D.	20	[blank]
26.	Joiner Francis M.	21	[blank]
27.	Jonson Thos. J.	18	R & 6S
28.	Jonson Wm. H.	30	[blank]
29.	Kellogg Saml. H	23	[blank]
30.	Lewis Andrew J.	26	R & 6S
31.	Lewis Jesse J.	26	R & 6S
32.	Lewis Geo. W.	19	on D.S. at Ft Lancaster Tex since Aug 31 61 fs. O.
33.	Lee Lewis	27	6S [on ds at Ft L as above]
34.	Laxson Thos. A.	18	[on dis at Ft L as above]
35.	McLamore Jas. B.	19	R & 6S [on ds at Ft L as above]
36.	Miller [T]hos B.	24	[on dis at Ft L as above]
37.	Miller Samuel	38	[on dis at Ft L as above]
38.	Miller Saml. R.	18	R & 6S [on ds at Ft L "since Sept.. 10 61. fs(?) detail."
39.	McWilliams Chas.	31	R & 6S

MUSTER ROLL Continued [separate document]

40.	Mattison Wm H.H.	22	Trans/f from Capt Hammers Co "H" july 1 61. fs. order Lt Col. Baylor to pay for musketoon
41.	Montague Chas	18[16]	Sharp's Rifle & 6S
42.	McNamara John	25	Minnie Rifle
43.	North Wm. Is.	18	on D.S. at Ft Lancaster, Tex since Aug. 31 61. fs. order.
44.	O'Bryant John W.	21	R
45.	Philips Jackson	23	R
46.	Pingenot August	29	R & 6S
47.	Pafford John R.	19	[blank]
48.	Pierce Joseph C.	30	Minnie Rifle
49.	Russell Wm R.	26	R, on D.S. at Ft Lancaster, Tex. since Aug. 31 61. fs. O.
50.	Russell Alonzo Is.	18	R, on D.S. [as above] rec/d to Pvt Aug. 31 61 from Baylore
51.	Read James H.	26	[blank]
52.	Richter John	28	R
53.	Rine Christopher C.	21	[blank]
54.	Robison James	21	"gun" & 6S
55.	Sier James W	33	R & 6S
56.	Schleyer Imil	21	[blank]
57.	Sauppe Gustavus	28	[blank]
58.	Soso Florintino	33	[blank]
59.	Sweitzer Chas L.	22	[blank]
60.	Smith John	27	[blank]
61.	Smith Patrick	25	on D.S. at Ft Lancaster, Tex. since Aug 31 61. fs. O.
62.	Thomas Wm. S.	21	[blank]
63.	Tilley Wm. L.	27	shot gun
64.	Vanpelt Wm. B.	25	on D.S. at Ft Lancaster, Tex since Aug 31 61 fs. O.
65.	Vanpelt David A.	26	R & 6S
66.	Weigle Earnest	38	R & 6S
67	Wheeler Wm C.	37	R
68.	Wilkins Mathew D.	25	R & 6S
69.	Watton Jos. A.	25	[blank]

70. Watson Wm. C.	41	6S
71. Wallace Peter	20	[blank]
72. West August	19	[blank]
73. Watkins Wm. M.	25	"Gun" & 6S, on D.S. at Ft Lancaster, Tex since Sept 6, 61. fs. O.

<u>Died</u>

1. Bowles John B.—26—Killed in an affray with mexicans at Presidio del Norte, Mexico. Oct. 16, 61. to pay for 1 army pistol, N.P, 1 screw driver, 1 wiper, & one Pistol scabbard.

2. Wren Thos. B.—30—Killed in an affray with mexicans at Presidio del Norte Mexico, Oct. 15, 61, to pay for 1 Army pistol, N.P. 1 Pistol scabbard, 1 Cartridge Box.

 I certify on honor, that I have at Fort Davis, Texas on this 31st day of October 1861, carefully examined this Roll, and as far as practible, caused the allowances, stoppages, and remarks to be justly and properly stated; and mustered the Company for the period herein stated.

W.C. Adams
Capt. 2T.M.R.
Mustering Officer

[No indication if Bowles and Wren were on official duty or on personal leave when killed. Years later Charles Montague Jr. had private possession of this roll and made this notation at the bottom of the roll:]

> Chas. Montague was born April 10th, 1845, but he was entered as "18" because the officers said he would be discharged by the war department, if he was enrolled as only 16 years of age.

[Charles Montague, Jr. does not say how he came to have the muster roll, but, in 1898, sent it with this letter to the Adjutant General:]

Office of
Chas. Montague
Notary Public and Land Agent

Bandera, Texas, 28 Dec, 1898
Adjutant Genl.
Austin, Tex.

Dear Sir,

Enclosed I hand you original Muster roll of Co. "C", 2nd Tex Mtd Riflemen and respectfully ask that you send me a receipt. I would have sent this sooner but have been sick.

Respectfully
Chas.Montague

The Indian Fight On The Seco

Indian raids were few in the early part of 1861, but increased towards the end of the year. The October 19, 1861 edition of the <u>San Antonio Herald</u> carried a letter to the editor from John W. De Vilbis of Leal with the heading, "More Indian Depredations." He described Indian raids in Uvalde and Medina counties, then said:

> I allude to that country between Camp Verde and Fort Inge, and extending down as far as Atascosa and McMullen counties, and thence to the Rio Grande. It is about 85 miles between Camp Verde and Fort Inge, and all the Indians who infest the country alluded to, pass down between these two posts - generally through the Sabinal and Frio Canons. Now, I would suggest that Fort Inge and Camp Verde be abandoned, and that in their stead a Camp be established either on the headwaters of the Frio or Sabinal, and another on the head-waters of either the Medina or Guadalupe, and a road established from Fort Mason past these new posts to Camp Wood, and from thence to Fort Clark. This would cover the whole region, and the same men now employed at Fort Inge and Camp verde could man these new posts.

During the winter months of 1861-62, Comanches encamped on the Pecos River made raids into the frontier counties. One of the largest raids involved 150-200 Comanches around December 1861. They raided as far south as Atascosa County before forming into two groups to head north again. One group headed straight up the Sabinal River before crossing the dry lands to the Devil's River, while the other group went up Seco Creek. William "Seco" Smith, a Medina County settler who later moved to Bandera County, recalled:

> This same band of Indians killed Mr. and Mrs. Stringfield, and carried their little boy, Tommy Stringfield, off into captivity. Mrs. William Hatfield,, now living [1922] at Medina, is a daughter of Mr. and Mrs. Stringfield, and was present when

her parents were killed, but managed to escape. The Indians came on up the country and divided into large parties. "Big Foot" Wallace, with a party of men, followed one of the bands which went out on the divide between the Sabinal and Medina Rivers. The Indians discovered their pursuers and laid ambush for them.

The other band of Indians had gone up the Sabinal, and I, in company, with several men, took their trail and followed them out to the head of Devil's River, out near where Sonora is now located. There were about 100 Indians in this band, and they made a very plain trail. A settlement fort had been constructed on the Sabinal for the protection of the few settlers there, and a company of rangers from Washington county, under command of Captain Meyers, was encamped about a mile below this fort at this time. We sent a runner to the ranger camp for assistance to help in chasing these Indians and Captain Meyers sent 25 men to join us. In the party of rangers were two men from San Antonio, Sam Maverick and a young man named Simpson.

Seco Smith with a few Medina County men and the rangers made a determined, but futile effort to catch up with the Comanches who had raced up the Sabinal. Meanwhile other men were gathering with Big Foot Wallace to confront the Comanches who had gone up Seco Creek. There are few sources beyond A.J. Sowell's biography of Big Foot Wallace and, in <u>Texas Indian Fighters</u>, the accounts of A.J. Davenport and Gideon Thompson:

This band of Indians had penetrated into the settlements as far as Atascosa County and killed many people. Around the little village of Pleasanton they had killed a man named Herndon, wounded Anderson and O'Bryant, and chased several others. On the way back they were fought by a small party of settlers, in which James Winters was killed and others wounded. Further on they killed "Mustang" Moore, near where Moore's station is, and Peter Ketchum, on the Hondo. They also killed Mr. Murray, tax assessor of Bandera County. Others were also killed and wounded by them, and horses gathered up all over the country.

James Thomas McMurray was elected Bandera County Tax Assessor & Collector August 5, 1861. The Election Return in the Archives has a rulered line drawn through his name. George Hay remembered him as "John" and gave this account in the <u>Pioneer History</u>:

> John Thomas McMurray came into my store one day and told me he was going over on the Hondo and Seco to assess taxes, and was going alone. I told him he might encounter Indians, and advised him to go with the mail carrier, but he said he was not afraid. McMurray had belonged to our ranger company and I knew him to be a very brave man. He had a crippled arm caused by the accidental discharge of a shotgun, which somewhat incapacitated him, so we elected him tax assessor and collector. After leaving me that day I never saw him alive again. He stayed all night at a ranch [Cosgrove's] over on the Seco, and next day, about 3 o'clock in the afternoon, while traveling along he came upon two men who were in camp and eating a late dinner. The men were coming from the Frio Canyon to mill at Bandera. They invited McMurray to take dinner with them, but he said he was in a hurry and did not have time to tarry, so passed on, and when about a mile from this camp he was attacked by a large party of Indians. He quickly turned and started back to the men who were eating dinner, but was killed before he had gone very far, being shot in the back with arrows. The campers heard the yells and saw the Indians, and became frightened and hastily left, going back to their homes. Whether or not they knew McMurray had been killed I do not know, but they never stopped until they reached the Frio. The weather was bitterly cold, it being winter time, and when word was brought to Bandera several days afterward that McMurray was missing, a searching party composed of P.D. Saner, Robert Ballantyne, O.B. Miles, myself, and others went out to the ranch of Henderson C. McKay, where we stayed all night, and the next morning we started out and found the body, laying face down. McMurray's pistol and assessment book had been taken away by the Indians, but he had not been scalped. We buried him there, and ever since then that draw has been known as Dead Man's Hollow.

A.J. Davenport gathered men to the Kinchaloe Prairie near D'Hanis and rendezvoused with Big Foot Wallace and the men from around the Hondo Creek area, as well as some men from Atascosa County. The Medina and Uvalde county men mentioned in the A.J. Sowell accounts were A.J., William, and Jack Davenport, Ross and John Kennedy, Frank Hilburn, Lewis McCombs, George Robins, Alonzo Moore, Bill Mullins, Manuel Wydick, F.G. Finley, Nathan

Davis, Malcom Van Pelt, Jasper Kinchaloe, and Harris. Most of the "many others whose names cannot now be recalled" were probably from Atascosa County.

The 30-40 men started up Seco Creek. Captain Wallace called a halt when they reached the bridle path that ran between Bandera City and Sabinal Canyon. He found indications that four Indians had left the main body of raiders and pursued someone (who later turned out to be J.T. McMurray). Tracking was continued to the head of Seco Creek where the men stopped for lunch. Unbeknownst to them, they were in full view of the raiders waiting in the heights above. The tracking was resumed as the men rounded a small hill on the approach to a high ridge with a long slope where they saw a horse staked part way up. In spite of being warned against it, some of the younger men in the group raced ahead to claim the horse. A volley of shotgun fire rained down the hill wounding William Davenport through the thigh and slightly wounding another young man named Harris. Both their horses were hit, but most of the shot went over their heads. As A.J. Davenport went up the hill to aid his son, the Indians rushed down upon their pursuers. Captain Wallace, who had been attempting to corral the young men, managed to slide and fall back behind a rocky ledge while the rest of the men hurried to secure their horses and began shooting at the Indians. The Davenports managed to reach the relative safety of the ledge where Captain Wallace had taken refuge. As the Indians began to take casualties from the settlers' return fire, they withdrew behind the rocks and bushes along the upper ridge. A few of the men who had long range rifles moved up the small hill in the rear where they began to inflict casualties from out of range of the Indians' weapons. Some men from below gradually reinforced Captain Wallace at the rocky ledge. They may have attempted a flanking movement on the Indians, who counter-attacked. Gradually losing their advantage in the battle, the Indians soon withdrew with all their horse herd. A norther had blown in and sleet had begun to fall. Captain Wallace and his men attempted no pursuit, taking the two wounded men to Waresville and sending Jasper Kinchaloe to the Anglin Prong to gather reinforcements.

While Captain Wallace and the others rested at Waresville, Gideon Thompson, Jack Kelley, and five other Anglin Prong men answered the call and set out in the cold night after unsuccessfully attempting to shoe a horse at Aaron Anglin's place. They could not keep a fire lit in the wind. Later as morning broke, they got the shoeing done while waiting at the Cypress Spring where they expected to meet Wallace and the others. A cold rain set in and as no one had shown up, they were going home when they crossed the trail of the others and caught up with them a few miles upstream along the main Sabinal River. As the temperature dropped again and the rain turned to sleet, the reinforced pursuers spent the next night at an abandoned ranch house. Some of the Atascosa County men were without coats.

Captain Wallace reasoned that the Indians also had to lay up during the bad weather and the next morning he led his men up the Sabinal River to the trail leading over the divide to the Frio Water Hole. The Indians had nearly 200 horses to move over a very rough region in central Bandera County. Meanwhile an ambush was set up and some tense moments passed as Wallace and his men could hear the horses clomping on the rocks long before the Indians were in sight. At two hundred yards the first few Indians came into view and Frank Hilburn raised up to look, firing his rifle in the process. The Indians all scattered, but the settlers' horses were recovered.

The horse trail across the divide in northwest Bandera County where Big Foot Wallace and his men set the ambush was known to Indians and rangers. It leads from the headwaters region of the Medina and Sabinal rivers, perhaps among the Lost Maples, over or around the divide eventually to the Frio Water Hole. From there raiders could dash for Mexico or the Pecos River with the horses they had gathered. R.H. Williams described a portion of the horse trail as he made his way to the Frio Water Hole in 1862, "It was, for the most part, desperate country to ride over, for we were well in the mountains, and frequently had to dismount and lead our horses down rocky slides."

According to Taylor Thompson who rangered around Uvalde County and most of West Texas during the Civil War:

> The head of the Medina was a rendezvous or gathering place for the Indians, a large body of whom would assemble there, and then dividing into small parties, would raid the country to the south, going by different routes and returning, meet again at the rendezvous.

On their typical way out of the settlements, Indian raiders, after reaching the Frio Water Hole, would ride to the Kickapoo Springs at the head of the West Nueces River or to the South Llano River. If they felt assured that they were not being pursued, they might camp long enough to barbecue some horse meat over a small fire sheltered by a cedar brake. Their next destination would be

Mexico or the Devil's or Pecos rivers. The Indians often made their crossing of the Rio Grande north of San Felipe (Del Rio).

The Lipan Apaches at this time ranged from around San Fernando, Mexico, to the Presidio del Norte and out to the Pecos River. Kickapoos were also in that area. Mescalero Apaches were there and in portions of New Mexico and the Texas Panhandle. Seminoles were around El Nacimiento, Mexico. Comanches generally went where they pleased, although most of their camps were north of the Red River by this time.

During 1861 Juan Castro led his diminished band of Lipan Apaches out of Mexico and joined the Tonkawas at Fort Belknap where they had a company of scouts in the Texas service. These few Lipans faded into obscurity among the Tonkawas in the Indian Territory. Costilietos and Chiquito were among the main chiefs of the Lipan Apaches remaining in Mexico.

6

The Frontier Regiment: Montel's Company

Company G (later Company D)
Frontier Regiment, Texas State Troops
February 1862 - December 1862

With the Mounted Riflemen, including Adams' Company, turned over to the Confederacy, the state of Texas raised a new regiment to protect its frontier regions. The bill was approved by the Texas legislature December 21, 1861. Since statehood, the Texas goal had been to have ranger protection paid for by the national government with control left in state hands. The Confederate congress approved that arrangement in legislation passed January 17, 1862, but President Davis vetoed the bill five days later. Control of, and fiscal responsibility for the regiment remained with the state of Texas.

The regimental officers were appointed: Colonel James M. Norris, Lieutenant Colonel Alfred J. Obenchain, and Major James Ebenezer McCord. In the summer 1862 Alfred Obenchain was murdered by friends of Captain Cureton who had quarreled with the Lt. Colonel. James McCord became lieutenant colonel and Buck Barry became major.

Meanwhile the individual companies were getting organized. Men mostly from Bandera, Blanco, Medina, and Uvalde counties formed Montel's Company in Bandera City February 17, 1862. Camp Bandera was set up for organizing, training, and outfitting the company. There was much to be done. Company officers were elected. As the horses were readied for service, four men were hired as blacksmiths. In the "Report of Persons and Articles employed and hired at Camp Bandera during the month of February 1862," John Kneipke was paid $40; John Funker, $15; C. Bauman, $10; and August Faltin, $8.20. Large quantities of corn had to be freighted to feed the horses. March 9, 1862, Quartermaster T.P. McCall paid Daniel McLemore $14 for hauling corn from Quihi to Camp Bandera. That same day Quartermaster McCall paid Paul Martin $24 for 24 bushels of corn.

The Oath of Capt Chas de Montel, Capt Comp Rangers, Frontier Regt

I Charles de Montel do solemnly swear that I will faitfull and impartialy discharge and perform all the duties incumbent on me a Captain of a Company of mounted Rangers in the frontier Regement of Texas aproved December 21th 1861 according to the best of my skill and ability, agreably to the Constitution and laws of the State of Texas and also to the Constitution and laws of the Confederate States of America so long as the State of Texas shall remain a member of that Confederacy.

And I do further solemnly swear that since the second day of March A.D. 1861 I being a Citizen of thise State, have not fought a duel with deadly weapons, within this State nor out of it nor have I send or accepted a chalenge to fight a duel with deadly weapons nor have I acted as second in carrying a challenge or aided or assisted anny person thus offending--so help me God.

Charles de Montel.
signed & sworn to before
me, this 28th day of february
A.D. 1862.-------- To certify which, I herewith sign
my name and affix the imprefs of the
seal of the County Court of Medina Co.
the day and year above written.

Louis Huth
Chief Justice, Medina Co.

Beginning in March 1862, the officers of the regiment inspected the frontier line for the best location of ranger camps. Colonel Norris was in Bandera City on at least two occasions. April 2 he paid David Monroe four dollars for four bushels of corn. April 16 he paid David Monroe three dollars for three bushels of corn. April 17 he paid August Klappenbach three dollars for nails and paid Daniel Rugh one dollar for shoeing a horse. Between March 17 and April 7 Colonel Norris posted his nine companies along a line of 18 camps (each company divided between two camps):

Company	Captain	Stations
A	A. Brunson	Northeast Wichita County. Southeast Wichita County and later moved eastward to Red River Station in Montague County
B	Jack Cureton	Camp Cureton (Archer County) Camp Belknap (near Fort Belknap)
C	John Salmon	Camp Breckenridge (Stephens County) Camp Salmon (Callahan County. This camp was later known as Camp McCord.)
D	T.N. Collier	Camp Pecan (Callahan County) Camp Collier (Brown County)
E	N.D. McMillan	Camp McMillan (San Saba County) Camp San Saba
F	H.T. Davis	Camp Llano (Mason County) Camp Davis (Gillespie County)
G	Charles De Montel	Camp Verde (two miles from old Camp Verde, Kerr County) Camp Montel (at the head of Seco Creek in Bandera County)
H	Thomas Robb	Camp Robb-The other half was split between Rio Grande Station and Fort Duncan
K	J.J. Dix	Camp Dix (Uvalde County) Camp Nueces

Charles de Montel's company was divided between Camp Montel at Ranger Springs, perhaps near the site of the recent "Indian Fight On The Seco", and Camp Verde, two miles from "old" Camp Verde. "Captain Charles" commanded from Camp Bandera (perhaps in or near Bandera City) at least in the early days of the company, while Camp Verde seems to have been his headquarters later. Lieutenant McCall, the second-in-command, served as quartermaster. Lieutenant Patton commanded Camp Montel and Lieutenant Gates commanded Camp Verde. For some time (at least June and July 1862), the men of Camp Verde were at Camp McCord and at least by November 1862 had returned to Camp Verde.

Detachments usually of five privates and one officer from each camp made regular patrols to the camp to their south every two days. Indian raiders got used to the routine after a while and the regular patrols were discontinued when the regiment reorganized the following year.

A.J. Sowell included accounts of Montel's Company in <u>Texas Indian Fighters</u>:

[A.J. Davenport]

> In 1861 Jack Davenport joined a company of rangers commanded by Capt. Charles de Montel. They were stationed at Ranger Springs, on the Seco. While they were here the Indians made a raid below the mountains and were followed by settlers from below to the head of the salt marsh in Sabinal Canyon, about five miles west from the present village of Utopia.
>
> In the meantime a runner had been sent to the ranger camp, and a scout was sent out to intercept them. The rangers and settlers got together at the head of the salt marsh and continued the pursuit. Among the rangers were Lieut. Ben Patton, commanding; Jack Davenport, Ed Taylor, Cud Adams, Demp Forrest, Dan Malone, Charles Cole, Jasper Kinchaloe, Lon Moore, and John Cook.
>
> The trail led in a northeast [means northwest?] direction over a rough, mountainous country, towards the head of the Frio River. At length, arriving on a high mountain in Sabinal Canyon, Lieutenant Patton discovered the Indians. They had camped in a valley, but on elevated ground, between two deep gullies, with a cedar brake in their rear. They were engaged in cooking horse meat, mending moccasins, etc.
>
> Without being seen by the Indians, Patton dismounted his men, left their horses, went down the mountain, and struck the creek about half a mile below the Indian camp, and came up keeping well concealed, until they approached the high banks of the gullies in less than fifty yards of the unsuspecting hostiles. Jack Davenport, having it on his mind to avenge his brother, kept his gun well in hand, and when the charge was ordered kept by the side of Lieutenant Patton, who led. The men went up the banks in various places and with great rapidity, and were almost among the Indians and firing upon them before they were aware of the presence of an enemy. The onset was so fierce and the firing so fast and fatal that the Indians made a

poor fight, and soon sought safety in the cedar brake near by. Davenport and Patton both fired their first shot at the same Indian, who fell near the fire. Another one fell fifty yards from the fire, and the third ran about 200 yards and fell. Many of the Indians were wounded but made their escape, leaving trails of blood behind them. One wounded Indian was found under the roots of a large cedar tree which had been blown down, and was pulled out and scalped alive by one of the white men. The Indian made a very wry face during the process of scalping, as if in much pain, and pointed towards the sky, as if threatening the man with the vengeance of God. In this fight John Cook shot twelve times at one Indian running, emptying two revolvers without bringing him down. Sometimes an Indian can carry off almost as much lead as a California grizzly bear. When the fight was over Jack Davenport went to the Indian whom he knew he had shot, and scalped him, saying as he did so that he was now even with them for his brother John. Be it said to his credit, however, his Indian was dead when he scalped him.

[Alonzo Moore]

The Indians made a raid in the Hondo valley again during the Civil war and killed a boy named Hood, who lived at the Redus ranch. The settlers followed them into the mountains and were joined in Sabinal Canyon by a squad of rangers under command of Lieutenant Patton of Captain Montel's company. Lon Moore was with the rangers and belonged to the company. The Indians were found in camp in the mountains. There were fifteen of them and twenty of the rangers and settlers. The charge was made on them with loud shouts. The Indians strung their bows and tried to outyell the whites, but did not succeed, and soon ran, leaving four of their number dead on the ground,--the chief, one squaw, and two warriors. Lon ran close to one Indian and shot him with a pistol, breaking his leg, and he fell off a bluff. Moore leaped off after him, but made a narrow escape, as the wounded savage made a dangerous thrust at him with a lance, but the active young ranger sprang to one side and shot the Indian three times more, and killed him. He and others ran one Indian some distance and shot him repeatedly with pistols, but could not kill him.

After the fight he told the men he had killed the chief, and showed them where he lay. Lon then tried to scalp him, but his knife was dull and he made slow progress. Some of the men told him it was not his knife but his heart that had failed him, but he finally got it off. The Indians had killed his brother-in-law, Pete Ketchum, and mutilated his face by cutting off his nose and skinning off the beard, and then, not being dead, dragged him through the prickly pears until life was extinct.

The men gathered up the spoils of the Indian camp, among which were twelve American saddles taken from men whom they had killed. Lon got a knife from the chief which had belonged to the boy Hood, whom they killed at the Redus ranch. It was brought back and given to the boy's mother. A party went back to this battleground some time after, who were not in the fight, to look at the dead Indians, and said the bodies of the Indians had been covered with brush. One lone Indian had returned and done this. It had rained since the fight, and all other tracks were obliterated but his, which had been made since the rain. Nearly all of the Indians who got away were wounded. There was so much shooting that Lon said he was as afraid of his own party as the Indians.

The Monthly Return for Montel's Company for the month of November 1862 was drawn up at Camp Verde by Lt. McCall, "Commanding the Company", as Captain Charles was away on a scout. Under "Absent Enlisted Men, accounted for by name", nine of the 44 privates were Bandera County men who are identified here by the addition of an asterisk:

Sergt. Hill & Harper, Corp. Pafford, farrier Brown, Privates Bates, Duncan, Wiley, Dodd, Dutcher*, Johnson, L. Moore, Owens I & II, Onion*, Peden, Reynolds, Reinhardt, Tomlin, Wilkins, Wight*, Ward, Zimermann, Forrest, Brewer, Bushall, Balentyne*, Bird*, Billharz, Burney, Casner I & II, Chipman*, Conrad, Gralen, Green*, Haller, Hicks*, Lauson, Nowling I & II, Pingenot*, Patterson, Stayton I & II, Swarz, Tondre, Wood I & II, Watson - on a scout 20 days

Commissioned Officers, present and absent, accounted for by Name:

Present

1. Thos. P. McCall 1 Lieut - A.A.Q.M. & A.A.C.S.
2. B. Patton 2 jr Lieut. - Comand/g Camp Montel

Absent

1. Ch. de Montel Captain - Comd/g a scout. party 20 days
2. A.V. Gates 2 Lieut. - with leave 46 days

Many similar scouts were made including one combined with other companies according to A.J. Sowell's account of Alonzo Moore:

> During the war, when Lon Moore was a member of Captain Montel's company of rangers, an expedition against the Indians on a large scale was gotten up. The intention was to invade the stronghold of the Comanches in the northwest. Thirty men were selected from each company on this part of the frontier, making 130 in all, and all under the command of Captain Montel. When the command arrived at a point high up on Devil's River some of the men wanted to come back. Montel stepped out and said, "All those who want to go on come and stand on my right." All of his own company came over and stood by him, and the other men turned back. Montel and his men now went on until they came to a place called the Black Hills, between the head of Devil's River and the Texas line. Here they saw many wigwams in a valley, and the captain said, "Now, all those who are willing to go down in there and fight them step to the right." All responded. "Now, boys," said Montel, "I see that I will have to say go back, you will not do it. I was in hopes you would say go back. There are too many for us."
>
> The Indians had discovered the presence of the rangers and followed them back to the Colorado, and one night while they were camped ran a thousand or more buffalo through the edge of their camp. The intention was to run them square over the rangers, but they turned. Six pack mules and two saddle horses were cut off, and went with the buffaloes. The design of the Indians was to stampede all the horses and leave the rangers afoot. They followed the trail of the buffalos thirty miles to rescue their stock, but came upon an Indian trail that turned in on the buffalo trail, and knew they would get them, so turned back.
>
> On this trip they subsisted on the return fifteen days on buffalo meat without bread. They were also without tobacco, and the first place they struck where they could get any was Fort Mason, and they had to pay $2.50 a plug for it in Confederate money.

Fabian L. Hicks, Bandera County Sheriff 1861-62, enlisted in Montel's Company July 7, 1862 at Camp McCord. The following excerpt is from Myrtle Murray's article about F.L. Hicks from a series she did in the Cattleman during the 1930s and republished in the September 1948 Frontier Times:

> During the war Mr. Hicks was a Texas Ranger and assigned to home duty to protect the women and children. He had to be away from home most of the time. When he told his wife and children "goodbye" he knew it was likely they might be attacked by the Indians before he returned.
>
> Mrs. Hicks knew [s]he was continuously in danger. Her people wanted her to move to town or to get some one to stay with her. But she felt that she must stay on the ranch and take care of things. Her brother, Gabe [Anderwald], stayed with her for a while. The rangers working with her husband knew they could always count on a good meal at the Hicks' home, when they were in that vicinity.
>
> The children were afraid of the Indians so it was easy for her to keep them in sight. The Indians, however, never bothered her except to steal horses when they knew Mr. Hicks was away. She tried to stake the horses at night so the Indians would not find them. She knew they were near when she heard the cattle running and bawling. She would put out the light, grab her ax and gather her children close about her. Mr. Hicks barely missed the Indians one time when he was returning from a long, hard trip. The Indians had stolen the horses, and left the house the way he usually returned home. This time he happened to come home another way, much to the relief and happiness of the family.
>
> Stampeding cattle sometimes meant that Indians were in the country. Often cattle would gather around the ranch house whenever Indians were about. It seems that before the Civil War, Indian raiders killed the settlers' cattle whenever they could. During the Civil War Indians learned they could sell Texas cattle to Union forces in New Mexico.

Two muster rolls for Montel's Company are in the Texas State Library. No ages are listed on these rolls; however, place of residence is listed on the 2nd roll. The muster rolls of Company G, Frontier Regiment of Texas Rangers (later Company D, F.R.):

Muster roll of Captain Charles de Montels Company in the [torn] Rangers Commanded by Col. [blank] called into the Service of the State by an act approved Dec. 21st 1861. Enrolled in the Countys Bandera, Blanco, Medina, [torn] serve for the Term of Twelve months from the date of organization unlefs sooner discharged. The Compagny was enrolled by Charles de Montel and organized by the [torn] tain Charles de Montel at Bandera on the 17th day of February 1862.

1. Charles de Montel	Captain
2. Th. P. McCall	I Leut/t
3. A.V. Gates	II Leut/t
4. P. Patten	2 Jun. Leut/t
1. Tucker	[no rank indicated–chaplain or surgeon?]
1. John Lawhorn	I Serg/t
2. G.W. Hill	II Serg/t
3. Rob Harper	III Serg/t
4. W. L. Cooper	IV "
1. Daniel Malone	1 Corp/l
2. Thom. Pafford	2 Corp/l
3. Thom. Bandy	3 Corp/l
4. R.W. Davis	4 Corp/l
1. W. Ganyon	Bugler I
2. Ch. de Montel, Jr.	II

1. Allen Hugh	40. Moore L.
2. Bates Felix	41. McKinney T.N.
3. Bowles D. C.	42. McKinny T.G.
4. Bowles G.	43. Masser Thom
5. Bates E. A.	44. Manning Wm
6. Bandy John	45. Moore J.T.
7. Ballantine Wm.	46. Nowlin K.W.
8. Bird Ch.	47. Norris J
9. Brewer L.	48. Owens W.P.

The Frontier Regiment: Montel"s Company

10. Bushnell Lester
11. Cude R.D.
12. Croke James
13. Cook Thom
14. Cook J.E.
15. Chipman H.
16. Carnahan D.S
17. Cooper W.L.
18. Duncan Benj.
19. Davenport W.
20. Dolch Louis
21. Dodd W.
22. Dutcher C.L.
23. Graylin A.
24. Grener N.J.
25. Green John
26. Grey J.D.
27. Heath Louis
28. Hegg Fr.
29. Hamilton G.W.
30. Johnson Oscar
31. Kenneday John
32. Kend D.B.
33. Lamon John
34. Long T.A.
35. Lindemann H.C.
36. Lindemann E.D.
37. Lindemann A.A.
38. Lundey M.R.
39. Lundey Wm.

49. Onion Jos.
50. Patterson D.
51. Pulliam B.
52.. Pingenot C
53. Patton B.F.
54. Reicherzer Th.
55. W.M. Reynolds
56. Stanford N.
57. Stayton J.A.
58. Smith H.R.
59. Jamson J.N.
60. Short Th.
61. Stayton D.W.
62. Schuckhard C.F.
63. Tondre Frank
64. Tilley E.
65. Thompson H.
66. Tomberlin A.
67. Taylor N.A.
68. Wilkins D.
69. Wight L.
70. Westfall W.R.
71. Wood W.B.
72. Wood C.P.
73. Westfall S.C.
74. Wyley I.
75. Watsen B.H.
76. Zorger Peter
77. Zimmermann A.

I Certify on honour that this muster Roll exhibits the true State of Captain Charles De Monteuls Company of the [torn] Frontier Regiment of Rangers for the period herein mentioned that [torn] man answers to his own proper name in person that the [remarks] [torn] opposite the name of each officer and Soldier are accurate and [torn] That the valuation of all arms and accutrements Horses [torn] equipments at the organization and Since the muster into Serv[ice] was made by disinterested and good judges and at fair and j[ust] [torn]

>Charles de Montel
>Capt
>Commanding the Company

I Certify on honour that I have at Bander City, Bandera Co., Texas on the 18 day of February 1862 Carefully examined this roll and as far as practicable caused the allowances and reasonable [torn] to be justly and properly Stated and enrolled the Company [torn] organization and it is hereby organized in Strict Compliance with the act approved December 21st 1861.

>Charles de Montel
>Enrolling officer

[torn] certify on honor that the men whose names appear [torn] Roll were duty sworn, in accordance with [torn] law.

>Charles de Montel
>Enrolling Officer

Supplement to Muster roll of Captain Charles de Montels Company in the Regiment of Rangers commended by Co. Norris called into the Service of the State by an act approved Decbr. 21 1861 Enrolled in the Countys of Bandera, Blanco, Medina & Uvalde to serve for the Term of twelve months from the date of organization unlefs sonner discharged. The Company was enrolled by Charles de Montel and organized by the Election of Captain Charles de Montel at Bandera on the 17th Day of February 1862.

1. Brown James [farrier]
1. Kreifsle John [blacksmith]
78. Adams P.
79. Brown John
80. Burney W.C.
81. Cole Wm.
82. Casner M.
83. Casner M.F.
84. Davenport A.J.
85. Harr Jeph
86. Horton Th.
88. Manning Th.
89. Miller John
90. Nowlin Sam
91. Peden H.
92. Rackly Wm
93. Reinhard John
94. Schwarz, Reinhard
95. Sanders Robert
96. Smith R.
97. Shorp G.W.
98. Schulz John

87. Morehouse E.   99. Taylor Th
                   100. Ward St. S.
                   67. Walker J.

I Certify on honor that thise Suplement roll exhibits the true State of Captain Charles Company of Texas Frontier Regiment of Rangers since February 17th 1862 for the period herein mentioned that each man answers to his own proper name in person, that the remarks set opposite the Name of each Officer and Soldier are accurate and just, that valuation of all arms and accoutrements, horses and horse equipments since the organization and muster in to Service was made by disinterested and good Judges and at faire and just rates.

      Charles de Montel
      Capt Com/g and Enrolling officer
      of Company G.

Muster Roll of Captain Ch de Montel's Company, in the Frontier Regiment of Texas mtd Volunteers, commanded by Colonel J.M. Norris called into the service of the State of Texas by Govern. F.R. Lubbock under the Act of Legislature approved Decbr 21st 1861, from the 17th day of February 1862, when mustered, to the 30th day of June 1862, the date of the present Muster.

		Enrolled	Mustered
1. Ch. de Montel	Captain		
1. Th. P. McCall	1st Lieut		
2. A.V. Gates	2nd "		
3. B.F. Patton	3rd "		
1. John Lawhorne	1st Serg	Blanco Co	Bandera
2. G.H. Hill	2nd "	Medina Co	"
3. Rob Harper	3rd "	"	"
4. J.W. Cooper	4th "	"	"
5. James Croke	5th "	Uvalde Co	"
1. Daniel Malone	1st Corp.	Medina Co	Bandera
2. Th. Pafford	2nd "	Uvalde Co	"
3. Th. Bandy	3rd "	Bandera Co.	"

4. R.W. Davis   4th "   Blanco Co.   "

1. W. Ganyon   1st Bugler   Uvalde Co   Bandera
2. Ch. Montel [Jr.]   2nd Bugler   Medina Co   Bandera

1. John Kreisfle   Blacksm.   Medina Co.   Camp Bandera
1. James Brown   Farrier   "   Bandera

Privates	**Enrolled**	**Mustered**
1. Adams Peter	Uvalde Co	Uvalde
2. Allen Hugh	"	Bandera
3. Bates Felix	"	"
4. Bowles D.C.	"	"
5. Bowles G	"	"
6. Bates E.A.	"	"
7. Bandy John	Bandera Co	"
8. Ballentine Wm.	"	"
9. Bird Ch.	"	"
10. Brewer L	Blanco Co	"
11. Bushnell Lester	"	"
12. Brown John	"	"
13. Burney W.C.	Kerr Co.	"
14. Billhorz Jos.	Medina Co.	Camp Verde
15. Cude R.D.	Uvalde Co.	Bandera
16. Cook Thomas	"	"
17. Cook J.A.	"	"
18. Chipman H.	Bandera Co.	"
19. Carnahan D.S.	Blanco Co.	"
20. Cooper W.L.	"	"
21. Cole William	"	"
22. Casner M.V.	"	"
23. Casner M.F.	Blanco Co.	Bandera
24. Conrad Peter	Medina Co.	Camp Verde
25. Duncan Benj.	"	Bandera
26. Davenport Wm.	Uvalde Co.	"
27. Dolch Louis	Medina Co.	"
28. Dodd W.	Uvalde Co.	"

29. Dutcher Ch.   Bandera Co.   "
30. Davenport Wm   Uvalde Co.   "
31. Dodd Curtis   "   Camp Montel
32. Dodd James   "   "
33. Forrest Demps   Atascosa Co.   "
34. Graylin Aug.   Blanco Co.   Bandera
35. Griner N.J.   Uvalde Co.   "
36. Green John   Bandera Co.   "
37. Gray J.D.   Blanco Co.   "
38. Heath Lewis   Median Co.   "
39. Hegg Fred   Blanco Co.   "
40. Hamilton J.W.   "   "
41. Horton Th.   Uvalde Co.   "
42. Harr Tepht.   Medina Co.   "
43. Haller Paul   "   Camp Verde
44. Hicks F.L.   Bandera Co.   "
45. Johnson Oscar   Medina Co.   Bandera
46. Kennedy John   Uvalde Co.   "
47. Kent D.B.   Blanco Co.   "
48. Kapper[s?] Franc. Medina Co.   Camp Verde
49. Lamon John   "   Bandera
50. Long T.A.   Uvalde Co.   "
51. Lindeman H.   Blanco Co.   "
52. Lindeman E.D.   "   "
53. Lindeman A.   "   "
54. Lundy M.R.   "   "
55. Lundy Wm.   "   "
56. Lindsay Andr.   Hays Co.   Camp Verde
57. Moore L.   Uvalde Co.   Bandera
58. McKinney T.N.   "   "
59. McKinney T.G.   "   "
60. Masfer Th.   Bandera Co.   "
61. Manning Wm   Blanco Co   "
62. Moore T.F.   "   "
63. Manning Th   "   "
64. Miller John   Medina Co.   "
65. Morehouse Ed.   Blanco Co.   "

The Ranger Companies Of Bandera County

66. Nowlin R.W.	"	"
67. Norris John	Bandera Co.	"
68. Nowlin Sam	Blanco Co.	"
69. Owens W.P.	Uvalde Co.	"
70. Owens Wiley	"	Camp Montel
71. Onion Jos.	Bandera Co.	Bandera
72. Patterson Dan	Medina Co.	"
73. Pulliam B.	Uvalde Co.	"
74. Pingenot C.	Bandera Co.	"
75. Patton P.	Blanco Co.	"
76. Peden H.	Medina Co	"
77. Reichezer Th.	Medina Co.	Bandera
78. Runnels W.	Uvalde Co.	"
79. Rackley W.	Medina Co.	"
80. Reinhardt J.	"	Camp Mondel
81. Roberts James	Blanco Co.	Camp Verde
82. Stanford W.	Uvalde Co.	Bandera
83. Stayton J.A.	Blanco Co.	"
84. Smith H.R.	"	"
85. Sansom J.W.	"	"
86. Short Thom	"	"
87. Stayton D.W.	"	"
88. Schuchardt C.F.	"	"
89. Schwarze R.	Medina Co	"
90. Sanders Rob	Uvalde Co.	"
91. Smith R.B.	Blanco Co.	"
92. Sharp G.W.	"	"
93. Shults John	"	"
94. Tondre Franc.	Medina Co.	"
95. Tilley E.	"	"
96. Thompson H.	"	"
97. Tomberlin A.	"	"
98. Taylor Th.	Uvalde Co.	Camp Montel
99. Wilkins D.	Medina Co.	Bandera
100. Wight L.	Bandera Co.	"
101. Westfall W.R.	Blanco Co.	"
102. Wood W.B.	"	"

103. Wood C.P.   "   "
104. Westfall S.C.   "   "
105. Wiley Isaak   "   "
106. Watson B.   "   "
107. Walker John   "   "
108. Ward St. S.   Uvalde Co.   "
109. Watson James   "   Camp Montel
110. Zorger Peter   "   Bandera
111. Zimermann A.   Medina Co.   "

[Four Monthly Returns of Montel's Company can be found in the State Library and are transcribed in the appendix.]

Doctors Shipp, Hoffmann, and Downs

Medical discharges for men in Montel's Company were signed by Drs. E.M. Downs, John Hoffmann, and A.A. Shipp at various and different times. On the outside cover of Uvalde County settler F.V. Mckinny's medical discharge:

F.V. McKinny of Company G Frontier Rgt T.R was enlisted by me at Bandera on the 17th Day of February 1862 to serve for one year. He is 49 years of age. during the last 40 days said Soldier has bin unfit for duty.

    Charles de Montel
    Capt Com/y G
    F.R.T.R.

[Inside:]
    Certificate of Disability for Discharge

F.V. McKinney of Capt Chas De Montell's Co. G. Front: Reg: of Texas Rifles was Enlisted by Capt Chas De Montell at Bandera City on the 17th Day of Feb: 1862 to serve one year he is 45 years of age - During the last two months said soldier has been unfit for Duty.

    Charles de Montel
    Capt Comp G
    Commanding Company

I Certify that I have carfully examined the said F.V. McKinney of Capt. Chas: De Montell's Company and find him incapable of performing the Duties of a soldier because of Leucoma of the Right Eye and frequent severe pain along the optic nerve when exposed to the heat of the sun and has Destroyed the sight of the Right Eye. I believe the cause or origin of the Disability was severe Ophthalmy.

       E.M.Downs
       act. asst. Surgeon
       Prov'l army C.S.

[The medical discharge of John Bandy of Bandera County:]

I Certify that I have Carefully exammed John Bandy of Captain Charles de Montels Company D and find him incapable of performing the duties of a Soldier in Consequence of his having received a gun Shot wound in the leg which So deprives him of the use of Said limb that he will be totally unfit for Service during the present term of enlistment,

A.A. Shipp Surgion
for Company D Texas
Frontier Regiment

I certify that John Bandy privat of Company D Frontier Regiment of Texas Rangers was enlisted by me on the 17th day of february 1862 to serve for the term of twelf months unlefs sooner discharged was born in the state of Tenesee, is 21 years of age and farmer [by o]ccupation, and that he received his [gu]nshot wound accidentaly by runing his horse after some other horses his Pistol striking against the Sadle, firing and taking efect in his leg and therefore not likly to be able to perform the duttys of a Soldier for the balance of his term of Service and that he is angious to be discharged & has bin unfit for Service about 35 days

       Charles de Montel
       Cap/t Com: D Com[?]:
       Camp Verde August 12th 1862
       F.R.T.R

Doctor Edwin M. Downs had established a ranch along the Verde Creeks south of Bandera City in 1857. He seems to have suffered from a progressive dystrophy or paralysis, but was able to get around quite well until 1866 when he was described as "too feeble" to ride a horse and was driven about in a buggy. He was among the volunteers who joined Paul's Company to take Camp Verde in 1861. He served as an assistant regimental surgeon during the remaining war years and left a long paper trail of medical reports and disability certificates across the West Texas frontier. He was often at Camp Verde and is known to have been at Fort Stockton. He was at Fort Lancaster to pull Thomas Laxson through a serious illness. He was one of three surgeons who signed a 60-day medical furlough for Levi Lamoni Wight in San Antonio. He was at Fort Clark August 10, 1862 when the Nueces Battle occurred.

The Nueces Battle

Following John Brown's Raid in 1859, the word "abolitionist" became a profanity in the South. Rumors of abolition terrorists were rampant across Texas in 1860. When Texas seceded, Levi Lamoni Wight joined a Confederate company that formed at Fort Mason. As he later recalled, "Times was warm. Union men and Southern men of note and princeple was read hot."

During June 1861, 18 representatives of different sections of Gillespie and Kerr counties met to plan the organizion of Union loyalists. August Klappenbach was an active Unionist in Bandera City where a petition to rejoin the Union was being passed around. The 1861 Bandera Resolutions sent to Texas newspapers let Seccesionists know that Bandera citizens were not abolitionists and may have spared Bandera County some of the grief that befell some of the other Hill Country counties. Charles de Montel's influence in the region may have restrained Union men in Bandera and Medina counties to some extent. Although at one point during the war he recommended martial law for Medina County.

When Kendall County organized February 18, 1862, Unionist John W. Sansom was elected county sheriff. (Curiously there was a J.W. Sansom on the muster rolls for Montel's and Lawhon's companies.) He was Kendall County Sheriff until June 18, 1862. He had lobbied for the post of enrolling officer for the area, but Jacob Kuechler was appointed instead. Both men may have had similar plans. It seems that loyal Secessionists could not find Jacob Kuechler when they wanted to enroll.

John James served in one of the Bexar County home guard units. His brother-in-law and former partner in a San Antonio merchantile venture, James R. Sweet, joined the Confederate Army.

May 10, 1862, the San Antonio Herald reported the 20th company raised for the Confederacy in San Antonio and listed the officers as James Duff, captain; J.R. Sweet, first lieutenant; Edwin Lilly and Richard Taylor, second lieutenants. R.H. Williams joined as a private. Near the end of May this company initiated the reign of terror known to Hill Country Germans as the Henkerzeit, the hanging times.

May 28 Captain Duff and his company left San Antonio and "took up the line of march" for Gillespie County. They reached Fredericksburg May 30 and declared martial law in Gillespie County and Precinct 5 of Kerr County. Captain Duff gave the citizens six days to come into town and take the oath of alliegence. In the meantime, he found he could not buy forage for his horses with paper money. He sent Lieutenant Lilly "to wait on Mr. F. Lochte", a leading Fredericksburg merchant, and the matter was resolved.

June 3 Captain Duff went to Medina County to arrest H.J. Richarz and other "certain citizens." His intention was to break up the leadership and communication lines of the Union sympathizers. Returning to Gillespie County he arrested Sheriff P. Braubach, F.W. Dobbler, and F. Lochte and sent them to a guardhouse in San Antonio. Another Union man, Jacob Keuchler, was still at large. According to Captain Duff's report, "He is a man of great influence; a German enthusiast in politics and a dangerous man in the community." A Union man in Kerr County named Nelson had "taken to the cedar brakes and escaped."

The political and cultural atmosphere of Sisterdale on Sister Creek in Kerr County was commented on by journalists and other writers who traveled along the West Texas Frontier in the 1850s. June 7, 1862, the home guard units of the 31st Brigade District in the counties of Blanco (southern portion), Kendall, Kerr (eastern portion), and Bandera abstained from the vote necessary to organize their companies into the Third Regiment. By apparent agreement only the militia men of Sisterdale, an intellectual center of the German community and the soon-to-be-formed Loyal Union League, voted with the following result:

Frederich Tegener	Colonel
Julius Schlickum	Lieutenant Colonel
E. Cramer	Major.

June 11 Captain Duff had moved his operation to Blanco County and declared martial law. His sources revealed that some Blanco County men, including Prescott, King, Howell, and two men named Snow and other armed men had gone to Fredericksburg intending to join with the Union men there to defeat Duff, but the Partizen Rangers had arrived first. Captain Duff believed that Guy Hamilton's ranch in Travis County near the Blanco County line was

headquarters for Union activity. June 18 Captain Duff moved into Kendall County where he arrested Julius Schlickum. By the 20th the company had returned to San Antonio.

Unrest was the order of the day. Earlier in June the men of the home guard units of Bandera, Kendall, and Kerr counties had refused to organize into a regiment as ordered. By June 28 Brigadier General Robert Bechem, in charge of the 31st Brigade, Texas State Troops, had gathered enough returns to report the results of the election of officers for the brigade's regiments and battalions to the Adjutant and Inspector General of Texas, Colonel J.Y. Dashiell:

The indep. Battalion in Medina County has also been organized, and Captain H.J. Richarz of Comp. A was elected Major with 135 votes; no return of his own Precinct (where no doubt he has received many votes) has been received, and the reason I understand, is, that he is at present a prisoner of State in San Antonio for political offence. I shall withhold his Certificate until hearing that he will have been acquitted; but if found guilty, I will have to order a new election. Two other Captains of the State Troops in my District have been arrested for the same offence, viz:

Capt. R. Radclift of Comp A Gillespie Co. S. T.
& " J. Schlickum "   B Kendall Co. S. T.

and from what I learned through Mr. Js. R. Sweet, Provost Marshall for Bexar & some surrounding Counties, they are after another Captain of State Troops in my Brigade District.

July 4, 1862, several hundred Loyal Union Leaguers met on Bear Creek in Gillespie County. Ranger companies were formed and officers elected. Their stated purpose was to defend themselves against Indian raids. An elected Advisory Board included Edward Degener. The officers of the three companies (according to John Sansom) were:

County	Captain	Lieutenant
Gillespie	Jacob Kuechler	Valentine Homan
Kendall	E. Kramer	Hugo Degener
Kerr	Henry Hartman	Phil G. Temple

Fritz Tegener was elected Major to command the battalion. Some of the Kerr County men left soon after the Bear Creek meeting to join the Union Army through Mexico. Not long after that, due to the overwhelming Confederate opposition, the Advisory Board met and disbanded the ranger companies. The only other alternative would have been to fight in the midst of their homes and neighbors. Some members met August 1, 1862 at Edward Degener's house on Turtle Creek in Kerr County. Sixty-five (?) men of the Loyal Union League set out for Mexico, rather than submit to the Confederacy.

Jacob Kuechler and John Sansom, both experienced rangers, led the men of the Loyal Union League (known as "bushwhackers" to Confederates) over the Indian trails on their way to Mexico. John Sansom had been to Mexico via the San Antonio-Eagle Pass road. Both men probably were well-informed about the Indian route, but may have never actually traveled its entirety. They had gone exactly to the Fio Water Hole, but when they reached the West Nueces River they were 10 to 20 miles off course if they had intended to reach Kickapoo Springs. Perhaps they knew an alternate route.

Unknown to the Union men a Confederate force was in pursuit. Lieutenant C.D. McRae, Captain Donnelson's Company, 2nd Texas Mounted Rifles led detachments from his own company, Captain Duff's Company, and Taylor's Battalion. Also included was a detachment of state troops from Davis' Company. R.H. Williams was among the Partizan Ranger detachment and described riding south from the upper Guadalupe River, crossing the divide between the Guadalupe and Medina rivers:

> The morning's ride led us over a tremendously rough and hilly country, and we could only follow the trail in Indian file, till we struck the head of the Medina River. Here the country became rough, rolling prairie studded with timber, and we pushed on along the wide trail at a smart pace, till we called a short halt at midday.
>
> Now as we rode along that afternoon, another trail came into the one we were following, showing the Bushwackers had been reinforced by another party [Tom and W.B. Scott, Howard Henderson, and William Hester].
>
> It was, for the most part, desperate country to ride over, for we were well in the mountains, and frequently had to dismount and lead our horses down rocky slides. Towards evening the trail led us to a large water-hole on the head of the Frio River; perhaps the only one to be found for many miles of its course,

which showed the enemy had good guides. Here we watered our thirsty horses and filled our canteens and, after a brief rest, pushed on again.

The Confederate force caught up with the Union men at the Nueces River and attacked in the early hours of the morning of August 10, 1862. The Union men threw up a wall of baggage and attempted a defense, but were out-gunned and in a bad position. The editor of San Antonio's Union paper, the <u>Alamo Express</u>, had been run out of town by this time. The <u>San Antonio Herald</u> reported The Nueces Battle August 16:

> By the El Paso mail this morning we learn that Capt. Duff's company has had a fight with the celebrated Mountain Guard, of that notorious scoundrel and Abolitionist, Jack Hamilton. The fight occurred a short distance above Fort Clark, and resulted in the entire defeat of the renegades, thirty-three were left dead on the field. One of Capt. Duff's men, Frank Robinson, of Uvalde, was killed, and five wounded.
>
> There were about 100 men on our side, detachments of Duff's and Donolson's companies and Taylor's Battalion; all under command of Lieut. McRae.

Anti-Confederate riots broke out in San Antonio and some Hill Country towns when the news was heard. Lieutenant McRae made his official report from San Antonio, August 18. [<u>Official Records,</u> Series I, Volume IX, pages 614-616.] Lieutenant McRae approached the Union camp in the early hours of the morning and divided his men into two forces who would deliver a deadly cross-fire at first light:

> Shortly after having secured our positions a sentinel on his rounds came near the position of Lieutenant Homsley's division, which he had the misfortune to discover, whereupon he was shot dead by Lieutenant Harbour, which caused an alarm in the enemy's camp, and a few shots were exchanged between the parties, and all became quiet again for the space of half an hour, when another sentinel hailed us on the left, and shared the fate of the first. It being still too dark for the attack, I ordered my men to hold quietly their positions until daylight. The enemy in the mean time were actively engaged preparing to resist us. The moment it became light enough to see I ordered the attack to be made by a steady and slow advance upon their position, firing as we advanced until

within about 30 paces of their line, when I ordered a charge of both divisions, which was executed in fine style, resulting in the complete rout and flight of the enemy.

They left on the field 32 killed. The remainder fled, scattering in all directions through the many dense cedar-brakes in the immediate vicinity. From the many signs of blood I infer many of those escaping were seriously wounded.

[The Herald reported more details of the battle August 28:]

The Battle with the Traitors

Since our last issue we have received more correct intelligence relative to the fight between our men and the traitors in the vicinity of Fort Clark. Our loss was two killed and 18 wounded. The traitors lost 33 killed on the field and many wounded of whom three are known to have since died. Their muster roll was found, containing 69 names. There were five Americans among them, the rest being Germans. The Americans, conscious of their [perfidy?], fled at the first fire. The entire outfit of the traitors, consisting of their horses, ammunition, guns and provisions, was captured by our men.

October 4, the Herald reported that Robert G. Elder was the other Confederate soldier killed in the Battle of the Nueces. According to historian Kevin Young, five of the 18 Confederate and State Troops wounded at the Nueces died at Fort Clark. The names of the Union men killed at the Nueces and the Rio Grande can be found on the Treue Der Union Monument in Comfort. As R.H. Williams recalled:

Immediately after the fight a couple of the boys were sent off, post haste, to Fort Clark, supposed to be some thirty miles distant, to fetch the surgeon stationed there. Till midnight I was off duty, but after that had to help tend the wounded, some of whom were in great pain; and we had no appliances with which to treat them, nothing much to give them except cold water.

Some of the Loyal Union League survivors made their way back to Kerr and Gillespie counties. Henry Schwethelm and others pushed on to Mexico. John Sansom went south along the Nueces River before heading back to Currys Creek. Of those that returned to their homes, some resupplied themselves and set out for Mexico again. Eight men were killed trying to cross the Rio Grande. John

Samsom returned to Kendall County many times during the war and smuggled recruits to Mexico and the Union Army.

In R.H. Williams' account the prisoners had already been executed before Dr. Downs arrived. His account continued with the next day when hand litters were made to carry the wounded to Fort Clark:

> That night the doctor arrived, and was promptly at work; but several of the cases were very serious, and would not, he said, live to see the fort.
>
> Betimes next morning, the litters, of long cedar poles with blankets laced to them, were ready with their sad loads, and the horses packed with the plunder. Four bearers were allotted to each litter, or thirty-two in all; sixteen of whom, being all that were fit for duty, were taken from our detachment.

After Lieutenant McRae was wounded, the Confederate officer in charge during the prisoner executions was, according to R.H. Williams, Lieutenant John Luck. The men who objected were detailed to carry the Confederate wounded. Lieutenant Luck left with the mounted men, promising to leave men ahead as relief for the stretcher-bearers. After several hours of trudging along in the heat, R.H. Williams and his comrades realized they had been deserted:

> The doctor, who was with us and behaved like a man, taking his turn at the litters, backed by some of us, at last got the men going again.
>
> [Louis] Oje and the three others of us picked up our litter and started, and the rest soon followed, the doctor bringing up the rear, to see that none lingered behind. To add to our troubles, and they were bad enough, we were in a dangerous Indian country, and had no arms with us, not even a six-shooter!

[The land north of Fort Clark was too rough for wagons. By sundown the group had reached level terrain near the fort:]

> Soon we had the wounded stowed in the ambulances, and ourselves, as best we could, in the wagons. We were five miles from the fort, and had come, they told us, a good thirty from the scene of the fight. It was the most awful journey I ever made. My shoulders were cut to the bone by the litter-poles, my feet were bleeding from the sharp rocks, and I was utterly broken down, as indeed were all of us, including the doctor, though he,

good fellow that he was, still had pluck and strength enough to attend to his charges directly we reached the fort.

John Sansom biographer, Frankie Davis Glenn, related Sansom's experience following the battle when he was detained by two sentinels of Captain Dix's Company, Frontier Regiment:

> But by knowing all the country well and knowing many of the officers and more of the men in Captain Dick's Company and Regiment, was able to secure his release in a short order.
>
> That done, he at once resolved to go to his brother-in-law's camp, [Lieutenant] Ben F. Patton, who was stationed in the Seco River area. Patton belonged to the same Regiment as Captain Dick's and were stationed 40 miles apart.
>
> When he got within 2 miles of the latter's camp he saw 8 Comanche Indian warriors driving some 60 head of horses and mules. They saw Sansom but moved on as to make it appear they were stockmen of the country. Sansom knew every man in Patton's Command and also knew half of them to be true Confederates, but they didn't like Indians. After Sansom reported the Indians, Patton and his men were after the Indians.
>
> Sansom stayed in Patton's camp to rest and eat, as he had been without food for 2 or 3 days and nights, since leaving Captain Dick's Company; then he proceeded on to his home in advance of the news of the Battle of Nueces.
>
> Sansom found out later, Patton and his men had "taken" the Indians the next day. Twelve men and Patton had killed 7 of the Indians, but [number] 8 had gotten away. Only one of Patton's men, John Cook, had been wounded. They then captured every bow, quiver, and anything the Indians had besides, recovering all of the 60 head of stock.
>
> The Governor was so pleased with [Lieutenant] Ben Patton and his men for this service that he thanked the men personally. This was quite an honor.

As a lieutenant (later captain) in the Union Army, John Sansom often traveled back and forth from Mexico to Currys Creek in Kendall County and other locations, gathering intelligence and Union recruits. By the end of the war he had an extensive spy network in Texas. According to John Sansom's account:

Soon after the "Battle of the Nueces," I took a squad of nine men out of the Confederacy, and later forty-eight, and still later thirty-six and into the ranks of the Union Army, where as commissioned officer, I had the honor of serving until the Union was re-established.

Supplies for the Texas State Troops

A Texas historian having just made a survey of the Civil War ranger vouchers at the State Library when asked what he had learned, replied, "It takes a lot of corn to feed a horse." Another thing the vouchers reveal is that most of the corn was grown by local farmers in the regions around the ranger camps. The large amounts of supplies needed by the Civil War ranger companies were freighted about mostly by the same or other local men.

June 16, 1862 Corporal R.W. Davis and four privates of Montel's Company had expenses of $7.50 when sent to Austin bearing a dispatch and to get powder for Company D. Six dollars and 50 cents was for 6 1/2 bushels of corn and $1 affadavit officers fees. This document was certified for 50 cents by P.D. Saner, Clerk of the County Court, Bandera County.

The San Antonio-Eagle Pass trade route employed many freighters during the Civil War. The importance of trade with Mexico and the general transportation of goods within Texas kept many Union men out of the Confederate draft. An A.J. Sowell account says that so many Medina County men had gone to war or were involved in freighting that no crops were grown there near the end of the war. J.P. Heinen gave this account in the Pioneer History:]

> During the war between the states I lived with my parents in Kendall County, near Comfort, I often passed through the town of Bandera hauling corn for the Confederate government to D'Hanis, driving a team of eight or ten yoke of oxen hitched to a heavy wagon, hauling three tons to the load.

Medical supplies of quinine, morphine, opium, and alcohol usually could be found in small quantities. Calomel (murcurous chloride) and other remedies were often used. The Federal troops before leaving Camp Verde insured that there would be no alcohol left there for the Confederate cause. Alcohol was one of the few drugs used at that time that actually had some real medical value. General Robert Bechem in New Braunfels made this report to the Adjutant General in Austin July 1, 1862:

> The Distillery of Messrs. Koester & Tolls has been closed, although Dr. Koester was in expectation that for reasons explained to his Excellency the Governor, permission might be granted to him, to continue the business. Reports have been received at this office, that there are no Distilleries in the following Counties of my District, viz: Blanco, Gillespie, Kimble, Medina, Atascosa, Frio, Uvalde, Dawson, Kinney, Maverick & Zavalla, but nothing to that effect has been heard in answer to my inquiries from the Assessor & Collector of the Counties of Kendall, Kerr, Bandera, Edwards, Llano, Mason, Menard, San Saba, McCulloch & Concho, and I am almost satisfied that no such establishments exist in these thinly settled Counties; or would it be necessary to take further steps for the purpose of better ascertaining this fact?

Ordnance officers scoured the countryside for firearms to buy. Many firearms of German make were bought or confiscated during this time. (Jaeger rifles were widely used by the men of Lawhon's Company.) In the same correspondence of July 1, 1862 General Bechem wrote:

> Manor F. Wrede at Fredricksburg, who has heretofore held the office as ordnance officer for Gillespie Co. writes, that he does not think a new appointment of an ordnance officer for that County necessary, as there are no arms that could be bought and which the State would be justified in buying.

> No further report has been received at this office from the ordnance officers of Medina & Atascosa Counties.

Bandera County was not mentioned and perhaps the idea of surplus arms there was not even a consideration.

Before the war broke out, most gunpowder and percussion caps in Texas had been imported from the northern states. Cap and firearm factories and powder mills sprang up across Texas in 1861. Two Fredricksburg men, E. Krauskopf, a gunsmith, and Adolph Lungkwitz, a silversmith, obtained the materials for making percussion caps (saltpeter and quicksilver) and made machinery to cut and form the copper. They supplied a wide region with caps during the Civil War.

The ingredients for gunpowder are saltpeter, sulfur, and charcoal. Some 60,000 pounds of sulfur were imported to Texas from Mexico during the war. Charcoal was easily supplied locally. Saltpeter was obtained from the many bat-caves of the Hill Country, including one about 14 miles south of Bandera City where the remains of three large stone vats can still be seen. Guano was layered with wood ashes and broom weeds in metal boiling pots and soaked with water. After sufficient boiling, the guano was placed in the shallow vats where it crystallized into saltpeter by evaporation. The product was then sacked and shipped to a powder mill.

The Texas Powder Company in San Antonio, William Friedrick, proprietor, supplied powder to much of the Frontier Regiment. In a letter August 24, 1863, he defended his product against charges of inferior quality, "When the ball of a sixShooter at a distance of 30 yards with a usual load went through 3--one inch boards it was considered to have sufficient force." Apparently this letter was presented to the Adjutant General in response to complaints from Major McCord. (A Civil War Texas powder mill is described in some detail in B.P. Gallaway's The Ragged Rebel, pages 58-68.)

Sophia Wight's letters to her husband illustrate that most clothing, blankets, and shoes or boots for rangers and soldiers in Texas were homemade:

[November 22, 1863]

> The baby is harty. She is begining to walk. She was only sick a few days. I think the reason she did not walk sooner was because I did not try to learn her more. I did not have time. I have got 24 yds cloth redy for the loom. It will be 30 yds that I have made and a plenty for winter. I am going to mak a blanket next and if you will not kneed it I will sell it. If you should need any clothes you must send me word and I will have them redy to sent any chance.

George Hay had married Amanda Minear in 1858. She died in May 1863 and in 1865, he married Amanda's sister, Virginia Elva Minear. Sophia Wight wrote again on December 20, 1863:

> George Hay and Vergina is verry thick. Mother went to Rodney's day before yesterday. The baby runs every where and begins to talk. You will [not] know her. She goes all the time and into all kinds of mischief. I have got 20 yds cloth in the loom.

[Interspersed with raising children, killing hogs, making soap and candles, and other chores, it could take a long time to spin a blanket. February 7, 1864:]

> I am spining your blanket as hard as I can work but if you should not kneed it by the time you write I can sell it for cows

any thime. I think I can get two cows and calves for a blanket but if you kneed it or like to kneed it I will keep it.

Wool production has a long history around San Antonio dating back to Spanish colonial times. As the settlement of the West Texas frontier began in the late 1840s and early 1850s, Peter Gallagher, H.J. Richarz, John James, George Kendall, Joseph H. Poor, and others pioneered sheep raising and breeding north and west of San Antonio.

Cotton production in Bandera County probably had its beginning on the Charles Jack ranch. Charles de Montel introduced cotton to Medina County. A receipt for cotton and woolen carders for Bandera County can be found in the Records of the Governor's Office. P. DeCordova was Secretary of the Military Board in Austin:

Bandera City March 16th 1864

P DeCordova

Sir you will pleas forward by Peter Sangar Sixteen (16) pairs of Cotton Carder and three (3) pairs of woolen if on hand for this County if not forward the Carder returned for for all of which the money will be Paid by said Peter Sangar. Per order Dated Austin Oct 28th AD 1863.

>OB Miles
>Chief Justice
>B.C.

[Reverse side]

Received of the Military Board Sixteen pair of Cotton and Three pairs of wool for which I have paid one hundred and [twenty-five?] dollars.

Austin March 28 1864---

>Peter Zorger

Peter Zorger from Uvalde County enrolled in Montel's company in 1862. His name appears on the rolls for Montel's and Lawhon's companies. On April 24, 1866 he was among 15 other men indicted in Bandera City for murder and highway robbery relating to an incident near the town in 1863.

Charles de Montel served as mustering officer for Lawhon's Company before leaving to take command of the Confederate steamship <u>Texas</u>. His commission is dated March 14, 1863 and Congressman Wilcox who had arranged for the letters of marquis, wrote from Richmond March 22, 1863, "I hope your Letters will reach you safely & that you may get your Ship and play hell and destruction with Yankee commerce." However, the vessel sank or was otherwise unavailable before Captain Montel reached it. He spent some time performing administrative duties for the C.S.A. before returning to the area in March 1864 to raise a company of Medina County men for the Confederacy.

As a legacy to the Frontier Regiment, it remained as such an ideal in Texan minds that every major ranger organization thereafter was at least initially referred to as the Frontier Regiment, including the Mounted Regiment, the Frontier Organization, the Frontier Force, and the Frontier Battalion.

7

The Mounted Regiment: Lawhon's Company

In an effort to get the Confederacy to pay for frontier defense and to answer the Confederate call for more men, Texas prepared to turn the Frontier Regiment over to the Confederate States Army. As required by the C.S.A. regulations, the nine companies were converted into 10 and mustered for a three-year term. Colonel Norris resigned and a regimental election replaced him with James Ebenezer McCord. The new force was officially the Mounted Regiment, but was often referred to as the Frontier Regiment or as McCord's Regiment.

While some of Montel's rangers entered the Confederate service or joined their local home guard unit, many remained to form Company B. The First Sergeant in Montel's Company was elected captain of the new company: John Lawhon and his wife, Jean, came from South Carolina and were among the early settlers of Blanco County. He had been foreman of Judge W.E. Jones' ranch before the war.

The reorganization of the regiment was completed by February 11, 1863. Colonel McCord made his headquarters at Camp Colorado. He placed Lieutenant Colonel James "Buck" Barry in command of the six companies of the northern sector. Major William J. Alexander was in command of the four companies along the southern portion of the line, from Camp Colorado to the Rio Grande. Colonel McCord discontinued the passive patrol system, using expeditions of larger units of rangers scouting west and northwest of their camps, while regular messengers kept the camps informed of contingencies.

Special Orders were usually hand-written notes to affect a particular individual or event. During the Civil War, General Orders were usually printed for distribution and affected larger numbers of people or events. In Special Order Number 57, August 9, 1863, Major W.J. Alexander appointed T.P. McCall quartermaster of Lawhon's Company replacing Lieutenant Adams. A bond was required to be posted. In Special Order Number 12, September 2, 1863, the major ordered Lieutenant McCall to make estimates for funds to supply Company B then "proceed to Austin and procure the necefsary funds and furnish Supplies for three months as early as practicable." Major Alexander's address is given as "Headquarters Southern Division, Mounted Regt. Texas State Troops, Camp Verde".

MUSTER ROLL of Captain <u>John Lawhon's</u> Company, in the <u>Frontier</u> Regiment of <u>Texas Mtd.</u> Volunteers, commanded by Colonel <u>J.E. McCord</u> called into the service of the <u>State of Texas</u> by <u>Govern.</u> <u>J.R. Lubbock</u> under the Act of <u>Legislature</u> approved <u>21st Decbr</u> 186<u>1</u>, from the <u>29th</u> day of <u>December</u> 1862, when mustered, to the <u>30th</u> day of <u>April</u> 1863, the date of the present Muster.

John Lawhon	Capt.	40	enrolled 12-29-62 at Camp Verde
Th. P. McCall	1st Lieut	32	by Ch. de Montel mustered into
T. Adams	2nd Lieut	21	service 12-29-62 at Camp Verde
Robt Harper	jr2nd Lieut	43	by Capt. Charles. Pay due from entry into Service

1. James Croke	1st Sergt	37
2. Th. Short	2nd "	32
3. M.V. Casner	3rd "	20
4. D.W. Stayton	4th "	25
5. H. Chipman	5th "	20
1. Th. Pafford	1st Corp	25
2. J.W. Manning	2nd "	26
3. L. Brewer	3rd "	36
4. R. Bird	4th "	21
1. Isaak Wiley	1st Bugler	20
2. J.W. Manning	2nd "	35
1. J. Shults	Farrier	45

Privates

1. Ballentyne Wm	38	26. Mannin Th	37
2. Bushnell L	26	27. Nowlin R.W.	21
3. Burney W.D.C.	33	28. Onion Joseph	19

4. Cooper W.L.	20	29. Pulliam B.A.	21
5. Cooper J.W.	30	30. Peden H.D.	24
6. Casner F.M.	20	31. Patterfon D.G.	23
7. Carnahan D.S.	25	32. Sharp G.W.	20
8. Cude R.D.	21	33. Smith H.R.	37
9. Click James	35	34. Sansom G.N.	22
10. Click T.L.B.	37	35. Stayton G.A.	22
11. Crawford Wm.	30	36. Stanford C.C.	34
12. Carson John	18	37. Tomberlin A.	35
13. Gralin Aug.	34	38. Tilley E.	34
14. Gray Wm.	18	39. Wilkins D.	19
15. Hegg Fred	37	40. Walker John	19
16. Hamilton John	21	41. Walker Riley	18
17. Johnson Oscar	20	42. Westfall W.R.	23
18. Lindeman H.C.	20	43. Westfall S.C.	17
19. Lindeman A.	26	44. Wood C.P.	26
20. Lindeman E.D.	25	45. Wood W.P.	23
21. Lundy M.R.	21	46. Wight L.L.	24
22. Malone Dan	19	47. Watson James	18
23. Mesfer Th. O.	21	48. Zorger Peter	22
24. Morehouse Ed	26	49. Zimerman A.	26
25. Moore T.G.	25	50. Ward S.S.	21

I Certify, on Honor, that this Muster Roll exhibits the true state [...] [The captain certifies that the men listed on the roll are actually in the company

I certify, on honor, that I have, at <u>Camp Verde</u> on this <u>30th</u> day of <u>April A.D.</u>, 186<u>3</u>, carefully examined this Roll, and, as far as practicable, caused the allowances, stoppages, and remarks to be justly and properly stated; and mustered the Company for the period herein stated.

      John Lawhon
      Capt.

[Extract of Muster Roll, June 30, 1863:]

The Mounted Regiment: Lawhon's Company

John Shults, farrier, "Dischgd. May 17.63. by Spec. Ord. No. 242. A.&G.G.O."

[Most of the men were paid April 30, 1863. Officers and non-commissioned officers remained the same as the last roll. The enrollment date was December 29, 1862 unless otherwise noted among the privates:]

1. Balentyne Wm	38	30. Nowlin J.B.	17 (6-20-63)
2. Bushnell L.	26	31. Onion Joseph	19
3. Burney W.D.C.	33	32. Pulliam B.A.	21
4. Cooper W.L.	20	33. Peden H.D.	24
5. Cooper J.W.	30	34. Patterson D.J.	23
6. Casner F.W.	20	35. Prim J.W.	37 (6-20-63)
7. Carnahan D.S.	25	36. Putnam M.D.	21
8. Cude R.D.	21	37. Ryan A.	37 (6-15-63)
9. Click James	35	38. Sharp G.W.	20
10. Click T.L.B.	37	39. Smith H.R.	37
11. Crawford W.H.	30	40. Sansom J.W.	22
12. Carson John	18 (1-15-63)	41. Stayton A.S.	21 (12-20-62)
13. Cole Wm.	– (6-17-63)	42. J.A. Stayton	22
14. Duveneck G.	33 (6-15-63)	43. Stanford C.C.	34
15. Gralin Aug	34	44. Tomberlin A.	21
16. Gray Wm.	18 (6-15-63)	45. Tilley E.	34
17. Hegg Fred	37	46. Wilkins D.	19
18. Hamilton J.W.	21	47. Walker John	19
19. Johnson Oscar	20	48. Walker Riley	18 (1-15-63)
20. Lindeman H.C.	20	49. Westfall W.R.	23
21. Lindeman A.	26	50. Westfall S.C.	17
22. Lindeman E.D.	25	51. Wight L.L.	24
23. Lundy M.R.	21	52. Watson James	18
24. Malone Dan	19	53. Wheeler W.C.	48 (6-6-63)
25. Mesfer Thom.	21	54. Wilson J.C.	16 (6-8-63)
26. Morehouse Ed.	26	55. Wenzel Charles	37 (6-22-63)
27. Moore T.G.	25	56. Zimerman A.	26
28. Manning Th.	37	57. Zorger Peter	22
29. Nowlin R.W.	21		

The men of the Mounted Regiment engaged more Indians and recovered more horses in their first few months than the Frontier Regiment had in a year, but now, particularly in North Texas, found their task compounded with a new problem. On July 4, 1863 the siege of Vicksburg ended in a Union victory. A flood of deserters, mostly Confederate and some Union, spread across the Texas Frontier. Texas State Troops were directed to arrest deserters, whenever found, and turn them over to Confederate authorities. A few commanders instead ordered summary executions out of exasperation, overzealous patriotism, or just meanness of spirit.

On July 25, 1863, eight Williamson County men, supposed to be Union sympathizers avoiding the Confederate draft and making an attempt to reach Mexico, were killed near Bandera City. According to some accounts, they had left their homes in response to a circular they had seen that gave Unionists an ultimatum to leave the state. J. Marvin Hunter, while a newspaper editor in Bandera during the 1920s, constructed the story from interviews with the few men still alive who had some knowledge of the incident. According to Marvin Hunter in the Pioneer History:

> This party of eight men and a boy passed through Bandera, and stopped here for a day or so, resting their horses and buying such supplies as they needed on the trip. They did not make any secret of their destination or the cause of their going, but openly stated that they were on their way to Mexico, to avoid conscription.

A different perspective on the story is provided by a descendent of William Sawyer, family historian Daniel Mahler. According to family tradition the Sawyer brothers were on furlough from their companies and, with their companions, were going to Mexico to buy horses to bring back to the Sawyers' companies. The price of horses in Texas had risen with the inflation of Confederate currency; however, horses could be purchased at a reasonable price in Mexico. Eight to nine hundred dollars had been raised among the men for that purpose. When they bought supplies in Bandera City, their wealth apparently became public knowledge. Major Alexander, in headquarters at Camp Verde, heard that these men had passed through the town. He began pursuit with 25 men from Lawhon's Company.

Perhaps one or more of the Williamson County men really intended to stay in Mexico and then there is the boy who was approaching draft age. The various accounts by Marvin Hunter give the age of the boy as 15 or 16. Clara S. Scarbrough gives the age as

13 in her history of Williamson County. Her research verifies that the Sawyer brothers were on furlough from their companies and that:

> William M. Sawyer, whose farm was eight miles west of Georgetown on the North Gabriel, had enlisted in the Confederate Army July 8, 1862, was in Gurley's Regiment, Company D, Texas Partisans of the Texas Cavalry. His brother, Coston J. Sawyer, was also in the Texas Cavalry, Company A, Morgan's Squadron, having enlisted March 26, 1862. Another of the group, George Thayre, was a brother-in-law of W.M. Sawyer.

J. Marvin Hunter told the story in the Pioneer History and in several newspaper articles, including this excerpt from the Houston Post October 17, 1937:

> Several days later Maj. Alexander and his men came through Bandera on the trail of the men, and went from Bandera to where Hondo is now located. Picking up the trail there they followed it to Squirrel creek, some 10 miles beyond, where they discovered the men they were seeking in camp. They had just finished their noonday meal and were quietly resting, some lounging around and others attending to the stock, not suspecting that they were being pursued and at that very moment in danger of being captured. Approaching under cover to within a very short distance of where the men were camped, Maj. Alexander stepped out into an opening, and swinging his saber over his head, called upon them to surrender, telling them that he had them surrounded and there was no chance for them to escape, and if they would quietly submit he would pledge his word that they should have a fair trial by court-martial at Camp Verde.

> The little party of nine promptly yielded up their arms, and were then forced to saddle their horses and immediately start back toward Camp Verde. All went evenly enough until the second night on the return trip, when, while in camp on the Julian, two miles southeast of Bandera, a suggestion was made that they hang the prisoners right there, without further ado. Some of Maj. Alexander's posse strenuously objected to this procedure, but they were over-ruled and some of them left the camp in disgust, being powerless to prevent the execution.

> The moon was shining brightly, and the prisoners were marched out a short distance from camp and hung, one by one.

A hair rope was used in hanging these men, and each one died by strangulation, being drawn up until choked to death.

[The rope became shorter after each hanging as it was cut from the victim's neck.]

Sawyer suggested to his captors that they shoot him. His request was granted, and five men in the party were detailed to do this. [The other Marvin Hunter articles suggest that only one ranger did the shooting and do not mention a firing squad.] Sawyer stepped off a short distance and a volley was fired at him, but only one shot struck him, in the arm. He fell forward on his face, and when it was found that he had not been fatally shot one man in the party shot him through the back with a rifle, the ball and the ramrod, which in his haste to reload, the murderer had failed to withdraw, passing entirely through Sawyer's body, killing him instantly. He was thus found the next day. The boy in the party, a lad about 15 years old, is supposed to have escaped, as his body was not found with the eight men who were executed. What became of him has remained a mystery to this day.

There is little firm information about Major Alexander or his reasons and intentions, but in Kerr, Kendall, and Bandera counties' historical traditions, he has been considered a rogue ranger responsible for other hangings and thefts as well. As represented by John Sansom biographer, Frankie Glenn, "Alexander and the men under his command would take over what they could appropriate from those they hung, for their use and benefit." In this incident, among possibilities, his choice of an execution site, where Bandera residents were sure to discover the bodies, was intended as an intimidation to Union sympathizers. Before making camp that evening, he may have promised Daniel Malone a promotion to corporal to incite the hanging. Possibly he supplied his men with alcohol for the occasion. According to Scarbrough's account:

Alexander's men drank heavily and, as the evening wore on, some of them became restive, suggesting that they hold a necktie party for the "deserters." One soldier wanted to hang all eight at the same time, but others wanted a longer ceremony and more "entertainment." A few of the soldiers opposed the action, but Major Alexander remained silent, thereby leading his men to believe that he gave tacit approval to the "gruesome proceeding." Troopers opposing the executions left camp and disappeared in the brush.

Joseph H. Poor, a sheep raiser who lived on the West Verde, was camped near the scene that night and next morning discovered the bodies while looking for a horse. Mistaking the ramrod for an arrow, he hurried into town to report an Indian raid. O.B. Miles, Robert Ballantyne, Daniel Rugh, George Hay, Amasa Clark, and other townsmen went out to investigate. Marvin Hunter's article in the <u>San Antonio Express</u>, January 29, 1922, contains the most complete statements by George Hay, Amasa Clark, and John Pyka. George Hay was a storekeeper and 2nd Lieutenant in the Bandera Home Guardes at the time:

> I have seen many foul crimes in my time, but this was the most revolting that I ever knew. A party of us went out from Bandera as soon as we learned of the occurrence, and found the bodies of those unfortunate men lying just as they had been cut down, pieces of the horsehair rope around each man's neck. They had all been strangled to death by the rope being placed over a limb and drawn up, possibly by somebody on horseback. One man, Bill Sawyer, was laying face down, shot through with a wooden ramrod, which had passed entirely through his body and penetrated into the ground for at least 10 to 12 inches. It was with great difficulty that I drew out this ramrod. Alexander's party passed through Bandera about 8 o'clock one Sunday morning, and in just a little while Joseph Poor came with the news that he had found some murdered men down on the Julian. We buried them as best we could, and in giving our verdict at the inquest we definitely placed the blame on Alexander's men, some of whom I knew, but they are all dead now.

Daniel Rugh was county sheriff and a private in the Home Guardes. Amasa Clark, a Bandera County constable at the time, recalled the incident:

> Oh, yes, I remember the hanging of the Sawyers and those other men. It was an outrage. They were murdered--yes, murdered in cold blood. Deliberately murdered without being given a chance for their lives. I knew all of the circumstances, and when Mr. Poor brought word to Bandera that he had found their bodies Mr. Daniel Rugh asked me to go with him down there. When we arrived there a gruesome sight met our gaze. Some had been partly stripped. I heard afterward that some of the men who took part in the hanging had worn the clothes of their victims while passing through Bandera. There was a report that some of them gambled for the clothing the night of

the murder, but I cannot vouch for this statement. This crime created a great deal of indignation here, but the citizens were powerless to do anything. The murdered men were strangers, peaceably passing through the country. They had committed no crime that I know of and should not have been molested. After the war diligent efforts were made to apprehend the guilty ones and bring them to justice, but without success. I knew several of them, but as soon as they were mustered out of the Confederate service, and before the civil courts were in good running order, they left the country. An attempt was made by New Braunfels officers to arrest one of these men [Daniel Malone] on warrant from Bandera County, but he resisted arrest and was killed.

Now, I do not charge this crime to Confederate soldiers. I do not believe a true Confederate would be guilty of such a heinous offense as deliberately putting to death an enemy without giving him every chance the law gives a man. I have lived in the South ever since I returned from my service in the Mexican War, in 1848, and I loved the South and the cause she fought for. I know the rules of warfare and how prisoners should be treated. Sawyer and his men were not treated as prisoners of war. They were hung without a trial, and it seems to me that robbery was the sole motive that prompted their execution. This all happened 60 years ago, but it made such a lasting impression on me that I will never forget it, and have many times wished to see the guilty ones brought before the courts and made to pay the penalty for their crime.

[Born in Polish Prussia, John Pyka was about 16 years old:]

At that time I was just a lad, large enough, however, to think I was about grown, and I distinctly remember when Mr. Joseph Poor came and notified us that he had seen the body of a man on the Julian with arrows sticking in him and he thought Indians were in the country. Mr. Poor lived on the West Verde, but was camped near the scene of the crime, and was out looking for his horses that had strayed off from camp when he came upon the bodies. He did not take time to investigate, but came right on to Bandera and notified the authorities. I went out with the crowd to the place, and we found seven of the men had been hung, and one had been shot through with a ramrod. It was an awful spectacle.

No, I do not think these men had been stripped of their clothing, because I remember seeing that the cattle had chewed the sleeve of the coat on one of the dead men, and if I remember rightly they were all in full attire. Their pockets were empty, showing that they had been robbed. A 16-year-old boy that was captured with the men was spared for the time being, I understand, and taken up about Fredericksburg, but as he was never heard of again, it is supposed that he, too, was killed. I knew some of the men who had a hand in this hanging, but they left the country when investigation started. I think all of the participants are dead now, for it has been a long time ago since all this happened.

We dug a shallow grave, laid the dead men into it, spread blankets over them and covered them up the best we could with dirt and stones to keep the wolves from getting to the bodies. I do not know of any persons now living who was present at the time except myself, George Hay and Amasa Clark. There may be others, but I do not remember.

In 1865 Bandera County citizens erected a tombstone at the gravesite. Traditional rhymed verses are rare as tombstone adornments in Texas, but this one can be traced back to 1376 and the tomb of Edward, the Black Prince, in England's Canterbury Cathedral:

C.J. Sawyer, W.M. Sawyer, George Thayre, William Shumake, Jack Whitmire, Jake Kyle, John Smart, Mr. Van Winkle: Died July 25, 1863. Remember, friends as you pass by; as you are now, so once was I. As I am now, you soon will be; prepare for death and follow me.

Many years later, Henry Nowlin, son of Dr. James C. Nowlin, wrote a letter to J.S. Piper, husband of William Sawyer's daughter, Ellen, "Do you and Ellen know that the young boy when released by the mob on Julian came directly to Curry's Creek and spent the night with us." Apparently, the boy was an uncle of Ellen's, on her mother's side, but his name is not mentioned in the letter.

Marvin Hunter repeats in each of his articles that no Bandera County men were among the men of Lawhon's company who stayed for the hanging. The documentary evidence seems to bear that out. Two men in Lawhon's Company were given promotions July 25, 1863. The timing of Bandera County resident William Wheeler's appointment to the position of company farrier on July 25, 1863, seems to have been coincidence or convenience. The position had been vacant for some time. William Wheeler's name is not listed on the 1866 indictment.

Daniel Malone enlisted in Montel's Company from Medina County and served as 1st Corporal. In Lawhon's Company he was a private, promoted to corporal July 25, 1863, while former corporal Brewer was reduced to the ranks. These promotions are stated in the following muster roll, but the Special Orders have not survived to reach the State Archives.

G.H. Noonan was District Judge of the region when the Reconstruction government directed grand juries to investigate war atrocities and injustices. Sixteen men were indicted in District Court April 24, 1866. The document in the Bandera County Courthouse gives no names other than "W.J. Alexander et al". The indictment was carried at the courthouse from term to term of the District Court since the men were never brought to trial. August 3, 1870, Sheriff T.C. Rine reported outstanding Bandera County warrants to Governor Davis:

> In district Court Spring Term AD 1866 Indictiment for Murder and highway Robbery against WJ Alaxander supposed to be in Matamoris Mexico   Sylvester Stayton   RD Cude   FL Cooper   Wm Gray   Augest Gralin   Adan. Bleaker   Whereabouts unknown   HD Peden supposed to be in Illinois   John Carson   Cal Putman   FM Casner   Osker Johnson   SC Westfall   Peter Zorger   Daniel Stayton   whereabouts unknown   Danl Malone dead

Except for Adan. Bleaker, all the names can be found on the muster rolls for Lawhon's company, although the first names or initials do not all match. The shooting of Daniel Malone took place when he resisted arrest in New Braunfels sometime after the April 1866 indictment and before Sheriff Rine's August 1870 report. The Comal County sheriffs in that time period were:

Charles Wiegreffe - August 1, 1864 through June 1866
William Schmidt - June 25, 1866 through May 1869
Charles Saur - December 3, 1869 through February 15, 1876.

Muster Roll of Captain John Lawhon's B Company, in the Mounted Regiment of Tex. State Troops, commanded by Colonel James E. McCord called into the service of the State of Texas by Gov. J.R. Lubbock under the Act of Legislature approved Dezember, 21st 1861, from the 1st day of July 1863, when mustered, to the 31st day of August 1863, the date of the present Muster.

The Mounted Regiment: Lawhon's Company

1. John Lawhon	Capt.	40	Present for duty
1. Thom. P. McCall	1st Lieut	32	Present for duty
2. P.T. Adams	2nd "	27	A.A.Q.M. Present for duty
3. R. Harper	3rd "	23	Absent with leave since 24 Aug. 63
1. James Croke	1st Sergt	37	Present for duty
2. Thom Short	2nd "	32	Present for duty
3. M.V. Casner	3rd "	20	Absent on detach/d Service since 24 Aug. 1863
4. D.W. Stayton	4th "	25	Present for duty
5. H. Chipman	5th "	20	Present for duty
1. Th. Pafford	1st Corp	25	Present for duty, on extr duty since 1st July 63.
2. B.F. Patton	2nd "	26	Present for duty
3. D. Malone	3rd. "	19	Present for duty, for duty, appointed Corp. July 25 63 by S.O. No. 48. f. R.H.Q.
4. R. Bird	4th "	21	Present for duty
1. Isaak Wiley	1st Bugl.	20	Present for duty
2. W. Manning	2nd "	35	Present for duty
1. W.C. Wheeler	Farrier	48	Present for duty, appointed Farrier July 25 63 by S.O.No.47 fr.R.H.Q.
1. Balentyne Wm	Private	38	Present for duty
2. Burney W.D.C.	"	33	Present for duty
3. Bushnell L.	"	26	Absent on detach. Service since 24 Aug. 63
4. Benton Wm.	"	40	Absent on detach. Service since Aug. 63
5. Brewer L.	"	36	Absent on det. Service since Aug. 63. Reduced to the Ranks July 25 by Spec. Ord No. 48 from Reg. Head Quart.
6. Cooper W.L.	"	20	Present for duty

7.	Cooper J.W.	"	30	Absent sick since July 30 1863
8.	Casner F.M.	"	20	Absent on det. Service since 24 Aug 1863
9.	Carnahan D.S.	"	25	Present for duty
10.	Cude R.D.	"	21	Present for duty
11.	Click James	"	35	Discharged July 24 by Spec. Ord. No. 258 from the A&GG Office
12.	Crawford W.H.	"	30	Present for duty, on extra duty since July 1st 1863
13.	Carson John	"	18	Present for duty
14.	Cole Wm.	"	34	Present for duty
15.	Click T.L.B.	"	37	Absent on detach/d Service since Aug. 24th 1863
16.	Callahan Wm.	"	26	Present for duty
17.	Duveneck G.	"	33	Absent sick since Aug. 20 63
18.	Gralin Aug.	"	34	Absent sick since Aug. 21 1863
19.	Gray Wm.	"	18	Absent on detach'd Service since Aug. 24 1863
20.	Green Wm.	"	18	Absent on detach/d Service since Aug. 24 1863
21.	Hegg Fred	"	37	Present for duty, appoint Hosp. Stewart July 2 1863 By Sp. Ord. No. 265 fr. A&GG Office.
22.	Hamilton J.W.	"	21	Present for duty
23.	Johnson Oscar	"	20	Present for duty
24.	Lindeman H.C.	"	20	Absent on detach/d Service since Aug. 24 1863
25.	Lindeman A.	"	26	Present for duty
26.	Lindeman E.D.	"	25	Present for duty
27.	Lundy M.R.	"	21	Absent on detach/d Service since Aug. 24 1863
28.	Mesfer Thom.	"	21	Absent on detach/d Service since Aug. 19 63
29.	Morehouse Ed.	"	26	Absent on detach/d Service since Aug. 24 63
30.	Moore T.J.	"	25	Present for duty
31.	Nowlin R.W.	"	21	Present for duty
32.	Nowlin J.B.	"	17	Present for duty

33. Onion Jos.	"	19	Present for duty
34. Pulliam B.A.	"	21	Present for duty, on extra duty since July 1st 1863.
35. Peden H.D.	"	24	Absent on detach/d Service since Aug. 24 1863.
36. Patterson D.J.	"	23	Present for duty
37. Prim J.W.	"	37	Present for duty
38. Putnam M.D.	"	21	Present for duty
39. Patton Charles	"	23	Present for duty, on extra duty since Aug. 16 63
40. Patton Sam	"	17	Present for duty
41. Ryan A.	"	37	Present for duty
42. Sharp J.W.	"	20	Present for duty
43. Smith H.R.	"	37	Present for duty
44. Sansom J.N.	"	22	Present for duty
45. Stayton J.A.	"	22	Present for duty
46. Stayton A.S.	"	21	Present for duty
47. Stanford C.C.	"	34	Present for duty
48. Tamberlin A.	"	21	Present for duty
49. Tilley E.	"	34	Present for duty, on extra duty since Aug. 31st 1863
50. Witkins D.	"	19	Absent on detach/d Service since Aug. 24 1863
51. Walker John	"	19	[blank]
52. Walker Riley	"	18	Present for duty
53. Walker Wm.	"	26	Absent on detach/d Service since Aug. 24 1863
54. Walker Dan	"	17	Present for duty
55. Westfall W.R.	"	25	Present for duty
56. Westfall S.C.	"	17	Present for duty
57. Wight, L.L.	"	24	Absent on detach/d Service since Aug. 24 1863
58. Watson James	"	18	Present for duty
59. Wilson J.C.	"	16	Present for duty
60. Wenzel Charles	"	37	Present for duty
61. Wiley Wm.	"	36	Absent with leave since Aug 29 1863

62. Zimmerman A.   "   26   Absent on detach/d Service
                                    since Aug. 24 1863
63. Zorger Peter   "   22   Present for duty

At an inspection of the arms of Capt Lawhon's Company (B) Mounted Regt Texas State Troops, stationed at Camp Verde, Texas, June 9th 1863. The arms and their condition were as follows, viz:

Names	Guns	Pistols	Condition
1. Sergt. Croke	Rifle	Holsters	good
2. Short	Shot gun	"	good
3. Casner	Yager	Navy S.S.	good
4. Stayton	Yager	Army S.S.	good
5. Chipman	Carbine	No Pistol	good
6. Corp Pafford	Rifle	Army S.S.	good
7. Patton	Rifle	Army S.S.	good
8. Brewer	Rifle	Navy S.S.	good
9. Bird	Yager	Army S.S.	good
[10. Bugler] Wiley	Rifle	No Pistol	Bad
11. Manning D.B.	Shotg	Navy S.S.	good
12. pt. Ballentine	Rifle	Navy S.S.	Rifle Worthlefs
13. Bushnell	Yager	No Pistol	good
14. Burney	Yager	Navy S.S.	good
15. Cooper I	Sharps R	Army S.S.	good
16. Cooper II	Yager	Navy S.S.	good
17. Cude	No gun	No Pistol	[blank]
18. Carnahan	Yager	No Pistol	Worthlefs
19. Casner	Yager	Army S.S.	good
20. Click I	Rifle	no pistol	good
21. Click II	Rifle	no pistol	good
22. Crawford	Yager	Navy S.S.	good
23. Carson	No gun	Navy S.S.	good
24. Graylen	D. Yager	Navy S.S.	gun bad
25. Gray	Minnie Rifle	No Pistol	good
26. Hegg	Shotgun & Rifle	no Pistol	good
27. Hamilton	Yager	Navy S.S.	good

#	Name	Gun	Pistol	Condition
28.	Johnson	No gun	No Pistol	[blank]
29.	Lindeman I	\\\\	Navy S.S.	good
30.	Linderman II	no gun	Navy S.S.	good
31.	Lindeman III	No gun	Navy S.S.	good
32.	Lundy	Rifle	one Holster	gun worthles
33.	Moore	Rifle	Navy S.S.	Rifel Worthlefs
34.	Mesfer	Yager	No Pistol	Worthlefs
35.	Morehouse	no gun	no pistol	[blank]
36.	Malone	five Shooting Rifle	Army Pistol	good
37.	Nowlin	Yager	Navy S.S.	good
38.	Onion	Yager	Navy S.S.	worthlefs
39.	Patterson	Rifle	Navy Pisto Rifle	good S. Brok
40.	Peden	Rifle	No Pistol	Worthlefs
41.	Pulliam	Yager	No Pistol	good
42.	Putnam	Yager	No Pistol	good
43.	Standord	Yager	Army S.S.	good
44.	Stayton I	Yager	Navy Pistol	good
45.	Stayton II	Yager	Navy Pistol	good
46.	Smith	Rifle & S.G.	Holsters	good
47.	Sanson	Rifle	no Pistol	good
48.	Sharp	Shot gun	no pistol	good
49.	Lilley	Rifle	Navy Pistol	good
50.	Tomlin	Minnie Rifle	Navy Pistol	good
51.	Wheler	No gun	No Pistol	[blank]
52.	Wilkins	Yager	Navy Pistol	Neither good
53.	Wilson	Rifle	5 Shooter	good
54.	Wight	No gun	Navy Pistol	good
55.	Westfall I	D.B.S. Gun	Navy Pistol	good
56.	Westfall II	Minnie Rif	No Pistol	good
57.	Walker I	Rifle	no Pistol	good
58.	Walker II	Rifle	Holsters	good
59.	Watson	Rifle	Army S.S.	Rifle not good
60.	Zorger	Rifle	No Pistol	No good
61.	Zimmerman	Yager	Navy S.S.	good

According to a voucher dated September 26, 1863, William Ballantyne, a skilled wheelwright and tracker and a private in Lawhon's Company, was paid $35 for repairing two wagons. In 1856, his Circle B was one of the first five cattle brands registered in Bandera County. His brother, Robert, was a 2nd Lieutenant in the Bandera Home Guardes.

As the time for the transfer to Confederate service drew near, the plight of the men of the Mounted Regiment can be illustrated by the men of Camp Davis, north of Camp Verde. H.T. Davis was the original captain of Company F, James M. Hunter was 1st Lieutenant and afterwards captain. A portion of Davis' Company under Second Lieutenant William Arbor took part in the Nueces Battle. When Captain Hunter was transferred to major in the Frontier Organization, Lieutenant Alonzo Rees became captain. The following is one of the few surviving documents in the State Archives written by Major Alexander:

Received   Camp Davis   Jan 27th 1864
the following orders

Fort Inge, Texas

Jan 17th 1864

Capt
    you will place all the men who were detailed by Lt. Rees to go on this Scout and who have failed to Come on Extra duty untill ordered to Relieve them by me unless they have been Released by you from the Scout
    Lt Rees hands me the following names who have failed   M.C. Alexander, WF Benson, JC Brown, H. Beekman, Joseph Friece, JM Neel, & R. White
you will carry out this order to the letter and assure them that the punishment will lefsend or increased on my Return according to the nature of their cases.

                Very Respectfully
                your obt srvt
                W.J. Alexander

Capt JM Hunter
Camp Davis
Texas

The extract of payroll for Lawhon's Company states that H.R. Smith died February 10, 1864. No cause of death is given.

Shortages of powder, percussion caps, and other supplies began to affect the morale and effectiveness of the regiment. March 21, 1864 Captain William Banta reported that he could not pursue Indian raiders because his company was out of caps. When the Mounted Regiment, also known as McCord's Regiment, became the 46th Texas Cavalry Regiment, C.S.A. in May 1864, Captain Banta was among a small group of deserters arrested by men of the Frontier Organization (home guard/ranger units).

[The letter Colonel J.E. McCord wrote from Camp Verde to Major General J.B. Magruder, C.S.A. is transcribed in the <u>Official Records</u>, Series I, Volume 34, Part III, Pages 802-803:]

HDQRS. Frontier Regiment of Texas Cavalry,
Camp Verde, Tex., May 2, 1864.

Maj. Gen. J.B. Magruder,

Commanding District of Texas, &c., Houston, Tex.:

General: I expect to leave in a few days for Austin, and before doing so I feel it my duty under the circumstances to give you in a few words my views of the present condition and future prospects of this immediate frontier, for of the destitute condition of the norther frontier you have already been apprised. In the first place, the good and loyal citizens of the southwestern frontier are very apprehensive for their personal safety, in the absence of any Confederate troops on the line. Their property they know will be driven to Mexico by deserters and renegades, and in the event of any provocation they themselves plundered and murdered. Very many of the men in the militia organizations are connected in some way with those who have fled the country, and I am credibly informed that bands of lawless men are already organized to rob and plunder the country as soon as the regiment is removed.

There never has been a time in my knowledge when regular organized troops were so badly needed here. Their presence at this time would be of incalculable benefit to the entire country, and without them I sincerely believe that the country will be devastated, and the good citizens reluctantly forced to retreat to the interior. The frontier will be broken up, and the outer line be thrown back to San Antonio and Austin, from 80 to 100 miles inside of the present line. Moreover, I believe that civil strife will be inaugurated on this border in less than three months from the present date, if troops are not thrown along the line from this post to the Rio Grande. The seeds are already sown, and they need but the absence of regular troops to insure a plentiful harvest of misery and devastation. In my opinion, general, it is of the utmost importance that one company at least should be ordered to the permanent occupation of Camp Verde, for the twofold purpose of protecting the camels, some 80 in number, belonging to the Confederate States, and for the protection of the surrounding country. That district is a key to several counties, and its occupation will afford protection to a large section of country.

Hoping that you will give this matter an early consideration, I am, very respectfully, your obedient servant,

J. E. McCORD,
Colonel Frontier Regiment of Texas Cavalry

[Three letters requesting the return of Lawhon's Company are transcribed in the Offical Records, Series I, Volume 34, Part III, Pages 816-819:]

[From Dr. E.M. Downs]

Rio Hondo, Tex., May 11, 1864

Col A.G. Dickenson:

Sir: In the capacity [of] commander of this frontier when stationed here, you manifested so much interest in our protection [that] you will excuse me asking you to use your influence with the commanding general of this department to continue the protection necessary to secure the lives and property of the loyal citizens of this frontier. Within two weeks and since the removal of the troops from Camp Verde, the Indians have made two visits to this neighborhood, killed two good, loyal citizens, killed and driven off nearly all our horses. We are not only exposed to the depredations of the Indians, but our worse foe the renegades and organized members of the Union League. We have very little confidence in the present partially organized troops of the frontier, as we believe many of them are men that have fled from the interior to avoid conscription and are and have been from the first, and are friends and sympathizers with the deserters and renegades that infest the mountains of this frontier and the Rio Grande.

We are fully convinced that regular troops only can keep down the spirit of disloyalty and vengeance that exists among the renegades that infest this frontier. Believing that you will generously use your influence in our behalf, and knowing as you do our dangerous and exposed situation, I have appealed to you. Camp Verde is the key to protection to all this portion of the frontier. If consistent to do so we would beg that Captain Lawhorn's company, with one other good company, be placed at Camp Verde, as we have full confidence in them as true, loyal Southern men and prompt and energetic in driving out the Indians. Captain Lawhorn's company has the entire confidence of all the loyal citizens of this frontier.

Very respectfully, your obedient servant,

E.M.Downs

[From Captain H.T. Edgars]

San Antonio, Tex., May 11, 1864.

Lieut. Col. A.G. Dickinson:

Sir: I have the honor to call your attention to the defenseless condition of that portion of the frontier between Camp Verde and the Rio Grande, which is being daily run over by bands of Indians and lawless white men with impunity. Having been stationed on this part of the frontier for more than two years, I feel it my duty to lay before you for your consideration a few plain, simple, and stubborn facts in regard to the condition of the good and loyal citizens of that portion of the frontier. You have already been informed of the removal of the Frontier Regiment; this leaves that entire scope of country destitute of any protection whatever, save the militia. This, in my opinion, in their present weakened condition, leaves them not only subject to lose their property by bands of lawless white men who are daily driving off their cattle by the hundreds, but their families are subject to fall victims to the savage foe at any time.

On the morning of the 6th of this month it was reported to me that these bodies of lawless white men and Mexicans had stolen and run into Mexico more than 5,000 head of stock cattle from and near Fort Clark, and that a body of the thieves was at that time camped on this side of the river. These lawless white men have been so lightly dealt with that they have already advanced as low down the country as the Rio Frio, and in my opinion, if these loyal citizens are not relieved from their present embarrassed condition by at least one well-organized company, to be stationed at some prominent point in said locality, they will be forced to move to the interior for protection.

This company should in my opinion be composed of men acquanted with all the water holes and whose interests are identified with that portion of the frontier.

And as Captain Lawhorn's company is composed chiefly of the bona-fide citizens of this frontier, I would move that they be assigned to that duty in preference to any other company, believing, as I do, that they would give universal satisfaction.

I am, very respectfully, your obedient servant,

H. T. EDGAR,
Captain Company F, Frontier Regiment.

[From W.A. Lockhart, Bandera County resident:]

San Antonio, May 11, 1864.

Lieut. Col. A.G. Dickinson:

Sir: I address you upon a subject of vital interest to our whole western frontier, stretching from the Colorado River to the Rio Grande. The withdrawal of the Frontier Regiment, and especially of the troops stationed at Camp Verde, has left the inhabitants wholly defenseless, being exposed not only to Indian depredations, which are now of frequent occurrence, but to the still more dangerous and destructive depredations of deserters, jayhawkers, and robbers, who already infest the whole country from the Colorado to the Rio Grande. Without some force to protect this frontier I have no doubt the whole country west of San Antonio will be deserted by every loyal citizen, and the beeves and horses in this region will be driven to Mexico, seized and carried off by the Indians, or destroyed. I live 4 miles beyond Bandera and 8 miles from Camp Verde, and I have no hesitancy in saying that if there be not at least one company of troops kept stationed at Camp Verde, or in that neighborhood, not only I but every loyal citizen in that part of the country will be sacrificed or compelled to abandon the country and fall back to San Antonio in less than sixty days. Already robberies and murders are of frequent occurrence.

On Monday night last Capt. William Wallace, an old Texan and one of our best and most skillful Indian fighters, was killed not more than 20 miles west of San Antonio, and very far within the lines of the frontier.

This was by Indians, who at the same time stole most if not all of his horses. It was only a week previous to this a party of Indians made their appearance on the Hondo, 30 miles west of San Antonio, and killed one man and scattered and drove off a large number of horses. But these occurrences have become so frequent that it would require too much space to mention all. Another danger equally as great, if not greater, threatens us on this frontier in our present defenseless condition, and it is from the vengeance threatened to every loyal citizen by the friends of the disaffected who have been forced to leave the country to avoid military service; nothing but the presence of an armed military can restrain this class of persons, and especially if their renegade friends and relations should return, as they would be sure to do if the military force be wholly withdrawn from this frontier. I address you, colonel, hoping you may use your influence at headquarters to secure us in our need some protection, and knowing that you are not unacquainted with our condition, I appeal to you in earnest language, because I am deeply impressed with a sense of the danger which now threatens every settler on the frontier. His life and property are daily at stake.

I rely on your influence because as a commander of this district you have ever appeared solicitous to protect the frontier. As the State troops or militia have been turned over to the Confederacy by the Governor, we of the frontier think we have a right to demand protection from the general commanding the department. I have no doubt Captain Lawhorn's company, formerly stationed at Camp Verde, if ordered back would give great satisfaction to the frontier inhabitants, at least to the loyal portion of them.

Very respectfully, your obedient servant,

W. A. LOCKHART.

[Endorsement:]

Respectfully forwarded, for the information of the major-general commanding, with the remark that many verbal representations being made upon this subject. He is an intelligent gentleman, and his views and representations worthy of consideration.

A. G. DICKINSON,
Major and Assistant Adjutant-General.

Big Foot Wallace joined the Confederate Army March 1, 1864. The rumor that he had been killed by Indians was apparently widespread. Ben Batot, an 18-year-old Medina County ranger at the time, may have embellished his memory in A.J. Sowell's account:

While we were in camp at Moss Hollow, about six miles below D'Hanis, we received a report that the Indians had killed Big Foot Wallace. It was about twenty miles to where Wallace lived [on Chachon Creek], but we immediately set out, about ten of us, and arrived at his place about dark. His lonely little cabin was deserted, no one there, and all we found in the way of provisions there was a small piece of bacon and a little corn meal in a sack. We prepared to camp, and in about an hour Big Foot Wallace came strolling in with his gun over his shoulder, his two pistols in his belt, his Mexican blanket on his arm, and leading his horse.

The military distribution of manpower in Texas in 1864 was a serious matter. The Union drives up the Red River and the Rio Grande required nearly every Confederate soldier in Texas for the defense of the state. Rip Ford gathered whatever men and boys he could in the San Antonio area (including Charles de Montel and Big Foot Wallace) to form the Cavalry of the West which fought the Union army in engagements from Laredo to the Gulf of Mexico.

The four southern companies of the Mounted Regiment were used to replace the Confederate coastal troops which were rushed to the Red River. Private Levi Lamoni Wight, Company C, First Texas Cavalry, C.S.A., was in camp near Goliad:

> In Feb of the following year (64) we were ordered on force march to reinforce Tom Green and Waker [Walker] who was then retreting up read river followed by Genl Banks of the fedral forse. We had ben durng the winter months so fare on the gulf cost holding the fedral gun boats at bay. Now that the boats were caled away to New Orleans in consideration of a heavy campain through Louisanna and Texas, while on the cost we had some active servis. The gun boats would ocationly land troops and we would chase them back.

To keep Governor Murrah apprised of a delicate situation, Major John Henry Brown, Frontier Organization, Texas State Troops, transcribed a letter he had received from Lieutenant Neel, formerly of the Confederate States Army (McCord's Regiment), speaking for about half the men of the four companies that had been moved to the coast:

March 25th, 1865

Major Jno. Henry Brown:

Sir:

I will report to you our present condition. I will report to you for the best, as I was requested by your friends. Col. McCord's regiment has, a large portion of them, come on the frontier to protect the frontier as their homes are on the frontier. They have come for no bad intention. I would like to do duty under you if I could. We are about 150 strong. We would like to stay on the frontier, if there is any chance. I was requested by your cousin (brother, I presume, J.H.B.) R. Brown, and if this matter can be straightened, we will return. We have not come to jayhawk or stay in the brush.

You can address me at Camp Verde

Yours, respectfully

    Lt. Neel

[Major Brown's notation to Governor Murrah:]

I have copied the letter so as fully to express the meaning. The original being so badly written as to be almost illegible.

    Jno. Henry Brown
    Major comd/g
    3rd F. Dist

[Major Brown wrote a long patriotic reply to Lieutenant Neel in which he exhorted the men to return to their regiment. He then wrote to Governor Murrah enclosing transcripts of his reply and Lieutenant Neel's letter:]

Fredericksburg, March 27, 1865

Governor:

The enclosed copies explain themselves. In the emergency presented for my consideration by the extraordinary note of Lt Neel, I adopted the course which seemed to me best and most judicious. Such a body of well armed men are of course beyond the reach of any force within my control, without a publicity and delay, which would insure defeat of the object - their arrest. Besides, many men of my command have relatives among those men, and the ordeal would be one through which sound discretion dictates they should not be part.

Until otherwise ordered, I shall continue the course thus begun- -to deal frankly with those men - endeavor to keep them embodied and instil into their minds a proper sense of their duty.

I address you directly, as you requested, whenever I thought proper.

    With great respect

        Jno. Henry Brown

Governor Murrah

Apparently, Lieutenant Neel and his men had moved on or dispersed before April 1865 when units of the Frontier Organization rendezvoused at Camp Verde for their last campaign.

8

The Bandera Home Guardes
(Mitchell's Company)

Company F, 3rd Regiment (unorganized),
31st Brigade, Texas State Troops
1862-1863

3rd Frontier District, Frontier Organization,
Texas State Troops
1864-1865

The Confederate State of Texas required each county to form a home guard unit. One had formed in Bandera County as early as June or July 1861, apparently unofficially. Charles Montague, serving as Justice of the Peace, Precinct One, wrote Governor Clark that this company "in case of invasion may prove of a dangerous character." This thirty-man company may have functioned as a county ranger company for a short time with O.B. Miles as captain, Robert Ballantyne, 1st lieutenant, and Thomas Bandy, 2nd lieutenant.

Perhaps the serious need for frontier defense convinced the Bandera men to conform to the Confederate-required company. Indian raids had subsided somewhat in the early part of 1861, but had increased again near the end of that year. The WPA history of Bandera County quoted from the Minutes of the Commissioners Court for January 8, 1862:

> State arms in the possession of the county clerk were placed at the disposal of Indian-fighters by instructions from Adjutant General J.Y. Dashiell, who ordered that, "should any forays be made by the Indians," these arms should be given "to those who have none and who are willing to follow the savages," the arms "to be returned immediately after the scout."

While many of the home guard units within Texas had little function, in the frontier counties, they were active as ranger protection against Indian raids. The mounted militia company known as the Bandera Home Guardes or Mitchell's Company formed in March

1862. Edward M. Ross, Chief Justice of Bandera County, may have been enrolling officer for the Home Guards at that time. The county mustered enough men for one company and one squad (perhaps 65-120 men). Some of the county's men had already joined the Confederate States Army or were in the Frontier Regiment or some other full-time companies of Texas State Troops.

E.M. Ross, O.B. Miles, and others in Bandera were army veterans. Most probably agreed with Polly Rodriguez' assessment of the situation:

> The Confederate authorities at San Antonio secured for me a commission as captain in that service and sent for me and offered it to me. But I declined. My heart was really with the United States, that I had served so long.
>
> They accused me of being a Union man. I said: "Now, it is like this: If I were out with ten men and nine should decide against me, I would be compelled to accept their decision. The State has seceded, and I accept the situation; but if I could have had my way, it would not have done so."
>
> So I went back to my home and joined the "Home Guards." We elected one of my neighbors, a Mr. Mitchell, captain.

The election of officers took place March 30, 1862. Bladen Mitchell, who had come to Bandera County from Virginia in 1857, was elected captain. Robert Ballantyne, who had come to Bandera County with Lyman Wight in 1854, was elected 1st lieutenant. His cousin, George Hay, was elected 2nd lieutenant. R.S. Perkins was elected junior 2nd lieutenant.

The state of Texas had been divided into 33 brigade districts in 1861 and the following year the brigade structure was utilized to organize county militia companies and, later, to administer the draft. The Bandera Home Guards were in the 31st Brigade then being organized by Brigadier General Robert Bechem, Texas State Troops. All or parts of 22 counties comprised the district including Blanco, Kendall, Comal, Medina, and Kerr. Due to the large German-speaking population of the district, the military law was distributed in English and German copies, but there was a shortage of both.

By April 15 Captain Mitchell still had not received a copy of the military law and there does not seem to be any record that he ever did. Polly Rodriguez remembered a consequence:

> Once during this service I asked the captain's permission to take my sister over into Mexico to her husband, who was over

there. He gave it, and I took her and came back by way of San Antonio. I had bought a fine buckskin suit over in Mexico, and a fine Mexican hat, beautifully fixed up in Mexican style. I was around a place of resort, a gambling and drinking place, one night, intending to leave early next morning for camp. The provost marshall for some reason (he was a bad man, a Captain De Hammond) attacked me. He demanded to know where I was from and where I had been. I told him a straight story-- that I had permission from my captain to be absent--and he wanted to see my permit. I told him it was only verbal.

"That won't do," he said. "You'll have to go to jail." I told him that was a place I never had been, and I was not going.

He said I would, and told the guard to take me. I determined to die rather than be put in jail. I offered to bring him any security from the best men in town. Nothing would do; I must go to jail. I was fully determined to kill him and die myself before I would go to jail. While the altercation was going on, an old man, Antonio Manchaca, who had known me from a child, and who was a kinsman of De Hammond, came up and took my part. He told De Hammond who I was, and that whatever I said was right. So the provost marshal let me go. Next day I started home.

Although supposed to be organized and operated according to C.S.A. regulations, the frontier ranger companies could be very democratic affairs. George Hay, a storekeeper in Bandera City at the time, later recalled:

Being an officer made no difference to me. I went into the ranks, stood guard and performed all the duties of a private. [His brother, Alexander, served as a private as did Polly Rodriguez who remembered:]

It was our business to defend the neighborhood from the wild Indians and to keep down the disorderly element at home. I served four years, the whole period of the war, in this company. We were almost constantly on the scout, and had many unimportant encounters with the Indians.

The men rotated turns at patrolling or "scouting", usually serving about ten days out of each month. Bladen Mitchell's ranch house may have served as their ranger station. Taylor Thompson, captain of a Uvalde County militia company, related a story of his Civil War ranger experiences in which he said of the Mitchell ranch, "I found twelve or fifteen men there preparing to start on a scout the next morning." The ranch was located along the east side of the Medina River. Ten miles from Bandera City, Mitchell's Crossing was strategically located.

General Bechem, headquartered in New Braunfels, was a reluctant citizen-soldier appointed to a difficult and thankless bureaucratic position. The war ruined his consignment business, yet he did not seek personal gain from his office as he said, "I disliked too much the way money was made by Speculators, Agents, etc." While writing often to the governor asking for a hardship discharge, he took advantage of every opportunity to postpone the required election of brigadier general which would confirm his position. He nevertheless made his best effort to perform his duties.

General Bechem's superior, the Adjutant and Inspector General in Austin, Colonel Jeremiah Yellot Dashiell, edited a newspaper before the war. He provided the general with advice, directives, and interpretation of the C.S.A. regulations. The mail between New Braunfels and Austin usually took no more than two days, but dispatches between New Braunfels and the various frontier locations in the 31st Brigade District could take weeks. General Bechem wrote to Colonel Dashiell, March 26, 1862:

> Enrollments from the Counties of Bandera, Edwards, Mavarick, Dawson, Kimble and of several precincts in the Counties of Llano, San Saba & Atascosa are still wanting and from other Counties the returns of election for Company officers have not been made, which detains me in completing the organization of this Brigade.

The Bandera Home Guardes had organized in March, but it was April 10 before General Bechem could report to Colonel Dashiell that a company had formed in Bandera County and April 15 before he could report the results of the election of officers for that company.

With the county militia companies successfully raised, General Bechem sent out an order in May for the companies to organize into regiments. On May 21 he confidently reported that the 3rd Regiment would hold elections June 7. By June 28 General Bechem had begun to express frustration:

> Only from one Poll the election returns for Field officers of the regiment under organization in the Counties of Blanco (southern portion), Kendall, Kerr & Bandera have been received, viz the return from Dr. E. Kapp, enrollg. officer at Sisterdale, Kendall Co., resulting in the election of:

Fredr. Tegener	for Colonel	20 votes
Capt. J. Schlickum	" Lt. Col.	20 "
E. Cramer	" Major	20 "

but I hesitate giving Certificates, as the election, having had to take place on the 7th inst., has not been a general one, although my orders of election had been forwarded to all the enrollg. officers on May 17th; and as regards the Certif. for Capt. Schlickum, I would have to withhold it until hearing the result of his trial for the political offence.

The indifference shown in these Counties displeases me very much, and will probably be the cause that I have to put off for some time the election for Brig. Genl.

How very strange that the entire regiment would abstain from voting while only the Sisterdale men voted. The town was the intellectual center of Union activity in the Hill Country. July 4, 1862, the Union Loyal League met on Bear Creek in Gillespie County. Whether General Bechem had any idea of what was going on, he did not say in his reports. With the 3rd Regiment still unorganized, he gave in and pronounced the Brigade organization completed July 5:

Not having succeeded to organize the 3d Regiment composed of:

1 Company	Blanco County	(southern portion)
3 "	Kendall "	
1 "	Kerr "	(eastern portion)
&1 "	Bandera "	

as with the exception of 1 Poll (Sisterdale) no election for Field officers has been held, and not being authorized by law, to make appointments for these offices, I better defer ordering a new election until the Conscripts may have been ordered into service, and considering the regimental & battalion organization completed, I intend in the course of this week to order in compliance with Sect. 13 of the military law an election for Brigadier General to take place on Saturday August 9th a.c.

O.B. Miles had been elected to his third, although not consecutive, term as chief justice of Bandera County in August. That same month new appointments for conscript enrolling officers were made with James M. Starkey for parts of Kerr County and O.B. Miles for Bandera, Edwards, and parts of Kerr County. Two months earlier General Bechem had reported that there were few men eligible for conscription remaining in some of the counties of his district and "no enrollments made in the Counties of Zavalla & Concho & only a small number enrolled in the Counties of Bandera, Kerr, Mason, Frio & Uvalde."

Unfortunately for all General Bechem's organizational efforts the events of the Civil War outpaced the usefulness of the militia structure he had struggled to complete. The Confederacy's requirement for men was enormous and desperate. After the August 1863 elections the Tenth Legislature of Texas took up the question of turning over the Mounted Regiment to the C.S.A., leaving the militia units of the frontier counties alone to face the Indians and deserters. The militia companies of the frontier would have to be reorganized to face the challenge. In his letter to Colonel Dashiell August 18, General Bechem seemed near a breakdown at the thought of going through another period of organization:

> Besides the five Counties of Comal, Blanco, Kendall, Medina & Gillespie, where the additional 25 per cent (resp. 50% of the undrafted men) have to be drafted, I would then have to order the enrollment & draft for organization for the local defences in the following 8 Counties of my District viz: Kerr, Mason, Llano, San Saba, Bandera, Atascosa, Uvalde & Maverick, which would again take up my time for several months with writing orders, corresponding, investigating petitions and exemptions, granting furloughs etc., etc.

September 16, 1863, citizens gathered in Bandera City to discuss a clear situation: The number of men defending the frontier was steadily decreasing. Montel's Company of the Frontier Regiment covering Bandera Pass at Camp Verde and the headwaters of the Medina and Sabinal rivers at Camp Montel had disbanded. Some of Charles de Montel's men went into Confederate service and the remaining formed most of Lawhon's Company which was stationed only to cover Bandera Pass. Now the proposals being discussed by the legislature could remove that protection and the rest of the Mounted Regiment. The conclusions of the meeting were sent to the civilian government in Austin in the form of resolutions. The Bandera citizens were apparently asking for a more traditional minuteman company under local control and exempt from the Confederate draft. The Bandera Resolutions were forwarded to Colonel Dashiell who forwarded them to General Bechem. The influence the resolutions had is uncertain, but the serious lack of men to defend the Bandera region is underscored by the number of county officials who served at various times in both the county government and in the county militia unit from which they were exempt:

	Office	**August Election**
W.S. Goodwin	district clert	1860?
George Hay	assessor and collector	1864
August Klappenbach	county treasurer	1864
H.C. McKay	county commissioner	1864
O.B. Miles	chief justice	1862
J.M. Phillips	county commissioner	1864
J.P. Rodriguez	justice of the peace	1864
Daniel Rugh	county sheriff	1862
P.D. Saner	county clerk	1861

The Tenth Legislature after much debate over states rights finally agreed to turn the Mounted Regiment over to the C.S.A. and made provisions for the reorganization of the frontier militia companies. An act of December 15, 1863 formed 59 counties from the Red River to the Rio Grande into the Frontier Organization. The act exempted these counties from the Confederate draft and directed their home guard units to organize into companies of 25-65 men with a captain and two lieutenants. Each company was to divide into roughly equal-size squads that would rotate time of service. Larger units could be authorized when necessary. The transfer of the Mounted Regiment to Confederate control should wait until the militia was ready to take over.

The Frontier Organization was divided into three districts with a Major of Cavalry appointed to command each. In the northern or 1st Frontier District was Major William Quayle, headquarters Decatur. The central or 2nd Frontier District was commanded by Major George Bernard Erath, headquarters Gatesville. The southern or 3rd Frontier District which included Bandera County was commanded initially by Major James M. Hunter, headquarters Fredericksburg.

Major Hunter, brother of John Warren Hunter who was the first of a line of Texas journalist-historians, had ranger experience as a captain in the Frontier and Mounted regiments and with ranger companies before the war. He was popular with the German settlers of his district, but his efforts to command in January and February 1864 were hampered by numerous Indian raids, disorderly deserter gangs, passive resistance by Union sympathizers, vigilante and other outlaw activity.

The companies of the Frontier Organization, as first formed, averaged 50-55 men each. O.B. Miles drew up a muster roll February 6, 1864 showing the following names, ranks, and ages for Mitchell's Company:

Captain Bladen Mitchell, 27
1st Lieutenant Orlando B. Miles, 37
2nd Lieutenant Robert Ballantyne, 35

Sergeants
1. Jackson M. Phillips, 33
2. W.H. Mott, 28
3. F.M. McKay, 19
4. George Hay, 27

Corporals
1. Thomas Bandy, 45
2. Loami Lemhi Wight, 30
3. Joseph Sutherland, 23
4. Albert Adamitz, 19

Privates

Walek Aunderwald, 28
Daniel Arnold, 66
Benjamin F. Bird, 36
Charles Bird, 38
Samuel Bird, 28
Ezra Alpheus Chipman, 46
E.P. Chipman, 19
S.F. Christian, 37
A.J. Click, 55
Meachem Curtis, 46
John Dugozs, 46
Horace V. Freiman, 21
Nicanor Garcia, 40
Erineo Gonzales, 38
Santos Gonzales, 42
W.S. Goodwin, 36
John Green, 23
Alexander Hay, 18

Thomas Hicks, 31
F. Juritzke, 37
Casper Kalka, 49
Joseph Kalka, 28
August Klappenback, 46
Blas Loya, 33
Henderson C. McKay, 46
Paul Martin, 64
Thomas Mazourick, 46
K. Merit [Merrets], 36
J.B. Miller, 46
Joseph Moravitz, 32
Joseph H. Poor, 37
Antone Pyka, 43
S.J. Rine, 56
Thaddeus C. Rine, 30
Jose Policarpo Rodriguez, 34
Edward Merritt Ross, 48

Lemuel Haywood, 37　　　　　　Daniel Rugh, 30
Andrew Hoffman, 37　　　　　　Patterson Douthit Saner, 41
Albert Hiduke, 49　　　　　　　Francis Woclawcyzk, 39

Each of the 53 men armed and equipped himself. All were armed with muzzle-loading black powder rifles or shotguns. Twenty-five men had rifles and pistols, while seven had shotguns and pistols. Twelve had only rifles and nine had only shotguns, probably the double-barrel type. The total armaments for the company were 37 rifles, 16 shotguns, and 32 pistols. The state provided some powder and percussion caps, but as George Hay pointed out, the quality of the powder was often poor.

In March 1864 as Civil War fighting raged on or near the Texas borders, the Confederate command called away the four southern companies of the Mounted Regiment, leaving only six of its companies along the Red River and the area of the 1st Frontier District. The 3rd Frontier District was mostly on its own and already off to a rough start. Raids by Indians and renegade whites during that spring and summer left the area in turmoil, particularly in Gillespie County. The people of Bandera County sent W. A. Lockhart to San Antonio to petition the Confederate authorities for the return of the Mounted Regiment or at least Lawhon's Company.

After a continuing series of crises in the 3rd Frontier District, Governor Murrah appointed Brigadier General John D. McAdoo to take charge. General McAdoo had served with the 20th Texas Infantry earlier in the war and had administrative experience as an assistant adjutant general of state troops in Houston. Since March he had been brigadier general in command of the 6th Brigade District.

The Confederacy had not recognized the state's right to grant exemptions from the draft. The men of Mitchell's Company may have continued a practice that was not uncommon in the frontier counties as General Bechem related to Colonel Dashiell August 7, 1863:

> I am sorry to say that in some Companies the commanding officers in making up their Rolls for the draft have not been very particular but have added the names of persons who were over age or otherwise by law exempted. Some of them were drafted & had to be withdrawn from the list; but at the other hand, about an equal number of such illegal names will be among the remaining undrafted.

The Frontier Organization had come under criticism by Confederate authorities as an unnecessary diversion of troops from the C.S.A. and as a haven for deserters and draft dodgers. To allay these criticisms one of General McAdoo's first steps was to ensure that the companies of the Frontier Organization conformed to the legislature's specifications. Any unqualified militia men were dropped from the rolls or transferred to an appropriate service. Paul Martin, 64, was spry enough to freight corn to Camp Verde, but his name does not appear on the muster of June 1, 1864. Captain Mitchell, rather than O.B. Miles, was enrolling officer and listed 13 fewer men than in February:

Captain Bladen Mitchell, 28
1st Lieutenant O.B. Miles, 37
2nd Lieutenant Robert Ballentine, 35

Sergeants
1. J.M. Phillips, 34
2. W.H. Mott, 28
3. F.M. McKay, 19
4. George Hay, 27

Corporals
1. [blank]
2. Benjamin Bird, 36
3. Joseph Sutherland, 23
4. Loami L. Wight, 30

Privates

Walek Anderwald, 28
Charles Bird, 38
George Calvert, 37
Ezra A. Chipman, 46
E.P. Chipman, 19
R. Click, 33
John Dugos, 46
Horace V. Freiman, 21
John Green, 23
Nicanor Garcia, 40
Santos Gonzales, 42
Erineo Gonzalez, 38
Alexander Hay, 18
Andrew Hoffman, 37
Thomas Haiduck, 31

Albert Haiduck, 49
F. Juretzke, 37
Casper Kalka, 49
August Klappenback, 49
Blas Loya, 33
Thomas Mazourick, 46
K. Merretts, 36
J.B. Miller, 46
J. Moravitz, 32
Henderson C. McKay, 46
Jose P. Rodriguez, 33
Daniel Rugh, 30
R.C. Rine, 30
P.D. Saner, 41
F. Waclawcyzk, 39

General McAdoo arrived in Fredericksburg June 23 and called his captains to a two-day conference to discuss problems and solutions. He then made an inspection tour of the district, trying to bolster morale along the way.

Mitchell's Company ordinarily did not patrol outside the boundaries of Bandera County before 1864. In April of that year Major Hunter had organized a scout of 60-75 men from the companies of his command and sent them to the upper Llano River region in an attempt to thwart raids from deserters and Indians. When General McAdoo took command, he assigned specific areas for each company to patrol on a regular basis. Apparently, the headwaters of the Llano River were assigned to Mitchell's Company.

Taylor Thompson was captain of a Uvalde County company and had some rivalry with Bladen Mitchell. Captain Thompson remembered:

> I was in camp with a party of rangers some sixty miles to the northwest of Bandera. One day I left camp alone to hunt deer, and about 10 o'clock that morning I met the Captain Mitchell above referred to. He was scouting in that same section with a squad of his company, for that was the territory assigned to him for scouting duty, while I was merely passing through, returning from having followed an Indian trail through there. The captain and I stopped and nooned together. After resting an hour or two we saddled up again and had ridden about half a mile when we came to where another valley ran into the one we were in, and riding up this other valley there came a party of twenty to twenty-five Indians. We were probably within 200 yards of each other before either saw the other. It was about half a mile up the valley to a clump of trees which grew right in the middle of it, and to these trees Captain Mitchell and I started at full speed, with the Indians in full pursuit yelling "As if all the fiends from heaven that fell, Had pealed the banner cry of hell."
>
> The Indians were armed with bows and arrows only, and they never got near enough to us to render these effective, though Mitchell and I fired several shots at them as we ran. We reached the trees safely, dismounted and tied our horses, while the Indians surrounded the small grove we were in with the apparent intention of laying siege to our position. Captain Mitchell, after taking a survey of the surroundings, remarked that he did not believe it was more than a mile or so to his camp, and that if we did much shooting his men would be apt to

hear it and come to the rescue, for sound travels far in those mountain districts. He and I kept up a pretty constant fire, more for that purpose than from the hope of doing the enemy harm, for they kept pretty well out of range. We had been there about an hour when Captain Mitchell, looking up, said, "Yonder they come." It proved, however, to be a squad of my own men instead of his. These men were out hunting and hearing the firing, came at once. They attempted to charge the Indians, but the latter did not wait the attack. Captain Mitchell returned to my camp with me and I sent four men with him to his own camp. A year or so later, I forget the exact date, the Indians caught this Captain Mitchell out and killed and scalped him, while I am left to tell The Record's 100,000 readers of the stirring scenes of those old days. [Thompson's overall veracity may be suspect. Bladen Mitchell survived an attack by Indians in 1866 and died of an illness while in Utopia in 1890.]

Besides patrolling against Indian raids, the home guard units were also responsible for apprehending deserters and "bushwhackers" (Union sympathizers avoiding the draft). Texas State Troops were under orders to turn any of these men found over to the Confederate authorities. From 1863 the number of deserters, both Federal and Confederate, roaming the frontier regions increased considerably. Many of them eventually went to California or Mexico. Others were sometimes troublesome along the northern and northwestern Texas frontier. Polly Rodriguez recalled the circumstances when a Mitchell Company patrol captured three deserters who were on foot near the headwaters of the Llano River:

> The captain had to put a guard over them to keep them from killing themselves eating. They were as ravenous as wild animals. We did not let them have all they wanted for about three days. In that time they had begun to change wonderfully. They were sound and well soon, and Captain Mitchell gave them up to the Confederate authorities. He was a great friend of the Confederacy, and did all he could to help them.

After a 10-to-20-day scout Corporal Loami Wight went on furlough to recuperate and get provisions. His wife, Martha, was staying in Burnet County near her sister, Sophia Wight, who wrote to her husband December 18, 1864:

> Loami is here. He has been here about three weaks. He was in Bandara 20 days. He had the chills when he came here. He is better now but is waiting for clothes. He will leave the last of

the weak. His time is out. There is about half of the Reg on Sick furlow. They are verry mytch discouraged and he thinks there will a great many disert if they are not better provided for.

Leadership was about the only resource made available to the home guard units as 1864 drew to a close. By December, General McAdoo was commanding the 2nd and 3rd Frontier Districts. He was still working to improve the effectiveness and morale of the Frontier Organization in his districts. After reducing the threat of various gangs of deserters in the Fredericksburg area, he set about to face an expected increase in Indian raids. He wrote to the new Adjutant and Inspector General, Colonel John Burk, December 15, 1864:

> The Indians are in the country. One hundred are known to be between this point and the headwaters of the Medina. The whole available force of the District has been ordered out, and are now in pursuit.
>
> As yet, their depridations, as reported to me are not considerable, excepting the killing of two women, whom they happened to encounter alone and at some distance from any settlement.
>
> Our forces may push them too closely to allow of much damage being done, but I fear they will escape, as heretofore, without receiving any signal punishment. I am preparing a General Order for the Districts under my command, for a System of Service which will remedy existing defects, and enables us hereafter to meet these forays more successfully, if not effectually stop them--I will transmit you a copy in a few days.

General Orders Number 3

For the purpose of rendering the service of the Frontier Organization uniform throughout the different counties of this command; to increase the efficiency of the service and to facilitate concentrated and combined movements of the troops when necessary, it is ordered by the Brig. Genl. Commanding:

I. That within each county or company district, there shall be established a permanent camp or rendezvous; and that the different companies be divided into four squads of as nearly equal strength as possible, which said squads shall succeed each other in the scouting service regularly every ten days; that each squad be required to report promptly at the said company camp on the day the preceding scout is to be relieved.

II. When said camps are located the company commanders will forthwith notify the commander of the district of its location, and also the company commander in all the adjoining counties.

III. It shall be the duty of the officers in command of said camp, to keep the forces thus collected constantly on scouting service, in those districts in which Indians, Bushwhackers, and Deserters are likely to be found--detailing from said force a sufficient number of men only, to keep camp and act as couriers, should it be necessary to communicate with neighboring camps on the appearance of Indians or other contingency.

IV. It shall be the duty of the officers in command of the camp detail, to dispatch immediately to the nearest county camp, by swift courier, any intelligence he may receive of Indians, or other danger threatening the Frontier, and such camp will communicate in like manner with the next, until the whole Frontier line is informed.

V. When Indians are known to have penetrated the settlements, the different scouts will guard particularly the passes through which they usually go out with horses. All experience has shown that the most effective plan of operations against an Indian enemy is to head off the raidng parties as they leave the settlements with their plunder and booty. If they are able to get in through the scouting lines, see to it that they go out without spoils, and with severe punishment.

VI. When camps are located they will not be changed without good reasons therefore, and when changed, the district commander and company commanders in the adjoining counties, will be notified of the location of the new camps. The commander of the district will be notified of the nearest Post Office to the different camps.

VII. The companies of Captains Gussett and King and Lieut. Haynes and Herring will form one common camp to be selected by Captain King. The companies will cooperate in the scouting service, and senior officers present commanding the men on duty.

VIII. When Indians have penetrated the settlements, the company commanders may call out a portion of their command not on their regular tour of duty, and if necessary the entire strength of their companies for the emergency. Let the Indians find themselves met by armed forces, not only on the outer line of the Frontier, but everywhere within those lines.

IX. The greatest promptness and diligence are enjoined upon the officers and men of this command. The Brig. Genl. commanding has good reason to believe the Indians of the North-West are incited and perhaps led to depredate on the Frontier of Texas by White men, who are agents, if not officers and soldiers of the United States. Extra efforts and watchfulness should be at that period in each moon, when Indians usually visit our Frontier. The country expects her Frontier Organization to protect the Frontier, and the Brigadier General commanding calls upon every officer and every man, to see to it that the public expectation is not disappointed.

> By Command of Brig. Genl. J.D. McAdoo
> Russell DeArmond
> Maj. & A.A.A.G.

The 1st Frontier District had undergone a change of command in September 1864 when Major William Quayle, in poor health and under great stress, was replaced by Brigadier General James Webb Throckmorton. Previously General Throckmorton had commanded the Third Brigade District. George B. Erath continued as major of the 2nd Frontier District, but James M. Hunter resigned in January 1865. John Henry Brown was appointed major for the 3rd Frontier District January 19. Earlier in the war Major Brown had served on General Ben McCulloch's staff and later served on General Henry McCulloch's staff, but illnesses and a surgery had kept him from active duty much of that time.

Some men from Mitchell's Company took part in the last campaign of the Frontier Organization. On March 10, 1865 General McAdoo ordered Major Brown to assemble 1/4 of the men of the 3rd Frontier District (400 men) at Camp Verde in one month. From 22 companies only 183 men described as "Americans, English, Irish, French, Poles, Germans, and Mexicans" showed up at Camp Verde with their 243 horses and pack animals.

Amidst news of the siege of Petersburg and Richmond, Major Brown arrived from Fredericksburg on April 10 and organized the men into four columns. He also undersigned the resignations of Samuel Mott and Bladen Mitchell who went to Houston to enlist in the Confederate States Army.

The next day with two 10-man squads ahead to protect the flanks, Brown's battalion rode north through Kerrville, turning west to follow Johnson's Fork of the Guadalupe River, then north again. The objective was to scout the area between the upper San Saba and Concho rivers and engage a large force of deserters reported to be gathering there to raid the settlements (Lt. Neel's men?).

The battalion arrived at deserted Fort McKavett on the San Saba River April 21. After a two-day rest the men moved out to scout the area. They encountered several small bands of deserters and rustlers and took prisoners when they could be caught. At the end of April the battalion was scouting in detachments along the upper Guadalupe and Llano rivers. Lieutenant Lacey's detachment found a group of men described as "bushwackers" holed up in a brushy creek bottom. A fierce firefight erupted which lasted most of the day as other detachments arrived to reinforce Lieutenant Lacey and his men. When it was over Brown's men had seven prisoners, two bushwackers were dead and at least two had escaped. The battalion reached the end of the campaign at Fredericksburg early in May after three and a half weeks on horseback. Major Brown referred to himself in the third person in the history of Texas he published in 1892:

> At the time of the surrender at Appomatox, Major John Henry Brown, who served in Arkansas, Missouri and Northeast Texas the first three years of the war, in command of about two hundred State troops, was on an expedition in the San Saba and Concho country, and knew nothing of the surrender of Lee and Johnston until his arrival in Fredericksburg in May. He then immediately disbanded all troops, from that point to Live Oak County, but retained in service a detachment from Burnet and Llano, until his arrival in Austin. These men were guarding about thirty State prisoners in his charge, who had been arrested under various requisitions, as bushwackers, deserters, and some as cattle thieves. Gov. Murrah had then left Austin. Confusion reigned supreme; the troops referred to were therefore disbanded, and the prisoners released, under a pledge that they would peaceably return to their respective homes.
>
> Thus ended the last manifestation of Confederate authority in Texas, excepting at and near Brownsville, on the lower Rio Grande. Major Brown, however, exercised authority in the frontier district until about the 30th of May, a little later than the last battle of the war [Palmito Hill: May 13, 1865].

Federal troops landed in Galveston June 18. The freedom proclaimed the following day is still celebrated as Juneteenth. Polly

Rodriguez remembered that a few months after Mitchell's Company disbanded, a company of Federal troops arrived in the county and camped on Bandera Creek near the town. George Hay looked back over the years:

> I have never received a cent for my services and none of my comrades ever received a cent of pay. We had to furnish ourselves, too. Some ammunition was supplied, but it was of such poor quality as to be almost worthless. The Indians often made raids down into this settlement and below here, and we would take their trail, sometimes inflicting severe punishment on the red rascals.

QUARTERLY RETURN
of Commfs/d Officers (as per Genl Order No. 4)
in 31st Brigade Texas State Troops,
for the quarter ending July 1st 1862

Brigade Staff Officers

Brigade Major	No Appointment made
" Adgt & Inspt Genl.	Herm. Seele, Commfsn received
" QuarterMaster	Fredr. Wrede, no " ", not liable to Conscription
" Commifsary	John F. Torrey, Commfsn. received
" Aid de Camp	G.W. Rittberg, no " " . is liable to Conscription
" Surgeon	Dr. Thead/re Koester, Commfsn recd

[Side notation:] if not his office as Depy. Post Master of P.O. Comal Rancho will exempt him, the PostMaster having removed from the State.

" Afst. Surgeon	Dr. W. Keidel for Gillespie County
" " "	Dr. Weifselberg was apptd For Medina County, but nothing heard from him

Field officers, 1st Regiment

Colonel	Jacob Schmitz	Commfsn received
Lieut Colonel	Herm. Heffter	"
Major	Chs. Floege	"

Staff officers 1st Regiment

Surgeon	Dr. Wm Remer	
QuarterMstr	Willm Leekatz	no commfsions received
Commifsary	C.W. Thomae	are not liable to conscription
Chaplain	Parson Aug Schuchard	
Afst Surgeon	Augustus Forke	
Adjutant	Gustf. Conrands	is liable to conscription

Field officers, 2nd Regiment

Colonel	Chs. Rothe	Staff officers no yet appointed
Lieut Colonel	C. Weyrich	
Major	J. Luckenbach	

F.O. 3rd Regt. Returns received only from 1 Poll
F.O. Indept. Battn. Llano County, R.S. Coon, Major
"   "   San Saba "   A. J. Rose, "
"   "   Medina   "   H.J. Richarz, "
Certifn of election for Major Richarz retained

Company officers

	Captains	First Lieut	Sec/d Lieut	Jr. 2nd Lieut

1st Regt. Comal County State Troops

	Captains	First Lieut	Sec/d Lieut	Jr. 2nd Lieut
Comp.A	H. Gunther	Hugo Loefs	Fr. Wunderlick	C. Ph. Georg
" B	J.J. Groos	C. Goebel	H. ZumBerge	Chs. Hergett
" C	G. Strempel	Bogislaw Hoym	Gg. Luersen	Erhd Mittendorf

The Bandera Home Guardes (Mitchell's Company)

" D	J. Heilmann	W. Rahe	Aug. Luerson	Christ. Page
" E	J. Scheider	A. Eiband	W. Sahm	Chr. Reile
" F	H. Coers	B.F. Smithson	C. Schuchardt	Carl Georg
" G	J. Mengdehl	F. Wagenfishr	Peter Becker	D. Knibbe

2nd Regt. Gillespie Co. S.T.

Comp A	R. Radeleff	F. Wilke	vacancy	J. Ahrhelger
" B	C. Weyrich.	Jac. Schmidt	J. Kunz	J. Metzger
" C	W.V. Hohmann	Sam Gnott	Chr. Althaus	Masc. Salomo
" D	C. Kothe	J. Dearing	N. Rusche	W. Cafs
" E	J. Kuchler	Joh. Schmidt	Fredr. Behr	Jacob Weber
" F	W. Feller	J. Luckenback	J. Brodbeck	J. Rusenberger

3rd Regt. not organized

Blanco County

C.A	A. J. Kercheville	John Carson	Tom Carson	Isaac Turner

Kendall County

C.B	J. Schlickum	Fredr. Lenz	R. Brotze	H. Wendler
C.C	Ottomar Labherd	Louis Breitenbauck	E. Beseler	Edgar Westfalen
C.D	M. Lindner	E. Schwethelm	W. Luckenius	Th[?] Brukisch

Kerr County

C.E	Thomas Saner	F. Metzger	Ed. Steves	Frank Selph

Bandera County

C.F	B. Mitchel	R. Ballentyne	Gge Hay	R.S. Perkins

1st Indept. Battalion Medina Co. S.T.

Comp A	H.J. Richarz	Jos. Finger	Paul Brotz	Hubd. Wienard
" B	George Meyers	Adam Blefs	Jul. Hartung	M.M. Saathoff
" C	Blasius Kieffer	Anton Schneider	Fredr. Mohr	Francis J. Miller
" D	Jacob Haley	John Libolt	Valenty Gully	Jos. Bendele

2nd Indept. Battalion Llano Co. S.T.

Comp A	John M. Smith	R.F. Holden	Wm. M. Riley	T. J. Bedford
" B	C. Haynes	T. Ward	D.J. Smith	W.L. Hendrick
" C	C.W. Dorsey	D.J. Owens	C.F. Mayes	A.A. Reichenau
" D	W.J. Johnson	W.C. Phillips	L.H. Cowan	W.M. Case

3rd Indept. Battalion, San Saba Co. S.T.

Comp A	W. Thaxton	A.J. Rose	Caleb Jones	J.L Tate
" B	W.R. Gray	W.H.H. Harrell	W.R. Gregg	J.T. White
" C	D.A. Harris	Howell Bafs	M.G.C. Keele	Dav. Hubbert

Indept. Companies

Mason County

Comp A	W. Chs. Lewis	C.W. Grooms	W.C. Hayes	Oliver Morrill
" B	John Anderegg	Otto Lange	Wm. Danheim	Herm. Fisher

Atascosa County

Comp A	J.W. Stayton	Jefse R. Smith	G.D. Gilliland	Saml. H. Niel
" B	Aug Durand	Ths. J. Adams	Leeson B. Harris	J.S. Fern

Frio County
Comp _ D. Lemons N. Terry   B.F. Franks   J.E. Bowen

Indept. Squads John A. Henderson & B. Sublett - seniority to Kerr Co. Prect No. 5 be decided by lots

Atascosa Co. Prect No. 2 not organized & Enrollg officer superseded

" " " No. 4 Elect. returns for One Lieutenant not received.

Gillespie Co. Prect No.6 F. Peterman apptd [1st Lt.] 2 Sgts & 2 Cpls

Kimble Co   B.L. Clements apptd   1 & 1

McCullock Co.   M.C. Trousdale   1 & 1

Dawson & Kinney Cos. J.B. Light [1st Lt.] John N. Grove [2nd Lt.] 2 & 2

Uvalde Co. Prect No. 1 James Hughs   2 & 2
   "   "   "   No. 3 J.C. Ware   2 & 2
   "   "   "   No. 2   1 & 1
   "   "   "   No. 4   1
Blanco Co. "   No. 2 & 7   1 & 1
   "   "   "   No. 3   1 & 1
Kendall Co. "   No. 4   1 & 1
Menard Co. "   1 & 1
Edwards Co. "   1 & 1
Maverick Co. " Election for Comp/y officers held June 30th & no returns rec/d as yet.

I certify that the above return is correct.

    New Braunfels, Comal Co., July 5th 1862
        Robert Bechem
        Brig. Genl. 31st Brigade T.S.T.

31st Brigade District   3rd Frontier District
(all or parts of the following counties)

31st Brigade District	3rd Frontier District
Atascosa	Atascosa
Bandera	Bandera
Blanco	Bee
Comal	Blanco
Concho	Burnet
Dawson	Dawson
Edwards	Dimmit
Frio	Edwards
Gillespie	Frio
Kendall	Gillespie
Kerr	Karnes
Kimble	Kerr
Kinney	Kinney
Llano	LaSalle
Mason	Live Oak
Maverick	Llano
McCulloch	Maverick
Medina	McMullen
Menard	Medina
San Saba	Uvalde

Some of these counties were unorganized or had become depopulated during the Civil War. The preliminary boundaries of Edwards County had been laid out, but no county seat had been designated and no government had been organized.

9

The Reconstruction Years

An incident that occurred in Texas during the last year of the Civil War had a long-term effect on the West Texas Frontier. Since the mid 1850s any Indians found on the Texas frontier were presumed to be hostile. Accordingly, a band of Kickapoos leaving the disturbed conditions in Indian Territory during the Civil War and peacefully proceeding to Mexico were attacked by rangers from the 2nd Frontier District of the Frontier Organization and Confederate troops. The Texans were routed in the 1865 Battle of Dove Creek. The Kickapoos established themselves in Mexico and made fierce raids on the West Texas frontier. They made peace with the Lipan Apaches and organized raids.

Amidst the postwar turmoil it seemed more people were moving out of Bandera County than were moving in. P.D. Saner's wife, Elizabeth, had died in 1863. In 1865 he moved with his four children to Boerne where he served a number of terms as Kendall County Judge. The stone house he had built on Bandera City's main street in 1855 became the Bandera County court house until the two-story Schmidtke & Hay building became available around 1874.

Although some Bandera City businesses expanded and some new enterprises were begun, there was little money in the postwar economy. James Booker Davenport and George Hay founded the mercantile store of Davenport & Hay. Hugh Duffy, an Irish immigrant, came to Texas from Wisconsin, settling in Boerne in 1864. He moved to Bandera City in 1866 where he practiced law and opened the Duffy Hotel. F.H. Schladoer moved from Kendall County and bought James, Montel, & Company's water-powered mill. John P. Heinen had freighted corn from Comfort through Bandera City to D'Hanis during the Civil War. With his brother Joseph in 1866, he started a mercantile store in Bandera City. Payment for goods was often made in shingles which he collected from store patrons all along the Medina River. West of Laxson's Creek, except for shingle crews, J.P. Heinen knew of only one settler, George Smith, who lived about two miles above the forks of the river:

The Indians came in almost every full moon, and when I left home I had no assurance that I would get back alive, but I was fortunate in never meeting the Indians face to face, although I have been very near them a number of times.

As Texas settled into the Reconstruction years, on November 16, 1866, the Bandera County Commissioner's Court ordered, "that the sum of $19.50/100 be paid to O.B. Miles for blank forms [amnesty oaths] purchased by him in San Antonio." The state was divided into 11 military districts, each administered by a general of the U.S. Army and by his appointed state officials. Bandera County was initially in the Seventh Military District, but a restructuring placed the county in the Fifth Military District.

Frontier protection was not a priority for the U.S. troops that moved into Texas as an occupying army to enforce the reconstruction of the South. The French presence in Mexico was also a concern that distracted the army from frontier protection. The U.S. peace policy towards the Indians further restricted the Army's conduct in regard to the Indian frontier.

General Philip Sheridan considered most appeals for frontier protection from Indian raids to be unfounded. He reluctantly ordered the Fourth U.S. Cavalry to Camp Verde and Fort Martin Scott in September 1866. The cavalry was removed in 1868 and Camp Verde was closed in 1869. Not until the early 1870s at the end of Military Reconstruction and after General Sherman's 1871 inspection of the frontier did the army become fully committed to frontier defense from Indian raids. All during this time the state was not allowed to raise troops or rangers. Governor Throckmorton discussed the situation with Buck Barry in a letter November 22, 1866:

> But for your own private information I will say that if the Indians continue to depredate and the government does not effectually stop them, in the Spring I contemplate a campaign even if it has to be done secretly. But there is not yet a company organized that I know of.
>
> But should a campaign be made, if the frontier companies are not raised, we can get the men.
>
> In the meantime I am trying to induce the Government to have a new Indian treaty and send commissioners from Texas, so that the Indians can be taught to know that Texas is a part of the U.S. If this treaty can be got up we may succeed in getting back our children and women who are prisoners.

The federal cavalry are now going out to Fort Mason, Inge, Camp Verde, Clark, etc. This is the 4th U.S. cavalry. The 6th cavalry, 11 companies, will have their Hd Qrs at Jacksborough. Those of them not gone are to leave here in a few days. I have requested that two companies or more of this force be placed at Camp Colorado--and also 2 companies in the corner of Erath or Comanche--somewhere in that vicinity--and a part of the 11 companies in Montague. I think this will be done--as soon as I learn the facts I will write you.

Truly Yr Friend,

J.W. Throckmorton.

P.S.--I have had a pretty broad hint that the State troops had as well not be sent out. This P.S. is private.

T.

Although militarily organized groups of civilians were not initially allowed by the Reconstruction government, the frontier settlers had mostly to depend upon themselves for defense in the postwar years. However organized or supported, any ranger company's success often depended on the men's ability to follow a trail. Many of them knew at least the rudiments of tracking, but few had the skill to follow hidden trails. Occasionally hunting dogs were used to follow a trail, but they could easily be thrown off the scent and lacked stamina compared to horses. Hombres del campo or frontier Tejanos like Policarpo Rodriguez and Macedonio Delgado were among the best trackers in West Texas. A man known only as Manuel served as tracker for Bandera County ranger companies in the 1870s. He had lived 15 years with the Comanches. Polly Rodriguez discussed tracking and the recommendations he made to the U.S. Army around 1865 when a company of U.S. troops camped on Bandera Creek:

> I recommended my cousin, James Tafolla, and he went, but he did not remain long in the service. I then recommended an American, William Valentine, who stayed with them some time. He was a good woodsman, and knew how to trail. It takes a keen, smart man to trail; not many can do it. Experience is necessary. A trailer must not look along under his feet, but keep the trail far ahead of him, by signs he must notice, by broken twigs and weeds. A good trailer can ride at a gallop. I have trailed where every other man said there was no sign, and would not believe I was on the trail until we came

upon the Indians. The Indian is very smart to cover up his trail. I don't know anybody that can equal him.

Young Frank Buckelew and his siblings were orphaned and came to Bandera County to live with their aunt and uncle, Mariana and Berry Buckelew. After their uncle was killed by Indians, the children were split up, Frank going to live on J.B. Davenport's ranch along the Sabinal River. He was captured there one day in March 1866 by Lipan Apaches. He recalled that the redbud trees were in bloom:

> Every part of their trail was covered so completely that a searching party would have been at a loss to determine even the direction in which we were going.
>
> [...]
>
> Our route still lay through the roughest and most difficult part of the region to travel.
>
> The Indian, in traveling, never followed a road or even a path if it was near a settlement, and never crossed either unless forced to do so, and then with considerable care he destroyed every sign of his trail before he would press on. This was perhaps the most successful means of eluding his pursuers. The white man, though eager for the chase and daring in his efforts to overtake the savage, was no match for him when it came to gliding over the roughs and canyons or in passing through dense cedar brakes or forests, and the savage well knew this.

Men from the Sabinal settlements tracked these Indians with John Ware's hunting dogs, but the dogs got diverted and lost the trail. Frank Buckelew was taken to a Lipan Apache camp on the Pecos River. Many Bandera and Uvalde county ranchers made pledges of cattle to ransom young Buckelew. By the time he returned to Bandera County in 1867, the cattlemen had cash on-hand to pay a reward to his rescuer. Perhaps they were already finding new markets for their cattle.

A.J. Sowell mentions several 1866 Indian raids in Bandera County in <u>Texas Indian Fighters</u>. In the account of M.C. Click, David Cryer was badly wounded with an arrow near Sugar Loaf Mountain on the trail between Bandera City and Hondo Canyon:

> There was no doctor near to attend Mr. Cryer and he suffered great pain, as the arrow was deeply embedded and could not be withdrawn by ordinary force or means. A man at Bandera

named O.B. Miles had been a hospital steward and generally attended men who were shot by Indians or any other way, and he was at once sent for and came, but Cryer had received a mortal wound and died in three days. Miles did all he could for him, extracted the arrow and dressed the wound, but of no avail.

In November 1866, Major George A. Forsyth arrived in Galveston to begin a tour of Texas to determine the validity of reports of Indian raids. He concluded that some additional army protection might be warranted, but the main problem was just a lack of pioneer fortitude along the frontier. Governor Throckmorton responded by requesting complete reports of Indian depredations from the county judges of the frontier counties. According to historian William L. Richter:

> On the basis of the replies to this circular, the governor declared to Secretary of War Stanton in August, 1867, that since the Civil War, 162 persons had been killed by Indians, 43 captured, and 24 wounded. An estimated 31,000 cattle, 2,800 horses, and 2,400 sheep and goats had been stolen during the same period.

[County Judge Eugene Oborske reported the Bandera County Indian depredations 1865-66. Document 93A, Volume 4, Texas Indian Papers:]

Citizen	# of horses lost	Date
L.L. Chilson	3	August 1
John Bandy	1	"last of" October
B.F. Langford	1	"last of"" October
John Green	9	September 15
Blanden Mitchell and E. Lane	15	September 15
Maryanna Bucklew*	4	during last 18 mos
Tho. Mimiko	10	during last 18 mos
A. Johns	12	during last 18 mos
Amasa Clark	3	June 2 & October 1
Jasper Norris	1	March 15
W. Ramsey	1	August 1

Joseph Rodrigues	1	August 1
E.M. Ross	1 (& 1 mule	June 2
Henry Ramsey	1	during last 18 mos.
George Smith	1	June
P. Rodrigues	47 horses & mules	last 18 mos.
M. Curtis	5	last 18 mos.
Perry Wilson	5	July
H.C. McKay	9	last 18 mos.
James Bandy	3	August

[* widow of L.B.C. Buckelew.]

Total amount of property [including 134 horses and mules]

consisting of horses and cattle stolen and Killed. Value Seven thousand Five hundred and Eighty Dolars curency.

Killed	Wounded
L.B.C. Bucklew	Rufus Click
George W. Miller	Bladen Mitchell
Thos. Click	Edwin Downs
Cryer	
Sullivan	

Captured

caried away boy about 13 years of age in captivity it is suposed that said boy by name Hubert itis amongst the Kickapoo Indjans in Mexico.

[Frank Buckelew] was abducated by Indjans, and is now in the Lipan Indian Camp in Mexico.

County Judge H.J. Richarz reported Medina County losses for 1865-66, "The number of stock stolen by the Lipan and Kickapoo cannot be ascertained, but will certainly number one thousand head."

The following excerpt is from a letter from J.B. Davenport, Bandera, to Hon. W.B. Knox December 22, 1866 asking for "assistance & advice" regarding the kidnapping by Lipan Apaches of a 13-year-old boy. He received [Document 93A. Volume 4. Texas Indian Papers:]

a letter from a friend of mine in Eagle Pass--James Moseley--informing me that the boy is in the hands of Kickapoo or Lipan who are encamped in the vicinity of Santa Rosa, Mexico, about 80 miles from Eagle Pass--

I will further remark that the boys name is Frank Buckelew & was captured close by his home in the Sabinal Canion---

[Document 100, Volume 4, Texas Indian Papers is another letter along the same line about Frank Buckelew dated January 28, 1867, from N.M.C. Patterson to J.W. Throckmorton.]

Frank Buckelew lived with Costilietos' band of Lipan Apaches as they wandered back and forth from the Pecos River to the Rio Grande and occasionally into Mexico. They traveled in a baggage train over a mile long and there were more than 100 wigwams when camp was made. Although Frank Buckelew greatly resented his kidnapping, he came to have some respect for Costilietos:

> The returned scout always went into council with Custaleta and one of the young warriors. I now learned that Custaleta was the retired chief, and that this young warrior was the young chief. He always went to Custaleta for advice and was very obedient to his commands.

Costilietos' people lived in constant fear of attack by Comanches, Kickapoos, rangers, and soldiers. Frank Buckelew was told of a recent battle in which they defeated Comanches on the Pecos River. He experienced false alarms that sent the women and children scurrying for the high ground as warriors gathered their horses. On one occasion a Kickapoo band under Chief Old Fox approached the Lipans in a threatening manner:

> Custaleta now gave evidence of the fact that he was by far the most important figure on this occasion, the young chief and every warrior placing himself immediately under his command, the wisdom and power of this great old war-chief now became evident.

Frank Buckelew may have inadvertently recorded some of the events at the time of the Kickapoo-Lipan Apache alliance. Old Fox and his warriors had come to talk peace, but later made off with many Lipan horses anyway. Some time after that, with the help of a Mexican national and a Texas rancher living near Fort Clark, Frank Buckelew escaped from the Lipan Apaches in Mexico. He saw his first U.S. soldiers at Fort Clark:

> I told them about the Indians watching a tribe in blue, and that I believed it was soldiers since I had now seen how the soldiers dress, for they were dressed just like the Indians had described the tribe in blue. The soldiers were astonished, and said they were in camp up on the Pecos for a month the summer before, and never saw a sign of an Indian.

[Frank Buckelew returned to Bandera County February 17, 1867, as he recalled:]

> The Indians were still making raids in Bandera county. Just before I came home, Charles Scheidemontel, was riding a wild horse and in crossing the Medina river it became frightened and threw him off, breaking his leg. Bladen Mitchell found him and took him to his house, and went after Dr. Downs. The doctor was too feeble to go alone, so his son, Ed Downs, drove his hack for him. The three started to the Mitchell ranch, the doctor and his son in the hack and Mitchell riding a mule. They were attacked by Indians in ambush, and Ed Downs and Bladen Mitchell were both wounded, but managed to stay in the hack and on the mule. The horses became frightened and out-ran the Indians, and they made their way to the Mitchell ranch. The doctor had three patients instead of one. Mitchell was shot with a poisoned arrow and his recovery was slow. All three of them finally got well, but Ed Downs and Bladen Mitchell were unable to work when I got home.

[According to the account in the Pioneer History:]

> While living on East Verde Dr. Downs, accompanied by his son, Ed Downs, and Bladen Mitchell, started over to Mitchell's ranch to attend Charles Scheidemontel, who had sustained a broken leg. They were attacked by a party of Indians, and Mitchell and Ed Downs were wounded, Mitchell being shot with a poisoned arrow. They outran the Indians and got back to the Downs ranch, and sent Calvin Dutcher to Bandera.

> A party of men went out there, among them George Hay, Robert Ballantyne, and O.B. Miles arriving about three hours after the fight. They followed the trail of the Indians for some distance, but the savages had such a good start they could not be overtaken. Both Ed Downs and Bladen Mitchell recovered from their wounds.

Judge Oborski's report of depredations of 1866 adds that they were "attacked by 8 Indjans on the Verde" and that Ed Downs "was shot badly first with the arow, 2d with bulet".

In the spring of 1867 some families pulled up and left Bandera County. Dr. Edwin Downs, David Monroe, William Curtis, their families, and perhaps others left in a group as Levi Lamoni Wight, living in Burnet County at the time, recalled the situation:

> I had a friend in Bandera, Dr. Downs, that was fiting up for going to Mo.[Missouri]. [He] had considerable properety and money. Said he would take me through in consideration of my help on the way. We struck a traid. I was to drive a team of 4 yoak of oxen and take my famely on the wagon. I took a portion of the team and got my famely and joined the Dr on the Selow [Cibolo Creek?] 9 miles from San Antonio in May, and we were soon on the road for Mo. That Indians were marauding the country, killing and robing the frontier, was one very great cause of our desiding to make this move, and they continued for ten years after we left. A great number of men, women and children were murderd in the amediat country that we left, Burnett County and the serounding countys. These with the unsetled condision of the late trobles, was our excuse for going to another country.

Charles Jack and Joseph Poor also left the county about this time. August Klappenbach moved to Austin where, some say, he served a term as mayor. O.B. Miles, four time chief justice and man for all seasons, also disappeared from Bandera County history.

Reading W. Black of Uvalde had spent much of the Civil War years in Mexico and continued to do business there after the war. He made a trip to Mexico as part of a negotiating team to convince the Kickapoo Indians to accept a reservation in the Indian Territory. Not long afterwards he was killed in his Uvalde store by G.W. Wall who held a grudge about a monetary transaction. In Document 101, Volume 4, <u>Texas Indian Papers</u>, J.W. Throckmorton wrote to L.V. Bogy, Commissioner of Indian Affairs, Washington, D.C. January 29, 1867:

> Having heretofore called your attention to the bands of Kickapoo and other Indians sheltering on the West bank of the Rio Grande in the vicinity of Eagle Pass, and above, and who are depredating upon the frontier of Texas, and presuming the Dept. desires all the information concerning them that is reliable, I take the liberty of forwarding herewith Copy of part

of a letter from the Hon R.W. Black of this State, who was requested by me to ascertain their disposition, locality, number and the prisoners among them.

Very recently the Comd'g officers of U.S. forces at Fort Clark attacked and broke up a band of these raiders while on one of their marauding expeditions. I approve of the suggestions of Mr. Black in regard to the removal of the Kickapoo and the probable chances of the others being induced to go with them.

Lipan Apache Chief Chiquito was killed by U.S. cavalry sometime in the late 1860s or early 1870s. Costilietos and other Lipans continued to raid the West Texas frontier. The Kickapoos had consolidated their position in Northern Mexico by staying on friendly terms with Mexican authorities and by making peace with the Lipan and Mescalero Apaches. The Mexican Kickapoos were not induced to go to any reservations until after Mackenzie's raid in 1873.

During 1867 many Comanches, Kiowas, and other Southern Plains Indians tentatively accepted reservations in Indian Territory. Comanche raiders left the reservations frequently until Quanah Parker's surrender in 1874. Chief Quanah's Kwahadi were the last Comanches to accept the reservation. Some Comanches, remnants of destroyed bands or young men seeking glory, were in Mexico or along the Pecos River, sometimes mixing with Kickapoos to make raids. Lipan and Mescalero Apaches still raided the Texas frontier, sometimes in Bandera County where Frank Buckelew recalled:

> In the fall session of district court in Bandera County, 1867, the grand jury found a bill of kidnapping against Custaleta, et al, and fixed their bond at $5,000. The case never came to trial for lack of the appearance of the defendants.

The Buffalo Soldiers were deployed that year. The 9th U.S. Cavalry took up positions along the San Antonio-El Paso road and escorted the mail stage and other travelers. A campaign by the 9th Cavalry against the Mescalero Apaches greatly reduced their raids into Texas. Meanwhile the 10th U.S. Cavalry patrolled the Red River in an attempt to cut off the Plains Indians who were raiding into Texas. The 10th Cavalry was also called upon to enforce peace on the reservations.

In the spring of 1868 Len Hough and his wife were camped on the Medina River, west of Bandera City, making cypress shingles as Frank Buckelew remembered:

One rainy day he decided to go hunting. He took a muzzle loading rifle, but left his pistol with his wife for protection. After hunting for some time he decided to go home. He was nearing his camp and to his surprise he saw an Indian standing on a hill just above him. The Indian's back was toward him and not seeing any more near, he took a shot at the redskin. When the savage jumped in the air and began yelling with all his might, four other savages appeared on the scene. Uncle Len had no time to reload his gun so ran with all his might toward his camp. His wife hearing the report of the rifle and the wild yells of the savage, seized the pistol and ran out to see what was the matter. Seeing her husband and the four Indians after him she ran toward him. When they saw she was armed they retreated. Uncle Len and his brother, Pleas, followed the trail, but were unable to find them any more or learn whether the Indian was killed or not.

[From the WPA survey of county archives:]

At a meeting of Bandera County citizens held at Bandera on Wednesday, March 25, 1868, with Judge James Davenport presiding, a resolution was presented and unanimously adopted, reading in part:

> Resolved that the general commanding the Fifth Military District be hereby memorialized; that our citizens are being frequently murdered by a remorseless foe, that our property is forcibly wrested from us, and our minds are constantly harrowed by painful apprehensions of empending danger. That since the removal of the cavalry from Camp Verde, we are without any protection. Wherefore knowing as we do the superior effectiveness of frontiersmen in protecting the frontier, we earnestly appeal to the commanding general, to encourage and assist us as far as may be consistent with his duty, in organizing Home Guards for our protection: respectfully representing that without such assistance, we are unable to organize effectually as the occasion requires. Without the approval of the military authorities, we dare not do the little towards organizing which might be within our power.

The resolution, signed by Chief Justice S.L. Chilson, lists four persons killed and two wounded, and numerous thefts and burnings. The depredations were chiefly in the valley of the Hondo, which at this time was "partially settled by industrious farmers and stock raisers." In consequence of these raids, these settlers "have abandoned the property they could not take with them and have moved their families to places of greater security," while "those who had preemption claims, with a view of settling, abandoned the idea, until they can feel more confident of effecient protection." The upper settlements of the Sabinal were also being broken up, and, the resolution recited, "a number of excellent families in the neighborhood of Bandera are, in consequence of these outrages, preparing to leave the country."

Indians were not the only ones to vex the settlers, whose troubles were ascribed also to Mexican and American outlaws and to the conflicting interests of cattle and sheep men. Whereas there had formerly been more than 50 families in the town of Bandera alone, there were now not more than 50 families in the entire county, of whom about 30 resided in the town.

Cattle, the staple of the barter economy in Texas, increased in value as new marketing opportunities opened up. Many cattlemen had sold cattle to isolated beef markets before the Civil War, but the main market for cattle in Texas before establishment of the Chisholm Trail had been the hide and tallow industry. Factories, mostly along the Texas coast, processed cattle hides for leather and turned the rest of the cow into tallow for candles and soap. With everyone's cattle roaming the open range, often across county and property lines, questions of ownership could be a problem. Each county's hide and animal inspector made important determinations.

In 1868 Leopold Haby went on his first roundup in this Marvin Hunter account:
> coming up in Bandera county to the ranch of August and Celest Pingenot. In the party with him were Jacob Koening, Louis and Ugust Rothe, Adolf Wurzbach, Ben Wernette, George Heyen, Bill Shoemaker and Justin Hans. August Pingenot joined the party and they hunted and rounded up cattle throughout the country around Bandera, penning at the ranch of Polly Rodriguez, at the Jack ranch, at the Bandy ranch, and at Bladen Mitchell's.

The Bandera region prospered as the cattle drives shifted westward from the Chisholm Trail. Bandera City was well-situated as many cattle herds were funneled through Bandera Pass to reach the Western or Dodge City Trail. In 1869 Charles Schmidtke, a New York miller, moved to Bandera County and formed a partnership with George Hay: Schmidtke & Hay, dealers in general merchandise. Charles Schmidtke also bought the Schladoer Mill. Like most general stores in the region Schmidtke & Hay took cattle, shingles, or other barter in exchange for their goods. Quite a few herds with Schreiner (Kerr County), Vance (Medina County), or Schmidtke & Hay brands went up the trail each year. In <u>The Trail Drivers of Texas</u>, C.W. Harris gave this account of a cattle deal Pat Saner and he made in Bandera City:

> In the spring of 1872 Pat Saner and I sold to Sam Jones and P.C. (John) Clark the GI and Circle S brands, estimating the cattle at 700 head, for a consideration of $5.00 per head cash. There were a great many three and four-year-old beeves in the herd, but it was considered a good sale. Pat Saner did all the trading--all I had to do with it was to rake half of the money into a shot sack, that being my interest in the brands. The money was counted out in Mexican doubloons, Mexican twenties and Mexican dollars on the table in the office of the county clerk.

Louis Schorp of Rio Medina became a fairly well-known cattleman along with his brother, Joseph, and brother-in-law, Joseph F. Spettel. Louis Schorp remembered:

> In the spring of 1873 John Vance, a merchant of Castroville, decided to drive a herd of cattle up the Kansas Trail. In company with my neighbors I helped to round up and deliver steers to Mr. Vance, this being my first work along this line. Bladen Mitchell, a pioneer of Bandera County, was engaged by Mr. Vance as trail boss. All of the cattle were received by Mr. Mitchell north of the Mormon Camp, where Mr. Mitchell had his herding pens, and what was known as the Mitchell Crossing.

> After delivering my bunch of steers I went over to Elm Creek, a tributary to the Medina River, where I found a crowd rounding up cattle for Perryman & Lytle, among whom were the Spettels, Habys and Wurzbachs. The following day five men out of this crowd, including myself, were going to Bandera to see the Vance cattle inspected and road branded.

10

State Police and Reserve Militia

In 1870 Edmund J. Davis was elected governor of Texas as a new phase of Reconstruction began. The U.S. military turned over authority to the civilian government of the state. Governor Davis set up state military and police organizations. A ranger regiment known as the Frontier Force was created. A Militia Act approved June 24, 1870 created two types of military forces, State Guard and Reserve Militia. A State Police bill was approved July 1, 1870. The Adjutant General of the state, James Davidson, was Chief of State Police and headed the militia and rangers for the governor. In the <u>Pioneer History</u> B.F. Langford remembered some of the Reconstruction years in Bandera County:

> All [state and county] officers were appointed by E.J. Davis, provisional governor of Texas, and they had to take the oath that they had never aided or abetted in the rebellion in any way, so there were very few who could hold office. The government would not allow us to organize ourselves into minute companies for protection against the Indians, and when Indians came into the country we had to send a courier to headquarters at San Antonio to notify the commanding officer who would send out a squad of soldiers, and these soldiers would march leisurely along the road for three or four days and go back and report that there were no Indians in the country. The Indians would be a hundred miles away before the troops reached here. [...]

> Indians have come right into the town of Bandera and taken horses since I have lived here. District court was in session at one time when Indians came in and stole horses out of a stable within fifty steps of the Duffy Hotel. The Indians that gave us the most trouble were the Kickapoos and Lipans who lived in Mexico, making their raids through this region and escaping across the border. Our government would not allow us to follow them into Mexico, but I remember one time our boys did follow

them across and severely punished them. One man of the party, named John Pulliam, was killed by Mexicans. I knew him quite well.

J.P. Heinen's store, located too close to the Medina River, was flooded out in 1870. He was getting by on carpentry work when he accepted the job of State Policeman for Bandera County:

> I was appointed to a position on the state police force, an organization created for the protection of frontier counties against outlaws. There were many bad men on the frontier in those days, generally in sparsely settled regions where they thought they could do as they pleased. To arrest and bring to trial these criminals was the purpose of the organization of the state police. From one to three men in each county were appointed on the force. I was the only one in Bandera county, and I served two years, resigning at the end of the second year. The pay was $60 per month, and we had to furnish our own equipment, horses, arms, etc. The pay was wholly inadequate considering the risks we were constantly called upon to face.

[H.J. Richarz, a ranger captain in the Frontier Force, wrote to Austin about problems south of Bandera County:]

Fort Inge 16th March 1871

General James Davidson
    Chief of Police [etc?]
    Adjutant General
    State of Texas

Sir:

I would most respectfully inform You that at the town of D'hanis in Medina County exists a state of lawlefsnes, which needs very much the action of Your Police Department.

Lately a freedman named Richard Edwards has been murdered in cold blood by a man named [J.?] Huberlin, about ten witnefses had been present, the Justice of the Peace of that Presinct had been informed at the same day, but he failed to take prompt measures to arrest the murderer who is still at large. An other good citizen named A. Porna was mutilated by a young man named Sam Lohman who lives at the Sabinal in Uvalde Co. but as yet the offender is not arrested. Fighting, nightly disturbances, assaulting peacefull citizens is a dayly occurence. Liquor is sold at the place by the dram without licence. Cattle stealing by a combination of men living in the vicinity of that town is going on with impunity, and the stock raisers are to much frightened to inform the Authoreties of it. The Justice of the Peace and Constable there are inefficient men and both connected in bufsnefs and by evry sanguinity with a number of the most dreded Rowdies there.

My own lands stock and residence is near that place. I am well aquainted with all the people there, so the lawabiding citizens of Dhanis and environs have entreated me to send this petition to Headquarters as my station as Ranger Captain may secure me of acts of violence and revenge by the above mentioned gang of desperados.

Therefore I would most respectfully suggest that two efficient policemen should be stationed at the town of D'hanis, but independent officcers from other Counties not related or connected in any way with the population there.

It is a central point, on the most frequented road to Mexico, the passage of most all fugitives from Justice, horse and stock thiefs.

Personnally aquainted with _all_ the people there I could not recommend any man from there for that Office who is a resident of Medina County.

I remain General
    Yours most respectfully
    H.J. Richarz
    Captain Frontier Force

P.S. I can give the assurance that the policemen to be stationed at that place will have the assistance and cordial sympathy of the great majorety of the people of Medina Co. who are in general a loyal, lawabiding people and the presence of State policemen at D'Hanis will have such a salutary effect upon that gang of lawlefs men that they will either leave or cease to commit outrages.

    Yours most respectfully
    H.J. Richarz

The Bandera County Reserve Militia: 1870-71

Governor Davis put forth plans passed by the Texas legislature for a voluntary State Guard of Texas. Any eligible men not enrolled in the State Guard were required to be in the Reserve Militia. These racially integrated military institutions foreshadowed the National Guard.

General Order No. 1 directed county sheriffs to enroll State Guard and Reserve Militia including all males between the ages of 18 and 45. Payment of a $15 fee granted exemption. According to the Act: "In time of war, rebellion, insurrection, invasion, resistance of civil process, breach of the peace or imminent danger thereof, the Governor shall have full power to order into active service the military forces of this State."

According to the State Library's catalogue information, Bandera County's Company E, 14th Regiment (infantry), Reserve Militia, formed on August 1, 1870. The muster roll gives the company's station as Bandera. The company's activities are unknown, but regulations required the men to have regular drills. Possibly they were only called into service by the governor to guard polling places during elections. Kerr County's company of Reserve Militia functioned as a ranger company, but this may have been unique.

Arthur Pue was appointed captain of the Bandera County company. He was the county's hide and animal inspector for many years. The inspectors carried the region's cattle brands and marks in their heads and made inspections at the roundups.

Samuel C. Mott was 1st Lieutenant, A.J. Stevens was 2nd Lieutenant. The sergeants were George Hay, John R. Preston, W.H. Mott, and Andrew Mansfield. The corporals were Samuel H. Davenport, W.H. Davenport, Henry Hamilton, and Hugh Duffy. Frank Fox was "musician" which usually meant bugler.

The names among the 95 privates reflect a rich ethnic and religious diversity in the county: There were Methodists, Catholics, and Latter Day Saints. Bladen Mitchell was among the Episcopalians. Ethnic origins included English, Irish, French, German, Mexican, Polish, and Scottish. The original Afro-American population of Bandera County had come as slaves and they were gone after the Civil War. The popularity of cotton as a cash crop brought a larger population of Black cotton workers in the 1880s, but only a few individuals and families of color lived in the county during the 1870s. Andrew Jackson was a buffalo soldier veteran who came to Bandera in October 1870 after serving three years in the frontier forts. He lived with his wife, Mariah, in Jackson Hollow and served as a school board trustee for Bandera County's Black schools during the 1880s.

The State Guards and the Reserve Militia were precursors to the National Guard, but in their time were not generally popular. April 12, 1871, an amendment to the Militia Act reduced the price of the exemption fee from $15 to $5.

According to the State Library's catalogue information, Company E, 1st Cavalry Regiment of Reserve Militia, formed July 5,

The Ranger Companies Of Bandera County

1871. There is also no record of activity by this company, but, as previously noted, Kerr County's mounted Reserve Militia deployed as rangers.

Arthur Pue was again captain of Company E, S.C. Mott and J.T. Stevens were lieutenants. Sergeants were George Hay, John Preston, Joseph Sutherland, and William Walker. Corporals were Isaac Stevens, Hugh Duffy, Joseph Rodriguez, and Samuel H. Davenport. There were 80 privates.

In the fall 1872, Adjutant General Davidson absconded with $37,454.67 of state funds, including $5,000 of ranger funds. He eventually surfaced in New Zealand where he died in 1885. Governor Davis appointed his nephew, Frank L. Britton, to the position November 15th.

Also in 1872, according to Adjutant General Britton's report to the governor, 46 counties had failed to comply with General Order Number 1. One hundred two regiments or 720 companies formed in 1872. Only 15 companies had arms and only 3 companies bothered with uniforms.

<u>Muster and Pay Roll</u> of Captain <u>Authur Pue</u> Company of Reserve Militia in the service of the State of Texas, from the <u>1st</u> day of <u>August</u> 187<u>0</u>, to the [blank] day of [blank] 187 [blank], both days inclusive

1. Authur Pue   Captain

1. Saml. C. Mott   1st Lieut.
2. A.J. Stevens   2nd Lieut.

1. George Hay   Sergt
2. John R. Preston   "
3. W.H. Mott   "
4. Andrew Mansfield   "

1. Sam H. Davenport   Corporal

2. W.H. Davenport   "
3. Henry Hamilton   "
4. Hugh Duffy   "

1. Frank Fox   Musician

Privates

1. Adamietz John
2. Andervald John
3. Anderval Walick
4. Austin W.H.
5. Andervald Anton
6. Bandy Hugh
7. Benton John T.
8. Benton Floied L.
9. Benton Geo. W.
10. Bandy John J.
11. Ballantyne Robert
12. Beakman A.M.
13. Click Rufus
14. Convoer A.C.
15. Casey Samuel
16. Cocke M.T.
17. Chipman David A.
18. Cebula Ignacio
19. Davenport W.H./// Corporal
20. Davenport Sam. H./// "
21. Doroma Antonio
22. Dugosz Constantine
23. Fagen Christopher
24. Fellows C.W.
25. Fox F.W. ///
26. Gibbons Redmond
27. Gobble James
28. Gonzales Santos
29. Gonzales E.
30. Hicks F.L.
34. Heinen Joseph
35. Hinds W.S.
36. Hester William
37. Hester Alexander
38. Heinen John
39. Hutchinson Granville
40. Jureski Leonard
41. Jones Saml.
42. Jackson A. W.
43. Jones W.H.
44. Jackson Andrew
45. James J. Jones
46. Kline Frederick
47. Knapick Frank
48. Kalka Joseph
49. Kindla Joseph
50. Langford Isaac B.
51. Laxson Thomas
52. Lewis G.W.
53. Langford J.B.
54. Laxson Dallas
55. Marquis Geo. W.
56. Martinez Felix
57. Myrick William Jun
58. Moncur A.M.
59. Moravits Joseph
60. Montague Chas. Jr.
61. Mefser Willia
62. Mefser Thomas
63. Mitchell Bladen

31. Hough J.P.
32. Hamilton Henry ///
33. Haiduk Chas.
64. Merrik Kinvan
65. Merchant James
66. Minear Joseph

[/// - indicates the name has been crossed through on the original document. Four names were crossed out as errors making the total of privates on this document 62. Numbers 61 and 62 above are "Messer". From the remarks section:]

#12–has joined John W. Sansoms rangers
#19–Corporal–[name entered as private in error]
#20–Corporal
#21–Mexican Birth
#25–Meusician
#26–Served 6 yrs in State Service before the War
#28–Nex birth
#32–Corporal
#34–U.S. Postmaster
#38–State Police
#45–joined Kelso's Rainging Company
#56–Mexican Birth
#66–joined Capt. J.W. Sansoms Ranger Co.

[supplemental roll (separate muster roll page):]

63. Mickle B.F.
64. North W.G.
65. Norris Jasper
67. Pue W.H.
68. Pue Robert
69. Pue J.A.
70. Pyka John
71. Pingenot August
72. Pingenot Celestin
73. Rodriguez J.P.
74. Ramsey William
75. Reed D.D.
76. Reed J.V.
80. Shirley George
81. Sutherland J.L.
82. Sheppard Joseph
83. Stevens Isaac W.
84. Shirley C.S.
85. Schmidtke
86. Tevim C.
87. Tafola James
88. Taylor R. M.
89. Taylor John M.
90. Taylor George B.
91. Witter L.H.
92. Wight L.H.

77. Rodriguez Joseph
78. Sheppard R.B.
79. Sheppard W.A. Jun.
93. Walker J.W.
94. Walker W.A.
95. White J.H.

[There are no remarks on the supplement.]

MUSTER ROLL of Captain <u>Arthur Pue's (E)</u> Company <u>1st</u> Regiment Cav. R.M., Organized in <u>Bandera</u> County, [blank] A.D. 187[blank]

Arthur Pue	Captain
S.C. Mott	1st Lieut.
J.T. Stevens	2nd Lieut.
George Hay	1st Sergeant
John Preston	2nd "
Joseph Sutherland	3rd "
William Walker	4th "
Isaac Stevens	Corporal
Hugh Duffy	"
Joseph Rodriquez	"
Samuel H. Davenport	"
Frances Fox	Musician

Privates

1. Adamitz John
2. Anderwalt John
3. Anderwalt Walick
4. Anderwalt Anton
5. Austin W.H.
6. Bandy Hugh
7. Benton John
8. Benton Floid L.
9. Benton George W.
10. Bandy John
11. Ballantyne Robert
41. Langford B.F.
42. Laxson Dallas
43. Marcus George
44. Martinez Felix
45. Myrick Wm. Jr.
46. Moncur A.M.
47. Morawitz Joseph
48. Messer Willis
49. Messer Thomas
50. Mitchell Bladen
51. Meret Kinyan

12. Click Rufus
13. Casey Samuel
14. Cocke M.T.
15. Chipman David A.
16. Cebula Ignacio
17. Dorame Antonio
18. Dugoz Constantine
19. Fagen Christopher
20. Fellows Charles
21. Gobble James
22. Gonzales Santos
23. Gonzales Erinear
24. Hicks F.L. senior
25. Hough Jm. P.
26. Haiduk Charles
27. Hay Alexander
28. Hinds W.S.
29. Hester William
30. Hester Alexander
31. Jureski Leonard
32. Jones Samuel
33. Jackson A.W.
34. Jones W.H.
35. Jackson Andrew
36. Jones James
37. Kalka Joseph
38. Langford J.B.
39. Laxson Thomas
40. Lewis Georg W.
52. Merchant James
53. Mickle B.F.
54. Morawitz Thomas
55. Mott W.H.
56. North Wm G.
57. Norris Jasper
58. Oborski Eugene
59. Pue W.H.
60. Pue Robert
61. Pieka John
62. Pingenot Auguste
63. Pue I.A.V.
64. Ramsey William
65. Reed D.D.
66. Reed Joseph
67. Sheppard Robert B.
68. Sheppard W.A.
69. Shirley George
70. Sheppard Joseph
71. Shirley O.I.
72. Trevinio C.
73. Tafolla James
74. Taylor R.M.
75. Taylor John
76. Taylor George B.
77. Witter L.H.
78. Wight L.L.
79. Walker John
80. White L.H.

[no remarks on this roll]

In January 1873 in the Thirteenth Legislature of Texas, Democrats gained control of the House. The Militia Law was amended to reduce the governor's powers. The State Guard was dissolved, those companies wishing to remain in existence were transferred to the Reserve Militia.

In January 1874, Governor Davis, defeated in the election, tried to remain in power. He called up the Reserve Militia. Only a portion of the Travis County company came to his aid. President Grant refused Federal support. Richard Coke became governor.

The dismissal of the full-time rangers of the Frontier Force in 1871 prompted many frontier counties to form minuteman companies. Although the mounted Kerr County Reserve Militia was active through the late 1870s, Bandera County apparently had discontinued its Reserve Militia company, forming instead, a minuteman ranger company in 1872.

11

The Frontier Force

A.J. Sowell gave this account of young captive Jack Hardy's close observation of 15 Comanches as they rode into Bandera County from Bandera Pass around 1870:

> From this point the Indians took the Bandera road and after darkness fell, passed through the town, two and two abreast, and crossed the Medina River. They stole a horse at the edge of town.

The U.S. Army lacked numbers and a commitment by the U.S. government to defend the Texas frontiers from Indian raids. The State of Texas determined to provide its own frontier defense. Among the discussions about how to proceed was General John J. Reynolds' recommendation for a telegraph line linking frontier minuteman companies (about 200 men). Contrastingly, on May 26, 1870, the state House voted unanimously for a bill providing for the formation of 20 companies of full-time Texas Rangers, about 1200 men.

There was still some ambiguity between civilian and military control of the state; the idea of a large contingent of full-time rangers met Federal resistance. In the compromise that was reached the state would pay the rangers and the army would provide some arms, equipment, rations, and forage. The rangers would be under state control, but their captains would occasionally make reports to the army to keep it informed.

Only 14 captains were appointed in July 1870 and they organized their companies of more or less 60 men each in August and September. Captains and surgeons were to be paid $100 per month, lieutenants $80, sergeants $54, corporals $52, and privates $50. Most of the 14 companies (about 740 men) were in the field by the end of September. Financing problems in November reduced the number of men in each company to 50 and by February 1871 the number of companies had been reduced to seven.

The captains of the Frontier Force were appointed by the state's Reconstruction Government. Lieutenants and sergeants were supposed to be elected by the men of the company, but there was some confusion among the companies in that regard and some were appointed by their captain. All officers had to take a loyalty oath, which was not unusual for ranger organizations, except that, since the war, some men had a problem with that.

While many of the men were recruited from the captain's county of residence, at least five Bandera County men served in these companies. James Jones served in Kelso's Company. Joseph Minear, Theodore Mimico, and A.M. Beakman served in Sansom's Company. Celestin Pingenot, a brother-in-law to Charles de Montel, was in Richarz' Company of mostly Medina County men. The companies were mustered into the service in Austin before being sent for "rations and forage" to the U.S. Army post nearest to their patrol areas. Captains Kleid, Sansom and others got their first supplies in San Antonio, while Captain Kelso had to go all the way to Fort Clark. They were given surplus military equipment when it was available, but the Secretary of War soon ended that arrangement, overriding the Department Commander, General Reynolds.

The effectiveness of the organization was hampered by poor coordination of supplies, lack or poor quality of field equipment, and weak state finances. Although the companies were generally cooperative with one another, they were further hampered, in view of indifferent leadership by the adjutant general, lack of a field commander. This situation was somewhat alleviated when the regiment was reduced in manpower and divided between the two most competitive captains. In some companies the men were inexperienced as outdoorsmen or were unfamiliar with the geography of their patrol areas. However, many of the men in the Frontier Force had grown up on or near the frontier and most became good rangers. They lived under the open sky, often without tents in all kinds of weather.

Although poorly supplied by the state in most respects, these were eventually the first companies of Texas Rangers to be equipped with repeating rifles. The new Winchesters were of a low caliber with rim-fire, low velocity bullets. They were subject to jamming without frequent cleaning. However, the rapid firepower of these rifles gave the often out-numbered rangers some advantage, particularly in December 1870 when large parties of Comanche, Lipan Apache, and Kickapoo Indians crossed into Texas from Mexico to raid the West Texas Frontier.

Like many of the ranger captains, John Sansom arranged for some of his men to get horses and equipment to qualify. The men supplied their own horses, but the state was supposed to provide weapons and food. By agreement, the U.S. Army would supply some equipment, but that was rare in practice and usually of poor quality. In some instances, the army actually asked for equipment, Richarz' Company's six tents, for instance, to be returned after a brief loan. Eventually official army support was withdrawn altogether.

Supplies were sometimes long in coming and it was often difficult to arrange transportation. Captain Sansom often bought food supplies in Bandera City, Comfort, and elsewhere. At one time he had to make explanation of his accounting and purchasing methods to the adjutant general. All the companies had problems with supply.

Captain	Residence	Company	Station
Franklin Jones		A	Fort Mason
A.H. Cox	Erath County	B	Camp Davidson
John W. Sansom	Kendall County	C	Camp Verde
John R. Kelso	DeWitt County	D	Camp Wood
H.J. Richarz	Medina County	E	Fort Inge
David P. Baker	Wise County	F	Thompsonville Station
Cesario G. Falcon	Nueces County	G	El Olmito, Lomo Blanco
E.H. Napier		H	(Zapata County)
James M. Hunter	Mason County	J	Camp Griffin
Jacob M. Harrall	Lampasas Co.	K	Camp Russell, Camp Pennall
H.R. von Biberstein	Gillespie Co.	L	Camp Degener
Gregorio Garcia	El Paso County	N	Camp Quadrilla
Peter Kleid	Comal County	O	Fort Territt, Camp Elm
James M. Swisher	Travis County	P	Camp Colorado

Sansom's Company

John William Sansom captained the ranger company stationed at Camp Verde in 1870. Born in Alabama in 1834, he was an early settler of the Currys Creek area where he married Victoria Helen Patton in 1860. He was a private in Callahan's Company in 1855 and captain of a minuteman ranger company in 1856 and another in 1858. During the Civil War he was sheriff of Kendall

County in 1862, a veteran of the Nueces Battle of 1862, and a Union captain. His brother, Jefferson T. Sansom, served as a private in the 1870 company.

The <u>Daily Austin Republican</u> reported August 25, 1870:

> Capt. John W. Sansom in command of Co. "C" Frontier Rangers, from Kendall county, reported Wednesday to the Adjutant General, to be mustered into service at once. The company with its full compliment of men reached here the night before, and as frontiersmen go into service with a full determination to do their part in suppressing Indian depredations on our western border.

[On the original muster roll the names are in one long list, last names first with rank, date of entry into service, and value of horses out to the side.]

Muster Roll of Captain <u>John W. Sansom</u>   "C" Company of <u>Texas Rangers</u> in the service of the State of Texas, from the <u>twenty fifth</u> day of <u>August</u> 18<u>70, for</u> the <u>term   one year in pursuance of G.O. No 3 Hdqrs state of Texas a.g.o. Austin Tex. August 3 1870</u>

John W. Sansom	Captain	$100
James C. Nowlin	Medical Officer	140
Charles A. Patton	Lieutenant	100

Lewis Nelson	1st Sgt	$100	Freeman Perkins	1st Cpl	$90
William Coston	2nd Sgt	100	John A. Nichols	2nd Cpl	75
Jas. K. Jones	3rd Sgt.	90	Albert Ammann	3rd Cpl	100
John F. Toller	Farrier	$65	John Colbaugh	4th Cpl	90
Gabe Munroe	Bugler	75			

Privates

Henry Baker	$75	William Manning	$115
Conrad Birchwale	80	Joseph Minear	60
A.M. Beekman	90	Geo. W. Nichols	65
James Benson	110	Wm. F. Nelson	90
W.H. Callahan	80	G.W. Nichols	50
Thomas C. Crews	110	John Parson	110
Sevano Chavice	100	Saml. B. Patton	100

Charles Cravy	$90	Geo. W. Patton	$50
John Davis	75	D.L.L. Prewett	50
J.C. Dollahite	100	Lewis Richardson	90
Thomas Frayne	80	John Rembling	75
Jas. T. Fanning	40	Serilda Ramides	50
Jessee A. Green	80	John Stukes	65
Benj. F. Green	50	Jefferson T. Sansom	75
Henry C. Gray	75	Simon Schneider	50
Wm. M. Gray	80	August Schaefereaster	90
L.C. Hearren	100	R.O. Tedford	110
Francis Keyser	50	Jacob Wesley	80
H.C. Lawrance	100	Charles Wagner	75
Lane Tarlton	100	Warren W. Worcester	100
Thos. M. Lacy	125	William Webb	80
John Light	80	A.J. Wilson	75
Frederick Leasman	125	Robert Wilson	50
Alexander Merritt	75	Joshua Welch	100
Theodore Mico [Mimico]	50	John Watson	90

I hereby certify that I have this day inspected and mustered into the service of the State of Texas, Captain John W. Sansom's Company "C" of the Frontier Forces of the State of Texas, for the period of one year in compliance with General Order No. 3. from Headquarters State of Texas, dated A.G.A. Austin Texas August 3rd 1870, and that the number of officers and men mustered in said company is as follows, viz: One Captain, One Lieutenant, One Surgeon, Three Sergeants, Four Corporals, One Farrier, One Bugler, and Fifty Privates,

Ira H. Evans
Austin Texas
August 25th 1870
[printed:]

I Certify, on honor that this Muster Roll exhibits the true state of the Company under my command for the period mentioned.

                                        John W. Sansom
  Place <u>Austin Texas</u>   Commanding.
  Date <u>August 25th 1870</u>   Capt. Co. "C"

The Frontier Force

Hodges Mills Kendall Co. Texas 2d Sept.

James Davidson
Adjt. General State of Texas

Dear Sr

    I have the honor to report that I proceeded to San Antonio with my Company in Obedianc to Orders from His Excellency E.J. Davis. Govoner and Commander in Chief.

    Immediately after my arrival in San Antonio I met with Mr Nuecom the Hon. Secretary of State. had an interud with him relative to General Rignalds furnishing my Company arms. Mr Neuecom Soon After talked with Genl. Regnolds about gitting Arms. The matter of owr gitting Arms was satisfactury as we thaught.

    So the next day Wednesday, 31 Aug. Secritay Nucom Capt. Jones - Capt. Clide - & my Self went to the U.S. Arsnal to Arrange about owr gitting Arms. And there were informed that the Arms that were there were the large Spencers, Cal 52 Armes that had been used and Condemed by the Government.

    For a little bit we did not know what to do, but Concluded that we had better not take the arms untill furthe Orders. That the State Arms would Soon reach Austin and That owr action in the Matter would be favourably [Consid due?] by the Adjutant general and Commander in Chief. & [---?] So I turned my attention as follows. I made Requesition for 30 days Rations and got them all except 18 days Rations of beef. I then asked for Transportation from Govrment. Could git non. I then Secured transportation from Mr Phillips, A Citizen of Bandara County. I Contracted with Mr Phillips to deliver in good order owr provifsion at Camp Verde at 75 cents per hundred lbs. I Sent a detail of men with the Supplys.

    I then proceeded to make Requisition for Corn - Obtained an order on William Steel (Governent Contractur to Supply Corn at that place) for the Corn - Soled the Order to William Steel - got the Money from Steel. I will by Corn at Camp Verde for my Comopany as far as my money [acs &c.?]

    I then proceeded to Kendall & Kerr County with my Co. where I expect to obtain Armes from the Citizens also Ammunition for the [pistols?] I will Start a Scout of 20 men to the Head waters of North fork of Neucesses & Sout fork of Llano Rvrs. the [---?] of this month.

    Also I made an effort to obtain Material from Goverment for Horse Shoing I could not git any assistance in that line, so on my own responsibility I purschaced of Elmendorf & Co. 1 Keg Hors Shoes - $9.00 1 Box Horse Nails $6.25 Ch - 1 hammer - 1 Rasp - 1 Piner 1 Draw Knife. Total Cost $18.75 Coin.

No Surgical Tools nor Medison Could be obtained from Govrnent for my Company So muy Physician on his own responsibility Mad a Small purchase &c until Some general arrangement could be made.

I will Communicated to Colonel Abram. C. Gillun at Fort Concho in a few days in Obediance to Colonel Reynols Orders.

Hoping that my action Since I left Austin will meet the approval of the Adjutant General and Commander in Chief and that as early as possible I may receive farther instruction from Head Quaters I will Conclude for the presant.

Yours Obt. & Respectfully

    John W. Sansom
    Captain Co.. "C" Frontier Forces Texas

P.S. Pleas addess me at Zanzenburg, Kerr Co.
    J W S
    C. C C

The patrols of Sansom's, Kelso's, and Richarz' companies formed a protection barrier around the northern, western, and southern boundaries of Bandera County whose hills, passes, and river crossings determined the routes of many Indian raids. The rangers found very little Indian activity their first few months of service. Some of the ranger captains on the western frontier began to think of making expeditions to the Devil's River or the Pecos River to attack the Indians and perhaps even crossing into Mexico to find Indians.

Sansom's company had reported to San Antonio at the end of August 1870 and the men were dispersed to their homes to find weapons. Soon detachments of the company were sent into the hills illustrating the captain's strategy to guard the passes and the Frio Water Hole:

Camp Verde Texas Sept 11th 1870
James Davidson
Adjutant General State of Texas

Sir

    This to inform you that I have Sent out Scouts as follows- Lieutenant Patton with 10 men is on Llanno Mntns 30 miles from this place Sargeant Costen with 6 men is on dividing Ridg of Guadaloupe

& Madena 20 miles from this place-- Corperal Colburv is on dividin Ridge of Madena & Frio mntns 45 miles from this place-- Sargeant Jones with 6 men is at the Head waters of Blanco-Curys Creek & Sisterdale Mntns-- Corperal Ammann with 5 men are at the extream head of Sibilo- Josana & Privilage Creek waters 15 miles from this place 2 men on Sick report-- 5 men on leave of Absence 4 day to Secure Guns. & the balance of my Company is in cam.

 I have large Arms Sutch as Spencers - Burnsides - Sharp - Shotguns Old fashioned Rifles & the like to arm about half of my Company. The other half have only 6 Shootim Pistols. I have Bought Some Powder & lead for my men, als[o] caps fo[r] which I will keep an account of.

 I have Conditionally Baught an Anvill Vice - Bellows - 1 pair Tongs - 2 hand hammers & hors Shoe Punch from Dr Nowlin (My Co.. Physician) by to Marvan Eauwing my Fariur will be ready to do owr own Horse Shoing. The Conditional pinch as of the Smith tools is provided it meets your approval.

 As Captain Jones passed near my Camp on his way up the Country & left 5 littl wild Spanish Mules for me an my Co.. for Pack Muls. I understand that they were furnished by Mr George Torrey. Without Saddles - Blankets - Cruprs - Ropes to pack with an to ty the mules with. I have baught Some Ropes & have taken the Saddles of Some of my Company for Pack Saddles. When will we git packing material.

 This is my Second report to you I think I have made mension of about all that you would wish to know of me. In my first Report [crossed out: to you & this: for which this is my] Second Report.

 I have written a Communication to Colonel Gillion to day at Concho.

 I have no late Indian news. You Shall hear from me as my Scouts returns.

 Yours Obt. & Respectfully

   John W. Sansom
   Capt. Co "C" Commding
    1870

[Captain Sansom:]

San Antonio, Tex., September 22nd 1870

James Davidson
Adjutant General Stat of Texas

Dear Sir

I will be at this place about next wednesday to git my Company Arms. Where will they be. I would like to have Pack Saddles. Cropers & Breast Straps for Pack Saddles - Blankets to go under Pack Saddles - Ropes to tye on Packs. And Ropes to tye up Pack Mules.

Docter J.C. Nowling of my Co.. has furnished himself with a Pack Mules to carry his meddisons. Lieutenant Patton of My Co.. & my Self have furnished our Selvs with an extra horse each for the good of the Service. Will you allow us Forage for them, And also Forage for 5 Pack Mules.

I have hired Citizen Teamsters to take our commissaries to Camp Verde, hope it will meet your approbation

When I return to San Antonio I will call at the Post Office for Orders from you.

My Company are all in the mountains above Camp Verde. There are no Indians in this Month on my part of the Frontier.

Hop you will come to See us After a while.

Yours Most Obediantly & Respecfl

    John W. Sansom
    Capt. Co. "C" Frontier Foces

P.S. I Received you Teligram Stating that my Arms will be at this place about next Monday. I will bring a wagon after them
    J W S
    C.C.C.F.F.

[In October Captain Sansom had the following inventory:]

58 Winchester Carbines, 12,000 cartridges, 5 McLellan saddles (old trees), 5 pack mules, 5 stake ropes, 1 horse rasp, 1 set of tools, 3 coarse files, 1 spade, 30 yards of picket rope, 2 axes and 1 common tent (worn).

Septer 27, 1870

Camp Verde Texas
Adjutant Gen.. James Davidson

Dear Sir

I have previously made a report of the Scouts I Sent out in the month of September, but have not mad a full report of what they done & of there discoveries. In the month of September there was no Indians in this Country between Llano River & Bandera Town on the Madena River. Lieutenant Patton found an Indian Old Camp some 80 miles from this place, and about due west, I Suppose the Indians camped there last winter there was 36 Camp Fires also wigwams, Cattle & Horse Bones in grate quantities. I do not know what Indians they were.

 I have the Honor to be your
  Obediant Servant

   John W. Sansom
   Capt Co.. "C" Frontier Forces

 Frank Kaiser and others raised around the Currys Creek area were in Sansom's Company. It was some time before Captain Sansom confidently reported, "I have my men well trained for rangers." Frank Kaiser's <u>Reminiscences of a Texas Ranger</u> illustrate the youthful exuberance the captain had to deal with:

> While searching for this village we separated so as to scout the country more throughly and were upon strict orders not to fire a gun on any account. There were about four men in my division while crossing a hill we came upon a bear of good size. We asked ourselves, and each other, what to do with him. Someone suggested roping him--which was no sooner said than we began to try it. He would throw the rope off but Bob Tedford let him run through his rope and caught him around the body. Mr. Bear began to march off, dragging Tedford and horse towards a deep ravine. We saw that something had to be done. Henry Gray and I threw out ropes on him but could not hold him with our horses. We had to get our ropes [off] but how? I got off my horse and tried to kill him with my dirk knife but could not.
> Then Gray tried it and failed. We were in a predicament. Knowing that the officers were waiting, and expecting Indians any minute, Gray jerked out his revolver and shot him. We got our ropes and scampered. We expected a dishonorable discharge but the Captain [or Lieutenant Patton?] didn't say anything [and] we were careful not to let anything like that happen again.

Kelso's Company

 John R. Kelso, a DeWitt County resident originally from Missouri, organized Company D stationed at Camp Wood. A.A. Kelso was his lieutenant. William W. Kelso served as a private in the company. It was a good time to get young men out of DeWitt County considering the hazards of the Sutton-Taylor Feud. The courts had ceased to function as witnesses were intimidated or killed. Many in the region tried to avoid the growing fury in their own way. A faction of the Taylor side, which included John Wesley Hardin, went on a cattle drive that year.

[John Kelso:]

>Headquarters Company D. Frontier Forces
>Camp Wood Texas, Oct 11th 1870

General James Davidfon
Adjt-Genl of Texas
Austin Texas

General:
    Upon my arrival at Fort Clarke, texas, after rations and forage for my company, I was informed by Capt Corbin, the Comdg Officer, that I would have to furnish my own transportation for the same, therefore I have the honor to inform you that I was compelled to keep two wagons for that purpose.
    The distance from here to Fort Clarke by the shortest <u>wagon</u> road is 75 or 80 miles, and I find that it will take <u>two</u> teams on the road all the time to Supply my company in rations and forage.
    I am unable to hire <u>heavy</u> teams for lefs than Six ($6.00) Dollars (coin) per day: if I can do So I will employ the cheapest I can find.

>Very Respectfully
>your Obt Servant
>
>>John R Kelso
>>Capt Comdg Co. "D" Frontier forces.

In the following muster roll, "Date of Entry into Service" is given as September 10, 1870 for each man. Their station is given as "Camp Wood, Kinney Co Tex". All are stated to have served one month and 20 days, except for Edward Stapp who served one month and 13 days. Rate of pay is stated as $50 per month for privates, including the bugler. Corporals' pay was $52 per month. Sergeants' pay was $54 per month. The surgeon's rate was $100, the lieutenant's was $80, and the captain's was $100. Written across the column headed "Last Paid" is the statement, "Pay due from Enlistment." The names are in one list down the left side.

Muster and Pay-Roll of Captain John R. Kelso's Company ("D") of Frontier Forces, in the Service of the State of Texas from the 10th day of September 1870 to the 31st day of October 1870, both dates inclusive.

Died: Stapp Edward. shot and killed accidently near Camp Wood, Tex. Oct 23d 1870

1. John R. Kelso Captain
2. A.A. Kelso   Lieutenant
3. A.J. Hodges Surgeon
4. Patrick Dolan 1st Sergeant
5. John Sugden Sergeant
6. Winceslan Garza Sergeant
7. Speed, Eustice H Corporal
8. Christall John Corporal
9. Letch Christian Corporal
10. Yonke, John Corporal
11. Davis Wm T. Bugler
12. Autrey G. T. Private
13. Antonis Estevan
14. Avant B.F.
15. Bush William
16. Colter Thaddeus
17. Cano, Encarnacion
18. Connoly James
19. Davis George
20. Delameter John
21. Esparta Eugene
22. Edgar John
23. Elius, Viciente
24. Frichs, Ernot
25. Felatta Simeon
26. Foster Buford
31. Houston James
32. Hodges, Samuel B.
33. Haelsbeck Adolph
34. Hahn, Joseph
35. Jones, J.A.
36. Jeffries, William
37. Kuykendall Samuel
38. Kelso, William W.
39. Kotmied, John [Kotwied]
40. Long A.N.
41. Mahood James
42. Marcos, Costes
43. McGee James
44. Macarrio Villenve
45. Milroy, John
46. McCarty William
47. McCloskey James
48. Nesbitt, Newton
49. Odom, James C.
50. O'Bryan T.
51. Parkerson August
52. Rodgers John W.
53. Smith H.E.
54. Swenson August
55. Starnonsky Henry
56. Snyder John C.

27. Gusman Manuel
28. Girron, Casimero
29. Gonzalas Antonio
30. Gerhart William

57. Samudio Antonio
58. Stone George
59. Williams Richard
60. Wiener, Saul H.
61. Weimers Christoph

I certify on honor that this Muster-roll exhibits the true state of the Company under my command for the period Mentioned.

Place = Camp Wood, Kinney County Texas
Date = October 31st 1870.

John R Kelso
Captain Commanding Company "D"
Frontier Forces.

[Captain Kelso reports:]

Headquarters Company "D" Frontier Forces
Camp Wood, Texas, October 4th 1870

Genl James Davidfon
Adjt Genl of Texas
Austin, Texas

General:
I have the honor to report my arrival at this place yesterday and encamped my Company on the right bank of the Nueses River. Owing to the heavy rains of the past ten days, and the limited amount of transportation under my control, I was delayed in my March; as I found it necefsary on account of heavy roads to lay over on the Medina River and made short-marches from there to the Rio Hondo.

From partial observation I am asfsured that this position my command now occupies is an important one, as it is near the main trail, and where the Indians separate into small bands in their incursions into the neighboring Settlements. The country on either side of the Nueses Valley is rugged and broken, the bare hills rising to a height of 600 or 700 feet, and all so nearly alike that for persons unacquainted with the country it is hard to distinguish land marks.

In this connection, I would respectfully invite your attention to the fact that I and my Command are perfectly unacquainted with the various trails and pafses through the mountains, and having come here determined to do my duty, I desire to be able to follow the Indians even into their haunts, in order to break up their excursions and theiving in our country. In order to do this it is absolutely necefsary that I have authority to enlist or employ one or two more men, who know this country throughly from here to the Rio Grande as Guides. I can obtain two men in this valley whom I am satisfied are conversant with the whole region of country around here.

    I find that my Company consists of 64 men rank and file. two men [Gor. Kildee?] and [Gro.?] Taylor having been mustered in by you a day or two after you mustered in my whole Company. One of my Men Private Hahn has never reported since the date of muster, and I would suggest that I be allowed to drop him from the Rolls, and to enlist a man in his place as guide.

    I have the honor to be
Very Respectfully your obt. Servt

    John R. Kelso
    Capt. Comdg Co. "D" F.F.

Headquarters Camp Wood, Texas,
December 3d 1870

General James Davidson,
Adjutant-General State of Texas,
Austin, Texas,

General:

    I have the honor to Submit the following Report of the operations of my Company ("D") from the 7th day of November to the 2d day of December 1870, for the information of the Commander in Chief, viz:

    On the 8th day of November, 1870, I ordered Sergt Sugden with [10?] men to take station near Pecan Lake, for the purpose of placing men on the high peaks nearby, to watch the several trails leading into this Valley. These points, from information which I gained from the citizens residing in this neighborhood, Seemed to have been a favorite pafs through which the Indians traveled to and from the Settlements northwest of here, consequently I deemed it advisable to have it closely watched: the high hills presenting great naturall advantages in aid of this object. The Sergeant, in addition to placing these look-outs, made Several Scouts out about 20 miles from Pecan Lake, acrofs the main river to the west Fork of the Neueses, in the vicinity of Pine oak creek. Pafsing up and down the main river. He failed to see any Indians nor learn of their movements. He returned to this place on the 11th of November.

On the same date I took [?] men, and proceeded down the river 15 miles; camped at a large Spring at the foot of some large Pecan trees, found good, grafs, and wood; on the 9th broke camp at 5 a.m. and traveled due South 23 miles, camping at an unknown Spring near Indian Creek finding plenty of good grafs and but little wood. On the tenth at 5 a.m. left here and traveled east of South about 18 miles camping at a lake about 15 miles South of the Neueses river. On the 12th left Camp at 6 o'clock a.m. and traveled a little west of the Llano, 20 miles, and camped where I found plenty timber and grafs. on the 13th traveled nearly west to heavy timber, distant about 18 miles from where I camped the previous night. [?] this rouge I could find no evidence whatever that there had been any Indians in that section for over two months. The citizens informed me that no Indians have been in Since the latter part of September; although, they are looking for them this Moon; and I hope to be able to catch them going in or out.

On the Same date (Nov. 8th) I despatched Sergt. Winceslan Garza in charge of ten men, up the main fork of the Neueses to its head thence in a Northeasterly direction to the head of the South Prong of the Llano River, returning midway between Kickapoo Springs and the main Fork of the Neuses entering the cedar breaks in the North Fork near Indian Hills (or Mountains) crofsing and following it to its mouth and then following the East Fork to Camp Wood. When crofsing the rough, rock Mtn (or divid) between the headwaters of the Nueses and Llano the Sergt came upon a trail which from following it for ten or fifteen miles he found, from coming upon some large rocks piled up with several names Scratched on them; to have been made by a party from Capt Sansom's Company. About eight or ten miles farther up the Sergt. came upon a herd of about 10 mules and 15 horses, which he found to be so wild that he nor any of his party could get near them. A little farther on he saw another herd of 3 Mules and of horses, which were as wild as the other. From Saddle Marks upon the Mules, he believes them to have been quite Gentle at one time. He saw nothing on his trip which Showed the presence of Indians in the country for a few Months past. The accompanying sketch will Show you the route [he] traveled. The nature of the Country is very rough, rocky and has plenty of good wood, water and grafs, except that portion lying between the head Waters of the Neueses [&] Llano. He found no Water between the Neueses and Llano.

On the 20th of November Lieut. A.A. Kelso, with 10 men proceeded up the East Fork of the Neuses to the Bullshead Mountain and thence to the Source of the North Fork, thence acrofs the Divide by painted Rock, thence through a dense Cedar thicket for 8 or 10 miles when he came into a more open and broken country and Soon came to the South Fork of the Llano near its Source crofsed the South Fork and traveled to the head of an unknown creek which he followed down to where it emptied into the South Fork, down which he continued to travel to where it formed a junction with the North Llano, up which latter Stream he traveled to [Elm], at which place he found the Camp of Captain Peter Kleid. Returning up the North Fork about 15 miles and thence acrofs the mountains traveled through Several dense Cedar brakes until he came to an unknown creek running east which he traveled down to where it formed a junction with another unknown creek; thence acrofs the divide to the edge of a cedar break, to the North Fork of the Nueces, down which he traveled to the Cedar Brakes, thence to Live Oak creek, down which he continued for about 20 Miles, from there crofsing over to the East Fork of the Nueses, coming in below Bullshead Fork, then following it down to Camp. He traveled about 250 miles and did not See any Signs where Indians had been during the present Moon. He was gone twelve (12) days.

In addition to these I have had several Small parties out acting as Scouts and Spies but there have been no Indians in here Since my company arrived.

Very respectfully
your Obt Servant

John R Kelso
Capt Comdg Co. D. frontier forces.

The red dots on enclosed map Shows the route traveled by Lieut Kelso

[The map Captain Kelso refers to is the basis for the map on page xv. The men were initially unfamiliar with the geography of their patrol area. The care with which the map was drawn shows their pride in mastering that geography.]

Headquarters Camp Wood, Texas,
December 26th 1870

Gen'l James Davidfon
Adjt-Genl State of Texas
Austin, Texas

General:

I have the honor to request permifsion to take 25 or 30 of my men, on or about the first day of February, 1871, and take Station at or near the Mouth of Devil's River and Sycamore Creek, on the Rio Grande, for 25 or 30 days.

I am Satisfied that I could do good Service in intercepting Indians at these Crofsing, besides the presence of troops would necefsarily compell the Indians to abandon these points as crofsing places to and from Mexico.

I am afsured by citizens of San Felipe, that I could get a fight at these points inside of a month, as the Indians are in the habit of pafsing and repafsing here with impunity.

I can forage my animals without any additional cost to the State.

Very Respectfully Your Obt Srv't

John R Kelso
Capt Comdg Co. "D" F.F.

[It is unfortunate that many of Captain Kelso's reports were written with a poor quality of ink and many of the surviving reports in the Adjutant General records have faded beyond readability.]

Richarz' Company

H.J. Richarz brought his family to Texas as refugees of the 1848 German revolution. From the ranch headquarters he established at old Fort Lincoln, he pioneered sheep raising and breeding in Medina County, sometimes in partnership with John H. Herndon. He commanded Medina County's Independent Battalion of home guards during the Civil War and later served as county judge of Medina County. The ranger company he commanded in 1870 was stationed at Fort Inge. From A.J. Sowell's account of Medina County resident Xavier Wanz:

> In this same year Capt. H.J. Richarz raised a company of rangers, of which Mr. Vance was Lieutenant. His commission was dated September 10, 1870. He was very active as a ranger, and recaptured many head of stolen stock and returned them to their owners. He was on a scout with twenty-three men when part of Captain Richarz's company had their desperate battle with Indians near Carrizo, and says if he had been there with his men they would have given the Indians a good whipping. When the Indians killed Riff and Captain Richarz's son (two rangers), Lieutenant Vance followed them, but could not over-

take them. He had just arrived at camp from a seven days hard scout when news of the death of the boys came, and although the men and horses were tired, they went that night to where the men were killed, and at daybreak took the trail and followed it to the Nueces. Captain Kelso had a company at this time at Camp Wood in Nueces Canyon. The captain was gone, and the Indians passed out near his camp.

[The names are listed in one column on the left side of the roll. Date of entry into service: September 9, 1870. Station: Fort Inge, Texas. Pay due from entry into service.]

Muster and Pay Roll of Captain <u>H.J. Reicharz</u> "E" Company of <u>Frontier Forces</u> in the service of the State of Texas, from the <u>Ninth</u> day of <u>September</u> 187<u>0</u>, to the [blank] day of [blank], 187[blank], both days inclusive.

1. H.J. Reicharz Captain

1. Haver Wanz [Xavier] Lieutenant
1. Woodbridge JE Surgeon
1. John Dickson 1st Sergeant
2. [Jltis ?] Seraphin Sergeant
3. Joseph Leman Sergeant

1. Jean Battot Corporal
2. Henry Hartman "
3. Alfred Eckhard "
4. E.G. Ritter "

1. Ben Andreas Farrier

1. William Byfield Bugler

1. Battot Crist Private
2. Bohls Frank
3. Bitiger Lorenzo
4. Brown Harry
5. Byri Joe
6. Blackney Tom
7. Brown James
8. Biggar James
9. Cox Ben
10. Decker Carl
11. Etter Guttlieb

12. Englehart Paul
13. Fox Frank
14. Hans Gabril
15. Huhner Albert
16. Husser Joseph
17. Haberie Frank
18. Haller August
19. Junjaman Peter
20. Krebaum D.
21. Kienlo John
22. Karn John

Muster Roll – continued

23. Leusmeyer Stephen
24. Lacey J.B.
25. Martin John
26. Munme August
27. Monge Frank
28. Myers Edward
29. Meuger Michael
30. Minder Emil
31. Nester Valentine
32. Priff Joseph
33. Postel Hermann
34. Pigenot Celestine
35. Reicharz Walter
36. Roerne Charles
37. Radke William
38. Sathof Jansen
39. Schott Ben
40. Witney Stanislaus
41. Hans Leonhard
42. Nagle Joe
43. Burl Joe
44. Burl Ben

I Certify that the above [is ?] True Muster of Capt H.J. Richarz Company of Frontier Rangers and that I this day Mustered Said Company into the Service of the State of Texas San Antonio

James Davidfon
Adjutant General
State of Texas
Sept 9-1870

I Certify, on honor, that this Muster Roll exhibits the true state of the Company under my command for the period mentioned.

H.J. Richarz
Capt. Front. Forces Commanding Co. E.

[Captain Richarz set up old Fort Inge as his ranger station and made this report (A.J. Sowell has related accounts):]

Fort Inge, Uvalde P.O. Oct. 15th 1870

Col. James Davidson
Adjutant General
Austin

Sir

I have the honor to acknowledge the rect of Your circular dated Sept 22 [?] and am ready to furnish You with the required statements as soon as the blanks come to hand.

This Company E. arrived at this station on the 24th Sept. I remained four days at the [camp?] to put the quarters in order as far as could be done the same being in a very dilapdated state having a long time served for shelter to cattle and hogs.

On the 28th Sept. having rec reliable information that on the day previous a Sheepraiser named B. Fossed had been atacked and wounded in the shoulder by a party of six Ki-Ka-poos. I started with 24 men whose horses had mean while been shoed to the Nueces river. The medical Officer of this Comp had the bullet extracted from out the shoulder of the wounded man. No trail visible, the Indians were on foot and the heavy rain during the night had washed out any sign. I went down Nueces River 40 miles from thence back in a Western direction crossing the Nueces to the Chaparosa Mountains touching Fort Clark where I reported to the Comm. Officer Col. Corbin who I am happy to state afforded us with the greatest Kindnef all nefsessities. From thence with the approval of Col. Corbin I proceeded through the mountains to the west prong of the Nueces River and from thence following Valley of said River I arrived here after thirteen days absense havig discovered no Indian Signs.

Meanwhile fif days after the departure of Scout No. 1. on the 3 Oct. Lieutenant Vanz proceded with 24 men to the Frio River up said River to the west prong from thence across the mountains in West direction to the dry Frio and Nueces from thence South to the Leona River springs and returned after 10 days absence. No Indian Trail found.

Upon my return from Scout I found a communication from Colonel Bliss Post Commander of Fort Duncan stating that a band of Indians hav plundered Benavidas and Callahan Ranchs near Fort Ewell eight days previous taking a number of horses away etc. It was to late to follow this party of Indians having ascertained that they had crossed the Rio Grande for Mexico

There is no good grazing near this Station. therefore I keep only the best conditioned horses here, ready for any emergency at an hours notice and have stationed 28 men and thirty horses at a camp at the Nueces River 10 miles South West from here, keeping up dayly communication Lieutenant Wanz is in command there.

I have suggested to Colonel Corbin at For Clark the practicability of an expidition to the Devils River Mountains eventually to the Pecos River with part of the garrisons of For Clark and Duncan and to be joined of detactments my Comp. E and Capt. Kelso Comp. stationed at Camp Wood Col Corbin is very much in favor of the plan and has already communicated this to Gen. Reynolds. The trails leading to that part show to a certainty that the Lipans, part of the Ki-Ka-poos, and some small Comanche Tribes are encamped there.

In case the General Government or the State of Texas will not furnish any hay to feed the horses during the long winter night. I am at a loss to know how to keep the horses in condition for service. I have either to change the camps from time to time or buy scythes and the other nefsessary tools and have hay made by the Company. I would respectfully await Your Order in the premises.

The required payrolls I will promptly forward by next mail.

Your decision in the case of Bugler Wm. Byfield as stated in my communication dated 14 Oct [?] awaiting. I remain

    Very respectfully
    I am
        H.J. Richarz
        Capt. Comm. Comp E.
        Texas Frontier Force

Fort Inge Dec. 4th 1870

Col. James Davidson
Adjutant General
State of Texas

In haste at midnight before leaving I feel it my duty to report the state of things here. On the 19th Nov. I returned with a scouting party towards the Rio Grande without having discovered Indians Signs. Though the Kikapoos who are encamped partly only twenty miles on the other Side of the Rio Grande had sent me a message by two Mexicans that they would come in force to fight me they did not cross the river to meet me then.

On the 22d of Nov. I ordered my Lieutenat out with twenty three men to proceed up the Nueces River and return in a circuit touching the Rio Grande above Fort Clark and from there back through the Caparosa mountains. Now the Indians in Mexico as is proved by facts are in league with border Mexicans and have undoubtetly been informed by the same of our movements.

Instead to cross the Rio Grande River between the mouth of San Felipe creek or more above as they have done since twelfe months they with a force of about One hundred warriors forded the River a few miles above Fort Duncan, then divided in three parties, from which one consisting of thirty warriors or more have atacked Spears Rancho on the Turkey creek between this station and Fort

Duncan and driven away three horses. As soon the Spears brought the report fourteen men of my company who were at the detached camp under command of Dr. Woodbridge and Corporal Eckard startet to pursue the band of Indians. To day one man of this party has returned his horse beig lame and reports that they had found the trail and had pursued the Indians to the Clarissa creek about fourty miles from Fort Duncan and had recovered fife horses from the Indians. That the scout was in hot pursuit of the murauders, who had met Mr David Adams a settler on the Clarissa creek and had killed him and that the Indians had recrossed the Rio Grande four miles above Fort Duncan almost under the eyes of the strong <u>U.S. garrison there</u> a few hours before my men reached the river.---
Whether this scout Nov 2 has succeeded to get more horses from the Indians as where they are now I do not Know as yet. But I got information just now that those Indians have been seen at Piedras negras boasting that the rangers have been in their way but they would surely recross again to have more scalps and horses. Piedras Negras is only a rifle shot distance from Fort Duncan.---

 Tomorrow morning (I had made preporation this evening.) I was going to start towards the Rio Grande with the remaining force I held as reserve consisting of eight men, as just I had commenced this report three citizens residing one hundred miles from here near Fort Ewel on the Nueces, arived here at 11 o clock p.m. and reported that an other band of Kicapoos and Lipan Indians had run off all their horses, and they required my assistance to intercept them before crossing into Mexico. So I will take the last man I can dispose off at day break to moorow morning, and hope to succeed on my return. I will report minutely and correct any errors I may have made in this statement caused by errounos report.

 But meanwhile, Colonel, as these two tribes have declared war, seeing that the troops stationed at Fort clark and Duncan who could if they are not disposed to fight the Indians, at least guard the Rio Grande and send me report if the Indians have crossed. I am at a lofs how to protect 200 miles of frontier and 10,000 miles of teritory with my fifety men, if the United States Government alows these savages to hover on the bank of the Rio Grande watching my movement and crossing into Texas where they please? and recross when pursued near the U.St. Military station, and dispose of their plunder in sight of the U.St troops. I challenge any ranger company now on the border to show a greater amount of work done than my Company since I am here and I am determined to go on as long as my horses can walk on their legs, but I am convince that in order to punish these red devils from the other side one Company either Capt. Kelso' or Kleid's or any other ought to be stationed some wheres near the mouth of the San Fellipe. Capt Kelso s company at Camp wood it seems to me is to far from the Rio Grande to watch the upper fords above Fort Clark and it would not be advisable for me to locate my camp further than the Nueces River in which case I could hardly with my small command effectually protect the densely settled Counties of Medina Atoscosa and the Counties west from there.

In order to keep my horses in condition while not on scout I keep them in a detached camp for grazing day and night under strong guard, the only shelter I have for rations and forreage are six old tents I got the loan of by the Kindnefs of General Reynolds and now in the midle of our heavy work I have received order to turn in those six wretched tents. I hop Colonel that by Your Kind interferens General Reynolds will let us have these tents at least during the winter months. I remain Colonel

Yours respectfully

H.J. Richarz
Capt. Comm. E Comp
Texas Frontier force

[Kickapoo raiders killed Captain Richarz' son and another ranger who were on their way back to Medina County on furlough.]

Fort Inge, Tex. Dec. 9th 1870

Col. James Davison
Adjudent General.

Sir:

Since my last report we had hard and bloody work here. I will endeavor to make this as short as possible, at day break on the 5th Dec. I started on a scout with fourteen men, and three citizens who had volunteered to scout the country between the Nueces and Rio Grande in order to intercept that band of Indians who stole the horses a hundred miles from here near Fort Ewel. That same day I met messengers from Fort Dunkan who brought the news that about 300 Comanches and Kiowas and about 200 Kickapoos and Lipans divided in parties from 50 to 100 warriors all armed with Rifles, spencer Rifles, and pistols besides their customary arms are sweeping this part in every direction. Before I left I had ordered my Lieut. to keep the force held in reserve at the Post in readinefs to mount on a half-hours notice. This party had just come in from a fifteen days scout to the devils River Mountains.

Twenty Five miles from the Rio Grande, I met a messenger & some U.S. Officers who informed me that the scouting party of my Co. I had mentioned in my last report under command of Dr. Woodbridge, our medical officer who had volunteered, & Corporal Eckhart consisting of fourteen men (one man having been left behind, his horse got lame) On an open prairie twelve miles from the Rio Grande had overtaken that band of Comanches who killed David Adams & two mexicans near the Pendencia, had gallantly charged them, and had stood their ground against seventy well armed savages and defeated them killing eight warriors and wounded about fifteen. I ascertained at the same time that this band of Indians after they were beaten had retreated towards the Rio Grande, and that Dr. Woodbridge party had buried one of my Rangers, Lorenze Biediger who fell in the commencement of the battle, and were camping near the battle ground to rest their worn out horses. So I turned with my Command towards the lower Chaparosa creek; not finding the trail of the Indians there, I made for the Nueces. During the night of the 8th December, my guide whom I had sent towards the Eagle Pass Road to meet a spy there returning to my camp, informed me that another band of Indians had appeared near my Post at Fort Inge in overwhelming Numbers had attacked two of my Rangers at the Blanco, 16 miles east of Fort Inge, and had killed them. Their names are Walter Richarz (my son) and Joseph Riff. Another band being Kickapoos had been seen near Uvalde riding in the direction to the Frio River. I broke up in the night arrived before daybreak at the Post and found to my satisfaction that Lieut. Wanz had started with the Reserve force on hand in hot pursuit of the murderers of my son & Joseph Riff. Before day-break the same night that party who returned with me, had started in a Northerly direction to fall in the trail of the Lieut. or eventually to intercept the savages on their way to the Canadian River or Indian Reserve. With the last three men I had I intended to start at Day Break the same night towards the Rio Grande to assist Dr. Woodbridge's party, as I was informed that old Castro the Chief of the Lipans had avowed at Piedras Negras that he would revenge his red brethren for the loss inflicked by Dr. woodbridge's party upon their allies. But I met the Doctor coming back into the Post, who had no loss than the man above mentioned, and carrying the shield of one of the Commanche Chiefs killed in the action as a Trophae. The report as above stated is correct in substance. Dr. Woodbridge reports that he can not praise enough the bravery & fighting qualities of my men. Without a moments hesitation this little band had charged seventy well armed savages (three of my men were absent on a reconoitering scout when the fight commenced.) The savages had formed two battle lines on a rising ground, and had soon outflanked my small band. The Indians fought like Demons first, & when an Indian tumbled down his horse dead or got wounded, their places were instantly filled out with warriors from out the second line. Dr. Woodbridge stunned by a blow upon his forehead by an Indian fell off his horse, but several of my braves though fighting themselves against overwhelming numbers came to his rescue, and in a second the Dr. had recovered himself so to join in the work again. His horse got wounded & lost. The Indians meanwhile seeing that they had to deal with a new sort of combatants gave up the contest & fell back, so did my men, they rallied about three hundred yards from the battle ground. I have to mention that when the action was in progress the three men who were on the reconoitering tour, drawn on by the heavy firing, joined in the attack on the left flank, killing a chief of the Indians. I hope that this lection given to the savages by that heroic little band of Rangers will do some good, & I am pretty sure that I shall be able to report another succefs in a few days.

At the same time refering to my last report, I would like to have some reinforcement at any rate to be authorized to fill up my company to the number as organized at first. My men & horses have not had any rest worth speaking off since my arrival here. The grass is getting worse every day, and as the tribes protected by the Mexicans, have a secure base of operation two hundred and fifty miles long, watching my movements under the eyes of the U.S. Garrison, having distinctly & formally notified me that they had determined to drive me from the place, and sweep the country to Bexar County, it is not reasonable to be expected that I can always successfully operate in every direction against a half a thousand well armed savages with thirty eight privates, not to mention that I am not able to have two strong scouts out in different direction at the same time: Though we will not count numbers, if we fight, I may loose to many men without having the satisfaction to destroy the enemy. If it was not for this cursed international law, I know very well what to do, to clean out these bloody savages on the other side of the Rio Grande.

I Remain, Colonel

    Yours
    Very Respectfully,

        H.J. Richarz
        Capt. comm E Comp
        Texas Frontier Forces

Fort Inge 21th December 1870

Col. James Davidson
Adj. Genl.
State of Texas,

Sir:
    I hereby acknowledge the receipt of four checks on the San Antonio National bank. Nr 97. for $46.66 Nr 98. $61.66 Nr 99. $53.33 and Nr 100. 46.66 in favor of Ambros Bohls, Frank Haberle, John Rothmann and John Karm respectively which I will forward to said discharged rangers.
    My two scouts who have been pursuing that band of Indians who killed Joseph Riff and Walter Richarz both of my comp. came in the post on the 13th Dec. The Indians having changed their sattle horses almost hourly had gained a start of about forty miles when my scouts who had joined near Camp Wood reached the headwaters of the Nueces. Our horses having had no corn for about twenty day having been on scout gave mostly out, so the Lieutenant was compelled to cease pursuit.
    I think I will have the horses in serviceable condition by next moon as I anticipate some more work then.
    I remain Colonel

        Yours most respectfully

            H.J. Richarz
            Capt. comm. E Comp.
            Texas frontier forse

[About the time Richarz and Kelso's companies were actively engaged, things began to heat up for Sansom's company as well. John Sansom reported:]

Camp Verde, October 27th 1870

James Davidson
Adjut. Genl.
State of Texas

Dear Sir
    This to inform you that on the fourth of this month I sent out a scouting party to the upper waters of the Medina, Hondo & Saco.

They returned a few days ago, made no discoveries of Indians worth reporting.

The same day I sent Lieutenant Patton with thirty five men, to the waters of Llano, Perdenallis & Guadalupe to watch the passways of the Indians. and to wait for me to come up with twelve other men & supplies, unless it became necessary for me to leave in persuit of Indians. The fourth inst. about 9 o'clock at night, one Mr. Huebner, living eight miles from San Antonio, came to me at Camp Verde. Huebner had rode all that day & night to 9 o'clock to let me know that the Indians had stolen several saddle horses from him out of his pasture. At that time I had but few men in camp. In twenty minutes after I got the word of the Indians Sargeant Nelson & seven men were on the march with orders to travel the entire night & all next day in order to get in front of the Indians at one of their watering places, generally known as the Frio Water hole and to remain there four days, then strike for Paint Creek (waters of Llano.) to meet me with supplies. In a few minutes after I started Sargeant Nelson, I sent a Courier to Lieu. Patton, informing him that there were Indians in the country, & to catch them if possible; and also to meet me at Paint Creek . So I started from this place the fifth and reached Paint Creek the eleventh inst.

Met Lieu. Patton & Sargt. Nelson & all the men safe in camp. Lieu. Patton made no discoveries of Indians.

Sargeant Nelson"s report is this.

My men & I rode the entire night of the 4th inst and the next day until night without stopping more that a few minutes at a time; reached Frio Water Hole about night put out sentinels; no Indians seen or heard untill about 9 o'clock at night; then there was a noise made by the Indians something like cattle. So the next morning we looked out for a trail. Found that the Indians had passed within four or six hundred yds. of Camp. We took the trail followed about four miles, came in sight of them; charged them, the Indians ran,

I ran them about fifteen miles, gaining distance on them all the time, and would have cought them but they ran into the cedar breaks of the Nueces, one in a place.

There was but four Indians. I captured six head of saddle horses, and two mules. Four or five of the horses are Mr. Huebner's the bearer of the information that there was Indians in the country. The Brands are HU and one grey horse branded HH and 13 One mule branded INO & 69 -- One mule branded MD and P The horses that were captured were very much injured by the hard service while the Indians had them. When the Indians discovered that they would have to give up the stolen horses they lanced two of them; one of which has since died. After our horses had rested a little at Paint Creek, I moved on to the head waters of the Llano, Nueces, & then to the waters of Devils River; made a thorough search in all that country for Indians, found none, but little signs except what was some months old.

The result of this months work is this.

I have satisfied myself that there is no encampment of Indians nearer than those in Mexico & am glad that I can report this fact to Head Quarters. And also that I can report that the minds of the citizens of this part of the country are fast becoming satisfied that they are to have permanent peace. That is they have full confidence that my company will keep the Indians out of this immediate part of the country.

I am glad to report also that the citizens are better & better pleased every day with the Govonors Administration.

I have also to report of finding many cattle recently <u>killed</u>, (a part of which were full grown) for their hides. Some of my scouts, on the waters of the Llano, saw the men supposed to be engaged in the business. My scout reported who they had seen, but before I could aprehend them they had left & I could not get them without riding 60 or 70 miles; so I let them go for this time

The names of the partie principally engaged in this business, and that were seen by my scout, are Taylars of Galispie County. I learn from reliable authority that there are bills of indictment against these Taylors in Galispie Co. for "Maverick" killing, & Please inform me if I need any Special order for making the arrest of such men; and when taken what shall I do with them & with the hides that may be found in their possession?

Before Concluding this report I must [do?] Justice to Sargeant Nelson Say that I am well pleased with him. As a man promt in business - Obediant to Orders to the letter - full of energy. And one of the best Scouts I ever Saw. Shoul Make a good Lieutenant or Captain.

I have my men verry well drilled for Rangers.

I am yours most Respetfully & Obediont Servant

    John W. Sansom
    Captain
    Co.. "C" Frontier Forces

[Excerpt from Captain Sansom's report of October 30, 1870:]

This is to inform you of the condition of my Company ("C") Frontier Forces. The men are in fine condition.

About 30 of my horses are in midling condition, and 30 quite lean.

There has been considerable sickness in the company for this country; such as diarhea, & colds: also a little fever from colds. There was but one case however that came up, not able for duty for more than one day at a time. There has been a great deal of rain in this part of the country since we have been out, and my company has been exposed in all of it

My pack mules are small and poor The pack sadles are too large for the mules, and without croopers, breast straps or blankets.

Except for the loaning of rangers from one company to an understaffed company, concerted actions or cooporation among the companies of the Frontier Forces was usually limited to shared intelligence about Indian movements into the settlements. In November 1870, Captain Sansom tried to get captains Kelso and Richarz to join in an expedition to the Devil's River. Captain Richarz ignored Sansom's request for 30 men for the expedition and may not have passed along the request to Captain Kelso. He criticized Sansom's plan, but, in fact, each of the three captains had come up with similar plans. Each had implied a desire to attack the Indians in Mexico.

Adjutant General Davidson had apparently given Captain Sansom's plan a verbal approval when the two men met in San Antonio, but had failed to inform the other captains. Even though he had received no word from the either of the two, Captain Sansom set out for Fort Inge after sending 30 of his men towards the Nueces River as a screen against raiders and for a later rendevous with men from the other two companies. Meanwhile a large number of Lipan Apaches, Kickapoos, and Comanches crossed the Mexican border to raid the Texas Frontier. Few Indians found their way into Sansom's patrol area that month, but on the outer frontier the activity was hotter. Captain Richarz had 2 or 3 detachments on scouts and apparently all of Captain Kelso's company was out on scouts.

Captain Richarz pointed out in his criticism of Sansom's plan, there were not enough rangers to protect the settlements and launch large-scale expeditions at the same time. December brought "hard and bloody work" as Captain Richarz said and plans of expeditions were reluctantly tabled. John Sansom:

Camp Verde, Kerr Co. Texas, Nov. 26th 1870

James Davidson
Adgt. Gen.
State of Texas
Sir

    I have the honor to inform you that my whole Company, with the exception of a few men to keep camp, and scout in this immediate neighborhood, will start today on a scout to the westward.

    The Scout will go out, following the divide between the waters of the Llano, Guadalupe & across the head waters of the Neweces.

    I shall communicate with my <u>spies</u> at St. Felipe Springs; and if they have learned any thing that will warrant me to go to the Pecos River, or any where else within my bounds to find an Indian encampment, I shall then call on the companies at Ft. Inge & old Ft Wood to accompany me; but if I find no good prospect of finding the Indians at <u>home</u>, I shall not call on the other companies, but scout within my own specified bounds. I shall be gone from twenty to thirty five days; it is impossible to tell just how long I shall be out; but I will communicate to you immediately on my return. If you should send a Pay Master this way, it would be better if you could let me know some fifteen days before hand, so that I can have all the men together; without some such arrangments, all my men could hardly be found in camp at one time

    I leave Corporal F. Perkins in charge of camp.

        Very Respectfully yours

            John W. Sansom
            Captain Co.."C" F.F. Texas

Camp Verde, Kerr Co. Texas, Dec. 24 - 1870

James Davidson
Adjutant General
State of Texas

    This is to report the service of my Company of Rangers for the month of December, and to report that I most effectually failed to get Captains Richardz and Kelsaw, and my Company to act with and in concert with each other against the Indians. I have already reported to you of having sent spies, to get the run of the Kickapoos and other Indians of Mexico & Pecos country. My spies went by the way of Uvalde, carried a letter from me to Capt. Richardz and delivered it about the 11th of November.

The contents of my letter to captain Richardz is this in a few words. "Go and see, or send your Lieutenant to Capt. Kelsaw and let us by a joint effort of the three Companies, try to kill some Indians." That we would guard the crossing on the Rio Grande River, to catch the Indians as they returned with their stolen property to Mexico: and then make an expedition to the Pecos River if we possibly could: I remained at Camp Verde until the 26th of November getting ready to act with Capt. Richardz and Kelsaws Companies against the Indians. Not withstanding I never received any letter from Richardz that he would or would not act. So I took it for granted that the other Companies would be ready and willing to act together: so I drove on as though I knew all was right (I thought So)

But before I go any farther with my report I beg leave to say that I do not think it was from any bad feeling to me, or bad motive in any way that Capt. Richardz did not act with me. Neither do I know whether or not he communicated the contents of my letter to Capt. Kelsaw. I know this much, there was no concert of action. I think I have said enough above to give you to understand why my action for this is as follows.

November 26th 1870, I ordered Lieutenant Patton with 30 men 30 days rations and 12 pack animals to march about due west to the extreem head waters of the Nueces River and from that point to communicate with me at Fort Clark if circumstances would admit. Otherwise if he discovered a large party of Indians or their trail leading into the country to fight or follow them, and that I would join in with other Companies, and do the best we could.

So the same day 26th of November I started for Fort Inge, reached Uvalde 28th Nov. saw and talked with some of Richards men, was informed that his Lieutenant had started to head of Nueces River on scout with 25 men, the 23d of November, that Capt. R had gone home but was expected in Camp soon.

So I remained in Uvalde till the 1st of Dec. then started for Fort Clark, reached there the 2nd remained at Fort Clark until the 5th inst. recd. no word from my Company from Lieu. Patton, so I with three men struck north in search of my Company. The 7th instant reached the head waters of the Nueces River, found no company; traveled down the River two days hard riding; the 9th inst. at night found my Co. on a trail of Indians. I think there was from 40 to 60 of them from the signs. There was at each camp from 10 to 13 fires. My men found one horse on the trail; one bow several arrows, one file, and some dozzen mocasins, bullets, bullet molds, and many other trinkets.

My Lieu. found the trail about 30 miles above the head of the Nueces River, followed it about 80 miles over as rough a country as any in Western Texas. As soon as I reached the commmand, I at once was satisfied that they were the same Indians that were in the neighborhood of Ft. Inge the 30th of November. I at once turned my command to the North prong of the Nueces River.

When I reached that point, found the Indian trail and learned from Sargeant Dolan of Capt. Kelsaw's Co. that the Capt. with part of his company was after the Indians some four days previous to that time; which was the 13th day of December.

So I remained near the Indian trail several days, thinking that there might be some other Indians behind that would be an soon, but none came. So I struck for Camp Verde and reached there the 22d inst.

Corporal Perkins and twelve men that I left at camp was all well. The Corporal informed me that no Indians had been in this portion of the country during my scout.

Right here I will say that the Indians have not taken a horse from my district since I have been in command here. And I will further beg leave to report that Capt. Kelsaw, Richardz & my Company could have acted in consert this last month, and could have got some Indians in fact.

My plan is to guard the passes of the Indian when they are leaving our border, then if we can't catch them, follow them to their homes and there break them up. I should feel disgraced, were I to belong the the Frontere service eight or twelve months and kill no Indians, & they constatly coming on our border. I think there is a considedrable band of Indians living on the Pecos River, that are depredating here, besides the Lipans & Kickapoos that are in Mexico

General, I wish to make an expedition against the Indians, and will give you my plan inside of fifteen or twenty days.

I aprehend no danger of Indians visiting this country before the full moon in February next; then I shall look for a small party of them in my district; but as soon as warm weather comes, we may look for them

Report of buglar Munroe & Private Serilda Ramedes (Spies) are as follows. We proceeded to Ft Inge, thence to Ft. Clarke, thence to, and above the mouth of Devil's River on the Rio Grande River traveling North. Then we went down the Rio Grande and found that a party had crossed at St. Felipe thence down to the mouth of the Losmoras, and found that a party had crossed there. We satisfied ourselves that they were Indians, then we struck for Uvalde as we were ordered; reached Uvalde the 24th of November. We learned from many persons that the Indians cross at the above named places frequently. So says Gabe Munroe, Buglar Co. "C" Frontere Forces. Our horses are very tired and considerably worn.

Your most Obedient Servant

    John W Sansom
    Captain Co.. "C" FF

At the time Richarz and Kelso's companies were too busy to make any expeditions with Captain Sansom. A detachment of Richarz's company had a desperate firefight with Comanches. Two rangers, one of them Captain Richarz' son, returning to Medina County on furlough, were surprised and killed by Kickapoo raiders. Apparently, all of Kelso's Company was out on scout at the time. Frank Kaiser's account suggests Captain Sansom had word of large raiding parties gathering in Mexico and the purpose of the expedition was to head them off before they reached the settlements:

> Then the Captain received word from the Indian agent that there was a big bunch of Indians coming in. He sent the company, in charge of Lt. Patton, up in this country, while he with three other men, Jeff Sansom, Jim Jones, and myself, went to Uvalde to get a company that was stationed there to come out and help us. When we got there the Indians were ahead of us and had whipped Captain Richer [Richarz]. He had sent out his company in three divisions, not knowing there were so many Indians, so that they had been too much for him.

[Actually, the detachment from Richarz' company made a good showing of themselves in the firefight with the Comanches. The deaths of the two rangers on furlough cast a shadow over the engagment. Frank Kaiser continued:]

> We [Sansom and his men] stayed there a few days, thinking to hear from our company, then we went to Fort Clark, expecting to hear there but could get no word so the Captain decided to hunt the company.

> We went up the Nueces River several days' ride. One day we stopped at the head of a little draw, some two or three hundred yards from the river. The Captain lay down under a cedar tree to sleep and rest. He had been on constant duty with us boys for we did not know at what minute we would be attacked. While he was resting, Jeff (his brother), and myself went to the

river where we found a campfire that was just dying out. We found some tracks and decided to follow the trail to see what was going on. As we left the river going up to higher ground we saw a wigwam. We hid ourselves and watched and soon discovered there were more wigwams but saw no one in sight so we slipped up and entered the nearest one. We examined the interior and ground around [it] which showed it had not been used for some time. We went back to our nooning place in a hurry for we had left against orders. The Captain had waked up and discovered we had gone before we could report our find. We got a reprimanding and then we reported our find. We were ordered to saddle our horses and investigate. We supposed this was the village we had been sent to hunt some months before which was now deserted.

We then went up the river and crossed. The Captain told us to fill our canteens but we did not. We had crossed water every little bit and did not want to burden our horses with unnecessary weight so we went on but found no water. The second day we followed a dry run back toward the river. We came in sight of a bunch of cattle. The Captain ordered one man to go ahead and kill a beef, calf or yearling. Jim Jones went. When he shot it, it rolled down the hill and we saw the water splash. We were soon there but the Captain stood by and would not let man or horse drink but a little at a time. It was awful hot and it had been two days and nights since we had crossed water. We skinned the yearling and went to some oak trees a few hundred yards away to cook dinner. After eating we three were sitting around, resting and talking. The Captain disappeared. We waited about an hour and began to get uneasy but all at once he came up with a skull in his hand. He then told us that he had an uncanny feeling since stopping and went out scouting around and had found we were near an old battle ground where he had fought during the Civil War. He took us out there where we collected bones and boots and buried them with the other graves. He showed us the cedar tree where he was standing guard under when he was relieved, and he had only taken one shoe off when the man who had taken his place was shot. It was the same tree he had taken his nap under when Jeff and I slipped off and found the deserted Indian village near by.

[Captain Sansom reported Indian raids increasing again near the end of January:]

Camp Verde Kerr Co. Texas Jan 31, 1871
James Davidson
Adjutant General
State of Texas

    Dear General

My report for this month of January, of my operations, will be included in the movements of three separate scouts viz.--

1st The first day of Jan. I took ten men with me and went into Kendall Co. scouting near, and along the line of Kendall and Blanco Counties.

I found no Indians, nor their signs, so on the 23d I returned to Camp.

2nd On the third of January Sargeant Nelson with twelve men, went to the divid between the waters of the Guadalupe & Llano Rivers he stationed his men across the divide and guarded the passways untill the sixteenth, when he returned to camp and reported having seen no Indians.

During the time that the above named scouts were out, Lieu Patton was in command of this post, with the balance of the Company ready to march in any direction that occasion should require.

3rd The 22nd news came to Camp that signs of Indians had been seen above here to the North & West: so Sargeant Nelson with 25 men went out in that direction I heard nothing from him until day before yesterday, he sent in a courier stating that he had found a trail of some 12 Indians going down the country

I have sent him more provisions, with instructions to guard that part of the country until the Indians return; or as long as he thinks necessary. Mr Nelson also informed me that he sent a scout to Capt Clide's Company, on the Llano, to inform them that the Indians are below; so that they will be on the allert, to intercept them if they should attempt to go out to the North of where he (Nelson) has stationed his scout.

Since writing the above I have heard again from Sargeant Nelson; he informes me that Capt. Clide has divided his men into two parties; one between the head of the Llano & Nueces, and the other North of there across the Llano.

    Very Truly Your Most
    Obedient Servant.
    John W. Sansom

Capt. Co "C" FF

Kelso's Company was among those disbanded by February 1871. The remaining companies were re-deployed in an effort to cover territory exposed by the thinned ranks. Captain Richarz was given command of three companies along the West Texas Frontier and Captain Sansom was given command of four companies along the northern sector of the frontier. The last seven companies:

West Texas		**North Texas**	
H.J. Richarz	Co. E	John W. Sansom	Co. C
H.R. von Bieberstein	Co. L	J.M. Harrall	Co. K
Peter Kleid	Co. O	David P. Baker	Co. F
		A.H. Cox	Co. B

February 4th Captain Sansom acknowledged receiving Special Orders No. 8 placing him in charge of the four companies and assigning them to the area north of Fort Terrett, Kimball County. He wrote to the Adjutant General that he was preparing to move his company to Jones or Shackleford County. Increased Indian raids and the discovery of a cattle-stealing operation (the Taylor brothers and other gangs) caused Captain Sansom to postpone the move until late March. He had been reporting the cattle-stealing since October 1870 and finally received a directive from the adjutant general:

Camp Verde Kerr Co. Texas Feb. 17th 1871

James Davidson
Adjutant General
State of Texas

General
    Your communication of Feb. 11th is received: informing me that lawlessness exists in some of the border Counties; such as cattle stealing, killing and branding unlawfully; and directing me to take the necessary steps for the arrest of all such offenders, and turn them over to the civil authorities for trial.

In January last, Sargeant Nelson had occasion to visit Capt. Clide's camp on the Llano, to act with them against the Indians; while traveling in Kemball Co. he accidentally found over one hundred hides which had no doubt been placed there by cattle thieves. Since that time I have directed Mr. Larramore - who is well acquainted in that part of the country - to watch their operations, and report to me if he found cause; he came to camp yesterday with the report that he had information that a party of cow thieves are now at work in Kemball Co. So today I sent Lieu. Patton with fifteen men, to arrest all such men and do by them as you have directed.

I have good reason to believe that in a few days, I can report to you the arrest of the Taylors and the gang who run with them.- However those thieves work carefully and I have no doubt, they have their friends to let them know when danger approaches.

Allow me, General, to express my opinion that the declaration of martial law in those unorganized Counties, for the suppression of cattle stealing, would do much to intimidate, and help drive such lawlessness from the border. It is believed that many of those men who are engaged in stealing cattle, kill more in a year than they pay taxes upon; but some of them, when they are brought before the courts, carry quite an influence in their own favor.

I think they would have a wholesome fear of a military court, that they do not have for the civil.

I am Sir
Very Respectfully
Your Most Obt Servt.

    John W Sansom
    Capt Co. C. FF

[Page] No 1

Camp Verde Kerr Co. Texas Feb. 28, 1871

James Davidson
Adjutant General of Texas

Dear General
    My report of scouts & Indians for February is as follows.- Feb. 1st three Indians or some other persons wearing moccasins and killing a cow with arrows made their signs twenty miles north of this. They traveled east from that place ten miles; thence south 30 miles crossed the Guadalupe river 10 miles to the County site of Bandera

Co.- The Sherif of Bandera Co. came to my camp at 12 o'clock at night, 24 hours after the Indians were in at the latter place to inform me that the Indians had been there; so 2rd Feb. I started a scout of 10 men in charge of private Thomas Crews, after them.-

[Page] 2

The Indians traveled east from Bandera passing four miles south of the County site of Kendall Co. From one Mr. Charles Cole they took two saddle horses; from that place they went on east to within 20 miles of New Braunfels; at that point they killed a beef. From the latter place Mr. Crews reports that he could not learn where they went. So after scouting, and hunting over that country several days, returned to Camp Verde the 10th instant. Sergeant Nelson who went out on a scout in January, reported to this camp the 15th inst.-; he reports all quiate on the head of the Guadalupe river with the exception of what I call cow stealing which is conducted in a scientific plan, as well as on a low down midnight plan.-

There are men who watch their chances and kill stock for their hides; they drag the hides into some secluded place, and at night go and haul them to where they can sell. There are other parties that have from

[Page] 3

one to eighteen hundred marks and brands of stock that they claim to have the right to gather.- They gather everything that they can sell; if caught with stock not their own, they will make some excuse that they did not intend to take the stock off; at the same time they will propose to pay for the beeves.- The 16th of Feb. private Geo. Learramore reported that he was very certain that the Taylors and their companions (cow thieves) could be caught.-

I have had learramore watching for them

The 17th inst. I sent Lieu. Patton with 15 men to arrest the Taylors, and all the cow thieves that he might catch stealing and turn them over to the civil authorities having jurisdiction over the county where the crime was commited.- I have sent out other small scouts for two or three days at a time to reconnoiter for Indians and signs.-

I have sent out two scouts after Indians on hearing that they were certainly in the country, and ascertained that there was none.

[Page] 4

Malicious persons put out falce reports on purpose to get up an excitment.

26th Feby Came two Mexicans to me with a letter from Mr. George Gallaher citizen of Medina or Bexar County. Gallaher writes yesterday at 12 a.m. 15 Indians came within 200 yards of my house and taken 5 Mules and 7 Saddle horses then struck in the direction of San Antonio. I at once ordered Sargeant Jones to take 10 men and go to a point 20 miles of this place where Indians frequently pass and there to guard that point 5 days and then return to camp. Same day 11 o clock at night an exprefs came to my camp sent by Mr. Henry Smyth of Comal County informing me that 15 Indians came near his house in open day in the morning and taken two of his children prisoners. Clinton Lafayett and Thomas Jefferson are the names of the children Clinton is about 11 years old and Jefferson near 7 years. Curier did not know which way the Indians went at once I had all of my Company assembled sent 2 men Buglar Munro and private Surilda Rametis as Curier to Captain Richard at Fort Inge to inform him of the Indians. I ordered Sargeant Nelson to Captain Clides with five men to inform him that the Indians were in

[Page] 5

and what the[y] had done. and to take a stand at some of the Indian pafses and do the best the[y] could. at 12 o clock at night Sargeant Nelson started also Munro as directed also I started at same time with 16 men and one citizen in the direction of Austin from this place for the purpose of heading the Indians if the[y] went that way traveled the balance of that night all next day to 7 Oclock P.M. Stoped and purchased corn for my horses. 28th 10 Oclock A.M. reached the point I was making for, a pass way for the Indians some 15 miles S.W. of Pack Saddle mountain near the Colorado River where I learned from a lady that 12 Indians had passed late the evening before. I taken the trail followed it to the waters of Willow Creek. 28 inst. the Indians killed a man by the name of John McCormick and wounded his brother Edward McCormick in the leg near same place young Waldrope and young Allhouse exchanged shots severl times with the Indians. the Indians using Revolvers and Rifle Guns Mr. Allhouse thinks he wounded one Indian badly. from there the Indians went to the Sandys. 1st March I reached Sandys nothing for our horses to eat 2, taken the trail followed them some 35 or 40 miles over a very rough country they traveled in various points of the compas as if they wished to strike in with other Indians. we were at that time within 12 hours of the Indians. Camped- had nothing for horses to eat. 3rd March traveled West zig zag on Indian trail some forty miles Indians gained a little on us. that day got some corn for our horses we are at this time on Llano. 4th March taken trail traveled a little north of west to

[Page] 6

Llano river. Indians struck due north after crofsing the river we traveled about 40 miles that day. camped at night grafs good. same night it rained a little and put out the trail so that we could not follow it. at that point I was some 80 miles from this camp the way I had to travel 5th March struck for Camp Verde reached here 7th March the Indians I was following are I believe Commanches or Kiowas and I think the[y] are the Indians that got Mr. Smyths Children

I must in justice to my men with me on scout say that I never have seen men more determined. some were truly sick when the[y] saw that it was impossible to catch the Indians and recover the boys which we were satisfied they had. I had all of my company at work. while writing this report curier came to this place and reports that 20 Indians made there appearance near Sisterdale Creek 30 miles east of this place. 2 hours before courier arrived I sent Doctor Nowlin with 8 men to that place to watch for Indians. So I sent no other scout. my horses being so completly tired out from hard service. Courier Munro just arrived from Captain Richards camp. he informed me that his men were hard at work.

Lieutenant Pattons report is as follows.

After leaving Camp Verde on the 17th we proceeded to the Guadelpue about 10 miles where we camped for the night on the morning of 18th left camp for the perdinales where we camped for the night. Wood, water and grass plenty on 19th we left camp and proceeded about 20 miles where we found a party of 14

[Page] 7

men engaged in marking and branding cattle. they had under herd about 700 head fresh branded, and about 50 unbranded all of which were calves. in the name of Mosley & Williamson & others. after duly considering their statement that all of them owned stock in that vicinity and all of those calves belonged to them and that they would stop branding as I had informed them that such was positively prohibited they were allowed to return to their homes we remained at their camp over night as wood water and grafs was plenty. On 20th after traveling about 13 miles we came upon 3 men with a four horse wagon loaded with hides James Taylor Thurman Taylor and Ed Jaynes. all these I arrested and sent to Fredricksburg under charge of Sgt. Coston with five men with instructions to turn them over to the Sheriff and take his receipt for the hides &c It seemed that those men had gathered the hides wherever they could kill them in the woods. We then proceeded to the west prong of James River where we camped for that night. we found wood, water, and grafs good. On 21st we left camp for Paint Creek. we saw great many head of Cattle which had been killed I suppose for their hides a distance of about 25 miles we found wood water and grafs plenty on 22nd we struck a wagon track which we followed about 6 miles where we found the wagon and 8 men encamped on the upper waters of Paint Creek. they had built a pen for the purpose (they said) of gathering Beeves & Mavericks. they had not yet gathered any. I informed them that all illegal gathering driving or branding was positivley prohibited they at once agreed to abandon their purpose and return to their homes. Finding

[Page] 8
wood water and grass plenty we camped for the night. I left camp on the morning of 23rd for the south Llano. about 4 miles from camp we struck a wagon track leading west towards the west fork of the Llano. following it about 8 miles we came upon a party of 8 men according to their statement the[y] came out for the same purpose as that of the party we had seen the day before. they having nothing in their possesion I could do nothing with them. but gave them the same instructions as I had the others. we camped with them we found them to be very generous they gave us corn to feed our horses at night. on the 24th we turned back in the direction of our camp of 22nd. when about 5 miles from camp we came upon a party of five men with a herd of Beeves on their discovering us they abandoned their Beeves and fled to a Ceeder Brake not far off. the brake being so dense as to render no hopes of aprehending them so we scattered the herd and left them and proceeded to camp where we remained until the 28th on account of our horses being so tired I thought it best to graize them a while. 28th left camp and proceeded to the extreme tributary of Elm fork of the Llano wood water and grass plenty. on 1st March left camp for the head waters of Devils River about 15 or 16 miles where we camped for the night wood water and gras in abundance. 2nd. we returned to Camp Verde having seen on our way a great many Cattle fresh branded Killed and Skinned, from what I have seen and heard from good sources I think there are quite a number of Cattle being illegally driven off Killed and Branded. Kimbell & Edward Counties. Charles A. Patton Lieut Co C. FF.

[Page] 9
Sargeant Nelson's report is as follows After leaving Camp Verde on 26th Feby 12 P.M. with the message from you to Captain

Clide I stoped about 2 o clock A.M. where we remained until daylight it being so cold we were obliged to stop to warm on the Guadelupe a distance of 12 miles. on the 27th we made about 45 miles and camped on the head waters of Elm Fork of the Llano at daylight stopped a few minutes to make some coffee having nothing else until we reached our journeys end we reached Captain Clides camp about half after three O clock P.M. Captain Clide not being present I delivered his message to the lieutenant. I then started to the main divide south of Captain Clides camp to get on the regular Indian pass following it back to the nearest point from Camp Verde having made no discoveries arriving at Camp Verde on 2nd March 1871.

    H.L. Nelson

No report of Sargeant Jones who had 10 men with him I suppose it was in Consiquence of -Jones- being discharged Some day.

The men with Jones Say that a party of Indians pass them in daylight at the pass I Sent him to, but before they could git readyd & git after them the Indy they were gone & that they never got in Sight of them again

I think that if Sargt. Jones had done

[Page] 10
His duty that I could have reported Something good

On page 6 I report 20 Indians 20 miles below here near Sisterdale an other report has just arrived that cause me to think there was no Indians at that point, &c&c

Will Conclude by Saying I am Your Most Obediant Servant

    John W Sansom
    Capt Co. C Comanding FF

Was compelled to run my report to March [&c?] in order to make my Scouts & Service more plane.

[Bandera and Kendall counties petitioned Governor E.J. Davis:]

State of Texas
County of Bandera

    To his excellency E.J. Davis, Governor of the State of Texas.

    Comes the undersigned petitioners. Citizens of Bandera County who would respectfully represent that they have learned with the most unfeigned Sorrow, that the Company of Rangers Stationed at Camp Verde, and commanded by Capt John Sansom has been ordered away.

Now therefore, your petitioners would state that they repose entire confidence in the honesty, ability, and valor of the aforesaid company of Rangers knowing that they are men who live upon this Frontier and whose interests are identical with our own

Therefore your petitioners do most respectfully beseech and pray that your Excellency do countermand the order directing the aforesaid Company to leave their present position, it being one where their services are much needed and absolutely necessary to the protection and prosperity of this and adjacent counties.

Dated this the 27th day of February A.D. 1871

Chas Montague J.P. Pct No 1 B.C.
T.C. Rine sherriff B C
J.P. Rodriguez J.P. pct. NO 4
W.H. Davenport J P Pct NO 2
James J. Jones
J.B. Langford
Wm G. North
J. [H?] White
George Hay
W.H. Mott
Thos. L. Buckner C. C.C. B.C.
Frank Fox L.M.
H. Hamilton
G. Shirley
J.J. Rodriguez
CS Shirley
T.T. Andress
W.H. White
Santos Gonzales
Erineo Gonzalez
Bales [Blas] Loya
Catarino Trevino
Otabiano Trevino
Bentura Garcia

Dimas Munos
W.B. Biggs
Henry Munoz
John Andeveverti [Anderwald?]
Geo. B. Taylor
John Adamietz
Samuel H. Jones
J.W. Sier
S.T. Christian
Arthur Pue
F.M. Buckelew
L.H. Witten
MH Langford
James Tafolla
W. Schultze
B.F. Langford
Wm E. Westerful
James Goffer

Boerne, Kendall County, Texas

The Frontier Force

28th Feb., 1871

To His Excellency
Governor E J Davis;

    The undersigned citizens of Kendall County hearing with anxiety and regret that Capt. John Sansom's Company now stationed at Camp Verde has been or is to be ordered elswhere would most respectfully solicit a reconsideration of such order if issued or determined upon, if not incompatible with the public interests.

    We take pleasure in bearing testimony to the zeal and energy manifested by Capt Sansom in his efforts to give protection to our section of the frontier, but it is at the same time true that the incursions and depredations of the Indians are at this very period more daring and serious than ever. At this time there is a large party of Indians in the Country, having taken large numbers of horses, and on Sunday the 26th inst taking captive several children -five- between Boerne and New Branfels, while three citizens were killed by them near Leon Springs, Bexar County, on the same day. Other mischief has undoubtedly been perpetrated of which we have not yet heard.

    Trusting that this petition will receive your Excellency's kind consideration, and that Capt Sansom may be retained at Camp Verde, we subscribe ourselves, with great respect. It is ascertained that these are an organized band from Mexico.

P.D. Saner	AM Bawnam
Henry C. King	Ph. F. Theis
H. WeneGer	AC BeversVorff
Ph Zoeller	A.W. Toepperwein
J.N. Everette	F. Phillip
H.G. Froebel	G. Stephan
Jacob Theis	R. Weufering
Henry Theis	Ralph Martinez
Ch Dienger	Anavato Martinez
Aug. Pfeiffersen	John F. Standeback
F Senz	Carl Leiwald
G.A. Toipperweim	Wm [Thuhfufor?]
T. Minnert	Bryce Little
John C. Bonnet	J.B. O'Grady
Ferd Lohmann	W. Dietert
	F. Schulze

A. Phillip   C. Roggorshache
Adam Schmars   F. Dierter
Anton Bergmann   Charles Braun
                                  F.W. Phillip
                                  Chr. Humbolt
                                  A. Theis

[John Sansom:]

      Camp Verde Kerr Co. Texas
          March 9th 1871

James Davdsen
Adjt. General State of Texas

Dear General
    In addition to my monthly reports I beg to Say that from all accontz their have been many Indians in the County this moon Had I not been gitten my horses up a little I [should?] have had Som 30 men at the head of Nuesses River, which would I think have done Some good. The Indians went South of me & 40 miles & Swng round North Keepin Considerate distanc from my camp my Self after Indians this moon, Make it allmost in possible for me to Start the 10 inst up North with my Company.
    I will Moov as Soon as Can get [?] Transportation. I am very anxious to git nearer my other Companies.
    I hav not had any report from other Companies than Captain D.P. Baker Co F. F.F
    Yours Obediently & Servant

        John W Sansom
        Capt Co. C FF

[March 19, 1871 Sheriff Rine wrote a letter to Adjutant General Davidson:]

      Bandera Texas March 19th 1871

Mr James Davisdon
Adgt General commanding
 astin Texas

Dear Sir

    We have forwarded from this county to his excellency Governor E J Davis, asking that Capt Sansoms company might remain at Camp Verdy the Indians have been depredating in this vicinity for Some time past and without protection we will be compelled to Stop buisinefs of all kind and fortify ourselves against their raids we ask your aid in retaining capt Sansom & his company at camp Verde

    Your Obedient Servant
    T C Rine. Sheriff
    of Bandera County

[Captain Sansom reported the difficulties involved in transporting rangers, equipment, and supplies:]

    Kerr County Camp Verde Texas March 18 1871

James Davidson
Adjutant General State
of Texas

Dear General

    This is to acknowledge receipt of Communication dated 20th Feby/71 & mailed 12th March. And to inform you that your directions will be carried out with all the promptness possible. Sargeant George Laarrimore with 12 men will Start up the Line to morrow. Keppin out from the way I will travel up and on a parellel line where Indians are most likely to travel. I with 2 men will leave here Monday next for Captain Coxes Company that is Stationed in Erath County.

    The balance of my Company will leave 23rd inst. provided I am not again desappointe in gitting Transportation. I Contracted with a Mr. John Brown to haul with 3 Ox wagons & team Some of my Co. Supplies at $1.50 Cerency 100 lbs for evry hundred miles - That is the best I can do, & am lucky to do that well. I am anxious to get to my new home -more so than you might expect.

    If I succeed in gitting my April Supplies from this place & along with my company I will do well. I hope balance; of my Supplies can be furnished me at my new Station. All other Oders & Communications will be Sent to me at Fort Griffin unless Your Honor otherwise Order. I am General Your Most Obt Srvt.

    John W Sansom
    Captain Co. C FF

P.S. Since visiting the [?] I have the promise of three mule wagons & Teams which if I git will be better than the Ox wagons Charles Schmidtke are the men that have the mule Teams.

    John W Sansom
    Capt. Co. C FF

           Fredericksburg Gillespie Co
               March 26th 1871

James Davidson
Adjt. Genl. State of Texas

    General my Company is at this place on Our way to Shacklford or Jones County. One wagon broke down or would have been a little ferther on our way. al is right now. All of my Co. here except Sargeant Lammons & 11 men that I Sent out Some days since - I will leave my Company in charge of Lieutenant & go to Captain Coxes Co. as quick as possible Will Send out Scouts on right & left of rout all the way up to where my Co. Stops. I just receive a letter from Rhodius & Co. to wit-

    Captain John W. Sansom, Dear Sir please let us know by return what arrangement have been made for your ferther Supplies. becaus from us you can expect none at or near Fort Griffin without an other Contract with the Govaner. Rhodius & Co. Therefor pleas let me know how & by whom my Company is to be Supplied in the future.

    Mr Mangald will delive this letter to you Mr Mangald is quite well accquainted with how we are gitting on & knows quite well what we need. General if you pleas give Mr Mangald an Audiance of 15 or 20 minuites for the benefit of the Frontier Service.

    Would be glad to hear from you as Soon as Suits your Convenance in regard to owr next Supplies

    Yours Respectfully
        John W Sansom
        Captain Co. F FF

Muster and Pay Roll of Captain <u>John W. Sansom</u> "C" company of <u>Texas Rangers</u> in the service of the State of Texas, from the <u>First</u> day of <u>March</u> 187<u>1</u>, to the <u>Thirtieth</u> day of <u>Aprile</u>, 187<u>1</u>, both days inclusive.

No. Names	Rank	Date of Entry Into Service	Remarks
1 Sansom John W.	Cpatain	August 4th 1870	
1 Patton Chas. A.	Lieutenant	August 20th, 1870	
1 Nowlin Jas. C.	Medical Officer	August 4th 1870	
1 Nelson Lewis	1st Sergeant	August 25th 1870	Reduce to ranks by request Apr 2nd 1871
2 Coston William	2nd "	"	
3 Jones Jas. K.	3rd "	"	Discharged Mar 5th. By Special Order No 20 Dated Austin Feb 25 1871
1 Perkins Freeman	1st Corporal	"	
2 Nichols John A.	2nd "	"	
3 Ammon Albert	3rd "	"	
4 Coopwood B.F.	4th "	Feb. 4th 1871	By order of the Adjt Genl State of Texas Appointed 4th Corporal Feb 4th Promoted to 1st Sgt. Apr 2nd 1871
1 Tollen John T.	Farrier	August 25th 1870	
1 Monroe Gable	Bugler	August 25th 1870	
1 Baker Henry	Private	August 25th 1870	

2 Brershuale Conrad	"	"	
3 Beekman A. M.	"	"	
4 Crews Thos. C.	"	"	
5 Chavice Siveana	"	"	
6 Cravy Charles	"	"	
7 Davis John	"	"	
8 Dollahite J.C.	"	"	
9 Frayne Thomas	"	"	
10 Fanning Jas. T.	"	"	
11 Gray Henry C.	"	"	
12 Gray Wm. M.	"	"	
13 Cerron L.C.	"	"	
14 Halloway Felix	"	Mar 14th 1871	(By Special Order No 22, from the Adjt Genl State of Texas, Dated Feb 16th 1871
15 Keyser Francis	"	August 25th 1870	
16 Lane Talton	"	"	
17 Larremore Geo	"	"	
18 Lacy Thos. M.	"	"	
19 Light John	"	"	
20 Merritt Alexander	"	"	
21 Manning William	"	August 25th 1870	
22 Minear Joseph	"	"	
23 Nichols Geo. W.	"	"	
24 Nelson Wm. T.	"	"	
25 Patton Saml. B.	"	"	(Promoted to 4th Corporal Apr 26th 1871)
26 Patton Geo. W.	"	"	
27 Richardson Lewis	"	"	
28 Rembling John	"	"	
29 Ramedis Sirelda	"	"	

30 Sansom J.T.	"	"	
31 Schnider Simon	"	"	(Discharged Mar 14th 1871 Special Order No 22 from the Adjt Genl State of Texas Dated Feb 22d 1871 at Austin Tex)
32 Tedford R.O.	"	"	
33 Wesley Jacob	"	"	
34 Wagner Chas	"	"	
35 Worcester W.W.	"	"	
36 Wilson A.J.	"	"	
37 Welch Joshua	"	"	Discharged by Order of Adjt Genl Feb 6th 1871 Special Order No 23 dated Austin Feb 27th 1871
38 Watson John	"	"	
39 Welson W.D.	"	February 7th 1871	By Special Orders No 23 Dated Austin Feb 27th 1871
40 White George	"	Mar 5th 1871	By Special Order No 20 Dated Austin Feb 25th 1871

I Certify, on honor, that this Muster Roll exhibits the true state of the Company under my command for the period mentioned.

Place <u>Fort Griffin Shackelford Co Texas</u>   <u>John W. Sansom</u>
Date <u>Aprile 30th 1871</u>   Captain Co. "C" FF

Muster and Pay Roll of Captain H.J. Richarz "E" Company of the Frontier Forces in the service of the State of Texas, from the First day of May 1871, to the Fifteenth day of June 1871, both days inclusive.

1 H.J. Richarz Captain
1 J.E. Woodbridge Surgeon
1 Haver Weinz Lieutenant
1 Rugg John 1st Sergeant
2 [Jltis ?] Seraphin Sergeant
3 [Lammer ?] Joseph Sergeant
1 Andreus Ben Farrier

1 Battot John Corporal
2 Hartmann Henry Corporal
3 Ritter E. G. Corporal
4 Brucks Henry Corporal

1 Battot Chr. Private
2. Bohl Frank
3 Brower Harry
4 Biry Joseph
5 Blackney Tom
6 Bunell Joseph
7 Cox Ben
8 Cox Hugh
9 Decker Charles
10 Dickson John
11 Engelhardt Paul
12 Husser Joseph
13 Etter Gottlieb
14 [Lungevann ?] Peter
15 Kieule John
16 Martin John
17 [Maemier ?] Frank
18 Menger Michael
19 Meyer Edward
20 Minder Emil
21 Macgelin Joseph
22 Nester Valentin
23 Poster Herrmann
24 Pingenot Celestin
25 Roene Charles
26 Rodke William
27 Saathoff Jansen
28 Schoff Ben
29 Witney Stanislaus
30 Linsmeyer Stephan
31 Cox William
32 Miles [Paulach ?]
33 Robert L. McCown
34 Hemhling Julius
35 Bader Emil

Place Fort Inge   I Certify, on honor, that this Muster Roll Date June 13th 1871 exhibits the true state of the Company under my command for the period mentioned.

> H.J. Richarz
> Captain Comm/g Comy E
> Texas F.F.

[From A.J. Sowell's account of Dr. J.C. Nowlin:]

In 1870 Dr. Nowlin was appointed surgeon to a company of rangers commanded by Capt. John W. Sansom and stationed at Camp Verde. In the spring of 1871 the company was ordered to Fort Griffin, on the Clear fork of the Brazos, and soon after arriving there went on a long scout to the head of the Big Wichita River. The Tonkaway chief, Castile, was along, as was also one of his warriors named Bill. This fellow was a good scout and trailer, and kept ahead of the company all of the time.

A detachment of the company had a skirmish with Comanches. Captain Sansom was planning a coordinated drive with the army into Comanche territory when his company was discharged from the service on May 30, 1871. By the middle of June all the companies of the Frontier Force had been disbanded. John Sansom sent this letter to the paymaster in Austin July 25, 1871:

Curys Creek Kendall Co Texas
Captain Evans

Sir
    Joseph Minear late of Company F Visits Austin for the purpos of having a Settlement with the Stat Paymaster for Ranging Services You will pleas wate on Mr Minear as readily as possible & Oblige -
    If you will Send me Certified Account for all that is due me from men of my Company you will Oblige
    There is due me from

        A. Schaeffereaster $10.00 $12.00
        A.M. Beekman   8.85
        F Liaseman $15 - or about that.

Liaseman was discharge befor you becom Pay Master
J.A. Green 4 or 5 dollars - Green was discharged at the time Liasman was - Also Certified Account for $100.00 for Transportation in the name of C.A. Patton. I am Captain Yours
Most Respectfully

        John W Sansom

After his ranger service Joseph W. Minear went on many cattle drives to Kansas and Iowa and in 1881 recorded his own brand in Bandera County. He settled on Laxons Creek and in 1888 married Harriet Emily Wight, daughter of Levi Lamoni and Sophia Wight who had returned with their family to the Bandera area in the mid1880s.

Before leaving office, Governor Davis made some attempts to revive the Frontier Force, raising companies from time to time along the north Texas frontier.

12

The Second Ballantyne's Rangers and Phillips' Company

Governor Davis had to find a system of frontier defense that was cheaper to maintain than a full-time regiment of rangers. November 25, 1871, he approved "an Act to muster into service minute men for the protection of the frontiers." Most of the frontier counties had 20-man minute companies at one time or another after 1872. Designations of companies included most of the letters between A to Z and numbers one through five including:

Company C Kendall County	1872-73	Lieutenant C.A. Patton
Company C Kendall County	1873-74	Lieutenant James C. Nowlin
Company #1 Edwards County	1873-74	Lieutenant William C. Calloway
Company E Kerr County	1872-73	Lieutenant Henry Schwethelm
Company E Kerr County	1874-77	"
Company #1 Kerr County	1873	S.R. Merritt (W/O Pay)
Company #2 Gillespie County	1873	George Laremore (W/O Pay)
Company F Gillespie County	1872-73	Lieutenant B.F. Casey
Company K Bandera County	1872-73	Lieutenant Robert Ballantyne
Company Y Uvalde County	1872-73	Lieutenant B.A. Bates
Company V Medina County	1872	Lieutenant George Haby

John Green, Bladen Mitchell's ranch foreman before the Civil War, was Company V's First Sergeant. Leopold Haby was a private and remembered in the <u>Pioneer History</u> that the company enrolled at Boerne November 6, 1872:]

> During the next few months we were kept busy scouting and trailing Indians. A bunch of redskins came down on a raid and stole horses near San Antonio and as far out as the Culebra. They secured 110 head and started west with them, camping the first night at Mescal Spring. Here they killed a horse and ate it. From here they went by Mitchell's Crossing, up Cypress Creek, thence west over the Verdes. They passed within two miles of the Davenport ranch, and near there killed another horse and had a feast, and then went on to Sycamore Spring, about five miles from where Tarpley is now located.
>
> John Green and some of the minute men were in camp on the Culebra, and George Haby and men were camped on Elm Creek when this raid took place. There were about twenty men in the two companies. We immediately took the trail which led out towards the head of the Hondo and Verde Creeks, the route being known as the old Indian trail. It was late in the afternoon, and after getting our supper we took a direct course to the Davenport ranch, where F.L. Hicks, a noted scout and Indian fighter, joined us, and we followed the old cattle trail to the Hondo, stopping about two hours before daylight to secure sleep and rest. Mr. Hicks stood guard and made coffee for us while we slept.
>
> We turned out and again got in the saddle at daybreak and made our way to Sycamore Spring, and just as we reached there we saw three Indians coming over a hill. They discovered us about the same time and took to the brush and got away. We made diligent search for the remainder of the band but did not find them, but we got the stolen horses, 110 head. After scouting around for sometime we decided the Indians had made good their escape, so we started back home with the recaptured horses, coming via Bandera. Some of the men went back on the trail in hopes of finding horses that the Indians had abandoned and we all met at Pingenot's that night. We received our discharges in 1873 and the company disbanded.

The second **Ballantyne's Rangers** were officially known as Company K Minute Men. They served from July 2, 1872 - June 1873. Twenty rangers were furnished with arms and ammunition. The ammunition was procured in Boerne, which may have been a regional organization and supply headquarters or just the nearest terminus of the stage from Austin. Each man furnished his own horse, food, and necessary equipment. They were paid two dollars a day to scout up to 20 days each month. According to J.P. Heinen who was a private in the company, the men often scouted more than the allotted number of days, but were not paid for any days over 20. The muster rolls indicate that they never reported more than 10 days of scouting each month. The days often coincided with the time of the light moon.

Full Moon	Scouting Days Reported
July 20	[no report]
August 18	13th - 23rd
September 17	14th - 20th
October 16	6th - 16th
November 15	1st - 10th
December 14	13th - 22nd
January 13	9th - 19th
February 12	11th - 21st
March 14	10th - 20th
April 12	13th - 23rd
May 12	9th - 19th
June 10	10th - 20th

During the early 1870s, settlers, including the Moore family, had begun to move as far west of Bandera City as the North Prong of the Medina River. Elizabeth and Joseph Walker Moore were killed July 4, 1872. Andrew Jones narrative of Ballantyne's Rangers:

> When the Indians killed Mr. and Mrs. Moore on North Prong of the Medina River, we took their trail the next day and followed it across the mountains. They went into a dense cedar brake where it was impossible for more than one or two men to go together. F.L. Hicks was with us on this scout and when we came to the dense cedar brakes our captain said it was unsafe to go in, and several of the men turned back, but Mr. Hicks said to me: "Andy, let's go in; we can whip every red rascal in there," so we went. It was a risky thing to do, but Mr. Hicks

was a man absolutely without fear and when duty called he was always ready to respond. It is said that Indians will not kill a crazy man, so I guess they thought we were crazy for entering that big thicket.

[From the Pioneer History:]

Not long after the killing of Mr. Moore and his wife the Indians made another raid and killed Mr. Moore's mother. The old lady was going to see Mrs. Curtis who was sick and a band of Indians attacked and killed her near the house of Mr. Walker. He heard her screaming and armed himself and repaired to the scene as soon as he could but the Indians had done their work quickly and were gone. Mrs. Moore was lying on her face, having been lanced to death. These raiding bands were followed by settlers but the county being mountainous and brushy eluded a successful pursuit and made their escape.

Eleven "muster and pay rolls" (August 1872 through June 1873) are at the Texas State Library. Even though the company organized July Second, the July muster roll is not in the state archives and may have been disqualified for some reason. Due to another unknown irregularity, the August roll seems to have been submitted to Austin a second time (in March 1873). As with each of the eleven rolls, it was written on pre-printed forms, each having the same preamble. Along with the roll for August 1872 are two statements made in March 1873:

State of Texas
County of Bandera
    Before me the undersigned authority this day personally came Robt Ballentyne Lt Comd/g Co. K. minute men, Bandera County, to me well known, and he declared that the foregoing muster & Pay roll was true and Correct and that he had Signed the Same as the Commanding officer of Said Company.
    Witness my Official Signature at Office in Bandera this 24th day of March AD 1873.

    Chas. Montague
    J.P. Prect No. 1.
    Bandera County

State of Texas

County of Bandera

I Charles Montague Justice of the Peace Prect No. 1. Bandera County do hereby Certify that Lt Robt Ballantyne with his men actually performed the Services Charged for, on the reverse hereof, and that they performed Scouting duty at that time, in accordance with the Law

Chas. Montague, J.P.
Prect No. 1, Bandera County.

Muster and Pay Roll of Company K, Minute Men, Bandera County Mustered into the service of the State of Texas on the 2nd day of July 1872.

1. Robert Ballentyn Lieut
2. Wm E Westerfield 1st Sergt
3. I.W. Stevens 2nd Sergt
4. Alphonse Gysels 1 Corporal
5. S H Jones 2nd Corporal

Privates

6. J.B. Langfort
7. Emiel Biancki
8. Leon Raccurt
9. H C McKay
10. Andrew Jones
11. James Merchant
12. Thom Click
13. Geo Lewis
14. J.P. Roduriguiz
15. A. Muncur
16. E.M. Ross
17. Jasper Norris
18. John Heinen
19. P.C. Clark
20. Roman Sanchez

I hereby certify that the foregoing Muster and Pay Roll of Company K, Minute Men, Bandera County, is correct, and that the services were rendered as above stated

Robert Ballantyne
Lieutenant Commanding Co. K, Minute Men,
Bandera County.
Station Bandera Date March 17th 1873.

I hereby certify that the above Muster and Pay Roll of company K, Minute Men, Bandera County, for the sum of $400.00, is a true and correct copy, the original of which is filed in the office of the Comptroller of the State of Texas.

W.H. King - Adjt. Genl.

According to the muster roll notations, the entire company was "on scout" from August 13 to August 23, 1872; 10 days, $20 for each ranger, total $400. Under the heading "Last Paid" is the notation "December" for each man. The dates on the accompanying statements seem to indicate this roll had been resubmitted in March 1873, perhaps before the February 1873 payment had been received.

Marvin Hunter has this account of Orlando Thallman (around 17 years old, if the date is 1872; if 13 years old, it was 1868):

> One morning, when he was about thirteen years old, he went out after the oxen, which grazed near the head of Privilege Creek. Seven of the oxen had bells on, and when he located these bells he went to the fartherest ones to round them up and drive them in, going at a gallop and hallowing them as he went along. He was gone about half an hour, and as he came back he found one of the oxen had been killed by Indians and they had hurriedly cut out and carried away some of the flesh. He dismounted and removed the bell, little realizing that perhaps savage eyes were watching his movements. Rounding up the remaining oxen he proceeded leisurely homeward, and when he reached town and informed Robert Ballantyne and some of the rangers of what had occurred they would not believe him, but in a few hours runners came in announcing that the Indians had stolen a lot of horses belonging to Bladen Mitchell and others.

Settlement of the county expanded east and west of Bandera City during the early 1870s. The Polly Settlement grew, and settlement along Pipe Creek began. J.P. Heinen:

> Polly Rodriguez sent a runner to town saying the Indians had chased a man named Gonzales to his place. As we were ready to go on a scout we went over to Privilege, six miles from town, in about an hour, but the Indians were gone. We followed them some distance. About a mile above where the San Antonio road

crossed Pipe Creek they killed a man who had been digging post holes. I think his name was Reeves, but I am not certain.

[Felipe Montez was killed in a raid remembered by Andrew Jones:]

>When in camp we had to stake and sideline each animal and put out a guard. A Mexican named Manuel, who had been an Indian captive for fifteen years, was our trailer and guide, and he was a good one. He knew just how to follow all signs and trails, and he thoroughly hated an Indian. One day we struck an Indian trail on Mason Creek and followed it to where the San Antonio road crosses Privilege Creek. Here the trail led up the creek, and we found a Mexican that had been killed by the Indians. The Mexican was at work building a fence when he was attacked, and when he was struck with a rifle ball he ran and took refuge in an old chimney which was standing where a frontier cabin once stood, and there he died. We found his body in this chimney in a sitting posture, with his pistol in hand ready to shoot. From there we went on and came to a house which the Indians had pillaged. They carried off a number of articles and trinkets, some of which we picked up as we hastily followed the trail. We then found where they stopped and painted themselves, preparatory to an attack on Jim and John Scott, who were clearing land, but they probably discovered our approach and fled, scattering in several directions, so that we could not successfully follow their trail. We then went to the Bladen Mitchell ranch and decided to go over to the Casey ranch on the Hondo and try to intercept the Indians as they came out of the country. We patrolled that region, two men each twenty miles apart scouting and observing signs, but without success. Then we crossed over to West Prong of the Medina, and here we found a bunch of wild beef steers. Our captain told us to kill them and we shot eight of the big fellows, and as wild as cattle ever got. Taking a supply of the beef we went on to the head of the Frio, Tom Click and I patrolling. We found a place where the Indians had left fourteen Indian saddles, and also where they had made a great many arrows and mended moccasins. We stayed there four days expecting the Indians to come and get their saddles, but as they did not show up we burned the rudely made saddles and left there.

The information in Document 235, Volume 4 <u>Texas Indian Papers</u>, Report of Indian Depredations, November 1, 1875, was compiled for use of the Constitutional Convention's committee on "Fron-

tier." The following excerpt of lists of names beginning January 1873, but includes at least a few names from 1872:
Bandera Co A H Barter & Chs Montague J Clk Dist CT reports

Jany 27 73	Ind Killed Joseph Moore & Wife & stabbed their 4 children & robbed horse of Santo Gonzalez. Killed Philip Gurtin Bernstein Ed Flores & Felipe Montez
Oct 6 73	stole from W J Weaver M. Montague & others 9H
May 74	" " Schmidke & Hay & others 30
Winter 74	" " W.W. Benton & S B Hugh 12
Summer 75	" " Preston 5
Sept 75	" " F.L. Hicks 2 L Schroder 2
	" " J.N. Elam 1 J Brooks 1 2

[Muster Roll, September 1872, with preamble and closing statement excluded:]

State of Texas
County of Bandera

I Charles Montague, a Justice of the Peace for the County of Bandera, do hereby Certify that all of the Scouts were in pursuit of Marauding bands of Indians, and that said Scouts or expeditions are necessary to the Safety and protection of the County.

Witness my hand at, Bandera this 11th day Nov. A.D 1872.

Charles Montague J.P. prc. No. B.C.

1. Robert Ballentyne   Lieut
2. Alphonse Gysels 1st Sergt
3. Isaac W. Stevens* 2nd "
4. H C McKay* 1st Corpl
5. S H Jones 2nd   "

Privates

6. J B Langford
7. Emile Bianchi
8. Leon Racourt
9. Wm Westerfield
10. Andrew Jones
13. George Lewis*
14. P. Rodriguez
15. Roman Sanchez*
16. A Moncure*
17. E M Rose

11. James Merchant
12. Thom Click*

18. Jasper Norris
19. John Heynen*
20. P C Clark*

[* absent with leave. Robert Ballantyne claimed $20 extra expenses. Perhaps to pay Manuel? John Heynen (Heinen) and P.C. Clark scouted September 18 through September 20 for four dollars each. The rest of the company scouted from September 14 to September 20, twelve dollars each, for a company total of $152. Under the heading "Last Paid" is the notation beside each entry "Never paid."]

Stationed Bandera. Dated, Sept. 30, 1872

[October 1872, summarized:

Robert Ballantyne claimed $30 extra expenses.

Robert Ballantyne, Alphone Gysels, S.H. Jones, William Westerfield, Andrew Jones, James Merchant, E.M. Ross, Jasper Norris, John Hynen, and P.C. Clark scouted from October 6 to October 16 for $20 each.

H.C. McKay, Emile Biauchi, Leon Racourt, Thomas Click, and A. Moncur scouted from October 11 to October 16 for $10 each.

George Lewis scouted from October 10 to October 16 for $12.

J.B. Langford scouted from October 13 to October 16 for six dollars. Polly Rodriguez and Roman Sanchez "went after ammunition to Boerne 2 days" for four dollars each.

Isaac W. Stevens was absent with leave.

Company total $276. Under the heading "Last Paid" is the notation for each man: "Never paid".]

Stationed Bandera, Date Oct. 31st, 1872.

[November 1872 summarized:

Alfoons Gysels, Emielie Biauki, Leon Raccurt, James Merchant, Tom Click, George Lewis, and P.C. Clark were absent with leave. E.M. Ross "Services two days" for four dollars. The rest of the company scouted November 1 to November 10 for $20 each and a company total of $244. Under the heading "Last Paid" is the notation "Never Pay/t".]

[December 1872 summarized:

Lt. Ballantyne claimed $30 for expenses. J.B. Langfort, Emielie Biauki, Leon Raccurt, Andrew Jones, James Merchand, George Lewis, and P.C. Clark were absent with leave. Three men, William Westerfield, Isaac Stevens, and John Heinen served from December 13 to December 15 for $15 each, while all the rest served from December 13 to December 22 for $20 each. The company total was $198. Under the heading "Last Paid" is the notation "Never Pay/t" for each man.]

Station Bandera Date Dec. 23d 1872

[January 1873 summarized:

I.W. Stevens, Emeil Biancke, Leuis Raccourt, Thos. Click, and George Lewis were absent with leave. The rest of the company scouted from January 9 to January 19 for $20 each. The company total was $300. Under the heading "Last Paid" is the notation "December" for each man.]

[February 1873 summarized:

Isaac W. Stevens, J.B. Langford, Emiel Bianchi, Leon Raccurt, and Thomas Click were absent with leave. The rest of the company scouted from February 11 to February 21 for $20 each. The total for the company was $300. The "Last Paid" column is blank.]

[March 1873 summarized:

The entire company scouted from March 10 to March 20 for $20 each. The company total was $400. Under the heading "Last Paid" is the notation "February" for each man. "Gysels" is spelled "Gyrels" on this roll and on the April roll.]

[April 1873 summarized:

The entire company scouted from April 13 to April 23 for $20 each. The total for the company was $400. Last paid - February.]

[May 1873 summarized:

The entire company scouted from May 9 to May 19 for $20 each. The company total was $400. Last paid - April. "Merchant" is spelled "Merchand" on this roll and on the April roll.]

[June 1873 summarized:

The entire company scouted from June 10 to June 20 for $20 each. The company total was $400. Last paid -April.]

Rangers were frequently frustrated by Indian tactics. Raiders coming into the country would often scatter if closely pursued, then regroup farther south or east. Indians going out of the country had the terrain to their advantage after a race for the passes. The outgoing raiders would also scatter if necessary. If rangers had not caught up with raiders by the time they reached the Frio Water Hole, they often gave up the chase. Minute man rangers could not ordinarily spend much time out of the county. Sometimes rangers would follow trails through the rough country as far as Kickapoo Springs, but the land from there to the Devil's River was even more forbidding. In his book *The Buffalo Soldiers*, William H. Leckie included this portion of a report by Captain Michael Cooney to the post adjutant at Fort Clark, November 28, 1872, describing a scout of Troop A, 9th U.S. Cavalry:

I marched from Fort Clark, Texas at 3 o'clock P.M. November 17 with my command consisting of 1st Lieut. Patrick Cusack and thirty enlisted men of Troop "A", 9th Cavalry, also a guide, with rations for seven days which was made to last ten days. I marched that night to Cope Ranch on West Fork of Nueces River to Kickapoo Springs with the intentions of crossing the country between the West Fork of the Nueces and Devils River. I found the country almost impracticable for travel being alternate mountain and valley with neither high land or valley favorable to travel. No permanent water between the two rivers. Some water was found in niches from recent rains. On the 21st we came in sight of Devils River but found great difficulty in getting down to it. However, after several hours search a place of descent was found and an Indian camp which appeared to have been abandoned about twenty four or thirty hours previous was found.

May 18, 1873, Colonel Ranald Mackenzie and 400 U.S. troops with Negro-Seminole scouts entered Mexico and attacked a Lipan and two Kickapoo villages along a tributary of the Rio Grande, Rio San Rodrigo, near El Remolino. Many of the Indian men were away on a hunting trip. Nineteen Indians were killed. Costilietos and 40 Lipans and Kickapoos were captured and brought to San Antonio. Except for Costilietos, the Lipans were eventually placed on the Mescalero Apache reservation in New Mexico. According to Mackenzie biographer Charles Robinson:

> In his report, Mackenzie stated that "three Villages averaging from fifty to sixty Lodges were destroyed. They appeared to be well supplied with stores, including ammunition." Sixty-five ponies were recovered, some of which had Ike Cox's brand. Government casualties included Private Peter Carrigan, mortally wounded; Private William Pair, "a splendid old soldier who has served in the Regiment since its organization," right arm amputated at the shoulder; and Private Leonard Kemppenberger, slightly wounded in the face but fit for duty.
>
> Although the majority of the Indians were away from the villages or escaped into the Santa Rosa Mountains, the raid was a success. Their base had been destroyed. Henry Strong recalled, "We just about exterminated what we did not bring back. The village looked like a cyclone had struck it."

The Kickapoo were soon compelled to negotiate and some moved to the Indian Territory. Lipan Apache raids continued and Colonel Mackenzie found it necessary to place a company of troops on the Sabinal River near present day Vanderpool. Camp Roberts, active for a year, consisted of a row of twelve rock chimneys 20 feet apart to which tents were attached. The site was known for many years as "the old soldiers' camp". The chimneys were razed in the 1940s.

Mackenzie's raid did not stop the Indian raids from Mexico, but marked the beginning of the end for that way of life. In succeeding years the remnant Lipans in Mexico gradually wandered north in small groups to the Mescalero Apache reservation in New Mexico. In 1905 a joint action of the U.S. and Mexican governments moved the last Mexican Lipans to the Mescalero reservation in New Mexico.

Meanwhile in June 1873, Costilietos escaped from the army at San Antonio. According to an oral tradition, he had refused to eat while in captivity and was found dead 13 miles west of San Antonio. Others say he survived his ordeal, reached Mexico, and once again led raids into Texas. The editor of the San Antonio Express sarcastically complained how dull he expected the Fourth of July to be in his "Local Affairs" column, July 3, 1873:

> We are not informed, but suppose the military will fire off a public spirited cannon. Old Costalitos should be led in triumph through the streets, but we believe we have already mentioned that he was absent.

The Economic Panic of 1873 put a lot of people out of work and out of their homes across the United States. Schmidtke & Hay were among those who sold cattle at a loss that year. Another wave of desperate men began to drift onto the frontier. While outlaw activity was on the increase, Indian raids began to decrease. September 27, 1874, Colonel Mackenzie's attack on Palo Duro Canyon removed Comanche access to their last refuge on the plains.

Some of Ballantyne's Rangers remembered by Andrew Jones in the Pioneer History were Robert Ballantyne, lieutenant; Manuel, tracker; J.P. Heinen, Ike Stevens, Andrew Jones, Tom Click, and Sam Jones. Jim Brown, Jim Gobble, and Lum Champion are mentioned in Andrew Jones' recollection of the company, but are not on the muster rolls for Ballantyne's Rangers. All except Lum Champion are in Tom Steven's account of Phillip's Company, so in Andrew Jones' account of the "last scout" the company seems to be Phillip's rather than Ballantyne's. Andrew Jones was in both companies.

Phillip's Company --Jackson and Martha Ann Phillips lived on Winan's Creek. Jack Phillips served in various county offices, the home guards, and was later a county deputy sheriff.

According to Tom M. Stevens the company was in service 1873-1875. He may have remembered most of the names, but did not include all their ranks. Jack Phillips' official rank might have been lieutenant and Sam Jones would then have been first sergeant, but the size of the company would seem to warrant a captain. The State Library does not have any rolls for this company.

Jack Phillips Captain
Sam Jones 1st Lieutenant
—-   [sergeant]
Tom M. Stevens Corporal

1. Jim Brown
2. Joel Casey
3. Sam Casey
4. Dave Chipman
5. John Clark
6. Joe Click
7. Jim Davenport
8. Charlie Gersdorff
9. Jim Gobble

16. John A. Jones
17. Jim Lewis
18. Jim McKay
19. Joe Miller
20. Monroe Moncur
21. Joe Reed
22. Will Ross
23. Jack Sheppard
24. Dave Weaver

10. Alex Hay
11. Bill Hester
12. Taylor Hester
13. F.L. Hicks
14. J.I. Jones
15. Andrew G. Jones

25. Mack Weaver
26. Pete Weaver
27. Laoma White [Loammi Wight]
[28. Hugh Bandy?]
[29. Lum Champion?]
[30. J.P. Heinen?]

[? Suggested by Andrew Jones' account]

[Tom M. Stevens:]

This Minute company was organized for protection against the Indians, and to put a stop to the cattle and horse stealing which had become very common in this country, the stealing being done by thieves who drifted in from other sections of the state. Indian raids at that time did not occur as often as formerly, but the redskins still came through occasionally.

Our first call was for ten men to scout for Indians. The second day out we jumped a big bear which took a tree. We ran up and Will Ross shot at the bear and missed it, but Will's gun was so near me that my face was powder burned. We got the bear, however, and Will had to guard the horses while we were in camp for being such a poor marksman. Finding no Indian sign, we returned home without accidently getting shot.

In the spring of 1874 Indians stole some horses from parties around Bandera. Captain Phillips and his men followed them out near the head of the Medina river to the headwaters of the Frio. There the Indians met another band of the red devils, who had been in camp several days at a fine spring which gushed out of a bluff of a mountain, which location afforded them an ideal lookout, as a splendid view of the whole surrounding country was obtained. Their spies had evidently seen us a long time before we reached there, for we never overtook them, although we followed their trail to the Nueces.

Along in 1873 and 1874 Bandera county was overrun with some bad hombres who were known to be cattle rustlers. Captain Phillips decided to break up some of their devilment. Four or five of these rustlers rounded up a herd of cattle along the Medina river above Bandera and started them west. We followed them and overtook the herd about where Leakey now stands, and we rounded up both cattle and men. They offered but little resistance, and it being late in the afternoon we went into camp for the night, Captain Phillips detailing some of his men to guard the prisoners. We had camped near a ranch, and while we were cooking supper a kind lady named McDougal, sent word that if any of our men would come over to the ranch she would cook supper for them. One of the prisoners, a man named Nichols, asked Captain Phillips if he could go over there and get supper if his guard accompanied him, and F.L. Hicks was detailed to go with him. Mr. Hicks consented but said, "I'll take you over there and I'll bring you back." But he never brought him back. When they went in and sat down at the supper table, Hicks left his gun near the door, Nichols seating himself nearer the door than Hicks. While Mr. Hicks was hiding the good things set before him, Nichols grabbed the gun and jumped for the door, and once outside he made a run for the brush. Mr. Hicks jumped up, knocking part of the dishes off of the table and turned over the bench on which he had been sitting, and dashed in pursuit, leaving his hat. It was too dark outside to see the prisoner, so he returned to camp and reported the escape. The joke was on Hicks, and we had lots of fun over the incident. We did not care if all the prisoners got away, just so we got the cows back home. Next morning we started for Bandera, and on reaching there we delivered the other prisoners to the sheriff and turned the cattle loose on their old range.

In the summer of 1874 we captured a young man named Waldroop on the river near where the town of Medina is now located. He was accused of finding ropes with horses at one end. There were also others accused of similar crimes, and we took them to San Saba where they were wanted, and turned them over to the officers at that place. A little broke-backed man by the name of Ace Brown, evidently the alcalde of the town, ordered the prisoners put in a hole in the ground, about 10x10 feet, which served as a jail. Guards were placed around this sweat hole to keep the inmates from escaping. And there we left them, and as we bade them farewell I could see the beads of perspiration standing out on their faces. I heard afterwards that these fellows left that hole one night and got away. I was glad of it.

We were disbanded in the spring of 1875, and the following winter Capt. Jack Phillips was killed by Indians, at Seco Pass, in the western part of Bandera county.

[Myrtle Murray gave this account of F.L. Hicks:]

> Mr. Hicks was among the group of men in that county who devoted much of his time to ridding the country of cattle thieves. One time he was reasonably sure that he knew who

was stealing his cattle, but he could not catch him. He went to another man in the community and offered to pay him to work with the suspected cattle thief. "And when you get ready to steal my cattle," he said, "let me know and I'll be there with the officers, but I'll see that you are freed."

Because of his reputation for law and order, Mr. Hicks knew he could do it. He had the courage of his convictions, and never hesitated to do what he considered the right thing.

By 1875 the U.S. Army and the Frontier Battalion of Texas Rangers seemed to be getting control of the Indian raids while on the West Texas Frontier fortunes were being made in the cattle business. Andrew Jones' account of Ballantyne's Rangers skips over to Phillips Company:

> The next scout we made we hired old man Smith with his three yoke of steers and went to the Frio Water Hole, where we built a good pen, and then went to Bull Head on the Nueces and gathered 400 steers which we intended to bring to Bandera and sell to Schmidtke and Hay for $2 per head. We appointed Sam Jones as our boss on this mavericking expedition. While on the Nueces we captured two government horses on the range with halters on. They had escaped from some post months or years before and had become wild. We brought the steers into the pen as we gathered them, and one night they stampeded and seventeen of them were killed by running against cedar stumps which had been left in the pen. About ten miles this side of the water hole was another pen which was called Post Oak, and we brought our steers to it. Four men had to stay with the wagon, and as we were coming to the Post Oak pen, Jim Brown, Jim Gobble, Lum Champion and myself intended to reach a spring at the head of the hollow. There were some Indians there, but I suppose they heard the wagon and hid out, as we did not see them. Near the spring I picked up a pair of moccasins and a small mirror which had been dropped by them. Leaving Champion and Gobble with the wagon, Jim Brown and I scouted around the spring to try to locate the Indians, but without success. We found where they had killed a cow just a short time before and taken some of the beef. They were afoot, evidently coming down into the settlements on a horse-stealing expedition. When we reported our discoveries to the captain he said we could not leave the cattle to follow the Indians, but to guard against attack. That night old Manuel and I stood guard

around the horses, and at different times during the night the horses showed signs of alarm and we made ready to secure an Indian scalp, but they did not come. We delivered our steers in due time and received $2 per head for them, and also received $50 for the two government horses we had captured, and we thought we were making money. Somebody reported that we had gathered the 400 steers, and our arms were ordered to be returned and we all got fired from the Ranger service.

13

The Frontier Battalion and the Special Force

General Philip Sheridan's Federal Indian Campaign across the Texas Panhandle 1873-75, and buffalo hunters in that area destroyed the Plains Indians' ability to wage war. Minuteman ranger companies and the organization of a new full-time force of Texas Rangers contributed to the end of Indian raids in Texas. Comanche raids were considerably reduced and ended completely by 1879. The line of settlement on the West Texas Frontier moved more steadily westward. Many of the older settlements began to record their last Indian raids as in A.J. Sowell's account of M. Saatoff, a Quihi settler:

> The last Indian raid was in 1874, and they carried off and killed together fifty head of horses in the Quihi settlement, and killed one boy on Black Creek. On one occasion Mr. Saatoff and others made a famous ride of eighty miles in one day after Indians, but the latter went one hundred and got away.

In May 1874 the Frontier Battalion of Texas Rangers and the Special Force of Texas State Troops were organized. In its early days the Special Force served under Leander H. McNelly mostly along the border, where Juan Cortina was still an item, and in the interior of the state quelling feuds. Initially the Special Force was more law enforcement oriented than the Frontier Battalion which was directed to patrol against Indian raids. The battalion consisted of six Ranger companies of 75 men each with John B. Jones as major. Although subject to the usual finance and troop reductions that seemed to plague all of Texas' ranger organizations, companies A-F were in service for 25 years, the first "permanent" Texas Rangers.

James Gillett joined these rangers in 1875 and later wrote an account of his experiences:

> At this time the captains received a salary of $100 per month, lieutenants $75, sergeants $50, and corporals and privates $40. Subsequently, as the legislature continually sliced into the ranger appropriation, the pay of privates was reduced to $30 a

month, a mere pittance for the hazardous service demanded of them.

[...]

Immediately after being sworn in the men were divided into messes, ten men to the mess, and issued ten days' rations by the orderly sergeant. These consisted of flour, bacon, coffee, sugar, beans, rice, pepper, salt, and soda. No potatoes, syrup, or lard was furnished, and each man had to supply his own cooking utensils. To shorten our bread we used bacon grease. Beef was sometimes supplied the men, but wild game was so plentiful that but little other meat was required. Furthermore, each recruit was furnished a Sharps carbine, .50 caliber, and one .45 Colt's pistol. These arms were charged to us, their cost to be deducted from our first pay. Our salary of $40 per month was paid in quarterly installments. The state also supplied provender for the horses.

James Gillet remembered how Major Jones inspected the line of companies with an escort of rangers who acted as a reserve force, additional manpower that could be injected into troublesome areas:

Nearly every ranger in the battalion was anxious to be at some time a member of Major Jones's escort company. The escort company was not assigned a stationary post nor did it endeavor to cover a given strip of territory. Its most important duty was to escort the major on his periodic journeys of inspection to the other companies along the line. The escort always wintered in the south and made about four yearly tours of the frontier from company to company, taking part in such scouts as the major might select and being assigned to such extraordinary duty as might arise. In 1874, when the Frontier Battalion was first formed, Major Jones recruited his escort from a detail of five men from each of the other companies. However, in practice, this led to some confusion and envy in the commands and Major Jones found it expedient to have a regular escort company, so he selected Company A for this purpose. This remained his escort until he was promoted to adjutant general.

The headquarters of the Frontier Battalion was wherever Major Jones happened to be at the time. He reported on the new bullet-firing pistols:

Headquarters Frontier Battalion
Kerrsville June 13th 1874

Gen. Wm. Steele
Adjt. Gen. of the State
Austin

Sir

    I have the honor to report that having tested the new pistols thoroughly, I find them entirely unreliable with the Smith and Wesson cartridge.

    As I have but few of these cartridges with me and presume the new ones have been received by this time I send a courier for them.

    Have to request that you will furnish him a pack mule and a cargo of the cartridges for the new pistols, not less than two thousand, with which he can meet me at Comanche.

    If the ammunition has not arrived yet, the courier can be detained several days as it will probably be ten or twelve days before I reach Comanche.

    I would suggest also that after sending twenty pistols to this place for Capt. Coldwell, you send the balance to Dallas and I will turn them over to the other companies and some pistol amunition, say eight or ten thousand rounds, to the Chief Justice at Fredericksburg for Capt. Perry and my detachment when I return from the North. Letters addressed to me at Jacksboro will reach me in two or three weeks.

    I have just learned that Indians attacked a party of Cow hunters on West Neueces last week, wounded one man, took some horses and made their escape, without being pessued. I get this from one of the party

    I am very respectfully
    Your obdt Servt,
        Jno. B. Jones
        Maj. Comdg. Battalion

[James Gillett:]

    [The .50 Sharps carbines] would heat easily and thus were very inaccurate shooters. The state furnished this weapon to its rangers at a cost of $17.50, and at that time furnished no other class of gun. The new center-fire 1873-model Winchester had just appeared on the market and sold at $50 for the rifle and $40 for the carbine. A ranger who wanted a Winchester had to pay for it out of his own pocket and supply his own ammunition as well, for the state furnished cartridges only for the Sharps gun.

The officers and stations of the original Frontier Battalion as set forth in General Orders Number 1 & 2:

Comp.	Captain	1st Lieutenant	2nd Lieutenant
A	John R. Waller	J.A. Wright	J.T. Wilsom

"near the Western corner of Erath Co., and patrol North to Stephens Co. and South West into Brown Co. P.O. at Stephensville."

B	G.W. Stevens	S.G. McGarroh	Ira Long

"at Hamby's Ranch, on Elm Creek, 8 miles North West of Belknap, and patrol North East, halfway to Buffalo Springs, and South to the centre of Stephens County. P.O. at Jacksboro.

C	E.F. Ikard	G.W. Campbell	L.P. Beavert

"at Buffalo Springs, Clay Co., and patrol North, to Red River, and South West, halfway to Belknap, P.O. at Henrietta."

D	C.R. Perry	W.H. Ledbetter	D.W. Roberts

"near Mason, and patrol North to Brady's Creek, and South, to South line of Kimble County, P.O. at Mason."

E	W.J. Maltby	J.C. Connell	J.H. Eckins

"In the vicinity of Santa Anna Peak in Colman Co., and patrol North East into Brown Co, and South to Brady's Creek - P.O. at Brownwood."

F	Neal Coldwell	Pat Dolan	F.H. Nelson

"in Bandera Co., and patrol North to Kemble Co., and South West to Nueces River, P.O. at Bandera

Captain Coldwell and family lived in Center Point. James B. Gillet described him:

> Captain Neal Coldwell was born in Dade County, Missouri, in May, 1844, and served gallantly throughout the Civil War in the Thirty-second Regiment, Texas cavalry, commanded by Col. W.P. Woods. At the organization of the Frontier Battalion in 1874, he was commissioned captain of Company F.

It is difficult, in a single sketch, to do Captain Coldwell justice or convey any correct idea of what he accomplished as a Texas Ranger. The station of Company F, the southernmost company of the line, was the most unfavorable that could well be given him. His scouting grounds were the heads of the Guadalupe, Nueces, Llano, and Devils rivers, the roughest and most difficult part of southern Texas in which to pursue Indians, yet he held them in check and finally drove them out of that part of the state.

Although Bandera City was originally designated as the station for Coldwell's company, the captain expressed concern that his men and horses would be worn out by the time they got out of Bandera County when pursuing Indians. He recommended a location closer to the corridor through which the raiders from Mexico came and went:

Centre Point, Kerr Co. Texas
May 22nd 1874

Maj. Jno B. Jones
Comdg. Frontier Battalion
Austin Tex.

Major,

I take the liberty to address you in regard to the Station of Co. "F" of your command. I hope that you will not regard it as a presumption on my part, when I assure you that it is for the good of the Service, and with a view that my company may render more effective Service in the protection of the Frontier that I will give you a brief Statement in regard to the Geography of the country, that is to be the Scene of action for my company.

The company will be stationed in Bandera Co and patrol north to Kimble Co and Southwest to the Neueces River. To Strike a line Southwest from any given point in Bandera Co above the town of Bandera will throw us into a country of dense cedar brakes through which are innumerable deep, narrow gorges that are almost impassable for a body of men. To turn more to the South of that line will throw us into a settled country and will leave many settlers on the outside of the line of Patrol. But to turn to the west of the line first indicated will give us a route above the cedar brakes and <u>outside</u> of all the Settlements.

None of the maps are correct in the location of the heads of the Guadelupe, Llano, Medina, Sabinal, Frio & Neueces.

The Gaudelupe runs round the head of the Medina and heads west of it and <u>even with the Frio</u>. From there a plain open "Divide" Starts off and runs <u>due west</u> for the distance of eighty miles. on the <u>right</u> hand Side of this "Divide" are the headwaters of the Gaudelupe, Paint Creek, Johnston's and South fork of the Llano. On the <u>left</u> of the "Divide" are the heads of the Medina, Sabinal, and Frio. all three of which head within a distance of Ten miles. After leaving the Frio going west the "Divide" heads the different prongs of the Neueces all the way to the extreme west prong of that river. After leaving the Head of the Neueces the country is generally open until the head of the tributaries of Devil's River are reached - and is very rough from there to the Rio Grande.

Indians depredating upon the counties of Uvalde, Bandera, Kendall, Kerr, Edwards, and Gellespie, <u>nearly always travel</u> the divide which I have described. To reach this thorough-fare of the Indians, a Scout from Bandera will have to travel at least forty miles

And to Patrol to Kimble Co, a Scout will have to pass out by the head of the Gaudelupe, which is the <u>true Key</u> to all the country East and South of it. A company at the head of the Gaudelupe can cover more country effectually than any other point that I Know on the Frontier. From that point Kimble Co would be distant twenty five miles and the West Neueces Eighty miles.

It would be outside of <u>all Settlers</u> and Indian trails can be easily detected going in or coming out of all the country lieyng South and East of there. It is easy of access from below, There being a good road nearly all the way from Kerrville, distant thirty miles supplies can be furnished as cheap as they can be furnished in Bandera. A great deal of time and travel would be Saved of going in and coming out by being located at the Head of the Gaudelupe.

I make this statement through no personal motives, but it is made with Sincere disire to render the State all Service in my power.

If it does not suit you to make the change I will do the very best that I can and cover as much country as possible.

Though Bandera is a central point on the map, it is a difficult point from which to operate.

I respectfully submit the following questions which I hope may have an early reply.

>1st Will the Company be allowed a Surgeon: If So will Capt's employ them. I have an opportunity just at this time to secure the Services of an excellent Surgeon who has Served a Such in the U.S. Army?

2nd will the horses of the company be Shod by the State?

3d will the men be allowed to furnish their own guns. if of the Same Kind & calibre of those furnished by the State?

4th Will the books and stationary of the company be furnished or bought at my own expense?

I think that I can have my company in camp by the 3rd of June.

I have the honor to be your

Most Obidient Svt.
Neal Coldwell
Capt. Co. F Frontier forces

Coldwell's company spent June and July operating from Camp Frio at the Frio Water Hole, patrolling the corridor between the headwaters of the Nueces and Llano rivers. By mid-August Captain Coldwell had moved his company's station to John Joy's ranch on the South Fork of the Guadalupe River, Camp Joy's Ranch, or Camp Joy, 28 miles west of Kerrville. From Major Jones' report to William Steele, September 14, 1874:

I have to report that I reached Capt Coldwells Camp on the Head of Guadalupe river on the 5th inst. Found the company in good condition but the horses worn out in a long chase after Indians, over a rough and rockey country they having captured all the horses belonging to a party of Bee hunters on the Medina a few days before. They were followed to the Nueces.

This company is not well situated for effective operations but I cannot post it to better advantage at present for want of grass. The whole country from the Llano [via?] the head of the Guadaloupe and Frio to the Nueces has been burned off in fact I may say that the whole country from the Brazos, along the frontier, to the Nueces has been burned off and there are very few places where water and good grass can be found together. I have traveled for a whole day at a time without finding any grass. Have been much retarded in my movements lately by rain. It has rained on [me?] every day for the last ten.

As Indian raids diminished, law enforcement became more of a priority for the Frontier Battalion. Prescott Webb:

The first serious trouble with outlaws and thieves encountered by Major Jones's men developed on the southern end of the line in the middle part of 1875. When the Frontier Battalion first went out, this region was occupied by Captain Neal Coldwell in charge of Company F. At the end of the first six months Coldwell's company had been disbanded in a reduction for the sake of economy. On May 19, 1875 Major Jones recalled Coldwell, and within eight days the company was full and stationed on Johnson's Creek, about twenty miles northwest of Kerrville. Five or six raids were made in that section between May 7 and June 1. Two of the parties were known to be Indians; and one was known to be white men.

Groups of desperadoes began to take over the Indian raiding routes to steal cattle and horses. An organized band of outlaws sometimes known as the South Fork Clan made raids into Kerr, Kendall, and Bandera counties. They stayed on friendly terms with settlers on the Frio and Nueces rivers where their operatives could dispose of their stolen livestock. Citizens of Kerr and Kendall counties organized to counter these raids. Phillip's Company was active in Bandera County. The restoration of Coldwell's company to the region was timely:

In camp June 28th 1875

Major Jno. B. Jones
Cmdg Front. Batt.
Kerrville Tx

Sir,
    I have organized a new company and will move to day to the head of Fall Branch, a tributary of Johnson's fork of the Guadulupe, and will be about Twenty miles North west from Kerrville, 12 miles from the head of North prong of the Guadelupe - and Twenty miles north of our former camp on the South fork.
    I do not know if this will Suit you. If not we can very easily move when you arrive. I think it is the best Station that we could have in this country. We will be nearer the Settlements of Gillespie & Kerr cos. and can be reached from Bandera Co. more easily, than at South Fork.
    Respectfully your obt Svt.

        Neal Coldwell
        Capt Co. "F"

[Major Jones:]

Headquarters Frontier Battalion
Camp in North West Corner of Kerr Co.
July 1st 1875

Gen Wm. Steele
Adjt. Gen.
Austin

Sir

I have the honor to report that Capt. Coldwells new Company, for the raising of which I sent him orders from Austin on the 18th ult., was organized and took up line of march for its post of duty on the 27th, five days from the time he received his orders.

He is now stationed on the head of Johnson or [Minters?] creek, tributary of the Guadaloupe, twenty miles N.W. from Kerrville. I regret that he was not authorized to raise a new company when the old one was disbanded. There has been great necessity for an organized force in this section of country during the last two months. Some five or six raids have been made on the Settlement here by Indians and white thieves since the 7th of May. About forty citizens have lost horses or mules by [them?] and there is great excitment and alarm among the people in consequence. Two of these raiding parties were Indians the others were beyond a doubt white men. One party of each have been overtaken and one Indian and one white man killed and all the Stock Stolen by both parties recaptured.

I found two companies of citizens under arms in this and Kendall County when I arrived and the town of Kerrville guarded and partoled every night. The raising of Capt Coldwells Co. has quieted the fears of the people to some extent and gives them a feeling of Security which they have not experienced for several months. I am Satisfied there is an extensive organization of thieves on this part of the frontier. The two fights alluded to above, one with the Indians the other with white thieves took place within ten miles of this camp. All the Stolen Stock has been taken out this way. The Leon Springs robbers were going in the direction of the head of the Llano. The white man who was [seriously?] wounded in the fight died near here. He confessed to being a member of an organized band of horse thieves and robbers. [Had? or He 'ad?] been in the clan but a short time and was not fully informed of their plans and operations but thought there were sixty or seventy of them, that they carried their Stolen stock out to the head of the Llano where it was kept for Some time, the brands and other marks by which they could be identified changed, and then sent off to different places and disposed of. Many suspicious parties have been known to leave these settlements and go out in that direction and others have been seen passing from the head of the Llano to the head of the Neuces where it is believed a branch of the Clan is operating. I have reason to believe that their connection extends interior as far as Burnet, Austin, and San Antonio. Their camp is supposed to be in the vicinity of old Ft. Terret.

I shall start tomorrow on a scout for them, will take part of Capt. Coldwells Company and some thirty citizens from this and Kendall Co. who have volunteered to go with me, will make a thourogh search of all the count[r]y on the heads of the Llano and will break them up if they are there.

I expect to be at Lt. Roberts camp near Menardville on the 10th inst. and have to ask that my mail or any orders you have for me may be sent to that place afterwards to Jacksboro.

Very respectfully your obdt. Servt.

    Jno. B Jones
    Maj Comdg Frontier Battalion

Headquarters Frontier Battalion
Los Moras Creek, Menard Co. Tex
July 9th 1875

Gen. Wm Steele
Adjt. Genl.
Austin

Sir

I have the honor to report having Scouted thoroughly the country on the heads of the Guadaloupe and Llano rivers during the last ten days in search of Indians and white robbers who have been depredating on the Settlements for the last three months.

I found no organized bands of robbers, as had been reported, and am Satisfied that the active robbers have all left the country. I found Some very suspicious people living in the mountains of the Llano who beyond a doubt are confederates of the robbers and harbor them and conceal their plunder. One of them is known to have furnished one of the Leon Springs robbers with a horse on which he made his escape from the country. I called upon these suspected persons and informed them that they would be visited occasionally by detachments of this command and would be dealt with if found harboring them or with stolen property in their possession. I think the good people of those Sections will not be molested by white robbers again Soon.

In addition to the Indians depredations on the Guadaloupe mentioned in my communication of the 1st inst. I have to report that Indians have been on the Llano four times this year. In March two of them were killed by a citizen below Ft. Terret, in April they wounded a citizen, Mr Cholston on Coperas Creek, in May they killed two men, Thackery and McCarty, at Ft. Terret and took horses from Rans, Moore and others lower down the river, in June they shot and wounded a woman, Mrs. Thackery, at Ft. Terret and took horses from Williams, Gregory, Smith and others on South Llano. None have been in since June 19th.

Capt. Coldwell will keep two Scouting parties moving during this moon from the head of the Nueces to the Llano and Lt Roberts is operating between the Llano and the Colorado and if the red rascals come in we hope to catch some of them.

On the Scout which I have just made I was accompanied by Lt. Henry Schwethelm and his company of Germans from Comfort. They were on the eve of Starting out when I reached Comfort and volunteered to go with me. They furnished their own rations, placed themselves under my command and acted in a very Satisfactory manner during the whole time.

I reached this, Lt. Roberts, camp day before yesterday, find the Company in good condition and doing good service, having one Scouting party out and another just starting. They are having or anticipating more trouble in Mason and at the request of the civil authorities I send Lt. Roberts and a few men to preserve order there during the Session of the Court which meets there next week.

No Indians have been in this section of country Since Lt Roberts last fight in December.

I leave this place tomorrow morning for Lt. Fosters camp in Coleman County, via Kickapoo Springs and the mouth of Concho river.

I am respectfully
Your obdt. Servt.

    Jno. B. Jones
    Maj. Comdg. Battalion

In August 1875 temporary budget cutbacks reduced captains to 1st lieutenants and in December companies were reduced to 20 men each. The size of companies fluctuated throughout the existence of the Frontier Battalion. Neal Coldwell and others were eventually returned to the rank of captain.

Incidentally a "capias" is a writ or warrant. Captain Leander McNelly, head of the Special Force, reported to William Steele from San Antonio, November 13, 1876:

> I have the honor to report that for the week ending Nov. 11th We sent one Scout to Bandera Co. to serve a capias placed in our hands by County Atty. Anderson. Another Scout to Gaudelupe Co. to serve papers for this court.
>
> The parties having left the neighborhood sometime since, no arrests were made.

H.H. Carmichael, a successful cattleman, bought an interest in Schmidtke & Hay in 1874. He bought Charles Schmidtke's remaining interest in 1875 and the firm became known as H.H. Carmichael & Company. Carmichael and his bride were planning to build a house just below the forks of the Medina River, but the Indian raids of 1876 changed their minds. They built the house in Bandera City and a later Carmichael house built there in 1890 still stands. From A.J. Sowell's "Trailing Indians":

> In the fall of 1876 they made their last raid through Sabinal Canyon. They first struck the settlers on Main Frio, and then came like a wave of destruction through this valley, and then made a circuit of many miles back towards the Rio Grande, sixteen persons meeting death at their hands during the raid. They came into Sabinal Canyon on the 10th of September, and stole quite a lot of horses, and then turned southeast below the foot of the mountains, playing havoc as they went.
>
> The Sabinal men gathered quickly and were soon joined by the scouts from Frio Canyon, who were coming rapidly on the trail. The following are the names of the men from both canyons: From Sabinal were James Thigpen, Phil Hodges, Albert Harper, C.S. Jones, J.H. Simpson, James Watson, Jack Kelly, and a German Schoolteacher named Lirch. From Frio were Henry Patterson, John Patterson, Riley Patterson, Joe Van Pelt, James Highsaw, Jack Grigsby, William Wall, John Kittnger, William Nichols, and Joe Richarz. Seeing the necessity of having a leader, the settlers elected Henry Patterson to fill that position, and they soon set out briskly on the trail, Phil Hodges and John Patterson being the trailers, taking alternate turns.

These Indians eventually escaped into Mexico. The troops at Fort Clark were notified, but a rise in the Rio Grande prevented their crossing. U.S. Army crossings of the border were not frequent, but had become more or less routine since Mackenzie's Raid and were sometimes made in cooperation with Mexican authorities.

Meanwhile other raiders came into the region from the north. Comanches based in Mexico or on the Pecos River made what may have been the last Comanche raid through the present boundaries of Bandera County. From A.J. Sowell's account of Kerr and Kendall County settler Dr. J.C. Nowlin:

> In 1876 Dr. Nowlin belonged to Capt. Henry Moore's company of rangers, and was stationed at the head of Bear Creek, fifteen miles from the present Junction City, in Kimble County. On the day before Christmas of the above named year, in the morning, the Indians made a raid into the settlement [Kimbleville] where Junction is now and killed a boy half a mile west of town, and two miles further killed a man on North Llano. The people were afraid to leave the settlement to notify the rangers until late in the day, but finally one man ventured out and arrived at the ranger camp about an hour by sun. The rangers at once got out and crowded the Indians so close they were compelled to abandon some of the stolen stock, which stood on the trail covered with sweat when the men came upon them.
>
> It was hard trailing through the cedarbrakes and over rocks, and finally the horses played out and the pursuit had to be abandoned. The rangers turned back at Wallace Creek (named for Big Foot Wallace, who owned a tract of land there), one of the tributaries of the Medina River. This was the band of Indians that killed Jack Phillips between the Hondo and Sabinal, ten miles or more south from where their trail was abandoned.

[From cattleman Jesse M. Kilgore's story in <u>The Trail Drivers of Texas</u>:]

> The following winter we gathered up and went to Frio county, about one hundred miles south of where we were. After two day's travel down the Hondo, fifteen redskins came by our old camp in behind us. A man named Phillips ate dinner with us and started back to Bandera and was killed and scalped by those Indians. No doubt they saw our herd and passed us somewhere near Frio City. We had eight men in our crowd.

[From A.J. Sowell's account of M.C. Click:]

> The Indians were followed by Hondo men, but not overtaken. The shoes of Phillips were found on the trail.

[Document #237, Volume 4 <u>Texas Indian Papers</u>. Report of Indian Depredations - Austin -- January 1, 1878:]

> Dec'b 76
>
> S.R. Merritt Kerr Co Vol Mil Co writes that on 24th 8 or 10 Indians stole a number of horses on Bear Creek & killed Sam Speers & Isaac Kuntz. They then stole a number of horses about 10 miles from Kerrville & on their way to the Frio, Stole some more horses & killed --- Allen.
>
> Geo. H. Grey Co Judge Kimble Co says of above raid that there were 13 Indians & that they got about 50 horses in Kimble Co
>
> Lt F M Moore & 10 men Co D front Batt. from 24 to 30th on trail of above raiders to the head waters of the Medina-- 12 horses picked up.
>
> Capt N. Coldwell & 10 men Co A front Batt. Scouting for Indians, struck trail on 31st as the Indians passed out behind the citizen Scout   Citizens recaptured 40 horses.
>
> [...]
>
> Wm Hudspeth, Co. Attorney Bandera Co writes that on 28th Dec. Indians Killed J M Phillips
>
> That on Jany 2. 77 a Mexican boy about 15 years old was captured alive by J B Hudspeth. Said boy was captured by Inds. when quite young & on raid above mentioned was lost from the party & in wandering about for something to eat, & as he says, also for a horse he was caught by Hudspeth. The boy Says he was with a party of Indians from Mexico. That on the Llano they killed a man & were pursued so closely...

So closely that in the rush through Bandera County the young man became separated from the Comanche raiding party. Perhaps his horse had given out. He made his way to Hondo Canyon, 18 miles southwest of Bandera. He was attempting to steal a horse when Joseph B. Hudspeth's dogs began barking. The rancher, in the <u>Pioneer History</u> account, "going out in the moonlight to learn the cause he discovered a blanket lying on the ground not far from his front door."

The Indian under the blanket was captured by Mr. Hudspeth after a struggle. Mrs. Hudspeth was standing by with a rifle and would have shot the young man, but the rifle failed to fire. The A.J. Sowell account:

> He was guarded all night, and next day carried to Bandera and placed in the house of Mr. James Hudspeth. The young Indian could neither speak Spanish nor English, and was kept here several days without being able to get any information out of him. About this time a squad of Texas rangers came along. Their guide could speak Spanish, besides several Indian dialects, and came in to see what he could make out of him. After trying him on several, he finally addressed him in the language or dialect of the Tuscalaro Indians.
>
> [...]
>
> Only a few days before this time the Indians had killed Jack Phillips six miles west of Mr. Hudspeth's house, and it was supposed this was the band he was with, although the young Indian said nothing about this killing. Now the rangers were after this band of Indians, and crowded them so close that several of their horses gave out and were left on the trail, and it was supposed it was at this time the boy was left, but before the killing of Phillips. The horses of the rangers gave out also, and they turned back at Wallace Creek.

[From the Pioneer History account:]

> The young Tuscalero was turned over to Polly Rodriguez, a well known guide and trailer for the rangers. He remained with Rodriguez many years and was known to all of our early settlers.

[Document 279, Volume 4 Texas Indian Papers. From a report of Indian Depredations, under "Citizens killed":]

J M Phillips	[Dec] 28 [76]	[reported by]	W Hudspeth
1 man in Llano	" 27	"	"
3 " Bandera	Jan 77	"	

Citizens recovered

1 Boy (Mex) Jany 2 77 reptd by W Hudspeth

[Captain Merritt of Kerr County's Reserve Militia made this report:]

W. Steel Adjudant Gen.
Austin Texas.

Sir!

    I have the honor to report to your office for the month of January 1877 for my Company.

    On Christmas Evening a Party of Indians, Mexicans, or Outlaws disguised as Indians 8 or 10 in number made their appearance on Bear Creeck a tributary of the North forke of Llano in Kimble County, Stole a number of Horses & killed two boys by the name of Sam Spears & Kuntz & thence proceeded Southeast by the way of Pedernales to a point near Hendersons Creek a tributary of the Guadaloupe river 10 miles above Kerrville, where they stole a number of more horses thence proceeded by way of Indian Creek & South forke of Guadaloupe River to the head of Walles Creek a tributary of the Medina river & from there proceeded in the direction of the Rio Frio Stealing many horses on the way & killing one more man on the Medina river by the name of Allen.

    Capt. Moore of the Frontier batalian on the killing of the two boy on Bear Creeck started imediatly in pursuit following the said trail for three days & trail for three days & nights leaving of at the head of Walles'es Creek owing to the Horses & men being unable to pursue further.

    Upon my learning of the Indians trails leading in the direction of the Rio Frio & believing them to turn toward the Head of Nueces or Devils river I detailed 6 men & started to the waters of the Rio Frio expecting perhaps to intersect possibly the trail or meeting the party.

    As it turned out however the Indians had passed further down on the Frio & I have since learnd had been pressed so hard as to leave all their stolen horses by a party of citizens near Frio City in Frio Co

    Our Scout not succeeding in our purpose, returned on the fourth day after traveling a distance of about 120 miles.

    Losses occured during the scout none.

    Closing I have the Honor to subscribe myself Respectfully Your Obediant Servant

    S.R. Merritt

Capt. Comdg. Comp. A.
Reserve State Militia
Kerr Co. Tex.

Jan. the 15th A.D. 1877.

[Pat Dolan:]

Camp Wood Tex Jan 5th 1877

Major Jno B Jones
Comdg Frnt Batt Austin

Sir

Since writing to you on the 1st I learn that Indians have been in East and South of here   Reports say that they came down the north Llano to Goudaloupe and Bandera from there they must have crossed over to the Hondo thence to Mr Kennedeys Pasture on the Sabinal and down to Frio Town   So far I am unable to say which way they went out   Capt Coldwell did not notify me and I only have this from report but believe it true

Very Respectfully

Pat Dolan
Lieut Comdg Co. F

The number of ranger companies monitoring the route of these raiders demonstrates the impossible situation the Comanche raiding tradition had reached. Their homeland was increasingly controlled by the U.S. Army and the buffalo were nearly gone. In March 1877 the adjutant general ordered the Frontier Battalion to cease regular Indian scouts unless in actual pursuit. In Bandera County and the rest of the frontier counties, control of lawlessness became a priority.

County sheriffs were limited by jurisdiction and the laws and customs of their time. Although Sheriff T.C. Rine was sometimes involved in manhunts for notorious criminals, he, like most sheriffs of the time, was often an arbiter, diplomat, and server of papers. Most often, it seems, Sheriff Rine would give a perpetrator a reprimand and say, "Vote for me in the next election." If he found it necessary to lock up anyone overnight, the prisoner was kept in his kitchen or chained to a tree. He reported only two outstanding arrest warrants during his tenure as Bandera County sheriff, appointed to office 1866-68 and elected to office 1869-73.

In 1869 82 out of 158 Texas counties had no jail and only 24 county jails in Texas were reputed to be secure. As the 1860s gave way to the 1870s, Bandera County found the need for stronger measures. B.F. Langford built the first jail in Bandera City which Marvin Hunter described in <u>100 Years In Bandera</u>:

> It consisted of a small room about 14x14 feet made of sawed cypress timbers, 6x6 inches in thickness, laid flat one on top of another. Only one small window, placed near the top, afforded light and ventilation. There was no door, only an opening in the flat roof, fitted with a lid. A ladder led to the top of the little square building. Prisoners were taken up on this ladder, then the ladder was pulled up and used to put the prisoner down inside the jail. A ring was bolted to the floor, and desperate prisoners were chained to this ring to prevent escape. This is one jail no prisoner ever escaped from, although one or two attempts were made by friends on the outside to release a prisoner.

Henry "Buck" Hamilton married Anne Phillips in Tennessee in 1856 and they moved to Kerr County in 1859. A farmer, rancher, trail boss, and entrepreneur, Buck Hamilton was Kerr County Sheriff 1862-64. In 1869 he moved his family to Bandera City where he established the Bandera Hotel and a stage line between Bandera and San Antonio. He was elected sheriff of Bandera County in 1875 and took his brother-in-law, Jack Phillips, as his deputy. Also serving as deputies at various times were Bladen Mitchell, John Pyka, Henry S. Hudspeth, and F.J. McCarthy. Buck Hamilton served from 1875 to 1888 when he died from a relapse of measles.

By the end of 1876 Neil Coldwell was leading the prestigious Company A. Later in 1877, Captain Coldwell deployed a detachment of five men to the Austin area where Company E needed help in the search for the Sam Bass Gang. In the meantime, Company F under Lieutenant Pat Dolan operated over a wide range of territory from Kimble County to Uvalde, Medina, Bandera, and Kerr counties. The men of Company F made their station, Camp Wood, the center of law and order on the West Texas Frontier. Lieutenant Dolan reported:

Camp Wood Tex Feb 19th 1877

Jno. C. Sullivan Esq}
Castroville   Texas }

Friend John

when you go to Kerrville to attend Court I would like for you to try and investigate the career of J.B. Johnson and Bros. in Kerr and Edwards Cos. and to enable you to arrive at some definite result have Al. McDonald, S.B. Rainey and Ed Hill summoned to appear before the Grand Jury of said co. question them as to their Knowledge about the Sale of hides by J.B. Johnson or any of his brothers to one R.L. Branclon a Puller [someone who arranges a sale or transaction?] if the ears of said hides were whole or were they cut entirely off also if they ever Saw Said Johnsons ever blotch the brands on any cattle if they Know of the Johnsons driving off 17 head of cattle from Dublens Ranche on the Llano if the brands of said cattle wer blotched I captured a young fellow yesterday who calls himself Franklin I believe he has been in jail some place there were two of them he says the other fellow was in jail in Castroville his name was Eckwood they were bothe riding stolen horses one a small Mexican Pony branded thus AR on left thigh white spot in forehead said to be stolen below the crossing of Austin Road on the Salado the other a Dun work horse branded thus JL left thigh 13 on neck and branded very dim J on left shoulder claimed to have been stolen from Norton in Bandera Co who lives near Bluff Creek at the next Uvalde Court have Bill Wells before the Grand Jury ask him if he ever saw 4 or 5 men have a bunch of Cattle rounded up and shooting them down and who were they

    Respectfully

    Pat Dolan

P.S. I sent a Pedler named Barten to Kerrville [having?] 30 beef hides on his Wagon without a Bill of Sale they were stolen hides he acknowledged that he bought 12 hides from Sam Rainey and Jim Goodman who were also sent over to Kerrville but all parties were turned loose simply with the loss of the hides is there no way of punishing thieves in this country the Puller could have been put through for Peddling and I learn an affidavit was made there setting forth that fact maybe it would be well enough to look into the actions of the county Attorney for Kerr Co

    Dolan

the hides were all sold in Edwards Co.
at Uvalde please See that Jim Goodman is Indicted <u>only</u> for the <u>offence</u> committed <u>in</u> <u>Uvalde</u> <u>Co</u> not for any offence committed in Edwards Co

    Dolan

Camp Wood Tex. Feb 19th 1877

Major Jno. B. Jones
Comdg Front Batt Austin

Sir

    I am in reciept of yours of the 10th and was very glad to hear from you as I was afraid you were not in Austin I wrote to you a few days ago asking more men and would again respectfully repeat the request as there is plenty of work to be done here but with the small number of men it is a hard matter for me to do much good as my camp is continually watched and all our movements are carefully noted by violators of the law or their friends I have got the run of things pretty well now and if you will give me the men I believe I can do a great deal of good for this section of country If you can give me 30 men it is all that I would ask I have a man in arrest that we caught yesterday for theft of a six shooter I believe he is a horse thief his name is Franklin he had the Pistol on when we captured him there were two of them they both ran off and left their horses - we got both horses and one man

    I am informed by a truthfull man that Baird has sold out and left but can not Positively say that it is so he is verry wild since McNelleys men went to his house and arrested the wrong man if you can possibly do so send about 3. pair Shackles or leg Irons for Prisoners if you could furnish a part of my men with improved Winchester Carbines and charge them with them they would be glad to have them if not too dear

    the only fault I found to Kingsbury was that every man he messed with Kept coming to me complaining about him being so trifling in the mefs and he run his horse to death every time he got out of my sight I tried him in my own mess while I would sit and watch him he would cook and no longer I made him help clean up around the mefs a couple of times and each time I done more than he did but it seemed to grate on his sense of honor very much to have to help to do anything in that line that was all the misunderstanding we ever had the simple fact of the matter was that he was a Kind of a Pest to all the men

    would respectfully solicit an immediate answer as to recruiting more men

    Respectfully

        Pat Dolan
        Lieut Co F Front Batt

P.S. the Prisoner Franklin has just admitted that the horses we captured last night are both stolen one was taken on the Salado near the San Antonio and Austin crossing a small sorrell mexican Pony branded thus on left thigh AR small white spot on forehead the other a dun horse stole near Bluff Creek Bandera Co from a man named Norton branded thus on left thigh JL and 13 on neck one colts Pistol the owner of which lives 4 miles from here what shall I do with the horses

    Pat Dolan
    Lt. Co. F

I believe I can trace the theft of 17 head of cattle to J.B. Johnson who lives at Camp Wood the Cattle should have been stolen from a man named Dublen on the Llano if you Know any one of that name it would be well to refer him to me

    Dolan
    Lieut Co F

[King Fisher was sometimes an outlaw and sometimes a lawman in the Uvalde area. He was captured by Texas Rangers more than once, but never convicted in a court. Lieutenant J.L. Hall of the Special Force made this report:]

    Castroville Medina Co July 29th/77

Hon Wm Steele
Austin Texas

    I have the honor to report my arrival here on Wednesday 25th. I found Sergt Parrott in Camp with Eighteen men, he having arrived a few days before from Uvalde with King Fisher, his detachment having scouted over Uvalde, Bandera, Maverick, Medina & Atascosa. he also sent a scout into Mexico in pursuit of the Trimble murderes but did not effect their arrest. I find Sergt Parrott has made about five arrests but his time has been principally occupied <u>w</u> guarding prisoners in the jails of this and Uvalde Counties
    I have reports from Lieut Armstrong & Sergt Watson in which they mention a number of arrests made in their section, but it will be impossible for me to send in a monthly statement of arrests for this month they command being so much scattered, but will forward it as early as possible. Valdes and Escobedo having disbanded their forces on the Rio Grande, they have turned loose a herd of thieves & cutthroats of whom the people of that section are very much

alarmed. I shall endeavor to arrest such of them as we can identify and will report to you as soon as I reach that Section. I understand that one of their camps is situated about twenty miles from Eagle Pafs & they are Killing cattle promiscuasly I will report more fully so soon as I visit that Country.

Very Respectfully, Your obed't Serv't

    J.L. Hall
    Comdg Sp'l Co S. Troops

We have both the Cavias & they have made confessions implicating about twelve other men in murders in various places for whom I have this day procured a bench warrant from Judge Paschal and will proceed to execute at once.

    Hall

In the summer heat Captain Coldwell and three other Texas Rangers rode into Bandera County. On August 16, 1877 Major Jones reported to Adjutant General Steele:

> I learn from one of my men just in from Frio that Capt. Coldwell started on ten days scout to Bandera County on the 12th inst. Had two other Scouts out at same time in different directions all for ten days and only three men in camp when my informant left.

[Incidentally there was a county commissioner named Jack Hamilton at this time. James B. Gillet remembered Sheriff Buck Hamilton as "Jack":]

> I remember a scout I was called on to make with Captain Coldwell over in Bandera County. The captain took with him John Parker, Hawk Roberts, and myself. In one week's time we caught some ten or twelve fugitives from justice and literally filled the little jail at Bandera. Captain Coldwell detailed Hawk Roberts and myself to capture an especially bad man wanted in Burnet County for murder. The captain warned us to take no chances with this man--this meant to kill him if he hesitated about surrendering. I can't remember this murderer's name at this late date, but I recall perfectly the details of his capture. Sheriff Jack Hamilton of Bandera County sent a guide to show us where the fugitive lived. The guide led us some fifteen miles northwest of Bandera and finally pointed out the house in which the murderer was supposed to be. He then

refused to go any farther, saying he did not want any of this man's game, for the fellow had just stood off a deputy sheriff and made him hike it back to Bandera.

It was almost night when we reached the house, so Roberts and I decided to wait until morning before attempting the arrest. We staked our horses, lay down on our saddle-blankets without supper, and slept soundly till dawn. As soon as it was daylight we rode over near the house, dismounted, slipped up, and, unannounced, stepped inside the room. The man we wanted was sleeping on a pallet with a big white-handled .45 near his head. Hawk Roberts kicked the pistol out of his reach. The noise awakened the sleeper and he opened his eyes to find himself looking into the business ends of two Winchesters held within a foot of his head. Of course he surrendered without a fight. His wife, who was sleeping in a bed in the same room, jumped out of it and heaped all kinds of abuse on us for entering her home without ceremony. She was especially bitter against Sheriff Hamilton, who, she said, had promised to notify her husband when he was wanted so he could come in and give himself up. She indignantly advised her husband to give old sheriff Hamilton a damned good whipping the first chance he had.

In 1878 Albert Maverick, a grandson of Samuel Maverick, bought the Mott Ranch, "several thousand acres of land on Winan's Creek and the Medina river between Bandera and Medina City, which was afterwards known as the Maverick ranch". Mrs. Jane Maury Maverick recalled when John King Fisher stopped by the ranch:

He arrived late one evening with a lot of cowboys and a good sized bunch of cattle.

[...]

To my inexperienced eye he was a very innocent looking cowboy, tall and thin and dark. He and I had a very pleasant conversation about his wife and babies before I knew who he was. Not very long after this visit he was shot in San Antonio in the Jack Harris theater with Ben Thompson.

In January 1879 John B. Jones became Adjutant General of Texas. The rank of major of the Frontier Battalion was abolished. Neal Coldwell, the last of the original captains, became Quartermaster. (Pat Dolan was promoted to captain of Company F.) Captain Coldwell, as quartermaster, was responsible for administration of the Battalion and oversight of its personnel. Like Major Jones before him, he constantly moved to various trouble spots until his retirement in 1883. He retired to his ranch in Kerr County where he died in 1925. He is buried in the Center Point Cemetery.

14

The Last Minutemen

In 1876 near the present town of Divine, Annie E. Brown, a widow since 1863, sold her boarding house to Big Foot Wallace who had been one of her boarders. She located a homestead near the community of Hondo Canyon, which eventually became the town of Tarpley. Jack Phillips had been killed a short distance away just two weeks before she took possession of her land:

> Having filed on land as a homestead, I felt that I should go and live on it, as the law required it, and, over the protest of my neighbors, I took my son and camped under a large oak tree. While here Grandpa Cazey came and begged me to leave; said he was afraid he would have to come and pick up my bones some day. I replied that if it was to be my fate I would just as soon have him pick them up as anybody, but this was my home and I intended to stay.

In the wake of the Indian raids of 1876 there was much discussion across the West Texas Frontier about the need to raise minuteman companies. Rio Frio was no exception. The town was just inside the southwestern corner of Bandera County as the boundary existed at that time, but it was many miles and several divides from convenient access to Bandera City. Uvalde was the nearest town of any size.

Rio Frio Uvalde Co. Texas

Aug 20th 76

To Hon Richard Coke Gov of the State of Texas

Dear Sir
    we the Citizens of Rio Frio ask your Friendly aid to assist us in repeling the frequent raids by hostile Indians Our locality is too far distant from the United States Forts to render us any available protection Fort Clark being the nearest post distance 85 miles from this locality and unfortunately for us we reside in a passway for the Indi-

ans to the interior and of late neither life or property is Secure can we get any assitance from you in regard to protection can you arrange for us to have a minute company if not can we get Some arms and ammunition by giving the proper Security for return of them we ask your advice and friendly aid to assist us. The population of this locality is about four or five hundred inhabitants and we request Mr J.J.H. Patterson of Rio Frio to correspond with you for the purposesen herein Stated and at the Same time hoping you will notice our requsnt and meet your approbation

    Yours Most Truly
        Many Citizens

During January 1877 Medina County citizens debated the need for a minuteman ranger company. Captain Coldwell investigated and found that the old-time residents did not feel any need for one, but the newcomers in the county did. The old-timers were more aware of the changes that had taken place. As Comanche raids into Texas decreased, Lipan Apache and Kickapoo raids, which also had been tapering in number since the mid1870s, continued mostly around the outer settlements of West Texas.

In fall of 1878 Indians thought to be Lipans and/or Kickapoos made their last raid into Kerr County and killed several children on Johnson's fork of the Guadalupe River. The Kerr County citizens asked for ranger protection and got Company E of the Frontier Battalion which had recently been involved in the hunt for Sam Bass. The ranger company, including Second Sergeant James B. Gillett, was stationed in Kerr County during the winter of 1878-79. Lieutenant N.O. Reynolds reported from Camp Contrary (on Contrary Creek) that he did not think his company was doing much good there. James Gillett said that it was the quietest winter he had spent in the ranger service. Lieutenant Reynolds resigned in February due to a medical problem and First Sergeant C.L. Nevill took over Company E reporting from Camp Johnson's Creek and later from Camp Billings.

In January 1879 Captain Pat Dolan at Camp Wood had many of the men of Company F out on various assignments, mostly after outlaws, and had just found out about a "crowd of vagabonds in the Kingfisher neighborhood who are stealing horses and cattle promiscuously." Another large band of outlaws was discovered to be operating from the Devil's River. Captain Dolan was concerned about having enough men on hand at Camp Wood as it was "getting near full moon (Indian time)." A detachment from Company E temporarily bolstered the force of Company F. James Gillett explained the situation:

> The fund appropriated for frontier defense two years before was now running short, and in order to make it last until it could be ascertained what the legislature would do, it became necessary for General Jones to order the various captains to discharge three men out of each company. A week later a similar order was promulgated, and this process was kept up until the battalion was reduced to almost one-half its former strength.

Camp Wood had attracted a few settlers as early as the army camp days. While some came and went, other remained permanently, particularly after the Civil War. R.S. Johnson and his family were among those living around the ranger station on the Nueces. He wrote to the adjutant general:

Camp Wood Tex
June 8th 1879

General John B Jones
Austin Tex.

Dear Sir
    in my Letter of the 3d written at Brackett I stated, Colston's two "Girls" but I had been missinformed. The youngest in its third year was a "<u>Boy</u>" & the Girl was in her (12th) year. its not posatively known which way the Indians went as they were not followed. when I started to Brackett the Neighbors, said they would start that Evening but failed todoso I believe I am warranted in saying if the State does not afford this section "Protection" that in a very short time half of the best Citizens will leave, & all the New comers, their has been 10 or 12 families moved in this section & ,2, of them had every Horse stole that they owned. I have heard <u>Hatch</u>, <u>Mulkey</u>, <u>Pullen</u> & <u>Webb</u> say they would not stay in the country as they could not leave home & feel that their families were Safe The "Rangers" while here did all that could bee done & the People felt safe. I understand the same feeling exists on the Dry & Main Frios that does in this Section--
    Respectfully Yours
        RS Johnson

P.S. Since we have lived here, four years the first of "January" their has been <u>Seven Persons</u> killed ,2, wounded & ,5, Shot at all by Indians & we alone have lost <u>32</u> head of Horses. RSJ

In 1878 the first house went up in the area that became Medina City near the forks of the Medina River. B.F. Bellows, a sheep-raiser, bought the land in 1879 and began selling parcels and town lots. James W. Walker and Thomas J. Sheppard opened a store. James Walker, a cattle-raiser, sold his interest to a Mr. Cunningham. By 1881 the store was advertised in The Bandera Bugle as "Sheppard & Bro., Medina City, Texas, dealers in general merchandise." Frank Buckelew remembered the times:

> The year of 1879, I went to live with Uncle Billie Sheppard and family, whose home was then on the old Jack Ranch, some seven or eight miles north of Bandera. That summer when the crops were laid by the men folks went to the shingle camps. They left me to guard the women in case of an Indian attack, and as no occasion presented itself to test my fighting qualities while thus entrusted, I passed for a fairly good guard.
>
> After crops were gathered we all moved to the shingle camps at the mouth of Sheppard's Creek on the Medina. Jack Sheppard and I were close friends and about the same age. We both liked to hunt, so kept the camp supplied with meat. We usually worked in the shingle camp all week and Saturday evening we would go out on a hunt. Wild cattle were plentiful and we had little trouble getting plenty of meat. Sometimes we killed deer and bear. We often found wild honey, and would case a deer skin and pack it full of honey.

By 1880 two Italians, Martin Cereghetti and Frank Roboles, were living in the mostly Hispanic community of Polly. Another Italian immigrant, Francisco Gerodetti, bought land from Polly Rodriguez and set up a general store in Polly in 1885. Mico Mimico, Camp Verde camel driver and Texas Ranger, is buried near Bear Creek on land that was the Gerodetti ranch.

A surveying camp established in northwestern Uvalde County by Charles de Montel in 1870 eventually became the town of Montell in the early 1880s. Before that, Camp Montel was the station for Company G, 37 men commanded by Captain A. Wilkerson, 1st Texas Volunteer Cavalry, also known as the Montel Guards, organized in Uvalde County in 1880. The governor authorized the county sheriff (probably J.J.H. Patterson, in office November 5, 1878 to August 31, 1881) to enroll the company. The minutemen appointed Major Montel as their advisor.

Florence Fenley wrote about many early settlers of the Uvalde area including Wyatt E. Heard who, at the age of 18, served as first lieutenant of the company. He remembered that they were sworn in by George Baylor, son of John R. Baylor.

> After a year's service, our company was disbanded and the guns returned to Austin. For this service we were to get $60 a month, furnishing ourselves with everything but the guns. We got what the little boy shot at.

In her account of another member of the Montel Guards, William Wall, Florence Fenly said, "Not only did they follow Indian Trails, but they were successful in subduing outlawry in this territory where it had been a profitable business and pastime." John R. Baylor's letter to Adjutant General King suggests that things were a little more complicated:

Montel [P.O.?] Sept 10th 1881

GenL
     I return the Muster Roll of the Montel Guards with two additional names. The men were sworn in as the other men by a magistrate. If you ship us the arms Send them to Frank Burkett, Uvalde. he is a prominent Merchant and responsible. I think it my duty Genl to offer a suggestion that if acted on may save trouble. There is at the head of this Canon a nest of theives who are robbing openly. We have made several attempts to arrest them without succesf and in consequence there is a bad feeling between us there are writs for several of them and there are escaped convicts. the[y] are splendidly armed and mounted and always on the alert. It is almost imposfible to go from here and catch them. they never sleep in houses and have spies on the look out all the time. If you can spare a half dozen of [?] men and station them in that neighborhood the men would either be caught or the clan scattered. If any of our Company attempt to make an arrest the result will be a fight and most likely end in a war of neighborhoods which would not be the case if the rangers should kill or wound any of them in making arrests. I learn they are getting up a Company of Guards and as over half are [notable?] theives the Co. wont work much good to the State. I hope you will think best to act on this suggestion and at once.
     Respectfully
     Jn. R Baylor

No one in the Bandera region was killed by Indians for some time after 1879. Lipans continued to make mostly isolated horse stealing raids, mostly west of the Frio River. A.J. Sowell gave an account of the Lipan Apache raid into Frio Canyon that took place about six miles north of Leakey April 19, 1881:

> At the time [John] McLauren left home that morning a band of Indians came around on top of the mountains and stopped on the cliff which overlooked all the valley and house, and no doubt saw the settler when he left home. The family at home consisted, besides the mother and boy Allen [Lease], of Maud, 6 years old; Alonzo, 3 years, and Frank, the baby in arms. The eldest daughter, Mary, was away boarding with the family of Richard Humphreys, near Leakey, and going to school.

[Friday, April 22, the San Antonio Daily Express printed a vague report from Uvalde:]

> Mysterious Triple Murder: Mysterious Mob Kill Three Persons in Edwards County--McLaurence and Wife and a Mr. Case.
>
> Special to the San Antonio Express.
>
> Uvalde, Texas, April 21st, 1881.-On last Teusday afternoon, a party of fifteen men rode up to the McLaurence's house, on the Frio, in Edwards county, and took the lives of McLaurence, his wife and a young man living with them, named Case. The whole affair is shrouded in mystery, as everything pertaining to the household was left undisturbed. The above news was brought here this afternoon by parties living in that neighborhood. The particulars have not yet been received.

[The paper received more particulars for its April 24th edition:]

> The McLaurin Ranch Tragedy
> Another Account of the Frio Canon Horror
>
> Special Correspondence San Antonio Express
>
> Rio Frio, Texas April 20.-On yesterday about 40 Indians visited the upper part of this canon, fifteen miles above this point, and killed Mrs. John McLaurin and Allen Reiss, of Uvalde, while in the garden near the house at work. When they discovered the Indians, Mr. Reiss started to the house to get his gun, but was shot down before he could reach it. Mrs. McLaurin started to run for [her] life and was shot down also.

Her three little children were with her, and the oldest, six or seven years old, "Little Maud," when her mamma fell, ran to the house, and taking a pillow from the bed placed it under the lady's head and then placed the two small children by her side, and started for G.W. Fisher's house to give the alarm.

Little Maud says when she was in the house after the pillow, that it was full of men, "big black men". They did not seem to take any notice of the child. They destroyed everything in the house of any value, even the sewing machine.

There will be a party of men leave here to-day in pursuit, but with very little prospects of overtaking the murderers.

Mr. D.W. Ward and wife were in the vicinity looking at the country, and have not been heard from. Fears are entertained for their safety. Everybody is greatly excited over the sad affair.

The weather is dry, with very high winds. The crops are in good condition but will need rain in a short time.

L.C. Neel

Young Maud brought help for her dying mother. Allen Lease, the 15-year-old boy who worked for the McLaurens, had been killed instantly. Catherine McLauren, 32, died shortly after help arrived. Their burials were the first recorded at the Florel-Leakey Cemetery where their gravesites are a short distance apart. The A.J. Sowell account states:

> Twenty men assembled to follow and fight the Indians, if possible to overtake them. The trail was taken up at the McLauren ranch, and it led back up the mountain the way they had come down. Among the pursuers were W.J. McLauren, captain; Tobe Edwards, James Hicks, -- Coryell, H.T. Coston, Henry Wall (better known as "Boy" Wall), Frank Pollard, George Leakey, M.V. Pruitt, John Thompson, and Frank Sanders. John McLauren, husband of the slain woman, was not of the party, the reason of which he says was his horse running into a stooping tree the day of the killing and nearly putting his eyes out, so that he could hardly see for several days.
>
> [...]

Coryell left them where the trail crosses the road that runs from Brackett or Fort Clark to Howard's Well, and went to Fort Clark and informed Lieutenant Bullis, who commanded the Seminole scouts, of the raid, and where they last saw the trail, which he was satisfied led into Mexico. Bullis at once took his scouts, and getting on the trail followed it out of Texas and five days into Old Mexico to a place called by the Seminoles "Horseshoe Bend." Here the Indians were in camp in a little valley on a creek.

> [...]

A general charge was now made on the camp, and some were killed before they got up from where they were lying, and others as they ran.

As the railroad built west of San Antonio in the late 1870s, Charles de Montel campaigned to have the line go through Castroville. The railroad's demand of $50,000 soured the deal as Castroville citizens refused to pay. To this day the railroad makes a long loop around the town. (Charles Scheidemontel died in Castroville August 3, 1882 and was buried in the family cemetery on his nearby ranch.)

Although Indian raids and outlaw activity continued along the outer settlements, the older West Texas settlements began to feel more secure. While social and technological changes were gradually taming the West, the Bandera region could still be a very rough place. Polly Rodriguez remembered March 23, 1880, when Arthur Pue went:

> to the barroom in Bandera, and there came a stranger there--a gambler--and Arthur gambled with him all day. Late in the evening he at last won all that Arthur had, and as he raked the money in some one made a sign to Arthur that the man had some cards up his sleeve. Arthur drew his pistol and leveled it at him and cursed him for a cheating scoundrel, and told him to shake those cards out of his sleeve. He shook his sleeve and three aces fell out, and Arthur took back his money. The man stood around awhile and went out. After dark Arthur stepped outside the door, and while standing there the man shot him in the dark without warning. The ball struck him in the side. Arthur turned toward the flash of the pistol, drawing his own as he turned. As he turned around, the man fired again. The ball struck Arthur in the breast below the heart, and he fired at the same time. The bullet from Arthur's pistol struck the man in the eye and killed him on the spot. Arthur died next morning.

A few years later stage lines in Kerr, Uvalde, and Bandera counties were experiencing hold-ups. The man believed responsible for these hold-ups, referred to only as "the lone highwayman," in newspaper accounts, stopped by the Hay ranch September 10, 1888. George Alexander Hay whose father had come to the county with Lyman Wight, had married Sarah Elizabeth Gibbons of Castroville a few years previously. They had two children by this time. The Lone Highwayman intended to plunder the ranch house, but Lizzie Hay stepped up with a Winchester in hand. After a scuffle, the wounded highwayman staggered back to his horse. He carried a bullet in his chest, Lizzie was left with a knife cut across her forehead. The next day lawmen found the man dead a couple of miles away.

The railroads widely advertised the availability of land along their routes and attracted many immigrants from the British Isles. Robert Maudslay and his brother, Harry, staked a homestead on some unoccupied land next to the land they had bought in Bandera County. They encountered a challenge from a claim jumper. Although the dispute was eventually settled peacefully in court, the brothers from England experienced some Wild West excitement before it was done. After an incident between the plaintiff and Harry Maudslay, Sheriff Buck Hamilton came by the Maudslay place and asked Harry if he carried a gun.

> On being told that he didn't, the sheriff said, "Then take this one; I think you're going to need it." Whereupon he gave Harry a .38 calibre pistol with all its chambers loaded.

[After another event Sheriff Hamilton visited the Maudslay ranch again as Robert Maudslay recalled:]

> After this incident, I was also presented with a pistol, and thereafter I might be seen following my peaceful occupation of plowing with a six-shooter partly exposed from my hip pocket. I practiced with it a little, too, and sometimes came quite near to hitting what I shot at.

The Maudslay brothers had come to Texas with their highly-educated mother and four sisters. Mrs. Maudlay's School For Girls became well-known for academic excellence in the region. Robert Maudslay said his mother and sisters, "did a good job with French, music, drawing, literature--mostly English--and mathematics, but when it came to history it seems that the American story was largely neglected in favor of a thorough knowledge of the British rulers from the first to Victoria."

The Literary Club had formed in Bandera City at least by 1879, holding meetings every Saturday night in the courthouse. Polly Rodriguez remembered when James Tafolla "organized a society, which was for mutual help and instruction" which met once a month on Sunday in the Polly schoolhouse.

> James Tafolla, my cousin, now lived in the same neighborhood with me on Privilege Creek. He had been educated in Georgia, and had been a bugler in the army, and when he settled down after the war he was elected a petty officer of the peace, and although, like the rest of us, he had been pretty wild, he wanted to do better as an officer.

Women became involved in public life through their church groups and other organizations. A branch of the United Friends of Temperance formed in Bandera City in 1879 and remained active through the 1880s. The charter membership included 13 men and 20 women.

December 5, 1881, Adjutant General W.H. King sent out letters to the frontier counties asking if they still needed their state-provided firearms. Charles Schreiner and Henry Schwethelm recommended keeping Kerr County's for a while longer, perhaps a year, for the sake of citizens in the "upper portion" of the county. At the same time S.R. Merritt of Kerr County's Reserve Militia felt the arms were no longer needed. Medina County was ready to turn in its state arms if someone would say where to send them and pay for the transport. Bandera County was reported free of most outlaw activity and probably had not had state arms since 1875.

Agricultural developments brought other changes. Cotton became a more popular cash crop in Bandera County until the boll weevil came in the 1890s. George Alexander Hay was among the ranchers who initiated raising and breeding of goats, expanding the wool and mohair industry in West Texas. Cattlemen associated to regulate their industry, ending disputes over who could brand which cattle and when roundups began, but a new contention arose. Barbed-wire fencing came to the Bandera region beginning in the late 1870s and its use became widespread during the early 1880s. Robert Maudslay recalled:

> About this time, fencing of land became general all over the country. Mr. Albert Maverick was the first to commence in our county and Mr. Charles Montague followed suit. Mr. Strickland also fenced some of his land.

The "Big Pasture Men," those who fenced large tracts of ranch land with barbed-wire, were sometimes ruthless or careless individuals or conglomerates. Common roads were sometimes fenced across and access to water became a serious issue. Smaller ranchers with no water on their land and livestock raisers who owned little or no land, but had cattle running on the once-open range were faced with hard decisions, particularly in the drought year of 1883. Most of those without land moved farther west, while others made accommodations to their way of life. Before all was resolved, fence-cutters made their own gates and long stretches of barbed-wire fences were cut. A fall 1883 issue of the Bandera Enterprise editorialized:

> It appears to us that it is high time some effective steps were being taken to settle the troubles between the pasture men and their enemies. Considerable blood has already been shed, and dangerous sentiments are rapidly assuming such proportions as to become a rational source of alarm.

Texas Rangers were called upon to keep the peace in some areas of the state, but eventually calmer heads prevailed: Gates were made for common roads, water rights and boundaries were worked out, and the new methods of livestock raising, breeding, and marketing were established.

People continued to move west "settling up" all the arable land of West Texas. Many of the second and third generations of the Medina County pioneers went west, some settling in the area that became Real County. The region became part of the early form of Edwards County with Leakey as the county seat in 1883. Under the leadership of James Hunter, Rock Springs became the county seat in 1891 and the settlements along the upper Frio River were once again a long way from the county seat. After an unsuccessful attempt to form Beulah County around 1895, the upper Frio River citizens organized Real County with Leakey as the county seat in 1913.

As the trail drives ended in the late 1880s and the railroad economy quickened the pace of U.S. society, Bandera County was a well-established and thriving agricultural area. The region had long been considered as a potential health resort area. A fledging tourist industry had begun as people from San Antonio made the train trip to Center Point and the stage ride from there to Bandera City. A buggy ride out to Amasa Clark's orchards in springtime made a pleasant excursion for guests at the Duffy Hotel. The town had about 600 residents and was frequently visited by people from all over the region for business at the county seat and for use of the saw and grist mills and cotton gins. H.H. Carmichael & Company had moved into new and separate buildings for the store and saloon. The old Schmidtke & Hay store building was used as the courthouse from around 1874 until the present one was built in 1890. The county built a new stone jail and county office in 1883. William Hudspeth edited the Bandera Enterprise. The rival newspaper was the Bandera Bugle, edited by John Guthrie, a Scottish immigrant who also dealt in real estate and described Bandera City in 1888:

> Within its boundaries it contains four stores, lumber yard, two blacksmith shops, two carpenters, a saddler, three druggists, three house builders, two butchers, one surgeon, a catholic chapel and school taught by Sisters of Charity, a Methodist church, and a large school house, one saloon, a court house and jail, two large and fully equipped hotels. There is also one saw and two grist and flour mills, two cotton gins, two worked by water and one by steam; and two weekly newspapers published, the Bugle, the county paper and the Enterprise.
>
> The city is laid out in lots, and these can be obtained at from $40 to $80 each. Outside of the city there is no vacant land in large bodies, but there are a number of desirable farms for sale.

Appendix

Appendix Contents

A Word About Muster Rolls

Settlement Dates

Muster Roll, Mitchell's Company

Tales of bones dug up and reburied

Monthly Returns for Montel's Company

Monthly Return for Lawhon's Company

Confederate Trials

Letter from Major James Hunter

Resignations of Samuel Mott and Bladen Mitchell

Undated Bandera County Petition

Letter From August Pingenot

Various Minuteman Muster Rolls

Reports Regarding the Last Minutemen

Letter From George Hay

Statement by Mary Leakey Miles

A Word About Muster Rolls

A muster roll is a list of the names of the men in a military company. A ranger muster roll was occasionally a multipurpose document. The roll for Davenport's Company in 1856, served, through postscript, as the captain's report of the company's activities. Sometimes a roll incorporated the information usually presented in monthly returns. Separate monthly returns accounted for the whereabouts and condition of every person and animal in the company. Monthly returns were not often made except in some large organizations such as the Frontier Regiment. Payments to the men were sometimes recorded on the muster roll and sometimes on separate quartermaster or pay rolls. The number of men in a ranger company varied from around 20 to around 100. Most often their muster rolls had a preamble stating the name of the commander of the company (a captain or lieutenant, depending on the size of the company) and usually something about legislative or executive approval. If the company were part of a larger organization, the preamble might include the name of the captain's commander. Most rolls were written on large, sometimes newspaper-size, sheets of paper, sometimes with preprinted preambles with blanks to fill in, while others were entirely handwritten. Preprinted preambles herein transcribed are indicated by an underlining of the handwritten parts. The lists of names, sometimes with the men's ages, place of enrollment, or other information, is usually followed by a concluding statement in which the signatories verified the document as true. Usually it was signed by the company's commanding officer, the enrolling officer, and/or other officiaries.

Settlement Dates

Castroville, 1844, Medina County
New Braunfels, 1844, Comal County
Haby Settlement, 1846?; Rio Medina, 1900?, Medina County
Quihi, 1846, Medina County
Vandenburg, 1846; New Fountain, 1850s, Medina County
San Marcos, 1846, Hays County
Stringtown, 1847, Hays and Comal County
D'Hanis, 1847, Medina County
Fredericksburg, 1847, Gillespie County
Pedernales, 1847, Gillespie County
Sisterdale, 1847, Kerr County
Currys Creek Settlement, 1847; Hodges Mills, 1850s, Kerr County

Zodiac, 1848-1851, Gillespie County
Tusculum, 1849-51; Boerne, 1852, Kendall County
Patterson Settlement, 1852; Sabinal (six miles south), Uvalde County
Ware Settlement or Waresville, 1852; Montana; Utopia, 1880s, Uvalde County
Bandera City, 1853, Bandera County
Encina, 1853; Uvalde, 1856, Uvalde County
Pittsburgh, 1853; Blanco City, 1858, Blanco County
Comfort, 1854, Kendall County
Brown Settlement, 1854; Zanzenburg, 1859?; Center Point, 1872, Kerr County
Wight's Settlement; Mountain Valley (The Mormon Camp) 1854-1858, Bandera County
Kerrsville, 1856; Kerrville (spelling gradually in use from the 1860s), Kerr County
Hondo Canyon, mid-1850s; Tarpley, 1900, Bandera County
Polly, 1859, Bandera County
The Ditch, 1868; Rio Frio, 1875, Real County
Pipe Creek, mid-1870s, Bandera County
Florel and Leakey settlements, 1875; Leakey, 1883, Real County
Medina City, 1879, Bandera County
Bugscuffle; Vanderpool, 1880s, Bandera County

The 1860s

[No muster rolls for the home guards can be found at the State Library. The two rolls that are summarized in Chapter Eight are from the Frontier Organization period. The following is a more complete transcription of the February 1864 muster roll for Mitchell's Company. R = rifle, S = shotgun, P = pistol.]

Muster Roll of Captain B. Mitchell, Bandera County, District No. 3, Texas State Troops, for the month of Feb 1864.

No.	Name	Rank	Age	Arms	Remarks
1.	Adamitz Albert	4th Cpl	19	R	
2.	Aunderwald W	Pvt	28	R	X
3.	Bandy Tho	1st Cpl	45	R & P	X
4.	Bird Charles	Pvt	38	R & P	X
5.	Bird B F	Pvt	36	R & P	
6.	Bird Samuel	Pvt	28	R & P	X

7. Ballantyne Rbt	2nd Lt	35	R & P	X	
8. Christian S F	Pvt	37	R & P	d.	
9. Chipman E A	Pvt	46	R & P		
10. Chipman E P	Pvt	19	R & P	X	
11. Dugozs John	Pvt	46	R		
12. Freeman H V	Pvt	21	R & P		
13. Green Jno	Pvt	23	R & P		
14. Gonzales Santon	Pvt	42	R & P		
15. Hay Geo	4th Sgt	27	R & P	X	
16. Hay Alexander	Pvt	18	R & P	X	
17. Hoffman A	Pvt	37	S & P	X	
18. Hiduke Thos	Pvt	31	S	X	
19. Haywood L	Pvt	37	S & P		
20. Juritzke F	Pvt	37	S	X	
21. Klappenback A	Pvt	46	S & P		
22. Kalka Casper	Pvt	49	R		
23. Kalka Joseph	Pvt	28	R	X	
24. Loya Blafs	Pvt	33	R		
25. McCay H C	Pvt	46	R & P		
26. Miles O B	1st Lt	37	R & P	==	
27. Mott W H	2nd Sgt	28	R & P	XX	
28. McCay F M	3rd Sgt	19	R & P		
29. Mitchell B	Capt	27	R & P	X	
30. Martin Paul	Pvt	64	S		
31. Mazourick Thos	Pvt	46	S		
32. Merit K	Pvt	36	R	X	
33. Moravitz Joseph	Pvt	46	S	X	
34. Phillips J W	1st Sgt	33	R		
35. Poor J H	Pvt	37	R & P		
36. Pika Antone	Pvt	43	S		
37. Rodriguez J P	Pvt	34	R & P	X	
38. Rofs E M	Pvt	48	S & P		
39. Rugh Daniel	Pvt	30	R & P	==	
40. Rine S J	Pvt	56	S & P		
41. Rine T C	Pvt	30	R & P		
42. Saner P D	Pvt	41	R & P	==	
43. Sutherland Joseph	3rd Cpl	23	R & P	X	

44. Wight L L	**2nd Cpl**	**30**	S		
45. Woclawczk F	Pvt	39	S		
46. Curtis M	Pvt	46	R & P		
47. Goodwin W S	Pvt	36	S & P	==	
48. Arnold Daniel	Pvt	66	R		
49. Hiduke Albert	Pvt	49	S & P		
50. Miller J B	Pvt	46	R & P		
51. Garia Nicanor	Pvt	40	R		.d.
52 Gonzles Erineo	Pvt	38	R		.d.
53. Click A	Pvt	55	S		.d.

[The following handwritten comments precede the printed closing statement:]

All the names marked thus x is Conscripts Furloughed by order No.4

All marked thus == is County officers Exempt from military Service and Volenteered

xx conscript [applied for disability] certifacate

all [others?] on this Roll is volenteers Except those marked .d.

and belonged to the former Company known as Bandera Home Guardes

I certify, on honor that this Muster Roll exhibits the true state of Captain <u>Bladen Mitchels</u> Company of <u>Bandera</u> County, Texas State Troops, <u>mustered into state service on the 6th day of Feb 1864 and that the remarkes is Correct.</u>

OB Miles
Enrolling Officer, B. Co.

> [According to a muster and payroll for Mitchell's Company, one man died during the company's existence. No name or cause of death was given.]

[Candelario Trevino and James W. Walker herded camels along the slopes leading to Bandera Pass during the Civil War. One day they found what they believed to be the grave of the Comanche chief killed in the 1841 Battle of Bandera Pass:]

"Candelario wanted to dig the Indian up, and give him all the trouble he could, even though he was dead, for the wife of Candelario had been cut in the face by an Indian about the time of this fight took place with the rangers there, and he didn't like Indians any better than I do."

"This was the old chief who was killed in the Bandera Pass fight. Candelario and I took the dirk knife and dug up the old Indian. We found a whole hat full of beads and arrowheads and such stuff in the grave. We took all the beads we wanted and just left the old chief there with the rest of his junk."

[From Murtle Murray's account of F.L. Hicks:]

One day while going through Bandera Pass he found the skeleton of an Indian which had been dug up by some one. Beads and other things evidently buried with the Indian were scattered promiscuously about. Mr. Hicks dismounted and collected everything he could find that came out of the grave and placed them in the hole from which they were dug. Then, he reverently covered the remains and marked the grave by placing two stones above it.

[Four Monthly Returns of Montel's Company can be found in the State Library:]

Monthly Report of Charles de Montel's Company for April 1862. Fron. Regt.

Enlisted men on extra or dayly duty acct for by name:
Private Th. Reichezer, Clerk of the Company.
Private E. Taylor, Escorting post team.

Absent enlisted men acct for by name:
Sergt. R. Harper, Corp. D. Malone, Privates Tumlin, Runnels, J. Long, Cook, F. Kennedy, Davenport, Nowling, T. Mefser, Wight, Ward, Thompson, Rackley, Reinhardt, Manning, Onion,J., Ch. Dutcher, T. Terger - On a Scout after Indians.

H. Peden, A. Zimmerman, W. Cole, Osc. Johnson, Croke, J., F. Davenport - Patroll.

D. Bohls, J. Bohls, Bates I, Bates II, L. Heath, Tilly - Sick.

C. Pingenot, Fr. Tundre, R. Schwarz, H. Chipman, Balentyne - Patrol.

Corp. Davis and Private Stayton - Going to Austin under Order.

Commifs. Officers present & absent acct for by name:
1. Charl. de Montel Captain - en route to St. Antonio for Subsistence & Ammunition, etc.
2. Thom. P. McCall 1 Lieutenant A.A.Q.M. - bying forage.
3. E.V. Gates 2 Lieut - Commd. Camp Verde.
4. B. Patton 2nd Brevt. Lieut. - Commd. Camp Montel.

Present:
Com Offic. - 2
Enl. men - 68 for duty
    2 on extra or dayly duty
    0 In arrest
    2 Sick
    72 Total

Absent:
Comm. Offic. - 2 en detached service.
Enl. men - 32 on detach service
    0 with leave
    0 without leave
    0 In arrest
    4 Sick
    39 Total

Present & Absent:
Comm. Offic. - one Captain, one 1st Lieutenant, one 2nd Lieutenant, one 2 Br. Lieutenant
Enl. men - four Sergeants, four Corporals, two Bugler, one Farrier, one Blacksmith, 99 Privates
    111 Total
    115 aggregate

Alteration since last monthly return:
    Gain - one enlisted in Regt.
    Lofs - one by discharge, one by disease.

Memoranda:
    Horses - 118 servicable
    Mules - 19 recruits required, 4 servicable

Charles de Montel
Capt of G Company
F.R.T.R.

Return of Captain Charles de Montels Comp. D, Fr. Rgt. stationed at Camp McCord & Camp Montel for the month of June 1862.

Enlisted men on extra or dayly duty acct for by name:
  Th. Reichezer - Clerk Comp.
  E. Taylor - Esc. post team.

Absent enlisted men acct for by name:
  32 Privates
  D. Bawels, P. Bawels, S. Heath, Telley, McKinney I, McKinney II, R. Sanders, Sanson, Brown, Nowling, Casner, Shuchards - Sick.

  Wiley - absent with leave on acct of his sick family.
  Watson II to procure equipment.
  Jam. Brown, H. Allen, Brewer, Balentyne, Burney, Dolch, Hamilton, Harr, Lindemann, Hanning, Pingenots, Pullham, Tundre, Westfall I, Duncan, Davenport, Horton, Hiller - [on scout].

Commifs. Officers accounted for by name:
  1. Ch. de Montel Captain - absent on businefs with the military Command. Dept. of Texas.
  2. Thom. P. McCall 1st Lieut. A.A.Q.M. - buying forage.
  3. A.V. Gates 2nd Lieutenant - absent on a scout.
  4. B.F. Patton 2nd Br. Lieutenant - Commanding Camp Montel.

Alteration among enlisted men since last return:
  F. Watson, private, enlisted at Camp McCord on the 29th.
  E. Dodd, private, enlisted at Camp Montel on the 24th.
  W. Owens, private, enlisted at Camp Montel on the 24th.

Present:
  Comm. Off. - 1

Enl. Men - 73 for duty
  2 on extra or dayly duty
  3 Sick
  0 In arrest
  78 Total

Absent:
    Com. Off. - 3 on detach. service

Enl. men - 18 on detach. service
    2 with leave
    0 without leave
    12 Sick
    0 In arrest
    32 Total

Present & Absent:
    Com. Off. - one Captain, one 1st Lieutnant, one 2nd Lieutenant, one 2nd Br. Lieut.

Enl. Men - five Sergeants, four Corporals, two Buglers, one Blacksmith, one Farrier
    100 Privates
    113 Total
    117 aggregate
    114 aggregate last return

Alteration since last monthly return:
    Gain
    Enl. men - 3 enl. in Regt.
    Lofs 0

Memoranda:
    Horses - 120 servicable
    Mules - 19 Recruits required
    5 servicable

        Charles de Montel
        Capt Com/d Comp. D.
        F.R.T.R.

Return of Captain Charles de Montel's Company D, Frontier Regiment Stationed at Camp McCord & Camp Montel for the month of July 1862.

Commifsioned Officer prefent & absent accounted for by name:
    1. Ch. de Montel Captain
    2. Thom. McCall 1st Lieutenant
    3. A.V. Gates 2nd Lieutenant
    4. B.F. Patton 2 Br. Lieutenant

Alteration among enlisted men since last return:

F.L. Hicks, P. Conrad, Jos. Billharz, Sam Roberts, Fr. Kappert - enl. in Regiment [at] Camp McCord [July] 7.

John Grey, Private - discharged for disability by Special Order No. 44 from Head Quarters.

Lindsey, Private - enl. in Regt. [at] Camp McCord [no date].

Enlisted men on extra or dayly duty accounted for by name:
Th. Reicherzer - Clerk Comp.
B. Pullham - Post teamster
H. Allen - Afs. Black.
Kreifsl - Blacksmith

Absent enl. men accounted for by name:
H. Peden, J. Bendy, L. Heath, R. Sanders - Sick.

Present
Com. Offic. - one - for duty
Enl. men - 36 - for duty
    4 - on extra or dayly duty
    0 - Sick
    0 - In arrest
    49 - Total

Absent
Com. Offic. - 3 - on detached service
Enl. Men - 71 - on detached service
    0 - with leave
    0 - without leave
    4 - Sick
    0 - In arrest
    75 - Total

Present & Absent
Com. Offic. - one Captain, one 1st Lieutenant, one 2nd Lieutenant, one 2nd Br. Lieutenant
Enl. men - 5 Sergeants
    4 Corporals
    2 Bugler
    1 Farrier
    1 Blacksmith
    102 Privates
    115 Total
    119 aggergate
    117 aggregate last return

Alterations since last monthly return:

Gain
Enl. men - 6 - Enlisted in Regiment
Lofs
Enl. men - 4 - for disability

Memoranda
Horses - [blank]
Mules - [blank]

  Charles de Montel
  Com. D. Comp
  F.R.T.R.

RETURN Of Captain Charles de Montels Company D of the Texas Frontier Regiment stationed at Camp Verde & Montel Army of the Confederate States, (Colonel James N. Norris,) for the month of November 1862

Enlisted Men on "Extra or Daily duty," accounted for by name:
Th. Reicherzer - 30 days det. to afs. the A.A.Q.M. & A.A.C.S.
Cooper, Norris 30 days - post teamsters
L. Lee - blacksmith 13 days
Patton afs. blacksmith 13 days
Morehouse afs. Blacksmith 12 days
Lundsey - act. Clerk for Lieut. Col. McCord 1 day.

Absent Enlisted Men, accounted for by name:
Corp. Davis sick 34 days, Priv. Harr 98 days, Long 30 days, Dodd 6 days, Nowlin 20 days, Pullam 4 days sick.

Taylor, Davenport I, Torger, Shulz - after mail 2 days; Davenport II, Dodd II, L. Heath - det. after provisions 2 days; Lindeman III - hunt. horses 8 days.

D. Carnahan 5 days, Cude 7 days, Manning II 5 days, Roberts, Lindeman II 2 days - absent with leave

Sergt. Hill & Harper, Corp. Pafford, farrier Brown, Privates [44] Bates, Duncan, Wiley, Dodd, Dutcher, Johnson, L. Moore, Owens I & II, Onion, Peden, Reynolds, Reinhardt, Tomlin, Wilkins, Wight, Ward, Zimermann, Forrest, Brewer, Bushall, Balentyne, Bird, Billharz, Burney, Casner I & II, Chipman, Conrad, Gralen, Green, Haller, Hicks, Lauson, Nowling I & II, Pingenot, Patterson, Stayton I & II, Swarz, Tondre, Wood [I & II ?], Watson - on a scout 20 days

Present

Commissioned Officers - 2 - for duty
Enlisted Men - 39 - For duty
    7 - On extra, or daily duty
    2 - Sick
    0 - In arrest or confinement
    48 - Total

Absent
Commisioned Officers - 1 - On detached service 1 - With leave
Enlisted Men - 8 - On detached service
    5 - With leave
    0 - Without leave
    6 - Sick
    0 - In arrest or confinement
    48 - On Scout
    67 - Total

Present and Absent
Commissioned Officers [as before]
Enlisted Men
    4 Sergeants
    5 Corporals
    2 Musicians
    1 Artificers, Farriers, and Blacksmiths
    103 Privates
    114 Total Enlisted
    119 Aggregate
    120 Aggregate Last Monthly Return

Alterations Since Last Monthly Return:
    Gain - 0
    Loss - 1 - For disability

Memoranda
    Horses - 119

Commissioned Officers, present and absent, accounted for by Name:

Present
    1. Thos. P. McCall 1 Lieut - A.A.Q.M. & A.A.C.S.
    2. B. Patton 2 jr Lieut. - Comand/g Camp Montel

Absent
    1. Ch. de Montel Captain - Comd/g a scout. party 20 days
    2. A.V. Gates 2 Lieut. - with leave 46 days

Alterations Since Last Return, among the Enlisted Men:
 Rob. Sanders, Private - discharged for disability by Special Order No. 106 dated October 27th 1862 [at] Camp Montel

Station: Camp Verde
Date: Decb.

    Thos. P. McCall, 1st Lt.
    Commanding the Company.

RETURN of Captain <u>John Lawhons</u> Company <u>B</u> of the <u>Mounted</u> Regiment of <u>Texas State Troops</u> Army of the Confederate States, (Colonel <u>James E. McCord Comdg</u>,) for the month of <u>August</u> 186<u>3</u>.

Present

Commissioned Officers.
    For duty   2
    On extra or daily duty   1
    Sick
    In arrest or suspension
    Total   3

Enlisted Men.
    For duty   47
    On extra, or daily duty   5
    Sick
    In arrest or confinement
    Total   52

Absent

Commissioned Officers.
    With leave   1

Enlisted Men.
    On detached service   17
    With leave   1
    Without leave
    Sick   3
    In arrest or confinement
    Total   21

Present And Absent.

Commissioned Officers.
    Captain   1

First Lieutenants	1
Second Lieutenants	1
Brevet Second Lieutenants	1
Total Commissioned	4

Enlisted Men.

Sergeants	5
Corporals	4
Musicians	2
Artificers, Farriers, and Blacksmiths	1
Privates	61
Total Enlisted	73

Alterations Since Last Monthly Return.
    6 enlisted men re-enlisted
    1 enlisted man was transferred

Memoranda.
    No. of blank Company returns on hand 2
    Enlisted Men on "Extra or Daily duty," accounted for by name.
    one corporal, one artificer or farrier, and three privates
    Pafford, since 1st August 63. Issuing Sergt.
    Crawford since 1st August 63. Asfistant Blacksmith
    Pulliam, since 16th Aug. 63. Attending Publ. Anim.
    Tilley since 31st Aug. 63. making Cayaces for the A.A.Q.M.

Absent Enlisted Men, accounted for by name.
    Sergt. Casner, Priv. Bushnell, Casner, Gray, Brewer, Lindeman, Peden, Lundy, Marchanse, Walker I, Wight, Zimmerman, Green, Walker III on Scout since 24th of August 63.

    Benton, Mesfer since 19th Aug. 63. Burning Coal for A.A.Q.M.

    Click, since 21st Aug. 63. hunting runaway horses
    Cooper I, absent sick, since 30th July 63.
    Gralin, absent sick, since 21st August 63.
    Duvenick, absent sick, since 20th August 63.

    Wiley, absent with leave since 29th Aug. 63.

Station: Camp Verde
Date: Septbr. 1st, 1863.

        John Lawhon

Capt.

Confederate Trials

The men who were rounded up by Duff's Partizan Rangers were held in San Antonio. The trials began there June 28, 1862, and continued through October. James Sweet, temporarily detached from the Partizan Rangers, sat as one of the judges. Many were acquitted for lack of evidence. Some were fined and dismissed, some served jail time. Many of those acquitted or dismissed were turned over to the army as conscripts.

Edward Degener of Kendall County, charged with conspiracy and disloyalty, was released on a $5000.00 bond. H.J. Richarz of Medina County was found to have unsubstantiated charges and they were dismissed. Ferdinand Simon (stated as Bexar County resident) participated in the Nueces Battle and later was captured. He was sentenced to hang, but the sentence was suspended and he lived out the war imprisoned.

Three men sentenced to incarceration until the end of the war, escaped in August: Julius Schlickum, Kendall County, convicted of conspiracy, disloyalty, and refusal of CSA money. Phillip Braubach, Gillespie County Sheriff, convicted of depreciation of CSA money and disloyalty, received several sentences including incarceration until the end of the war. Ferdinand Doebbler, Gillespie County, was convicted of disloyalty.

[Captain Duff's reign of terror in Gillespie, Kerr, Kendall, and Blanco counties was known as the Henkerzeit or hanging times. The area was left in lawless turmoil. According to Biggers, Waldrip's Gang, who, as individuals had been trouble in the Fredericksburg area before the Civil War, took on a shield of Confederate authority as vigilantes during the war. James Hunter made some effort to bring justice to the Hill Country during that time. (Records of the Governor's Office. Texas State Library. Letter from Major James Hunter to Governor Murrah):]

Head Quarters Mch 31, 1864

To His Excellency Govenor Murrah

In obediance to your instructions on my return from Austin I proceeded to collect a force which I deemed sufficient to sustain the civil authorities in the investigation of the facts connected with the murder of Capt Schuitz and other murders and outrages perpetrated while I was gone to Austin. Accompaning this report is a copy of the evidence I have caused to be taken in relation to their transactions. The evidence it will be seen is full as to the outrages perpetrated, but defective in identifying the perpertrators. I found but one magistrate in the county and he the brother of one of the murdered men and very unwilling to act at all in taking the evidence of witness. I find a general feeling of terror exists in the country and an unwilingness to give evidence for fear of violence to their persons should they do so. Enough however has been developed to be made the base of further action on the part of the civil authorities and I have no doubt that if sustained by a sufficient force the whole of the perpertrators can be discovered--I have attempted to make no arrests. the order of your Excellency directing me to make none unless I deemed it necessary to do so to prevent escape. I do not think the perpertraters intend at present to attempt an escape. they believe themselves strong enough to resist any force that I have now at my command and as the process of the civil law is slow they believe their chances of escape by the power of combination sufficiently Strong to place them under no necessity to leave the country.

I have information from various sources that a secrete organization exists extending over a considerable district of country & embracing a number of Capt Banta's company at Camp Davis some belonging to my command some to the millitia & others belonging to no command. I believe that they engage to make comon cause with each other & to render assistance on to another in whatever they do to protect them from punishment. No evidence appears in the papers transmitted [except?] incidentally of the existance of an organization. It would perhaps been unsafe to have attempted it at present as the persons who might testify about it would be exposed to their resentment without adequate protection. As an evidence of the existance of an organization of this Kind I will state that in a conversation with Capt Banta of the Frontier Regmint who was invited by me to come to Fredericksburg to confer with me in relation to these matters. he told me that courers had been sent from evry point which I visited to collect men to his camp giving information of my movements and warning him that it was my intention to attact his camp and other things calculated to exasperate his men. after explaining my orders and the objects I had in view he said that he had been deceived and misled by these mesages he had received. I will further state that at least one active individual followed me to Fredericksburg - he belonging to no company whatever a distance of fifty miles and discouraged the proceedings indeavering to create the impression that the object was to protect and screne a few Unionists.

every thing was done that could be done to thwart and embarrass the action of the law and produce discontent and incipient mutiny among the men of my command and in the minds of others of the people of the country.

on my way to Fredericksburg from my tour collecting men I was called on by two officers from Burnet County belonging to my Command who was in command of Squads to state what was the object in collecting men. I told them that it was for the purpose of carying out an order for the Governor to investigate certain Outrages in Gillespie County. One of them said that he did not regard it as a legal order and would disobey it - that he would not put his hands to arrest a suthern man for hanging a tory and that he had understood that the man was hung for disloyalty. I asked them if they knew what disobediance of orders meant. he said he did and was willing to abide the consequences. after further conversation they went on to Fredericksburg and at the end of two days I discharged them.

The civil authorities of the county is powrless to do any thing. As before stated but one Justice of the Peace is now in office, two men killed, towit Schuitz and Feller and others have either resigned or left the county for fear of violence.

In relation to the case of Lewis Cass who was forcably taken from his house and has not yet been heard of and his house afterwards robed of a large sum of money. no evidence has been taken. The principal witness left town without making testimony and lives too far off to send for before making this report. I think the evidence can be better procured hereafter.

      James M. Hunter
      Major Comdg 3d Fr. Dist.
      Texas State Troops

[Samuel Mott's statement of resignation. Records of the Governor's Office. Texas State Library.]
    Bandera Texas
    April 10th 1865

Hon/l. P. Murrah
Austin Texas

Sir

I Samuel C. Mott native of the State of Louisana - resident citizen of Bandera County Texas - private soldier of Capt Bladen Mitchells Company 3rd Frontier District. Believing that I can better serve my country as a soldier of the Confederate Army and desiring to volunteer for that service forthwith - Respectfully request of you an honorable discharge from Frontier Service.

>Saml. C. Mott

I certify the above statement of facts - in regard to Samuel C. Mott a member of my company as correct in every particular. Bandera April 10th 1865--and approve the Same

>Bladen Mitchell
>Capt. Comdg Company

PS
>You will please to forward my discharge to the care of Marcus F. Mott--
>Houston Texas--   S.C.M.

[on the reverse side:]

Hd Qrs. in the field
3d Frontier District
April 10, 1865

Approved and respectfully forwarded with the remark that Mr. Mott has been recommended to me as a true & good man as I <u>know</u> his brother, Marcus F. Mott, to be.

>Jno. Henry Brown
>Maj. Comdg.

>[Bladen Mitchell's statement of resignation. Records of the Governor's Office. Texas State Library.]

Bandera April 10th 1865
Honl P. Murrah
Austin Texas

Sir
>For the purpose of offering my services immediately as a volunteer soldier in the Confederate Army I beg leave respectfully to tender my resignation as Captain of Company 3rd Frontier District.

>>Bladen Mitchell
>>Capt. Comdg. Bandera Com
>>T.S.T.

PS
>You will please to direct the acceptance of my resignation forwarded to care of Marcus F. Mott Houston Texas.

[on the reverse side:]

Hd Qrs. in the field
3d Fr. District
April 10, 1865

Under ordinary circumstances, I would be compelled under a sense of duty to recommend the non-acceptance of this resignation. Capt. Mitchell is a good officer, But the patriotism which prompts his course merits praise and I therefore respectfully forward & recommend the acceptance of his resignation.

      Jno. Henry Brown
      Major Comdg.

The 1870s

[After the Civil War, John R. Baylor lived for a time in San Antonio before moving to Montell in Uvalde County. An undated petition from Bandera County, is transcribed as document number 282 (Volume 4) in the Texas Indian Papers:]

TO THE SENATE AND HOUSE OF REPRESENTATIVES OF THE STATE OF TEXAS
We your Petitioners, beleiving that your Honorable bodies will adopt some measure for the better protection of the Frontier, do hereby recommend John R. Baylor as a suitable person to command a regiment of Rangers. knowing him to be a fine man, who has long lived upon the Frontier, and who is well versed in Indian warfare, And we believe his appointment would give universal Satisfaction to the people of the entire frontier--
    And your petitioners will ever pray, etc.--

      Chas Mentassa [Montague] Jr Clk Dist Court B. C

D M Philliy	Bladen Mitchell
S.H. Jones	Robert Pue
Thos. Fason	Joseph R. Dornstin
E.C. Clark	Sutton Pue Jr
George Hay	John J Bandy

J.A. Jones
J.J. Jones
Ch Schmidtke
G.W. Lewis
A.G. Jones
M Z Weaver
John Anderwate [Anderwald]
F. Jureothe [Juretzke?]
Charles Montague Sr
H.C. Duffy
Albert Admietz County Treasurer
Jno Montague
William Hudspeth
A J Hudspeth

Henry Guerra
T.C. Rine
B.F. Langford
Foster Hester
William Myrick
Logan Mynek
A. Mansfield
Edward M Ross
Harry Stevens
John Geo Hegan
A.W. Jackson
Amasa Clark
Albert Haidecker
M.C. Click

[Celestin Pingenot, private, Company E, Frontier Force:]
Fort Inge, Texas
Dec. 29th 1870

To the Adjudant Genl.
of the State of Texas
Col. Davison

Sir!
    With due devotion I allow myself to approach you with a demand personally to you, hoping as a favor to receive an answer. The Ranger laws says, "A horse killed in action with the Indians will be paid by the State." It has already happened in our Company in our last action, not telling whether killed or ran off by the Indians. One man for instance being killed and his horse lost; and another man being knocked off his horse, and did not see anything of the horse afterwards.
    Devoted I ask now, whether such horses as lost as stated will be paid by the State.   Hope to hear from you soon.
    With due Respect,
    I am
    your Obd Servant
        Celestin Pingenot
        Ranger Co.E.
        Fort Inge
        Texas.

1872+ Minuteman Companies

[Company V - Medina County Minutemen.]

John Green had been Bladen Mitchell's ranch foreman before the Civil War. See also A.J. Sowell's account of Jack Huffman, pp 832-833 in <u>Texas Indian Fighters</u>. In another account J.B. Wernette was living in Castroville, when "one night after the Civil war" Indians got:

> all of the horses on the east side of the river, but delayed so long in rounding up and getting them together that by daylight they had only proceeded with them as far as the head of Colevro Creek. John Green, a brave man and good Indian fighter, raised six men, and taking a near cut came upon them at the [south] Verde pass and at once charged them. Green was ahead of his men and first encountered the Indians, but soon scattered them with his revolvers, but was himself severely wounded. The other men soon came up and all the horses were retaken and brought back, and Mr. Wernette got old Bill again.

Green afterwards belonged to a company of minute men, and was first lieutenant. On one occasion he wanted to take a night scout and ordered the men to saddle up, but while saddling his horse, was shot and killed by a Mexican who belonged to the company, who then ran and made his escape into Mexico. What the trouble was about the writer has not been able to learn.

[The roll of Company V as the names appear in the <u>Roster of Minute Companies</u> at the Texas State Library:]

Haby, George	Lt.
Green, John	1st Sgt.
Wurzback, Adolf	2nd Sgt
Van Risser, James	1st Corp.
Leichling, Julius	2nd Corp.

[15 Privates]

Beck, Joseph	Korm, John
Bohm, Arming	Manchac Secundo
Braun, Charles	Munier, Frank
Braun, Fred	Van Risser, W.L.

Burrell, Joseph
Haby, Leopold
Jones, Taylor W.

Zapata, Jesus
Burrell James

[The roll for Company C Kendall County as the names appear in the <u>Roster of Minute Companies</u>:]

Patton, C.A. — Lt.
Worcester, W.W. — 1st Sgt
Nowlin, James C — 2nd Sgt
Parron, B.F. — 1st Corp.
Davis, John T. — 2nd Corp.

Besseler, Aug
Davis, Orin
Davis, J.W.
Epps, S.T.
Gray, H.C.
Grizzard, T.M.
Knibbe, Aug.
Knibbe, Herman

Kelly, William
Lawhon, J.W.
Piland, James W.
Sansom, T.J.
Sanders, G.W.
Swain, Joseph
Taylor, T.Y.

[The roll for Company E Kerr County (station: Comfort) as the names appear in the <u>Roster of Minute Companies</u>:]

Schwedhelm, Henry — Lt. [Schwethelm]
Ingerhutt, Thos. — 1st Sgt
Nelson, Lewis — 2nd Sgt.
Roggenbucke, Chas. — 1st Corp.
Henderson, Howard — 2nd Corp.

Brazil, James
Callahan, John
Doebbler, R.
Fischer, And.
Heinen, H.H.
Johnson, J.W.
Ingerhutt, M.
Kouger, E.

Schultz, N.B.
Steiles, G.
Teurknett, R.
Watson, James
Watson, John
Welsh, James
Walters, H.

[The roll for Company Y Uvalde County as the names appear in the Roster of Minute Companies:]

    Bates, B.A.   Lt.
    Cook, A.E.   1st Sgt.
    Pulliam, W.M.   2nd Sgt.
    Sanders, R.W.   1st Corp.
    Sessions, Jake   2nd Corp.

    Young, Matthew   Spencer, T.S.
    Evans, S.M.   Collins, J.B.
    Bates, F.C.   Grogan, A.P.
    McKinney, R.C.   Cox, Hugh
    Jones, Franklin   Cox, Henry
    Biggs, W.B.   Dolan, Pat*
    Hewitt, James E.

[*Served as 1st Sergeant of Kelso's Company, 1870. He was a lieutenant, and later, captain in the Frontier Battalion that organized in 1874.]

The Last Minutemen

Office of
Ferdinand Niggle,
Sheriff and Collector Medina County.
Castroville, Texas, Nov 17th 1881

W.H King,
Adjutant General
Austin, Texas.

Sir:
    There is a body of men armed with six shooters & winchester rifles operating in the Southern & Southwestern portions of Medina County They claim to have the right to carry six shooters by virtue of being members of Long's Minute Company of Frio County. I am advised by Attorney General Mc[torn] that they have no right to carry six shooters [o]n or about their persons unlefs they are militiamen in actual service; and I have been advised by him to apply to you for information. Are they militia men in actual service? They claim, so I understand, to be acting under your orders. Medina

County is quiet, peaceable & orderly; and I and my deputies are able to preserve the peace & enforce the laws. Please answer
Very Respectfully Yr obdst,

  Ferd Niggle
  Shff Medina Co Texas.

Frio Nov. 27. 81

W.H. King. Ajt. gen
 Sir in reply to Sheriff Niggli of Medina Co I see in his Statement to you he claims that there has bin a body of my men operating in medina Co. which is a fals except in one occutions one of my nearest Neighbors had four Horses stolen out of his field while at breakfast who is a member of my Companey he taken three other members of the Companey and went on trail of the Horses they followed the trail .7. or .8. miles and overtaken the Horses the band that had charg of the Horses had to leave to make there escap the Horses wer taken out of Frio Co. within a bout one mile of Medina Co line and was driven in the direction of Castorville the County Sit of medina Co. except this scout I claim that he is mistaken or hav bin mis informed my men has bin caring six shooters but hav bin on lookout for theives I ask you to inform me if I hav no right to follow theives out of my County or not if we if do not hav the right to follow desparados or thievs to any point in the stat we wish to be disbanded for we can not protect our selves and property if we can not crofs County lines if I dont do writ it will be threw a mistake
 Respectfuely

  Capt. J.E. Long

[Postcard to the Adjutant General:]

Castroville, Texas, Dec. 7/81.

Your letter of Dec. 5th to hand I have still 19 guns belonging to the State of Texas, subject fo your order, but you are the better Judge whether Medina Co. needs them than I am. There is no military company here, and if you pay ship them at you expense I will do so immediately, but I do not want to be at all responsible for the expense of shipping or the safe delivery to you of this property. Advice me how to ship them. Hoping to hear from you soon I Remain yours truly,

  Joseph Kenepf

Kerrville Kerr Co Dec 10th 1881
Adjutant General

Sir I Received yours of this Month. yesterday you wanted to know if we could Do without the State guns we have in posesion. the country is in peace now and have B[een?] for A few years the guns will Be Subject to Your Orders in as Short time as possible yours as

      Ever S.R. Merritt

CHARLES SCHRIENER,
Wholesale and Retail Dealer In
General Merchandise

Kerrville, Kerr Co., Texas, December 16 1881

Genl. W.H. King
Adjt Genl, State of Texas
Austin, Texas

Sir, In reply to your letter of the 2nd inst. beg to state that in my opinion the 40 Sharp's Carbines in posesion of the K. M. Rifles and for which I am responsible are still needed for the protection of the people in the upper portion of this County. in 12 months time I think they can be dispensed with.

    Yours Respectfully

      Chs Schriener

Kerrville Kerr Co Decb 19th/81

W.H. King
Adjt General of the
State of Texas.

Sir
    I have receaved your letter in regard to them 20 Sharps Carbines that my Company has. I would like to Keep them yet, because we have still a good many outlaws in ouer County, and no other protection. I would also like to have some Ammunition, for the Company. pleace sent the same to Emil Warmund. Fredrigsburg
    very respectfully yours truly

      Henry Schwethelm

Lt Comd Kerr Co Vol. M. Comp.

[H.H. Carmichael & Company went bankrupt after the Panic of 1893. George and Virginia Hay moved to Hondo where they opened a confectionery store. Later (1903?) they moved back to Bandera where George Hay served as Justice of the Peace well into his 80s. He wrote the following letter to the Adjutant General of Texas sometime between 1918 and 1925. The first page is missing.]

When our Detachment (Minute Men) Texas Rangers; were Mustered into Service, as afore Said; 15 men Lieut Robert Ballantyne Com'd'g, First Seargt George F. Towle made three (3) Muster Rolls, of said detachment. one was filed with the Adjutant General Austin, Texas. one filed in the Office of the Clerk of the County Court of Bandera County Texas. The 3rd Roll was kept by Sear'gt Towle; When the Civil War Commenced Seargt Towle joined the Army; placed the Muster Roll in my charge, which I kept untill the 18th day of June 1908. When I transmitted said Roll to E.M. Phelps, Asst. Adjutant General, Austin, Texas; Who after Coppying Said Muster Roll, transmitted it to the Adjutant General of the U.S. Washington D.C. and Said Muster Roll Should now be on file in the war Department Washington D.C.-

I have made Application to the U.S. pension division 3 times, Was refused the first (1st) time for the reason That the State of Texas had not reimbursed the United States for the payment of Texas Rangers. The Second Application was turned down and refused; for the reason That the authorities of the State of Texas had made no Official Acknowledgement of the Company of Lieut Robert Ballantyne's Company ever having Served the State of Texas as Rangers or Minute Men;- The third Application was refused upon and for the above mentioned reasons combined; and was advised that future applications would be N.G. Now if the fronteer of Texas was not entitled to protection against the depredations of hostile Indians in the year 1860.

Why was it not so stated in the Act of Congress of May 30, 1918? In the Treaty of 1848, between the Republic of Mexico and the United States. The Republic of Mexico "Aggred to defend and protect the fronteer of Texas against the raids of hostile Indians." which She (Mexico) failed to do-and hostile Indians did Continualy depredate all along the fronteer of Texas; from the year 1848, untill the year 1875. I know this to be a fact, I resided in Gillespie, Burnett, Llano & Bandera Counties during those years;

In the year 1855. The U.S. government appointed Commissioners who were Sent along the Fronteer, who took the Sworn Affidavits of Citizens of <u>Murders Committed; people Captured</u>, Stock killed and Stolen by hostile Indians; which aggreated an immense Sum the U.S. government made a demand on Mexico for payment. and received only $3,000,000 but our government did not pay us Settlers anything for our loss.

I put in a Claim to the United States Court of Claims, for mules and horses stolen by Comanche Indians in May 1874. I had the best of proof by Competent Witnesses who fought the Indians trying to recover said Stock; but my Claim was dismissed by said Court for want of prosecution, My Attorney John Wharton Clark, having died. I suppose just before Court Convened.

Now if you will please excuse this long "epistle" and assist me in getting a pension; for I need it in my old age; I will be exceedingly oblieged to you.

  Very Respectfully
  George Hay

P.S. I was born on the 17th of March 1836.
  Now I suggest that the Legislature make some provision for us old fellows so that we may obtain a pension without much delay by letting us make proff of our Service to the State as Rangers. Should we delay many years longer, we will be in the ground.
  Very Hopefully yours.
  George Hay

[Clerical notation:]

Record of service for Geo. Hay
has been sent to Washington.
  K.E.

  John Leakey's daughter, Mrs. Mary Leakey Miles, reminisced about the old days, "Many a thing happened that weren't ever told."

Sources

Almaraz, Felix D., Jr. "Islanders's Story Veiled In Myth." <u>The San Antonio Express-News</u>. August 1, 1993.

Baenziger, Ann Patton. "The Texas State Police During Reconstruction: A Reexamination." <u>The Southwestern Historical Quarterly</u>. Volume 72. Number 4. (April 1969) Pages 470-491.

Baker, T. Linsay. <u>The First Polish Americans: Silesian Settlements In Texas</u>. Texas A&M University Press. College Station. 1979.

"Bandera City--More Indian Depredations." <u>The San Antonio Herald</u>. September 11, 1855. Center For American Studies. UT. Austin.

Bandera County History Book Committee. <u>History of Bandera County, Texas</u>. Curtis Media Corporation. Dallas. 1986.

Bandera Resolutions of 1861. <u>The Daily Ledger and Texan</u>. July 26, 1861. www.rootsweb.ancestry.com~txbander/.

Bandera Resolutions of 1863. Brigade Correspondence. Records of the Adjutant General. Archives Division. Texas State Library. Austin.

"Bandera Valley and City." <u>The San Antonio Herald</u>. August 14, 1855. Center For American Studies. UT. Austin.

Banks, C. Stanley. "The Mormon Migration into Texas." <u>The Southwestern Historical Quarterly</u>. Volume 49. Number 2. (October 1945) Pages 233-244.

Bartlett, John Russell. <u>Personal Narrative of Explorations and Incidents in Texas, New Mexico, California, Sonora and Chihuahua, Connected with the United States and Mexico Boundary Commission, During the Years 1850, '51, '52, and '53</u>. D. Applton and Company. 1854.

Baylor, John R. Letter to W.H. King. September 10, 1881. Adjutant General Records. Archives Division. Texas State Library. Austin.

Bechem, Robert. Reports to J.Y. Dashiell: 3-26-1862, 4-10-1862, 4-15-1862, 4-20-1862, 5-13-1862, 5-21-1862, 6-11-1862, 6-28-1862, 7-1-1862, 7-5-1862, 8-7-1863, 8-18-1863. Brigade Correspondence. Records of the Adjutant General Archives Division. Texas State Library. Austin.

Bennett, Bob. Kerr County, Texas: 1856-1956. The Naylor Company. San Antonio. 1956.

Biggers, Don H. German Pioneers In Texas: A Brief History of Their Hardships, Struggles and Achievements. Press of the Fredericksburg Publishing Company. 1925.

"The bill for frontier protection." Austin Daily State Journal. May 27, 1870. Center For American Studies. UT. Austin.

"Biographies of Great Lipan Chiefs." http://www.lipanapache.org/Museum/museum_chiefs.html

Bitton, Davis. "Mormons In Texas: The Ill-fated Lyman Wight Colony: 1844-1858." Arizona and The West. Volume 11. Number 1. (Spring 1969) Pages 5-26.

Bitton, Davis, ed. The Reminiscences and Civil War Letters of Levi Lamoni Wight: Life in a Mormon Splinter Colony On The Texas Frontier. University of Utah Press. Salt Lake City. 1970.

Boyd, Eva Jolene. Noble Brutes: Camels On The American Frontier. Republic of Texas Press. Plano. 1995.

Brown, John Henry. History of Texas from 1685 to 1892. Jenkins Publishing Co., The Pemberton Press: Austin & New York. 1970 [1892].

Buenger, Walter Louis, Jr. Stilling The Voice of Reason: Texans and The Union, 1854-1861. University Microfilms International. Ann Arbor, Mi. 1979.

Burnside, Sabrina Rine. "Recollections of Sabrina Rine Burnside." Bandera County Historian. Volume 10. Number 1. (Spring 1987) Pages 1-6.

"Capt. John W. Sansom." Daily Austin Republican. August 25, 1870. Center For American Studies. UT. Austin.

Catton, Bruce. The Civil War. American Heritage Publishing Co., Inc. New York. 1960.

Chabot, Frederick C. With The Makers of San Antonio: Genealogies of the Early Latin, Anglo-Americans, and German Families with Occasional Biographies. Artes Graficas. San Antonio. 1937.

Chiodo, Beverly Ann. "Real County." The Southwestern Historical Quarterly. Volume 65. Number 3. (January 1962) Pages 348-365.

Citizens of Bexar County. "Petition of Various People." November 21, 1855. Archives Division. Texas State Library. Austin.

Citizens of Sabinal Canon, Bandera County. "Petition Protesting the Formation of a New County." 1895. Archives Division. Texas State Library. Austin.

Clark, Amasa Gleason. Reminiscences of a Centenarian. Naylor Company. San Antonio. 1930.

Coldwell, Neal. Reports to John B. Jones. 7-13-1874, 7-27-1874, 8-12-1874, 8-20-1874, 6-28-1875, 7-6-1877, 7-29-1877. Adjutant General Records. Archives Division. Texas State Library. Austin.

Cox, Mike. "Lizzie Hay and the Demise of the Lone Highwayman." Texas Escapes Online Magazine. February 9, 2012. www.texasescapes.com/MikeCoxTexasTales/Lizzie-Hay-Demise-of-Lone-Highwayman.htm.

Cox, Mike. "The Comanche War Trail: Terror In The Night." Texas Highways. Volume 44. Number 8. (August 1997) Pages 42-50.

Cox, Mike. The Texas Rangers: Volume I: Wearing The Cinco Peso. 1821-1900. Tom Doherty Associates. New York. 2008.

Cremony, John L. Life Among the Apaches. Commercial Herald Office. San Francisco. 1868.

Davis, John L. The Texas Rangers: Their First 150 Years. UTSA Institute of Texan Cultures. San Antonio. 1975.

Denman, Clarence P. "The Office of Adjutant General In Texas, 1835-1881." The Southwestern Historical Quarterly. Volume 28. Number [?]. (from July 1924 to April 1925) Pages 302-322.

Dennis, Mr. and Mrs. T.S., eds. Life of F.M. Buckelew, The Indian Captive, As Related By Himself. Hunters Printing House. Bandera. 1925.

Denson, Mrs. Howard, Mrs. Billy Burnes and Mrs. Howard Graves. The Bandera County Cemetery Records. Bandera County Historical Survey Committee. Bandera. 197?

De Vilbis, John W. Letter to the Editor. The San Antonio Herald. October 19, 1861. Center For American Studies. UT. Austin.

De Voto, Bernard. The Year of Decision: 1846. Houghton Mifflin Company. Boston. 1942.

Dobie, J. Frank. The Longhorns. University of Texas Press. Austin. 1987. [Little, Brown and Company.]

Dolan, Pat. Letter to John C. Sullivan. February 19, 1877. Adjutant General Records. Archives Division. Texas State Library. Austin.

Dolan, Pat. Reports to John B. Jones: 1-5-1877, 2-19-1877, 1-22-1879, 1-28-1879. Adjutant General Records. Archives Division. Texas State Library. Austin.

Dolch, Lois, et al. "August Klappenbach." The Bandera County Historian. Volume 6. Number 1. (Winter 1983) Page 4.

Edwards, Carolyn. "Bandera County's Silesians." The Bandera County Historian. Volume 15. Number 2. (Summer 1993) Page 1.

Edwards, Carolyn. "The Church In the Hearts of the Polish Immigrants." The Bandera County Historian. Volume 15. Number 2. (Summer 1986) Pages 5.

Edwards, Carolyn. "Few Markers Remain In Cemetery." The Bandera Bulletin. March 6, 1991.

Edwards, Jay. "A History of The Privilege Community." The Bandera County Historian. Volume 9. Number 2. Summer 1986. Pages 1-3.

Edwards, Jay. "E.F. Buckner Served As First District Judge." The Bandera County Historian. Volume 14. Number 1. (Spring 1992) Pages 3-4.

Edwards, Jay, et al. "The Last Days of Camp Verde." The Bandera County Historian. Volume 8. Number 2. (Summer 1985) Pages 2-3.

Edwards, Jay, et al. "Rio Medina." The Bandera County Historian. Volume 8. Number 1. (Spring 1985) Page 2.

Election Return. Bandera County. 1856, 1861, 1862, and 1864. Archives Division. Texas State Library. Austin.

Election Return. Uvalde County. 1856. Archives Division. Texas State Library. Austin.

Emmett, Chris. Shanghai Pierce: A Fair Likeness. University of Oklahoma Press. Norman. 1953.

Emmett, Chris. Texas Camel Tales. Naylor Printing Company. San Antonio. 1932.

Fehrenbach, T.R. Comanches: The Destruction of a People. Da Capo Press. New York. 1974.

Fehrenbach, T.R. Lone Star: A History of Texas and the Texans. The McMillan Company. New York. 1968.

Finley, Florence. Oldtimers: Their Own Story. The Hornby Press. Uvalde. 1939.

Friedrick, William. Letter to F.J. de Witt. August 24, 1863. Records of the Adjutant General. Archives Division. Texas State Library. Austin.

Gard, Wayne. "The Fence-Cutters." The Southwestern Historical Quarterly. Volume 51. Number One. (July 1947) Pages 1-15.

Garrison, Lora B. Davis. Pioneers In The Frio Canyon Hill Country: An Oral History Study. Copy in DRT Library. San Antonio. 1980?

General Orders Number 1 and 2. Frontier Battalion. 1874. Adjutant General Records. Archives Division. Texas State Library. Austin.

Gibson, A.M. The Kickapoos: Lords of the Middle Border. University of Oklahoma Press. Norman. 1963.

Gillet, James B. Six Years With The Texas Rangers. Von Boeckmann-Jones Company. Austin. 1921.

Glenn, Frankie Davis. Capt'n John: Story of a Texas Ranger. Nortex Press. Austin. 1991.

Graves, Rev. H.A. Andrew Jackson Potter, the Fighting Parson of the Texan Frontier. 1881. Reprinted in serial form in the 1933 Frontier Times magazine.

Greer, James Kimmins. Colonel Jack Hays: Texas Frontier Leader And California Builder. E.P. Dutton and Company, Inc. New York. 1952.

Greer, James K., ed. Buck Barry: Texas Ranger and Frontiersman. University of Nebraska Press. Lincoln and London. 1978. [1932]

Guthrie, John. Descriptive Account of Bandera City and Bandera County. Bugle Office. Bandera. 1888. (facsimile printing 1974?)

Hall, J.L. Report to William Steele. July 29, 1877. Adjutant General Records. Archives Division. Texas State Library. Austin.

Hardin, Stephen L. The Texian Iliad. University of Texas Press. Austin. 1994.

Henry, William R. Statement concerning property lost by F.L. Hicks. January 9, 1856. Records of the Adjutant General. Archives Division. Texas State Library. Austin.

Hunter, John Marvin. 100 Years In Bandera: 1853-1953. The Bandera Bulletin. Bandera. 1953.

Hunter, John Marvin. "A Bandera County Tragedy." Frontier Times. (August 1924) Pages 8-11.

Hunter, John Marvin. The Lyman Wight Colony In Texas. Bandera Bulletin. Bandera. 1937. [reprint of Heman Hale Smith's "The Lyman Wight Colony in Texas"?]

Hunter, John Marvin. "Bandera Mass Hanging Was Diabolical." The Houston Post. October 17, 1937. John Peace Library. UTSA. San Antonio.

Hunter, John Marvin. "Camel Driver's Son Was President of Mexico." Frontier Times. Volume 19. Number 1. (October 1941) Pages 1-2.

Hunter, John Marvin, ed. [From the Richard Irving Dodge memoir:] "Chased by Indians Through Bandera Pass." Frontier Times. Volume 25. Number 7. (April 1948) Pages 169-173.

Hunter, John Marvin. "Lonely Graves and Sentinel Oak Mark Grim Tragedy of Bandera Hills." The San Antonio Express. January 19, 1922. John Peace Library. UTSA. San Antonio.

Hunter, John Marvin, ed. Herman Lehmann: 9 Years Among The Indians: 1870-1879. Von Boeckmann-Jones Company. Austin. 1927. [1993]

Hunter, John Marvin. Pioneer History of Bandera County. Hunter's Printing House. Bandera. 1922. [The University of North Texas Library: http://texashistory.unt.edu/data/TBDP/UNT/meta-pth-27720.tkl

Hunter, John Marvin, ed. The Trail Drivers of Texas. Cokebury Press. Nashville. 1925.

"Indians Stampeded." The San Antonio Herald. April 26, 1855. Center For American Studies. UT. Austin.

Inspection of Arms. Lawhon's Company. June 9, 1863. Mounted Regiment, Texas State Troops. Archives Division. Texas State Library. Austin.

Jackson, A.T. "Confederate Gunpowder." Frontier Times. Volume 28. Number 2. (November 1950) Pages 32-43.

James, Vinton Lee. Frontier and Pioneer Recollections of Early Days in San Antonio and West Texas. Artes Graficas. San Antonio. 1938.

Jennings, Frank W. "A Pioneer's Story." The San Antonio Express-News. November 11, 1990.

Jennings, Frank W. San Antonio: The Story of An Enchanted City. The San Antonio Express-News Press. San Antonio. 1998.

Johnson, R.S. Letter to John B. Jones. Adjutant General Records. Archives Division. Texas State Library. Austin.

Jones, John B. Reports to William Steele. 6-13-1874, 9-14-74, 7-1-1875, 7-9-1875. Adjutant General Records. Archives Division. Texas State Library. Austin.

Jordon, Terry G. Texas Graveyards: A Cultural Legacy. University of Texas Press. Austin. 1982.

Kaiser, Frank C. (Edited and annotated by A.E. Skinner). Reminiscences of a Texas Ranger. Copy in Center For American Studies. UT. Austin. 1967

Kellner, Marjorie, Project Director. Wagons Ho! A History of Real County, Texas. Curtis Media, Inc. 1995.

Kelso, John R. Reports to James Davidson. 7-28-1870, 8-11-1870, 10-4-1870, 10-11-1870, 12-3-1870, 12-26-1870. Adjutant General Records. Archives Division. Texas State Library. Austin.

Kilgore, D.E. A Ranger Legacy: 150 Years of Service to Texas. Madrona Press, Inc. Austin. 1973.

Lackman, Howard. "The Howard-Neighbors Controversy: A Cross-section In West Texas Indian Afairs." Panhandle-plains Historical Review. Volume 25. (1952) Pages 29-44.

Leckie, William H. The Buffalo Soldiers: A Narrative of the Negro Cavalry in the West. University of Oklahoma Press. Norman. 1967.

"Local Affairs." The San Antonio Express. July 3, 1873. John Peace Library, UTSA. San Antonio.

Lockett, Landon. "Cool Cats." Texas Highways. Volume 50. Number 12. (December 2003) Page 13.

Long, J.E. Letter to W.H. King. November 27, 1881. Adjutant General Records. Texas State Library. Austin.

MacCormack, Zeke. "Find May Alter Texas History." May 27, 2000. The San Antonio Express-News. San Antonio.

Mahler, Daniel D. Phone Conversation Regarding The San Julian Creek Incident. October 9, 1995. Jolly, Texas.

Maudslay, Robert. Texas Sheepman. University of Texas Press. Austin. 1951.

McAdoo, John D. Letter to John Burk. December 15, 1864. Brigade Correspondence. Records of the Adjutant General. Archives Division. Texas State Library. Austin.

McDaniel, Niki Frances. "Clark's Daughter Reflects On Life." The San Antonio Express-News. November 11, 1990.

McNelly, Leander. Report to William Steele. November, 13, 1876. Adjutant General Records. Archives Division. Texas State Library. Austin.

Menke, Jim. Military History of Medina County. Copy in DRT Library. San Antonio. 1974.

Merritt, S.R. Letter to W.H. King. December 10, 1881. Adjutant General Records. Archives Division. Texas State Library. Austin.

Merritt, S.R. Report to William Steel. January 15, 1877. Adjutant General Records. Archives Division. Texas State Library. Austin.

Metz, Leon. John Wesley Hardin: Dark Angel of Texas. Mangan Books. El Paso. 1996.

Miles, O.B. Statement of discharge and accounting of state property for Ballentyne's Company. June 3, 1860. Records of the Adjutant General. Archives Division. Texas State Library. Austin.

Minear, Les. "Joseph William Minear's Service as a Texas Ranger, 1870-1871." The Bandera County Historian. Volume 15. Number 4. (Winter 1993) Pages 1-3.

Minear, Minnie Bruce. "Joseph William Minear." The Bandera County Historian. Volume 2. Number 1. (Winter 1979) Page 2.

Montague, Charles. Letter to William Clark. July 19, 1861. Records of the Governor's Office. Archives Division. Texas State Library. Austin.

Monthly Return. Lawhon's Company. Mounted Regiment. Texas State Troops. August 1863. Archives Division. Texas State Library. Austin.

Monthly Returns. Montel's Company. Frontier Regiment. Texas State Troops. Archives Division. Texas State Library. Austin.

Muir, Andrew Forest. "Diary of a Young Man In Houston." Southwestern Historical Quarterly. Volume 53. Number 3. (January 1950) Pages 276-307.

Murray, Myrtle. "John Leakey." The Cattleman. Volume 25. Number 6. (November 1938) Pages 31-37.

Murray, Myrtle. "Lucius Hicks of Bandera County." Frontier Times. Volume 26. Number 12. (September 1948) Pages 290-295. [reprinted from The Cattleman.]

Muster Rolls. Adams Company. 1861. Archives Division. Texas State Library. Austin.

Muster Roll. Ballantyne's Company. 1860. Archives Division. Texas State Library. Austin.

Muster Rolls. Callahan's Company. 1855. Archives Division. Texas State Library. Austin.

Muster Roll. Davenport's Company. 1856. Archives Division. Texas State Library. Austin.

Muster Rolls. Lawhon's Company. Mounted Regiment. Texas State Troops. Archives Division. Texas State Library.

Muster Roll. Mitchell's Company. Frontier Organization. Texas State Troops. February 6, 1864. Archives Division. Texas State Library. Austin.

Muster Roll. Mitchell's Company. Frontier Organization. Texas State Troops. June 1, 1864. Archives Division. Texas State Library. Austin.

Muster Rolls. Montel's Company. Frontier Regiment. Texas State Troops. Archives Division. Texas State Library. Austin.

Muster Rolls. Paul's Company. 1861. Archives Division. Texas State Library. Austin.

Muster and Pay Rolls. Company K, Minute Men, Bandera County (Ballantyne's Rangers). August 1872 - June 1873. Archives Division. Texas State Library. Austin.

Muster Rolls. Pue's Company. Reserve Militia. 1870 and 1871. Archives Division. Texas State Library. Austin.

"Mysterious Triple Murder." The San Antonio Daily Express. April 22, 1881. John Peace Library, UTSA. San Antonio.

Neighbours, Kenneth Franklin. <u>Robert Simpson Neighbors and the Texas Frontier: 1836-1859</u>. Texian Press. Waco. 1975.

Neel, Lieutenant. Letter to John Henry Brown. March 25, 1865. Records of the Governor's Office. Archives Division. Texas State Library. Austin.

Neel, L.C. "The McLaurin Ranch Tragedy." <u>The San Antonio Daily Express</u>. April 24, 1881. John Peace Library, UTSA. San Antonio.

Nelson, Christian G. "Rebirth, Growth, and Expansion of the Texas Militia, 1868-1898." <u>Military History of Texas and the Southwest</u>. Volume 2. Number 1. (February 1962) Pages 1-16.

Nelson, F.H. Report to Neal Coldwell. August 7, 1874. Adjutant General Records. Archives Division. Texas State Library. Austin.

Nevill, C.L. Reports to John B. Jones. February and March 1879. Adjutant General Records. Archives Division. Texas State Library. Austin.

Newcombe, William W., Jr. <u>The Indians of Texas</u>. University of Texas Press. Austin. 1961.

Newspaper accounts of the Nueces Battle. <u>The San Antonio Herald</u>. August 16, 1862 and August 28, 1862. Center for American Studies. UT. Austin.

Niggle, Ferdinand. Letter to W.H. King. November 17, 1881. Adjutant General Records. Archives Division. Texas State Library. Austin.

Nowlin, Henry M. Letter to John Samuel Piper. October 22, 1941. www.rootsweb.ancestry.com~txbander/. (Accessed 11-22-16)

Olmsted, Frederick Law. <u>A Journey Through Texas: Or, a Saddle-Trip on the Southwestern Frontier</u>. Dix, Edwards and Company. New York. 1857.

Ozment, N.G. "Texas Minute Man Blazes Way For Civilization." <u>The San Antonio Express</u>. October 10, 1915. John Peace Library, UTSA. San Antonio.

Patterson, N.M.C. Letter to Sam Houston. January 26, 1860. Records of the Governor's Office. Archives Division. Texas State Library. Austin.

Payment Receipts for Expenses Incurred by Callahan's Texas Ranger Company. 1855-56. Archives Division. Texas Library. Austin.

Pease, E.M. Message to the Texas Senate and House of Representatives. January 8, 1856. Records of the Adjutant General. Archives Division. Texas State Library. Austin.

Pease, E.M. Message to the Texas Senate and House of Representatives. August 4, 1856. Records of The Adjutant General. Archives Division. Texas State Library. Austin.

Petition from citizens of Sabinal Canyon, Uvalde and Bandera counties. May 30, 1860. Records of the Adjutant General. Archives Division. Texas State Library. Austin.

Pierce, Michael D. The Most Promising Young Officer: A Life of Ranald Slidell Mackenzie. University of Oklahoma Press. Norman and London. 1993.

Porter, Kenneth Wiggins. "The Seminole Negro-Indian Scouts 1870-1881." The Southwestern Historical Quarterly. Volume 54. Number 3. (January 1952) Pages 358-377.

Porter, Kenneth W. "The Seminole In Mexico, 1850-1861." The Hispanic American Historical Review. Volume 31. Number 1. (February 1951) Pages 1-36.

Quarterly Return of Commissioned Officers, 31st Brigade District. 6-1-1862 and 10-10-1862. Brigade Correspondence. Records of the Adjutant General. Archives Division. Texas State Library. Austin.

Ransleben, Guido E. A Hundred Years of Comfort in Texas. The Naylor Company. San Antonio. 1954.

Receipt for cotton and woolen carders. Bandera County. March 28, 1864. Records of the Governor's Office. Archives Division. Texas State Library. Austin.

Record Book of Camp Davis, Kerr County, Texas: July 10, 1862 - March 29, 1864: Letters and orders of James M. Hunter, William Banta, J.M. Hayes and W.J. Alexander. Photostat copies, 1928. Barker Texas History Center. Austin.

Reeve, Frank D. "The Apache Indians in Texas." The Southwestern Historical Quarterly. Volume 50. Number 2. (October 1946) Pages 187-219.

Report of Crimes. Bandera County. August 3, 1870. Adjutant General Records. Archives Division. Texas State Library. Austin.

Report of Hired Persons. Montel's Company. 1862. Archives Division. Texas State Library. Austin.

Report of Regional Indian Depredations. The San Antonio Ledger. September 8, 1855. Center For American Studies. UT. Austin.

Resignation Statement. Bladen Mitchell. April 10, 1865. Records of the Governor's Office. Archives Division. Texas State Library. Austin.

Resignation Statement. Samuel C. Mott. April 10, 1865. Records of the Governor's Office. Archives Division. Texas State Library. Austin.

Reynolds, N.O. Reports to John B. Jones. January and February 1879. Adjutant General Records. Archives Division. Texas State Library. Austin.

Richarz, H.J. Letter to Edmund J. Davis. December 29, 1870. Adjutant General Records. Archives Division. Texas State Library. Austin.

Richarz, H.J. Reports to James Davidson. 8-14-1870, 10-14-1870, 10-15-1870, 12-4-1870, 12-9-1870, 12-21-1870, 2-2-1871, 3-16-71. Adjutant General Records. Archives Division. Texas State Library. Austin.

Richter, William L. The Army in Texas During Reconstruction: 1865-1870. Texas A&M University Press. College Station. 1987.

Robinson, Charles M., III. Bad Hand: A Biography of General Ranald S. Mackenzie. State House Press. Austin. 1993.

Robinson, Charles M., III. The Men Who Wear The Star. Random House. New York. 2000.

Roberts, D.W. Report to John B. Jones. June 9, 1879. Adjutant General Records. Archives Division. Texas State Library. Austin.

Rodriguez, Jose Policarpo. <u>Jose Policarpo Rodriguez: "The Old Guide": Surveyer, Scout, Hunter, Indian Fighter, Ranchman, Preacher: His Life in His Own Words</u>. Publishing House of the Methodist Episcopal Church, South. Nashville and Dallas. 1898?

Rollings, Willard H. <u>The Comanche</u>. Chelsea House Publishers. New York and Philadelphia. 1989.

Rose, Victor. <u>The Texas Vendetta; or, The Sutton-Taylor Feud</u>. J.J. Little & Company. New York. 1880.

Roster of Minute Companies. [beginning 1872] Adjutant General Records. Archives Division. Texas State Library. Austin.

Saner, Jack. "Saner-Davis Family Reunion Set For September 4." <u>The Bandera Bulletin</u>. August 26, 1977.

Sansom, John W. Reports to James Davidson. 8-16-1870, 9-7-1870, 9-11-1870, 9-21-1870, 9-22-1870, 9-27-1870, 10-27-1870, 11-12-1870, 11-15-1870, 11-26-1870, 12-24-1870, 1-31-1871, 2-4-1871, 2-4-1871, 2-17-1871, 2-28-1871, 2-28-1871, 3-9-1871, 3-12-1871, 3-18-1871, 3-26-1871, 7-25-1871. Adjutant General Records. Archives Division. Texas State Library. Austin.

Santleben, August. <u>A Texas Pioneer</u>. The Neale Publishing Company. New York and Washington. 1910.

Scarbrough, Clara Stearns. <u>Land of Good Water</u>. Williamson County Sun Publishers. Georgetown. 1973.

Schilz, Thomas F. <u>Lipan Apaches In Texas</u>. Texas Western Press, UTEP. El Paso. 1987.

Schreiner, Charles. Letter to W.H. King. December 16, 1881. Adjutant General Records. Archives Division. Texas State Library. Austin.

Schumacher, M.J. PhD. "Our Polish Heritage: Rugged Individualism and Community Spirit. <u>Celebrate Bandera 2005/Bandera Bulletin</u>. August 31, 2005. Page C18.

Schwethelm, Henry. Letter to W.H. King. December 19, 1881. Adjutant General Records. Archives Division. Texas State Library. Austin.

Scott, Robert N., et al, eds. The War of the Rebellion. A Compilation of Official Records of the U.S. and Confederate Armies. 70 volumes in 128 books. Government Printing Office. Washington. 1891. [1971]

Shearer, Ernest C. "The Callahan Expedition, 1855." The Southwestern Historical Quarterly. Volume 54. Number 4. (April 1951) Pages 430-451.

Shook, Robert W. "The Battle of the Nueces, August 10, 1862." Southwestern Historical Quarterly. Volume 66. Number 1. (July 1962) Pages 31-41.

Skinner, A.E. "Forgotten Guardians: The Activities of Company C, Frontier Forces 1870-1871." Texana. Volume 6. Number 2. (Summer 1968) Pages 107-121.

Smith, David Paul. Frontier Defense in the Civil War: Texas's Rangers and Rebels. Texas A&M University Press. College Station. 1992.

Smith, Persifor F. Letter to Senior Don Emilio Langberg. December 6, 1855. Records of the Adjutant General. Archives Division. Texas State Library. Austin.

Smith, Thomas Tyree. Fort Inge: Sharps, Spurs, and Sabers On The Texas Frontier 1849-1869. Eakin Press. Austin. 1993.

Smith, Thomas T. The Old Army In Texas: A Research Guide to the U.S. Army in Nineteenth-Century Texas. Texas State Historical Association. Austin. 2000.

Smithwick, Noah. The Evolution of a State or Recollections of Old Texas Days. H.N.P. Gammel. Austin. 1900.

Sowell, Andrew Jackson. Early Settlers and Indian Fighters of Southwest Texas: Facts Gathered From Survivors of Frontier Days. Ben C. Jones & Co. Austin. 1900.

Sowell, Andrew Jackson. The Life of "Big Foot" Wallace. State House Press. Austin. 1989 [1899].

Special Order Number 2. Texas Mounted Volunteers (Callahan's Company). September 12, 1855. Records of the Adjutant General. Archives Division. Texas State Library.

Special Order No. 57. August 9, 1863. Southern Division, Mounted Regiment. Archives Division. Texas State Library. Austin.

Special Order No. 12. September 2, 1863. Southern Division, Mounted Regiment. Archives Division. Texas State Library. Austin.

Stevens, Tom M. "A Bandera County Minute Man." Frontier Times. Volume 3. Number 4. (January 1926) Pages 21-22.

Texas Historical Records Survey: Division of Professional and Service Projects: WPA. Inventory of the County Archives: Bandera County: No. 10. San Antonio. 1940.

Thompson, Jerry, ed. Fifty Miles and a Fight: Major Samuel Peter Heintzelman's Journal of Texas & the Cortina War. Texas State Historical Association. Austin. 1998.

Tise, Sammy. Texas County Sheriffs. Oakwood Printing. Albuquerque. 1989.

Tobin, Peggy, ed. "Bandera County Cattle Brands, 1856." The Bandera County Historian. Volume 6. Number 4. Fall 1983. Page 4.

Tobin, Peggy. "Early History of the Old Court House: 1868-1890." The Bandera County Historian. Volume 1. Number 4. (Summer 1979) Pages 1 and 4.

Tobin, Peggy, ed. "Frontier Reminiscences". The Bandera County Historian. Volume 6, Number 3. (Summer 1983) Pages 1-2.

Tobin, Peggy. "History of Bandera Pass." The Bandera County Historian. Volume 9. Number 2. (Summer 1986) Pages 4-6.

Tobin, Peggy. "The Medina River In Early History." The Bandera County Historian. Volume 7. Number 3. (Fall 1984) Page 3.

Tobin, Peggy. "Spanish Influence In Bandera County." The Bandera County Historian. Volume 14. Number 3. (Fall 1992) Pages 1 and 4.

Tumlinson, Peter. Letter to Sam Houston. April 2, 1860. Records of the Adjutant General. Archives Division. Texas State Library. Austin.

Turk, T.R. Mormons In Texas: The Lyman Wight Colony. Port Lavaca? Copy in DRT Library in San Antonio. 1987.

Tyler, Ronnie C. "The Callahan Expedition of 1855: Indians or Negroes?" The Southwestern Historical Quarterly. Volume 70. Number 4. (April, 1967) Pages 575-585.

Tyler, Ron, ed. J.D.B. Stillman: Wanderings in the Southwest in 1855. The Arthur H. Clarke Company. Spokane. 1990.

Tyler, Ron, et al, eds. The New Handbook of Texas. Texas State Historical Association. Austin. 1996.
http://www.tsha.utexas.edu/handbook/online/

Underwood, Rodman L, Death On The Nueces: German Texans Treue der Union. Eakin Press. Austin. 2000.

U.S. Census. 1860. Texas State Library. Austin.

"Voting Results." The San Antonio Ledger. August 18, 1855. Center For American Studies. UT. Austin.

Vouchers. Brigade Correspondence. Archives Division. Texas State Library. Austin.

Wallace, Edward S. "General John Lapham Bullis, The Thunderbolt of the Texas Frontier, I." The Southwestern Historical Quarterly. Volume 54. Number 4. (April 1951) Pages 452-461.

Wallace, Edward S. "General John Lapham Bullis, The Thunderbolt of the Texas Frontier, II" The Southwestern Historical Quarterly. Volume 55. Number 1. (July 1951) Pages 77-85.

Wallace, Ernest. Ranald S. Mackenzie on the Texas Frontier. Western Texas Museum Association. Lubbock. 1964.

Wallace, Ernest and E. Adamson Hoebel. The Comanches: Lords of the South Plains. University of Oklahoma Press. Norman and London. 1952.

Weaver, Bobby D. Castro's Colony: Impresario Development In Texas, 1842-1865. Texas A&M University Press. College Station. 1985.

Walton, Greg. Bear Meat `n' Honey: An Oral History of the Sabinal Canyon. Acorn Press. Austin. 1990.

Webb, Walter Prescott. The Texas Rangers: A Century of Frontier Defense. University of Texas Press. Austin. 1935.

Weiss, Harold J., Jr. "The Texas Rangers Revisited: Old Themes and New Viewpoints." The Southwestern Historical Quarterly. Volume 97. Number 4. (April 1994) Pages 620-640.

Weslager, C.A. The Delaware Indians: A History. Rutgers University Press. New Brunswick. 1972.

Wilcox, A. Letter to Charles de Montel, March 22, 1863. Montel Papers. Center for American Studies. UT Austin.

Wilkins, Frederick. Defending The Borders: The Texas Rangers 1848-1861. State House Press. Austin. 2001.

Wilkins, Frederick. The Highly Irregular Irregulars: Texas Rangers In The Mexican War. Eakin Press. Austin. 1990.

Wilkins, Frederick. The Law Comes To Texas: The Texas Rangers: 1870-1901. State House Press. Austin. 1999.

Wilkins, Frederick. The Legend Begins: The Texas Rangers 1823-1845. State House Press. Austin 1996.

Williams, Amelia W. and Eugene C. Barker, eds. The Writings of Sam Houston: 1813-1863. Pimberton Press; Jenkins Publishing Co. Austin. 1970.

Williams, Robert Hamilton. With The Border Ruffians: Memories of the Far West: 1852-1868. J. Murray. London. 1907.

Winfrey, Dorman H. and James M. Day, eds. The Indian Papers of Texas and the Southwest: 1825-1916. Pimberton Press. Austin. 1966.

Winkler, William, ed. Journal of The Secession Convention of Texas 1861. Austin Printing Company. Austin. 1912.

Wooster, Ralph A., ed. Lone Star Blue and Gray. Texas State Historical Association. Austin. 1995.

Wooster, Ralph A. "Wealthy Texans, 1860." Southwestern Historical Quarterly. Volume 71. Number 2. (October 1967) Pages 163-180.

Wooster, Ralph A. "An Analysis of the Membership of the Texas Secession Convention." The Southwestern Historical Quarterly. Volume 62. Number 3. (January 1959) Pages 332-335.

Young, Kevin R. To The Tyrants Never Yield: A Texas Civil War Sampler. Wordware Publishing, Inc. Plano. 1992.

www.ingramcontent.com/pod-product-compliance
Lightning Source LLC
Chambersburg PA
CBHW060500240426
43661CB00006B/862